Thank you for picking up volume 6. Drawing a game from beginning to end—no matter who the opponent is—leaves me in a mood that's hard to describe. I think to myself, "Aah, right. This was an official game..." I will keep giving this series my all so that I can draw all of the games as they are meant to be.

At least...that's what runs through my tired and sleepy brain sometimes. Man, I could really go for a beer right now.

HARUICHI FURUDATE began his manga career when he was 25 years old with the one-shot Ousama Kid (King Kid), which won an honorable mention for the 14th Jump Treasure Newcomer Manga Prize. His first series, Kiben Gakuha, Yotsuya Sensei no Kaidan (Philosophy School, Yotsuya Sensei's Ghost Stories), was serialized in Weekly Shonen Jump in 2010. In 2012, he began serializing Haikyu!! in Weekly Shonen Jump, where it became his most popular work to date.

HAIKYU!!
VOLUME 6
SHONEN JUMP Manga Edition

Story and Art by
HARUICHI FURUDATE

Translation ❶ **ADRIENNE BECK**
Touch-Up Art & Lettering ❷ **ERIKA TERRIQUEZ**
Design ❸ **FAWN LAU**
Editor ❹ **MARLENE FIRST**

HAIKYU!! © 2012 by Haruichi Furudate
All rights reserved.
First published in Japan in 2012 by SHUEISHA Inc., Tokyo.
English translation rights arranged by SHUEISHA Inc.

The stories, characters and incidents mentioned
in this publication are entirely fictional.

Printed in the U.S.A.

Published by VIZ Media, LLC
P.O. Box 77010
San Francisco, CA 94107

10 9 8 7 6 5 4 3 2 1
First printing, December 2016

www.shonenjump.com

www.viz.com

BANNER: DATE IRON WALL, Date Technical High School Volleyball Club Alumni Society

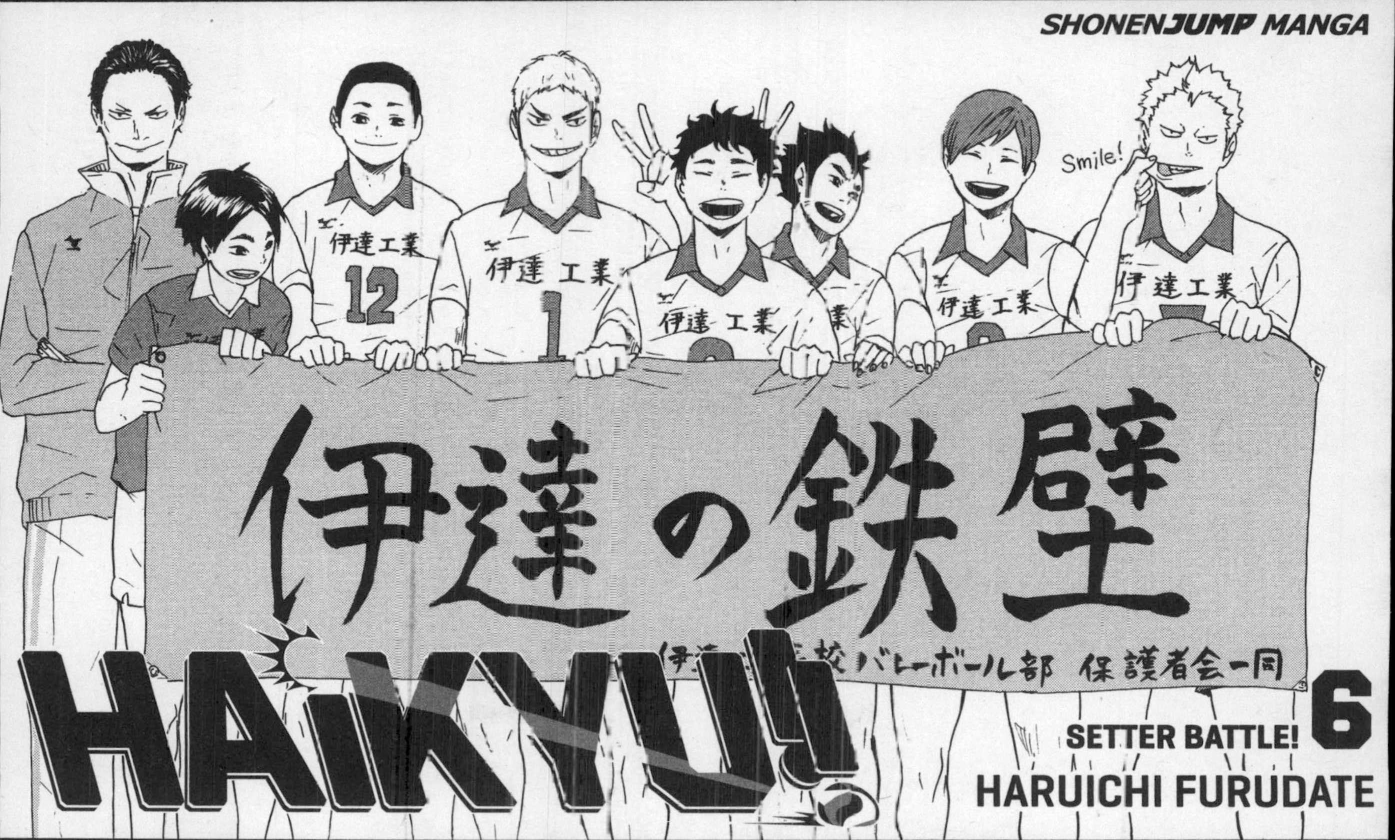
SHONENJUMP MANGA
Smile!
伊達工業
12
伊達工業
1
伊達工業
伊達工業
伊達工業
伊達の鉄壁
バレーボール部 保護者会一同
HAIKYU!!
6
SETTER BATTLE!
HARUICHI FURUDATE

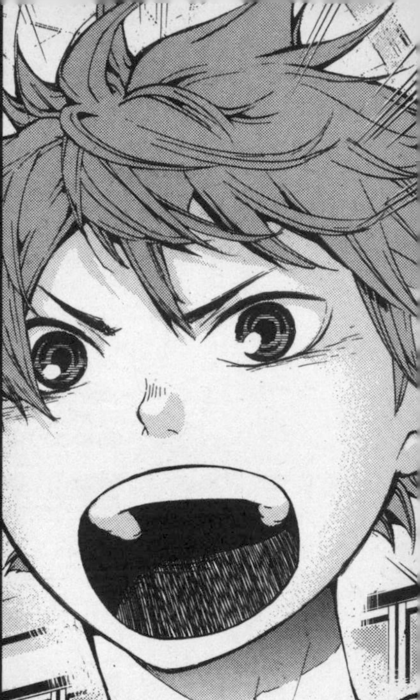
KARASUNO

SHOYO HINATA

1ST YEAR / MIDDLE BLOCKER

Even though he doesn't have the best body type for volleyball, he is super athletic. Gets nervous easily.

TOBIO KAGEYAMA

1ST YEAR / SETTER

His instincts and athletic talent are so good that he's like a "king" who rules the court. Demanding and egocentric.

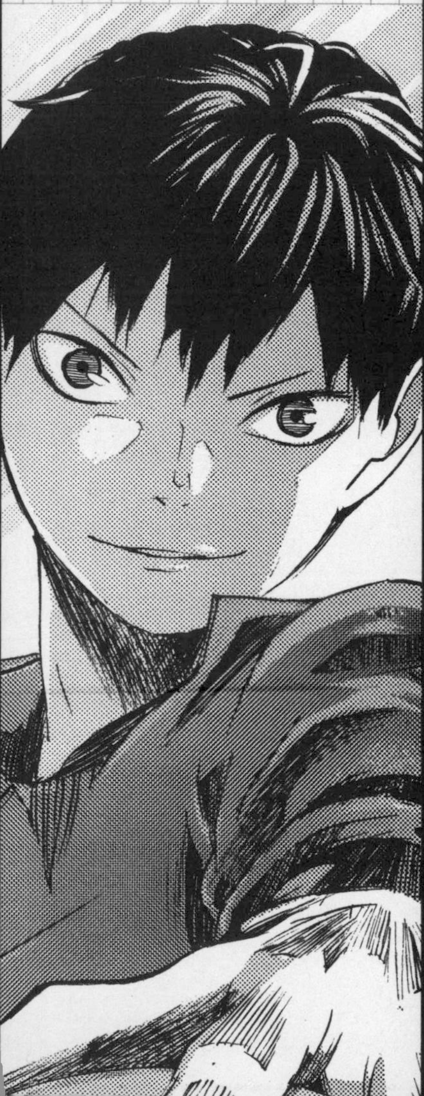

CHARACTERS

Karasuno High School Volleyball Club

YU NISHINOYA
2ND YEAR
LIBERO

KEI TSUKISHIMA
1ST YEAR
MIDDLE BLOCKER

KIYOKO SHIMIZU
3RD YEAR
MANAGER

DAICHI SAWAMURA
3RD YEAR (CAPTAIN)
WING SPIKER

ASAHI AZUMANE
3RD YEAR
WING SPIKER

TADASHI YAMAGUCHI
1ST YEAR
MIDDLE BLOCKER

RYUNOSUKE TANAKA
2ND YEAR
WING SPIKER

KOUSHI SUGAWARA
3RD YEAR (VICE CAPTAIN)
SETTER

Aoba Johsai High School | **Date Tech**

TOHRU OIKAWA
3RD YEAR (CAPTAIN)
SETTER

TAKANOBU AONE
2ND YEAR
MIDDLE BLOCKER

KEISHIN UKAI
COACH

ITTETSJ TAKEDA
ADVISER

Ever since he saw the legendary player known as "the Little Giant" compete at the high school national volleyball finals, Shoyo Hinata has been aiming to be the best volleyball player ever! He decides to join the volleyball club at his middle school and gets to play in an official tournament during his third year. His team is crushed by a team led by volleyball prodigy Tobio Kageyama, also known as "the King of the Court." Swearing revenge on Kageyama, Hinata graduates middle school and enters Karasuno High School, the school where the Little Giant played. However, upon joining the club, he finds out that Kageyama is there too! The two of them bicker constantly, but they bring out the best in each other's talents and become a powerful combo! In Karasuno's practice game against old rival Nekoma, Kageyama and Hinata figure out new ways to improve their skills but ultimately lose to their opponent's consistent teamwork. Promising to get payback on the national stage, Karasuno gets ready for the summer Inter-High Tournament! They crush their opponents in the first round. But now they must face an old enemy...the very team that shut down Asahi in the last tournament—Date Tech! Can Karasuno overcome the Iron Wall now that they have Hinata and Kageyama on their team?

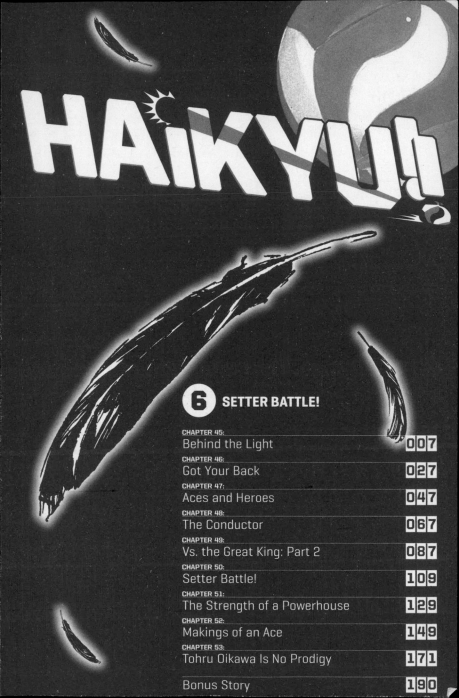

HAIKYU!!

6 SETTER BATTLE!

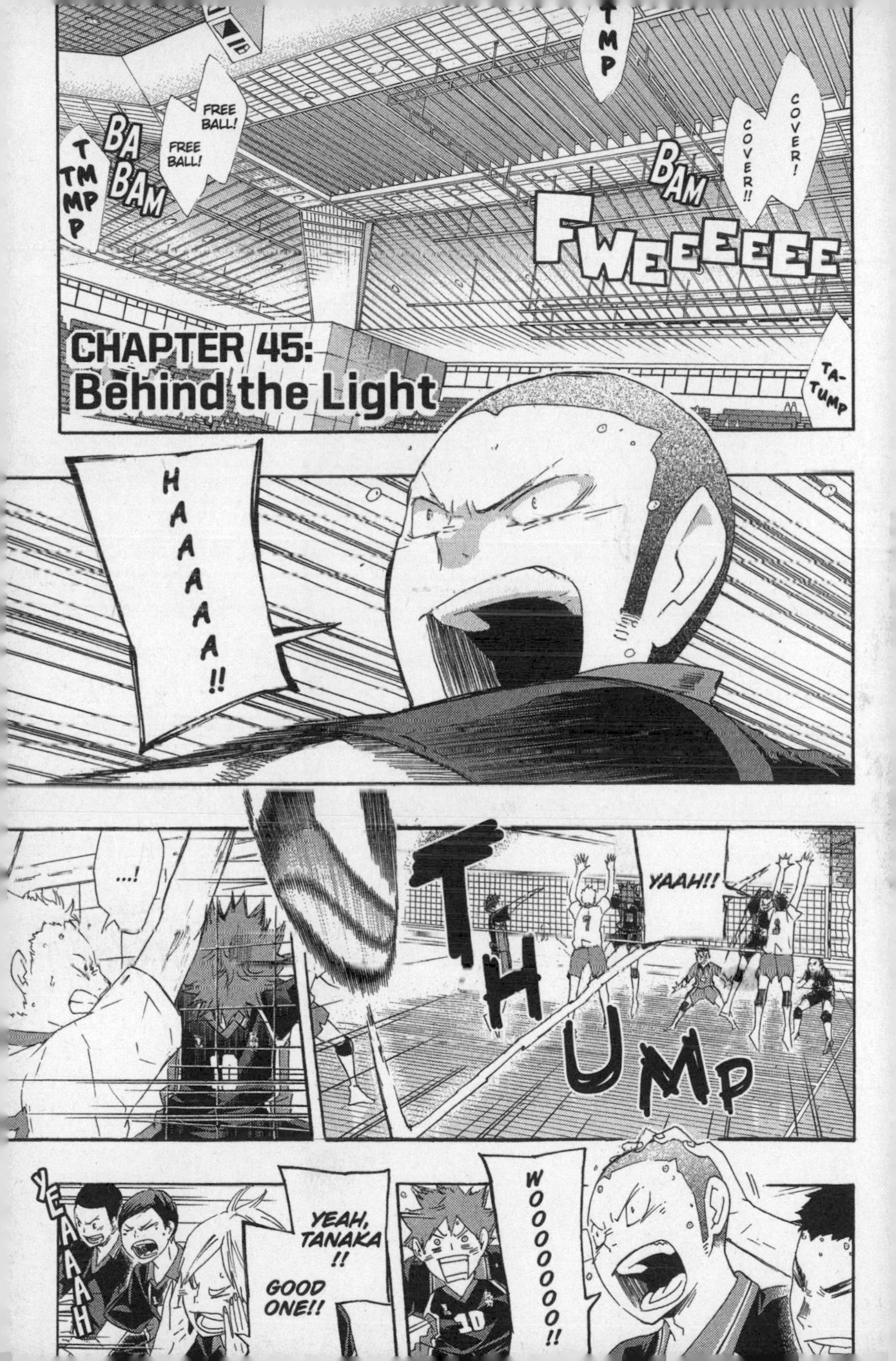
TMP
COVER!
COVER!!
BAM
FWEEEEEE
FREE BALL!
FREE BALL!
BA BAM
T TM MP P
CHAPTER 45:
Behind the Light
TA-TUMP
HAAAAAA!!
YAAH!!
THUMP
...!
WOOOOOOOO!!
YEAH, TANAKA!!
GOOD ONE!!
YEAAAAH

KARASUNO

SERVER UP! DO IT AGAIN, TSUKI-SHIMA!!

BOM

KAMASAKI (SAKUNAMI) | OBARA | MONIWA

SASAYA | FUTAKUCHI | AONE

NET

HINATA | TANAKA | KAGEYAMA

SAWAMURA | AZUMANE | TSUKKI (NOYA)

*CURRENT ROTATION

DATE TECH

2 3 1 9

BUT IF THEY WANT TO OPEN UP SOME SPACE ON DATE TECH...

HERE COMES NO. 7!

... KARASUNO IS PROBABLY GOING TO TAKE THE FIRST SET.

AT THIS RATE, IF THE USUAL "I SCORE, YOU SCORE" ROUTINE CONTINUES ...

TMP TMP

LY

FWIF

WHAP

GAPH ...!

... THAT'S EXACTLY WHAT THEY NEED!!

NICE DEFLEC-TION!

COUNTER!!

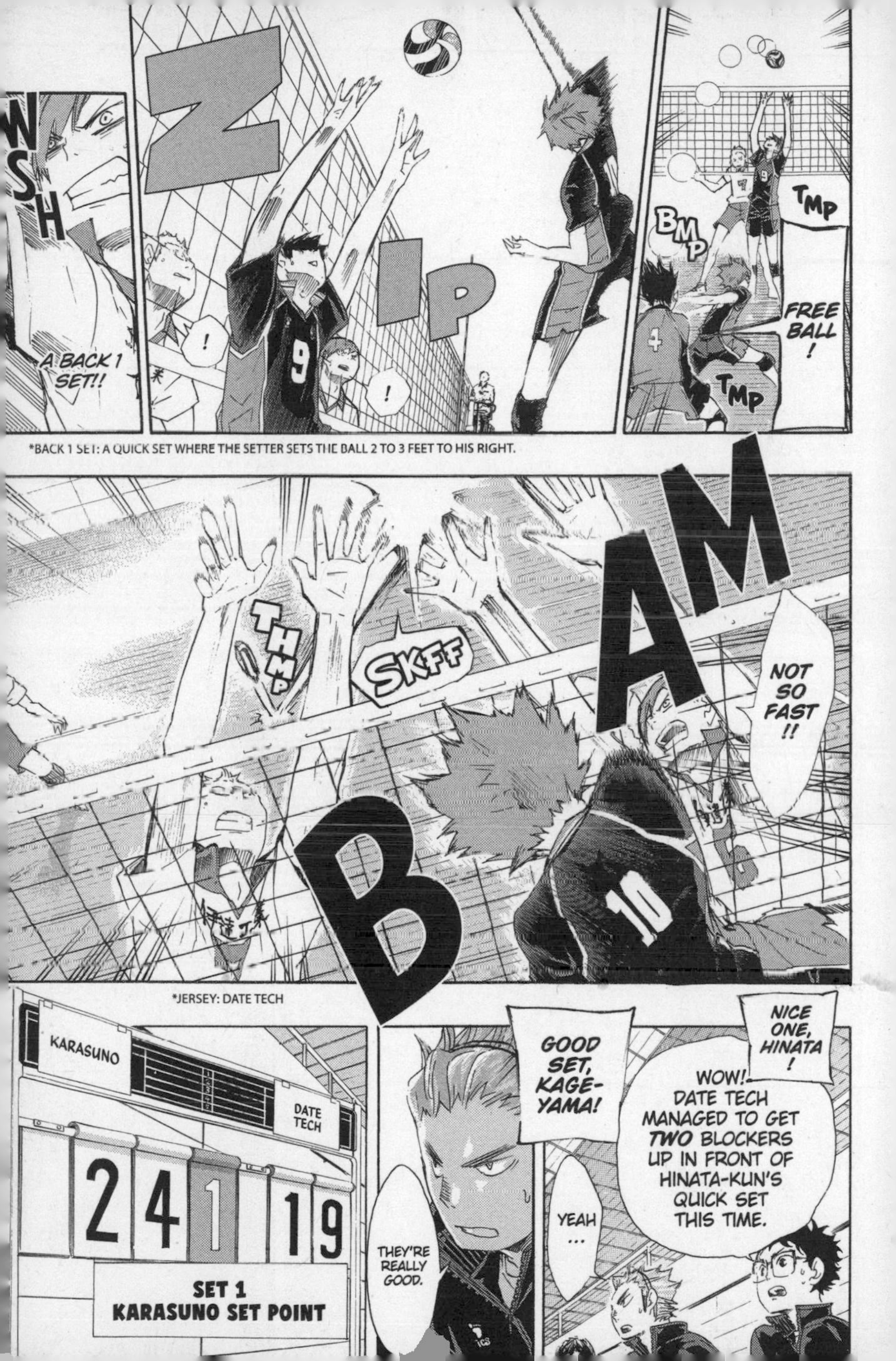
TMP
BMP
FREE BALL!
TMP
ZIP
!
!
WSH
A BACK 1 SET!!
BAM
NOT SO FAST!!
SKFF
THMP
NICE ONE, HINATA!
GOOD SET, KAGE-YAMA!
WOW! DATE TECH MANAGED TO GET TWO BLOCKERS UP IN FRONT OF HINATA-KUN'S QUICK SET THIS TIME.
YEAH ...
THEY'RE REALLY GOOD.
KARASUNO
DATE TECH
24 1 19
SET 1
KARASUNO SET POINT

*BACK 1 SET: A QUICK SET WHERE THE SETTER SETS THE BALL 2 TO 3 FEET TO HIS RIGHT.

*JERSEY: DATE TECH

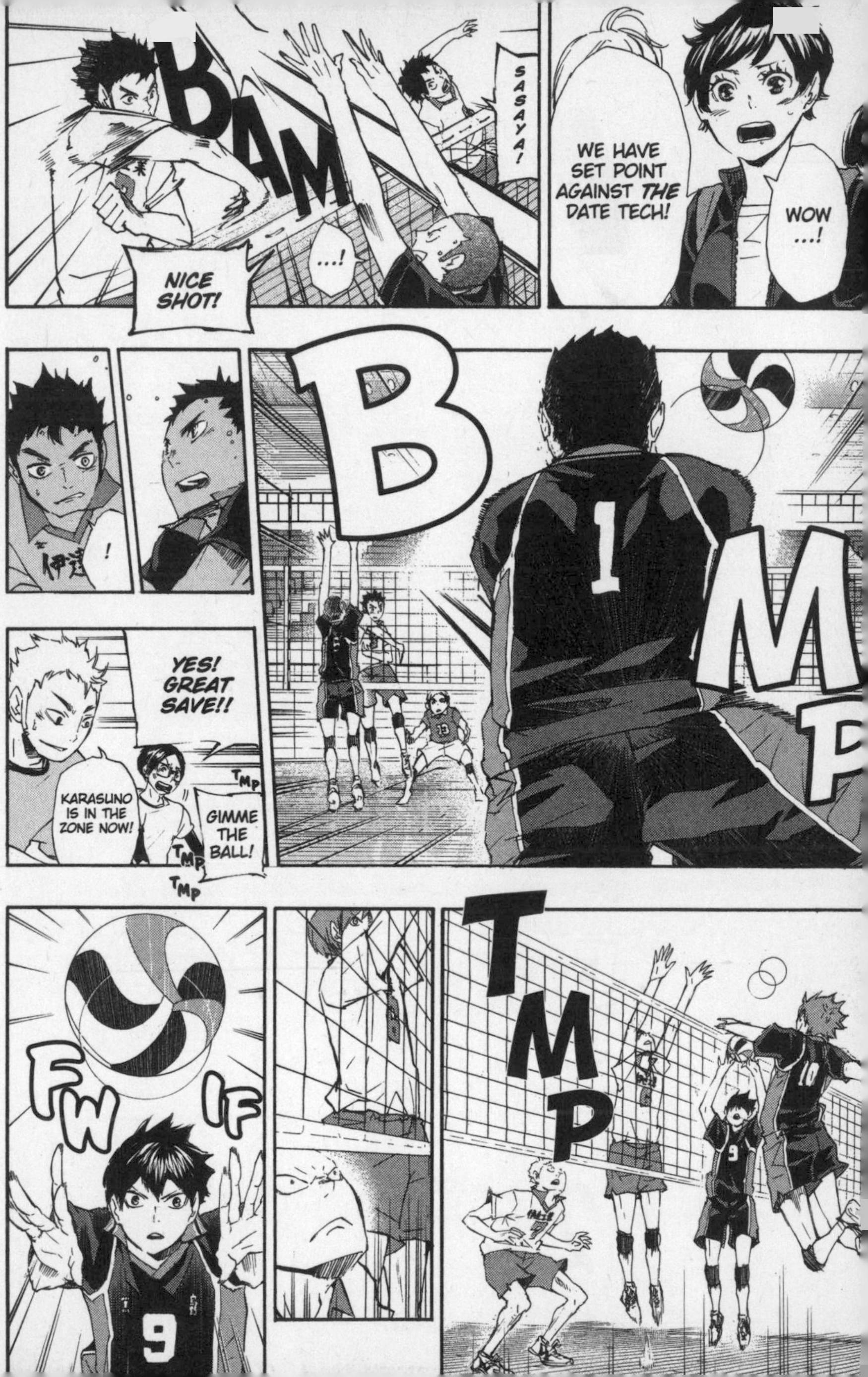
WOW ...!
WE HAVE SET POINT AGAINST THE DATE TECH!
SASAYA!
BAM
...!
NICE SHOT!
BUMP
!
YES! GREAT SAVE!!
GIMME THE BALL!
KARASUNO IS IN THE ZONE NOW!
TMP
TMP
TMP
TMP
FWIF

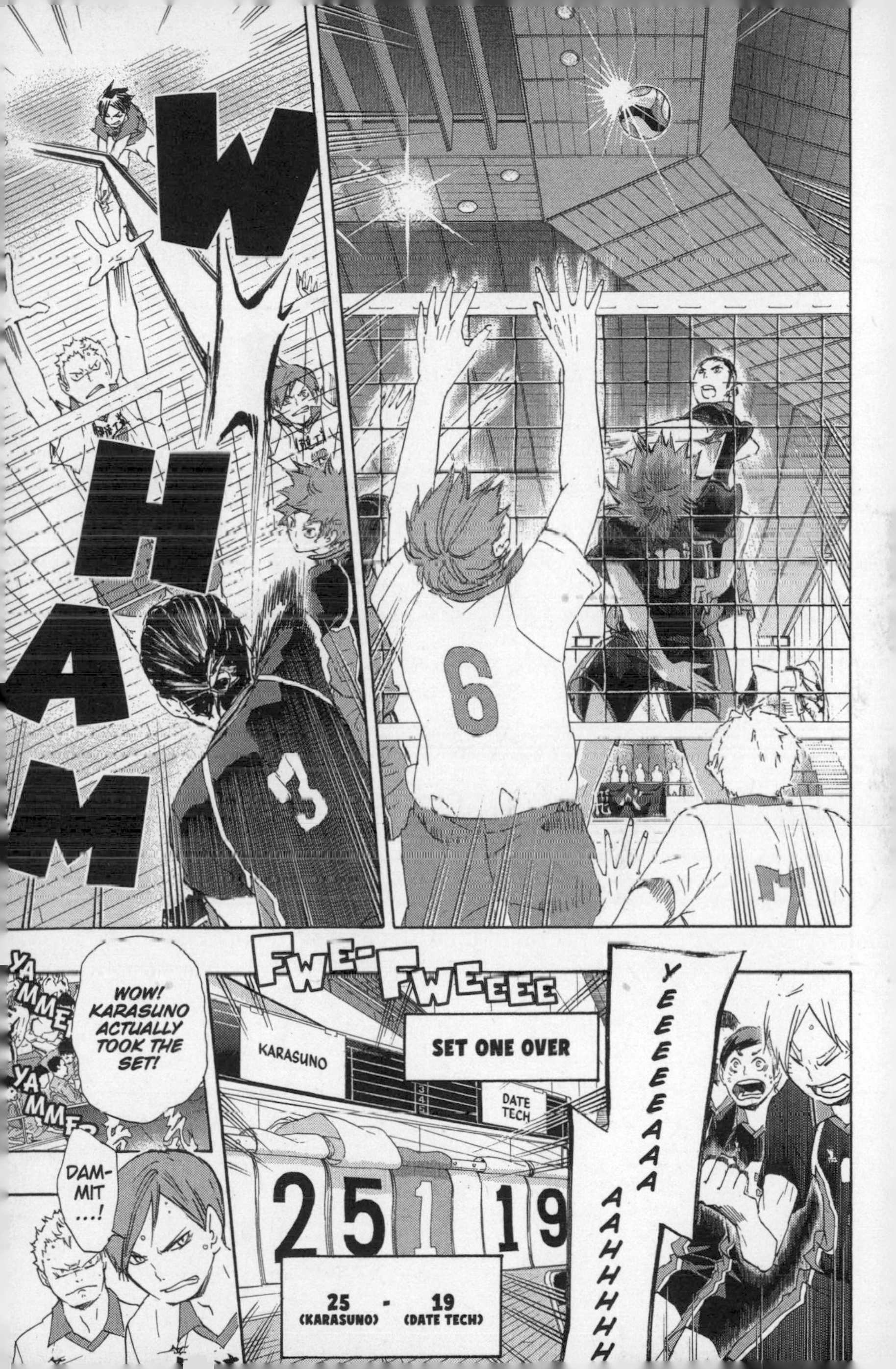
WHAM
YEEEEEEAAAAAHHHHHH
FWE-FWEEEE
SET ONE OVER
KARASUNO
DATE TECH
25 1 19
25 - 19
(KARASUNO) (DATE TECH)
WOW! KARASUNO ACTUALLY TOOK THE SET!
YAMMER
YAMMER
DAM-MIT ...!

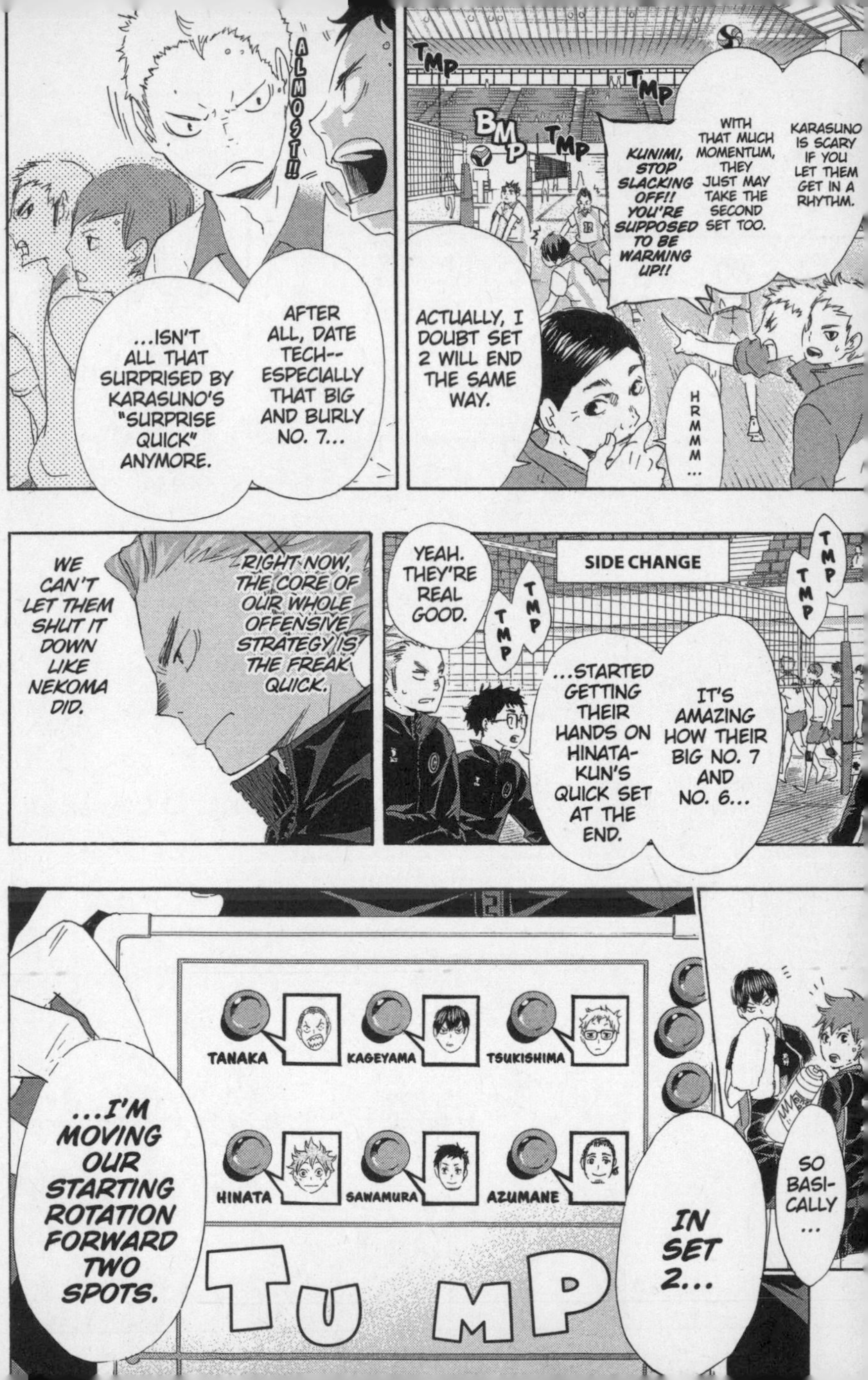
TMP
TMP
KARASUNO IS SCARY IF YOU LET THEM GET IN A RHYTHM.
WITH THAT MUCH MOMENTUM, THEY JUST MAY TAKE THE SECOND SET TOO.
KUNIMI, STOP SLACKING OFF!! YOU'RE SUPPOSED TO BE WARMING UP!!
BMP
TMP
HRMMM...
ACTUALLY, I DOUBT SET 2 WILL END THE SAME WAY.
ALMOST!!
AFTER ALL, DATE TECH--ESPECIALLY THAT BIG AND BURLY NO. 7...
...ISN'T ALL THAT SURPRISED BY KARASUNO'S "SURPRISE QUICK" ANYMORE.
TMP TMP
SIDE CHANGE
IT'S AMAZING HOW THEIR BIG NO. 7 AND NO. 6...
...STARTED GETTING THEIR HANDS ON HINATA-KUN'S QUICK SET AT THE END.
TMP TMP
YEAH. THEY'RE REAL GOOD.
RIGHT NOW, THE CORE OF OUR WHOLE OFFENSIVE STRATEGY IS THE FREAK QUICK.
WE CAN'T LET THEM SHUT IT DOWN LIKE NEKOMA DID.
SO BASICALLY...
IN SET 2...
TSUKISHIMA
KAGEYAMA
TANAKA
AZUMANE
SAWAMURA
HINATA
...I'M MOVING OUR STARTING ROTATION FORWARD TWO SPOTS.
TUMP

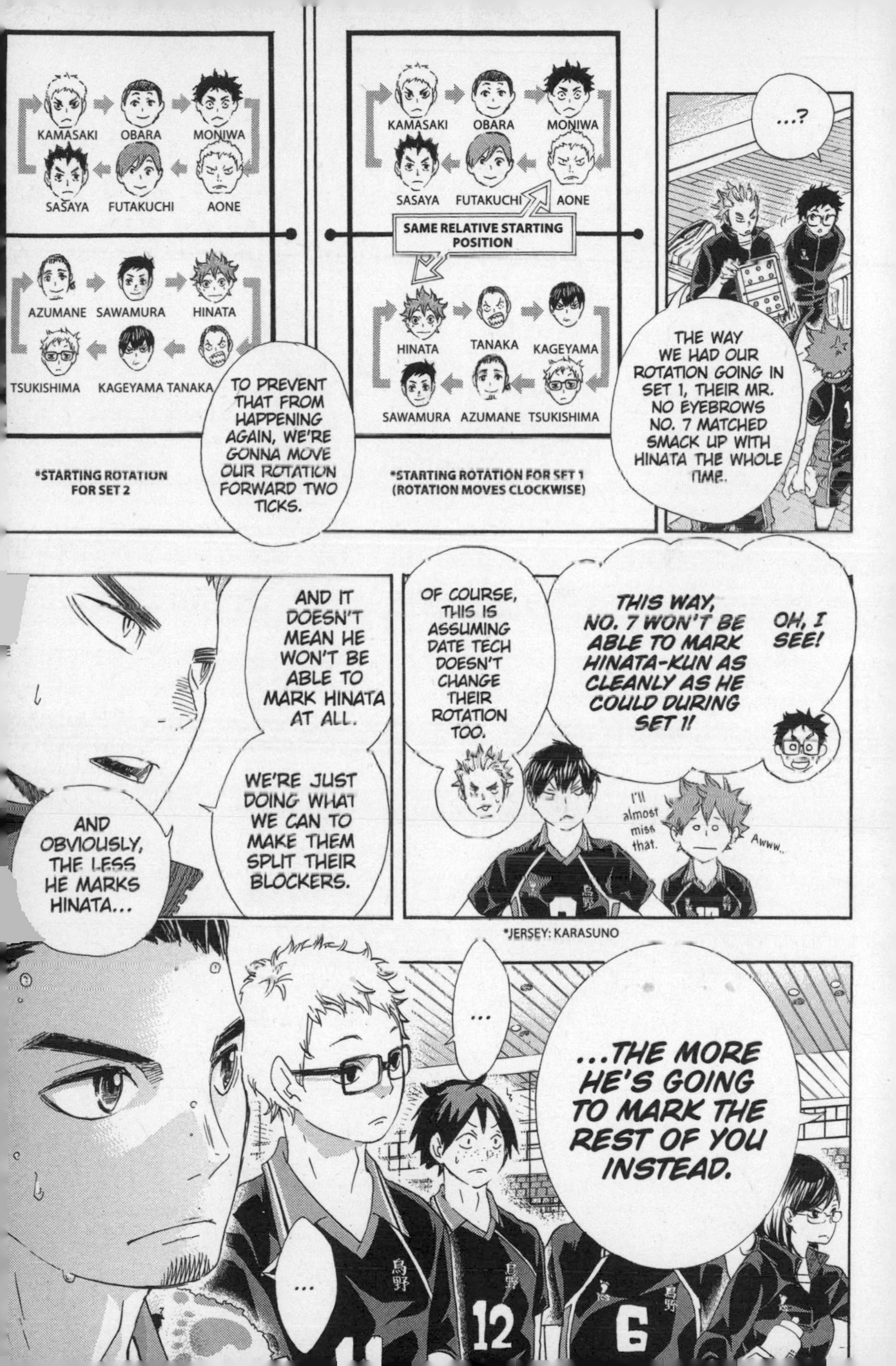

...?
THE WAY WE HAD OUR ROTATION GOING IN SET 1, THEIR MR. NO EYEBROWS NO. 7 MATCHED SMACK UP WITH HINATA THE WHOLE TIME.
KAMASAKI
OBARA
MONIWA
SASAYA
FUTAKUCHI
AONE
SAME RELATIVE STARTING POSITION
HINATA
TANAKA
KAGEYAMA
SAWAMURA
AZUMANE
TSUKISHIMA
*STARTING ROTATION FOR SET 1 (ROTATION MOVES CLOCKWISE)
TO PREVENT THAT FROM HAPPENING AGAIN, WE'RE GONNA MOVE OUR ROTATION FORWARD TWO TICKS.
KAMASAKI
OBARA
MONIWA
SASAYA
FUTAKUCHI
AONE
AZUMANE
SAWAMURA
HINATA
TSUKISHIMA
KAGEYAMA
TANAKA
*STARTING ROTATION FOR SET 2
OH, I SEE!
THIS WAY, NO. 7 WON'T BE ABLE TO MARK HINATA-KUN AS CLEANLY AS HE COULD DURING SET 1!
OF COURSE, THIS IS ASSUMING DATE TECH DOESN'T CHANGE THEIR ROTATION TOO.
I'll almost miss that.
Awww..
AND IT DOESN'T MEAN HE WON'T BE ABLE TO MARK HINATA AT ALL.
WE'RE JUST DOING WHAT WE CAN TO MAKE THEM SPLIT THEIR BLOCKERS.
AND OBVIOUSLY, THE LESS HE MARKS HINATA...
*JERSEY: KARASUNO
...THE MORE HE'S GOING TO MARK THE REST OF YOU INSTEAD.
...
...

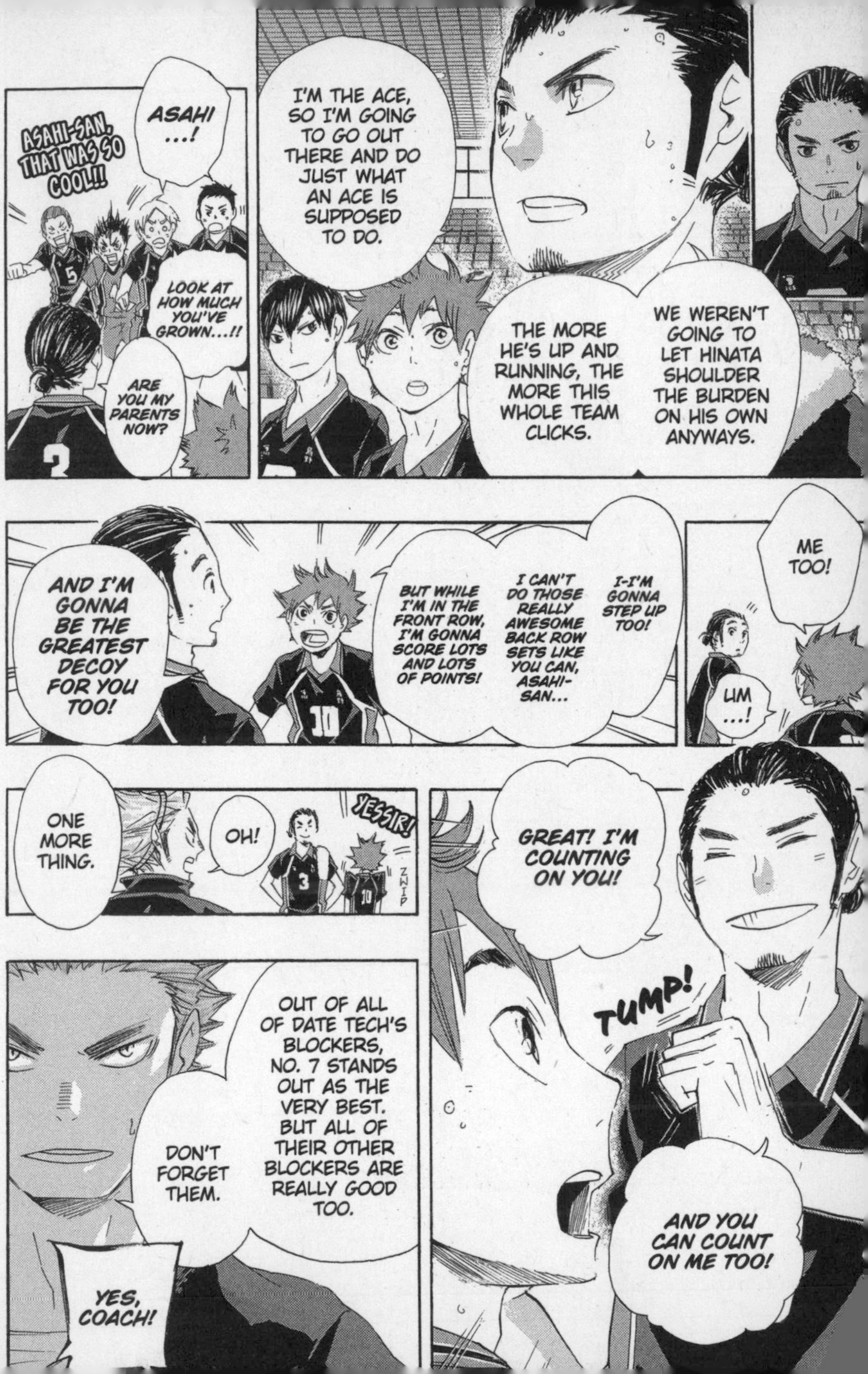
I'M THE ACE, SO I'M GOING TO GO OUT THERE AND DO JUST WHAT AN ACE IS SUPPOSED TO DO.
WE WEREN'T GOING TO LET HINATA SHOULDER THE BURDEN ON HIS OWN ANYWAYS.
THE MORE HE'S UP AND RUNNING, THE MORE THIS WHOLE TEAM CLICKS.
ASAHI ...!
ASAHI-SAN, THAT WAS SO COOL!!
LOOK AT HOW MUCH YOU'VE GROWN...!!
ARE YOU MY PARENTS NOW?
ME TOO!
UM ...!
I-I'M GONNA STEP UP TOO!
I CAN'T DO THOSE REALLY AWESOME BACK ROW SETS LIKE YOU CAN, ASAHI-SAN...
BUT WHILE I'M IN THE FRONT ROW, I'M GONNA SCORE LOTS AND LOTS OF POINTS!
AND I'M GONNA BE THE GREATEST DECOY FOR YOU TOO!
GREAT! I'M COUNTING ON YOU!
TUMP!
AND YOU CAN COUNT ON ME TOO!
YESSIR!
ZWIP
OH!
ONE MORE THING.
OUT OF ALL OF DATE TECH'S BLOCKERS, NO. 7 STANDS OUT AS THE VERY BEST. BUT ALL OF THEIR OTHER BLOCKERS ARE REALLY GOOD TOO.
DON'T FORGET THEM.
YES, COACH!

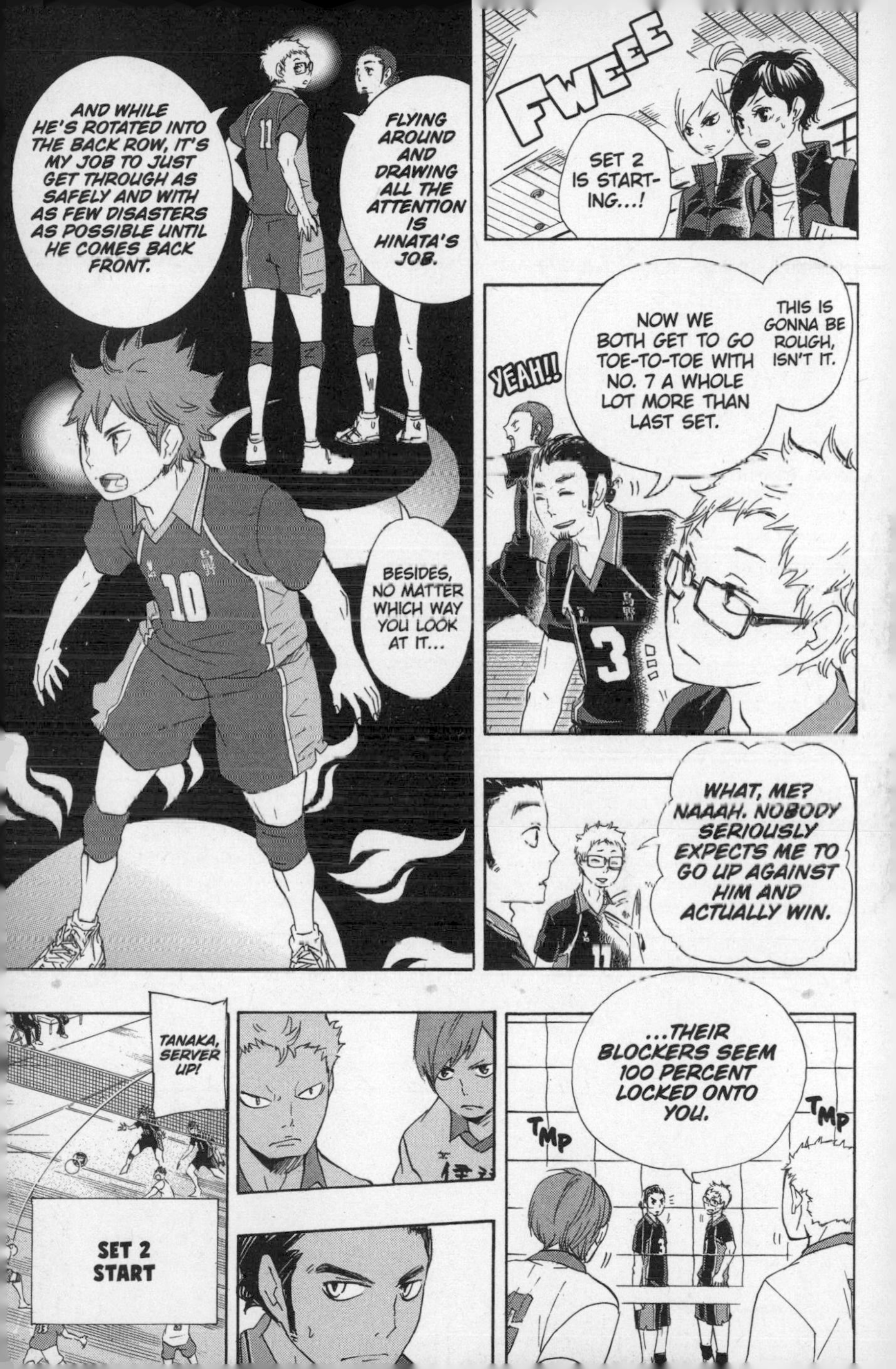
FWEEE
SET 2 IS START-ING...!
THIS IS GONNA BE ROUGH, ISN'T IT.
NOW WE BOTH GET TO GO TOE-TO-TOE WITH NO. 7 A WHOLE LOT MORE THAN LAST SET.
YEAH!!
WHAT, ME? NAAAH. NOBODY SERIOUSLY EXPECTS ME TO GO UP AGAINST HIM AND ACTUALLY WIN.
FLYING AROUND AND DRAWING ALL THE ATTENTION IS HINATA'S JOB.
AND WHILE HE'S ROTATED INTO THE BACK ROW, IT'S MY JOB TO JUST GET THROUGH AS SAFELY AND WITH AS FEW DISASTERS AS POSSIBLE UNTIL HE COMES BACK FRONT.
BESIDES, NO MATTER WHICH WAY YOU LOOK AT IT...
...THEIR BLOCKERS SEEM 100 PERCENT LOCKED ONTO YOU.
TMP
TMP
TANAKA, SERVER UP!
SET 2 START

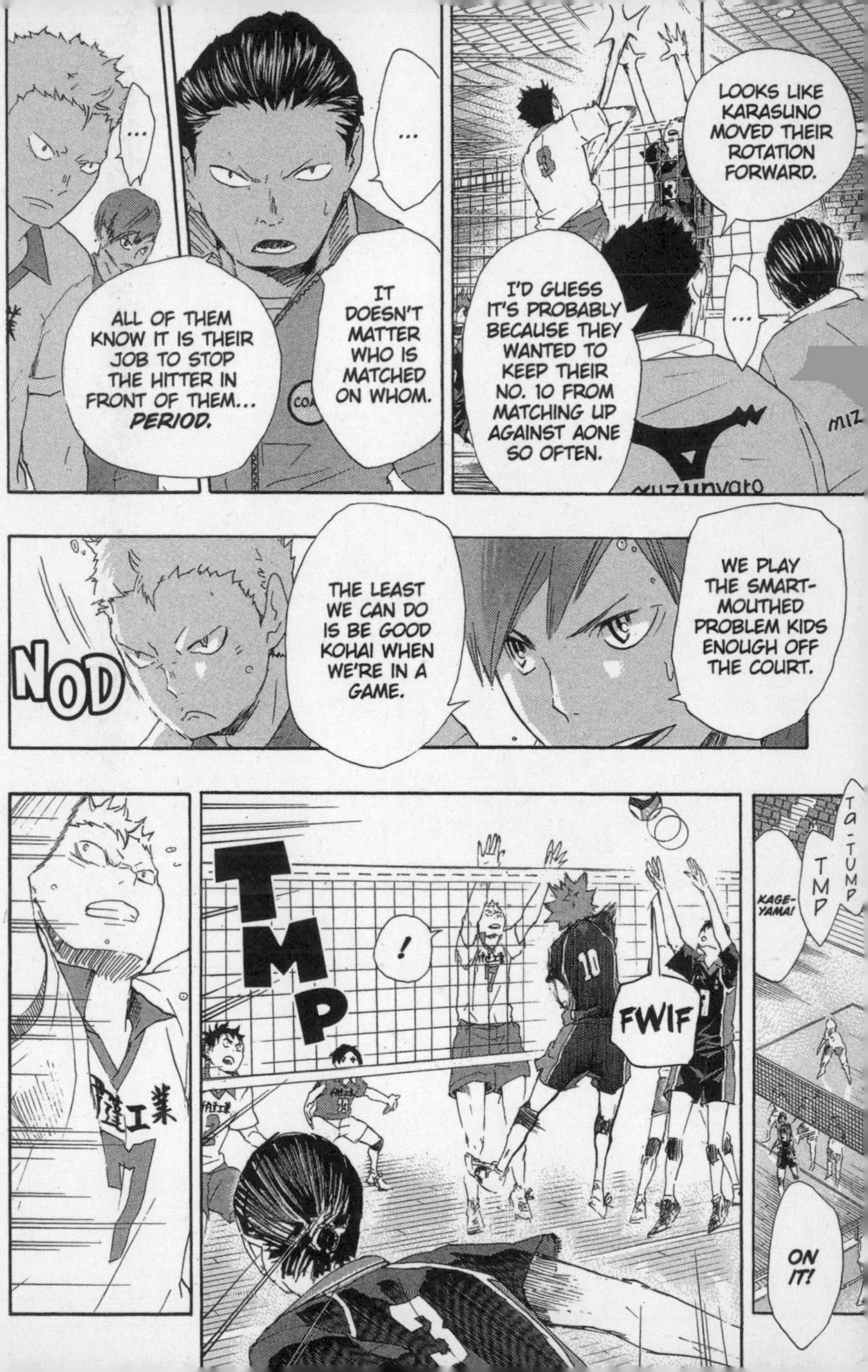

LOOKS LIKE KARASUNO MOVED THEIR ROTATION FORWARD.
I'D GUESS IT'S PROBABLY BECAUSE THEY WANTED TO KEEP THEIR NO. 10 FROM MATCHING UP AGAINST AONE SO OFTEN.
...
...
IT DOESN'T MATTER WHO IS MATCHED ON WHOM.
...
ALL OF THEM KNOW IT IS THEIR JOB TO STOP THE HITTER IN FRONT OF THEM... *PERIOD.*
WE PLAY THE SMART-MOUTHED PROBLEM KIDS ENOUGH OFF THE COURT.
THE LEAST WE CAN DO IS BE GOOD KOHAI WHEN WE'RE IN A GAME.
NOD
TA-TUMP
TMP
KAGEYAMA!
ON IT!
TMP
!
FWIF

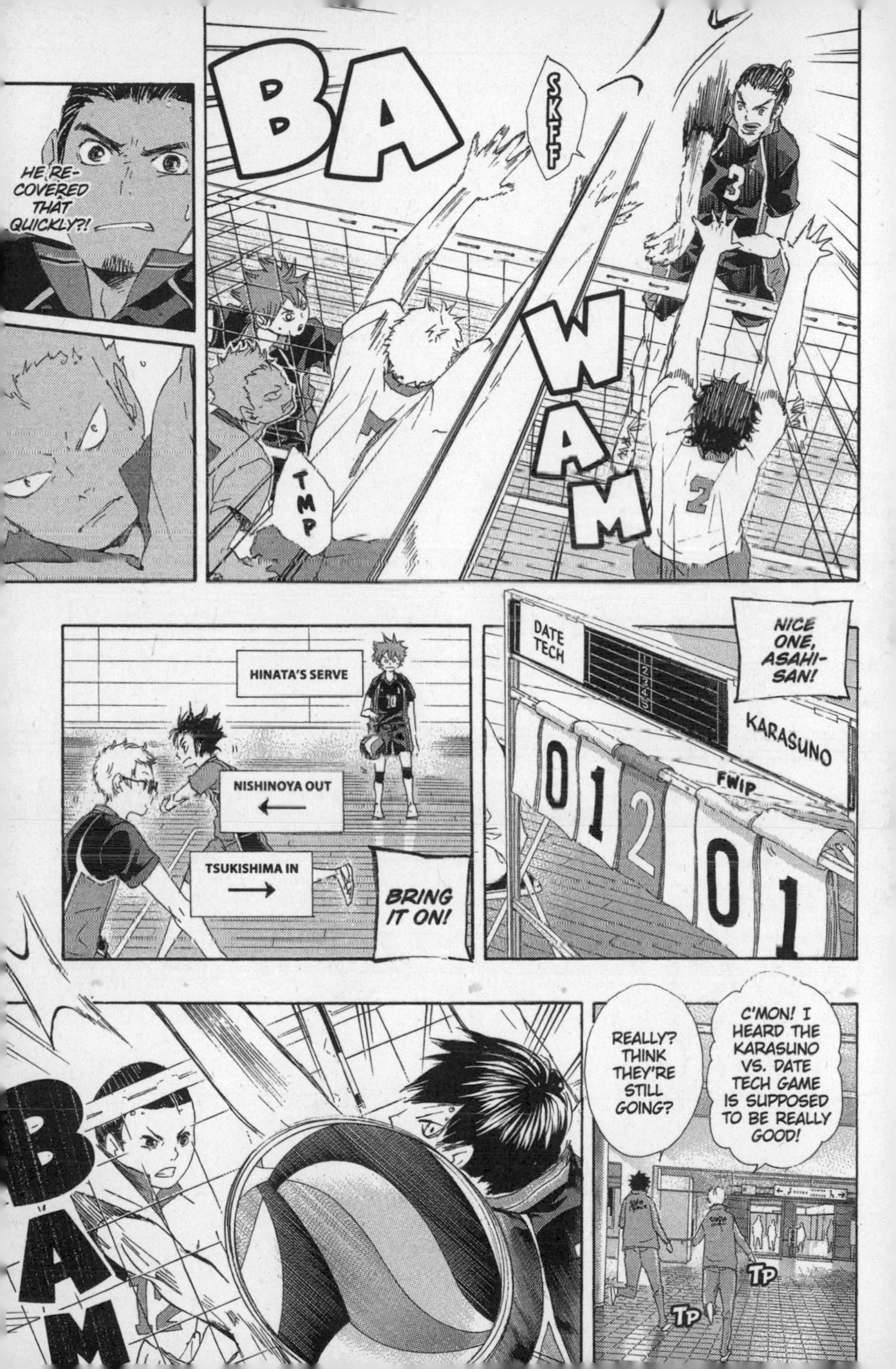

BA
SKFF
WAM
TMP
HE RE-COVERED THAT QUICKLY?!
NICE ONE, ASAHI-SAN!
DATE TECH
KARASUNO
FWIP
HINATA'S SERVE
NISHINOYA OUT
TSUKISHIMA IN
BRING IT ON!
C'MON! I HEARD THE KARASUNO VS. DATE TECH GAME IS SUPPOSED TO BE REALLY GOOD!
REALLY? THINK THEY'RE STILL GOING?
TP
TP
BAM

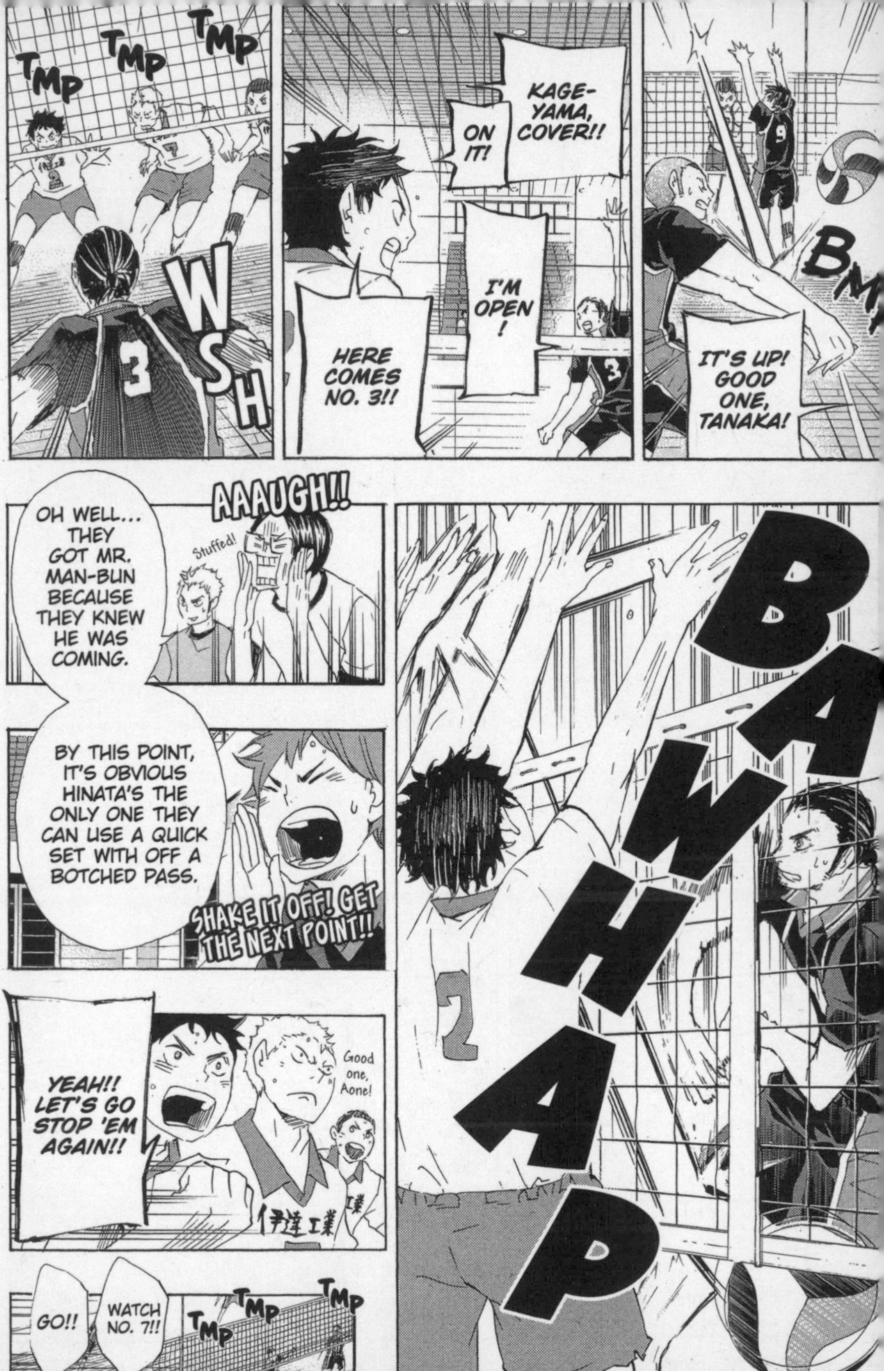
BMP
IT'S UP! GOOD ONE, TANAKA!
KAGE-YAMA, COVER!!
ON IT!
I'M OPEN!
HERE COMES NO. 3!!
TMP
TMP
TMP
WSH
BAWHAP
AAAUGH!!
Stuffed!
OH WELL... THEY GOT MR. MAN-BUN BECAUSE THEY KNEW HE WAS COMING.
BY THIS POINT, IT'S OBVIOUS HINATA'S THE ONLY ONE THEY CAN USE A QUICK SET WITH OFF A BOTCHED PASS.
SHAKE IT OFF! GET THE NEXT POINT!!
Good one, Aone!
YEAH!! LET'S GO STOP 'EM AGAIN!!
WATCH NO. 7!!
GO!!
TMP
TMP
TMP

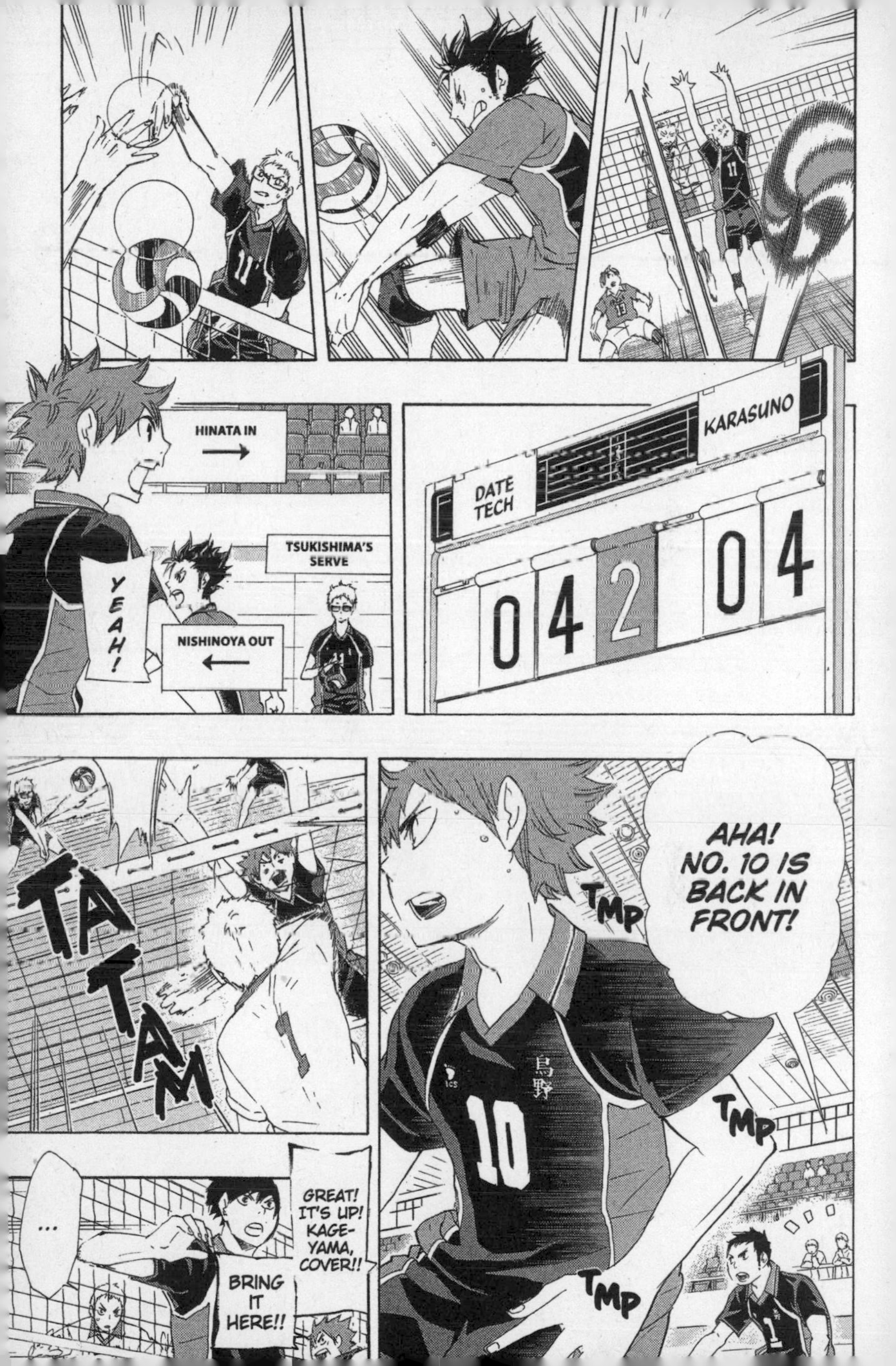

KARASUNO
DATE TECH
04 2 04
HINATA IN
TSUKISHIMA'S SERVE
NISHINOYA OUT
YEAH!
AHA! NO. 10 IS BACK IN FRONT!
TMP
TMP
TMP
TA TA TAM
GREAT! IT'S UP! KAGE-YAMA, COVER!!
BRING IT HERE!!
...

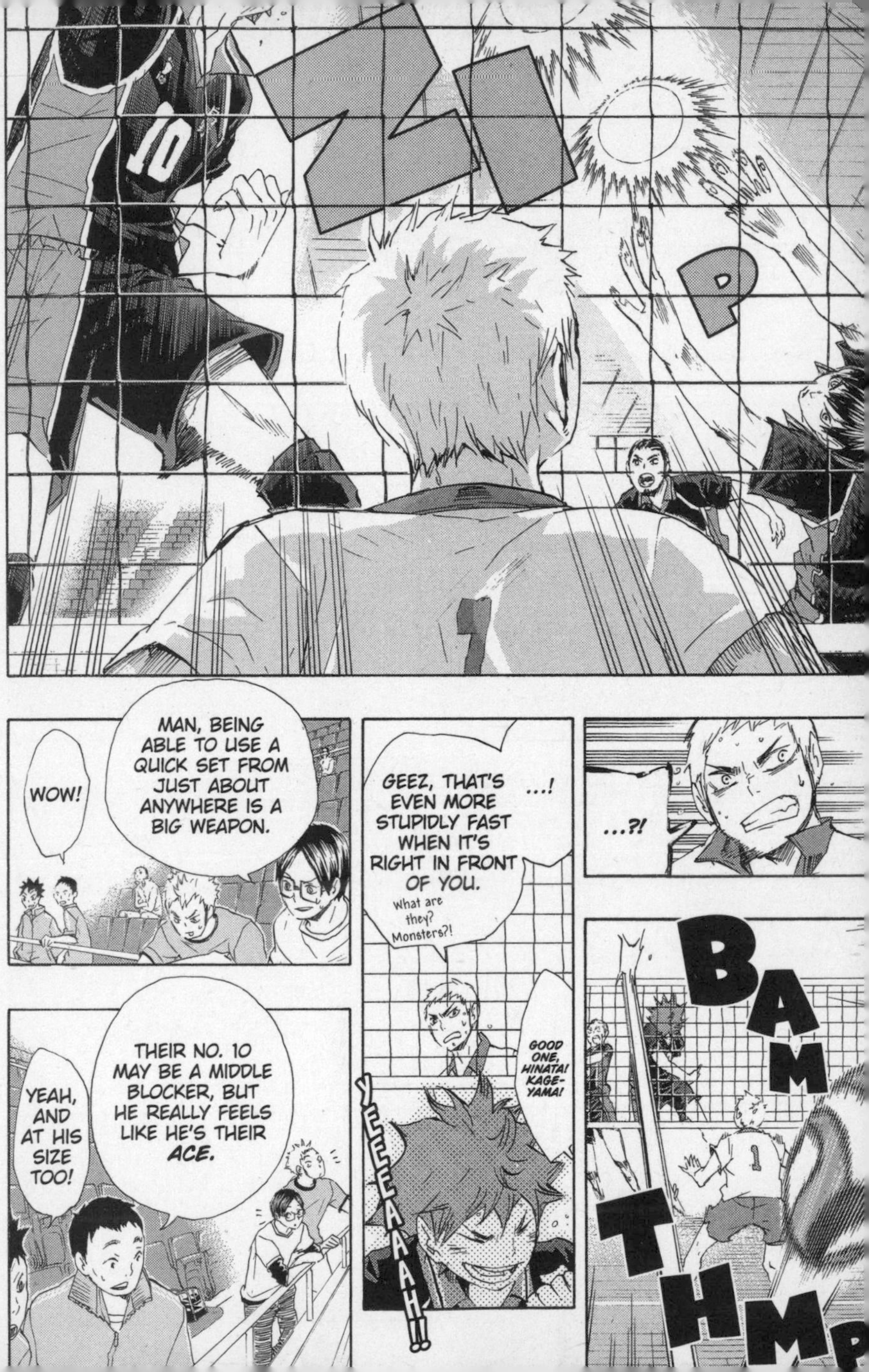
P
...?!
BAM
THMP
...!
GEEZ, THAT'S EVEN MORE STUPIDLY FAST WHEN IT'S RIGHT IN FRONT OF YOU.
What are they? Monsters?!
GOOD ONE, HINATA! KAGE-YAMA!
YEEEAAAAH!!
MAN, BEING ABLE TO USE A QUICK SET FROM JUST ABOUT ANYWHERE IS A BIG WEAPON.
WOW!
THEIR NO. 10 MAY BE A MIDDLE BLOCKER, BUT HE REALLY FEELS LIKE HE'S THEIR ACE.
YEAH, AND AT HIS SIZE TOO!

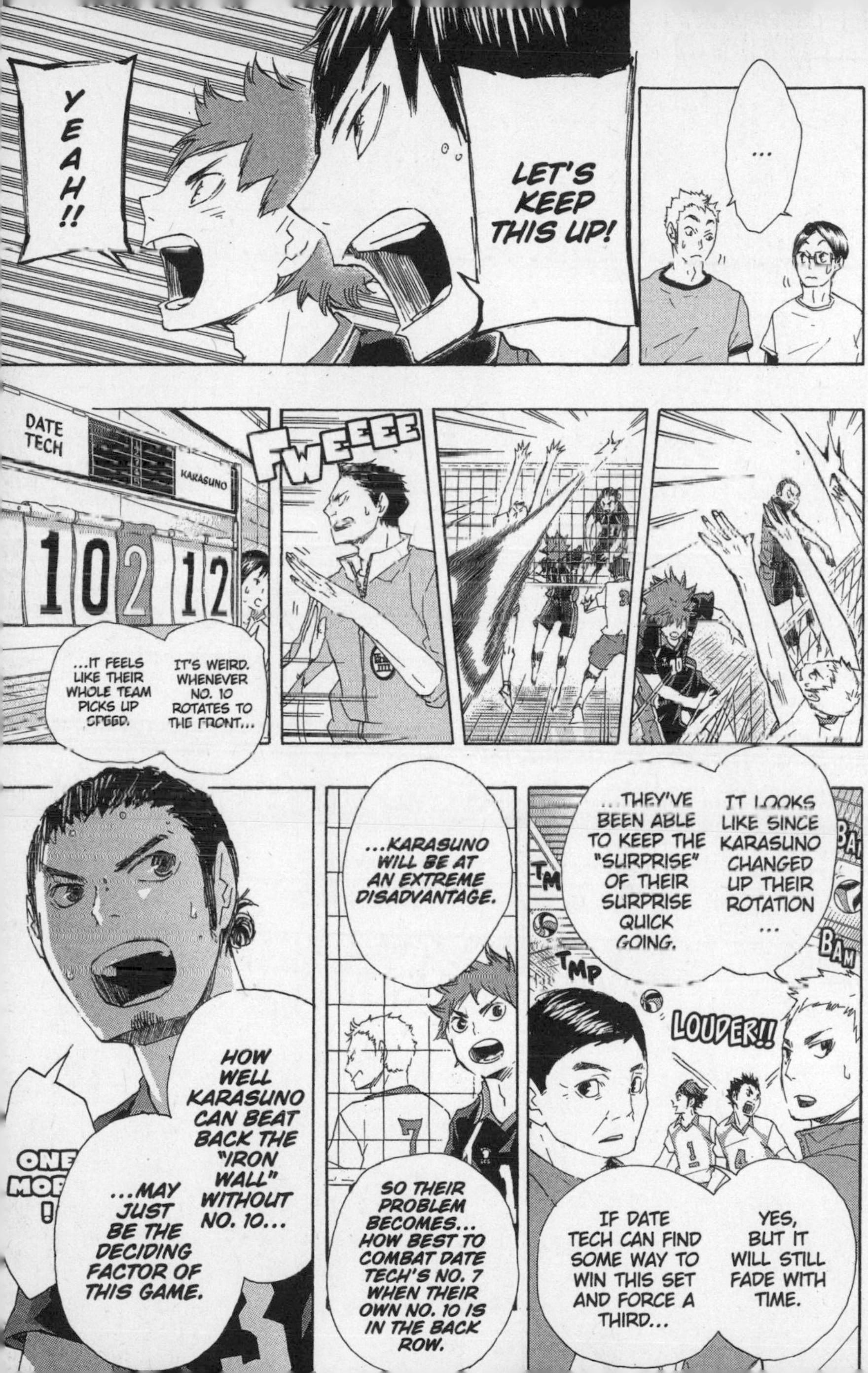
...
LET'S KEEP THIS UP!
YEAH!!
FWEEEE
DATE TECH
KARASUNO
10 2 12
IT'S WEIRD. WHENEVER NO. 10 ROTATES TO THE FRONT...
...IT FEELS LIKE THEIR WHOLE TEAM PICKS UP SPEED.
IT LOOKS LIKE SINCE KARASUNO CHANGED UP THEIR ROTATION...
...THEY'VE BEEN ABLE TO KEEP THE "SURPRISE" OF THEIR SURPRISE QUICK GOING.
BAM
BAM
TMP
TMP
LOUDER!!
YES, BUT IT WILL STILL FADE WITH TIME.
IF DATE TECH CAN FIND SOME WAY TO WIN THIS SET AND FORCE A THIRD...
...KARASUNO WILL BE AT AN EXTREME DISADVANTAGE.
SO THEIR PROBLEM BECOMES... HOW BEST TO COMBAT DATE TECH'S NO. 7 WHEN THEIR OWN NO. 10 IS IN THE BACK ROW.
HOW WELL KARASUNO CAN BEAT BACK THE "IRON WALL" WITHOUT NO. 10...
...MAY JUST BE THE DECIDING FACTOR OF THIS GAME.
ONE MOR !

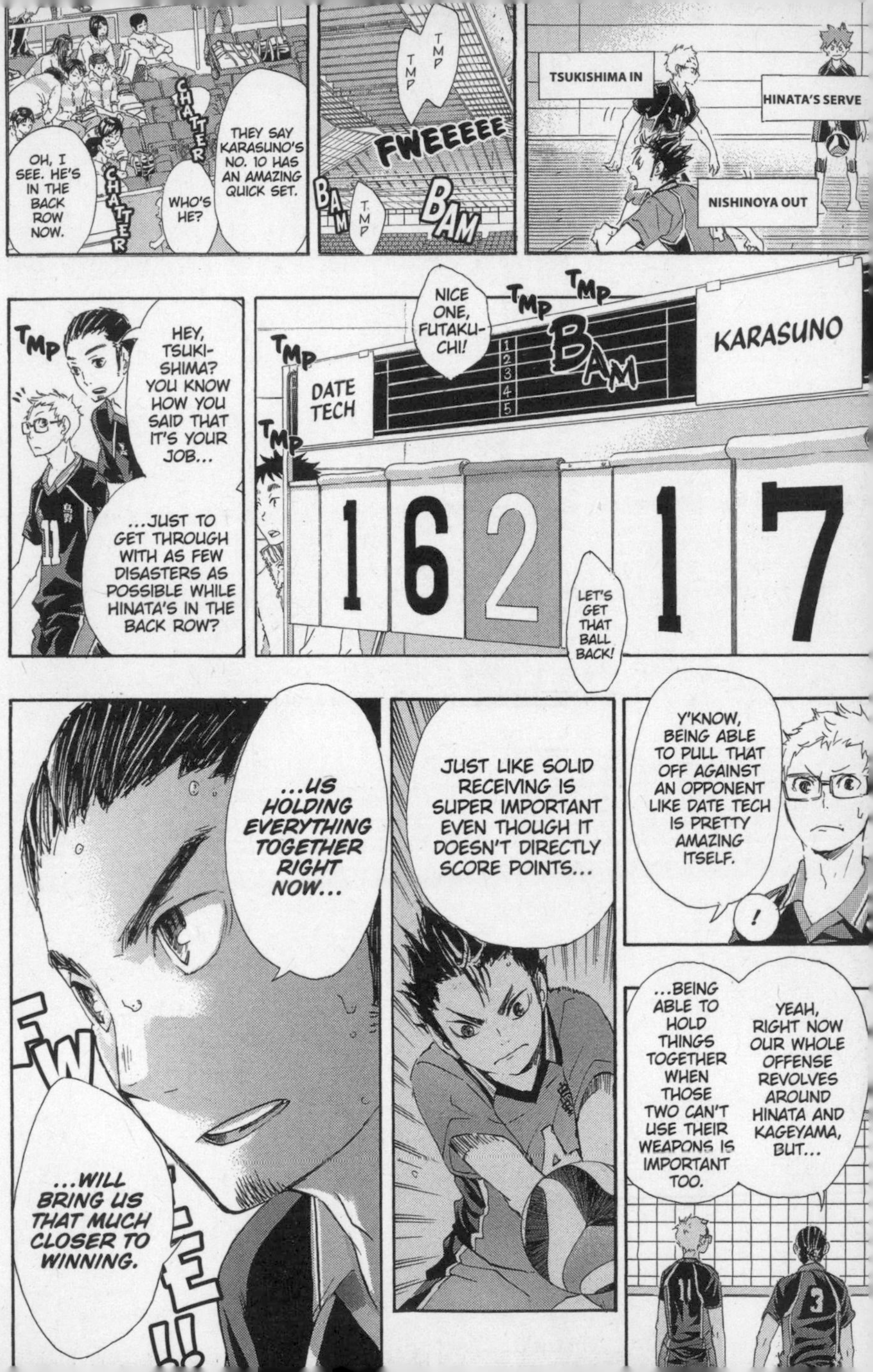
HINATA'S SERVE
TSUKISHIMA IN
NISHINOYA OUT
TMP TMP
FWEEEEE
BAM
TMP
BAM
THEY SAY KARASUNO'S NO. 10 HAS AN AMAZING QUICK SET.
CHATTER
WHO'S HE?
CHATTER
OH, I SEE. HE'S IN THE BACK ROW NOW.
KARASUNO
NICE ONE, FUTAKUCHI!
TMP
TMP
BAM
DATE TECH
TMP
TMP
1 2 3 4 5
16 2 17
LET'S GET THAT BALL BACK!
TMP
HEY, TSUKISHIMA? YOU KNOW HOW YOU SAID THAT IT'S YOUR JOB...
...JUST TO GET THROUGH WITH AS FEW DISASTERS AS POSSIBLE WHILE HINATA'S IN THE BACK ROW?
Y'KNOW, BEING ABLE TO PULL THAT OFF AGAINST AN OPPONENT LIKE DATE TECH IS PRETTY AMAZING ITSELF.
!
YEAH, RIGHT NOW OUR WHOLE OFFENSE REVOLVES AROUND HINATA AND KAGEYAMA, BUT...
...BEING ABLE TO HOLD THINGS TOGETHER WHEN THOSE TWO CAN'T USE THEIR WEAPONS IS IMPORTANT TOO.
JUST LIKE SOLID RECEIVING IS SUPER IMPORTANT EVEN THOUGH IT DOESN'T DIRECTLY SCORE POINTS...
...US HOLDING EVERYTHING TOGETHER RIGHT NOW...
...WILL BRING US THAT MUCH CLOSER TO WINNING.

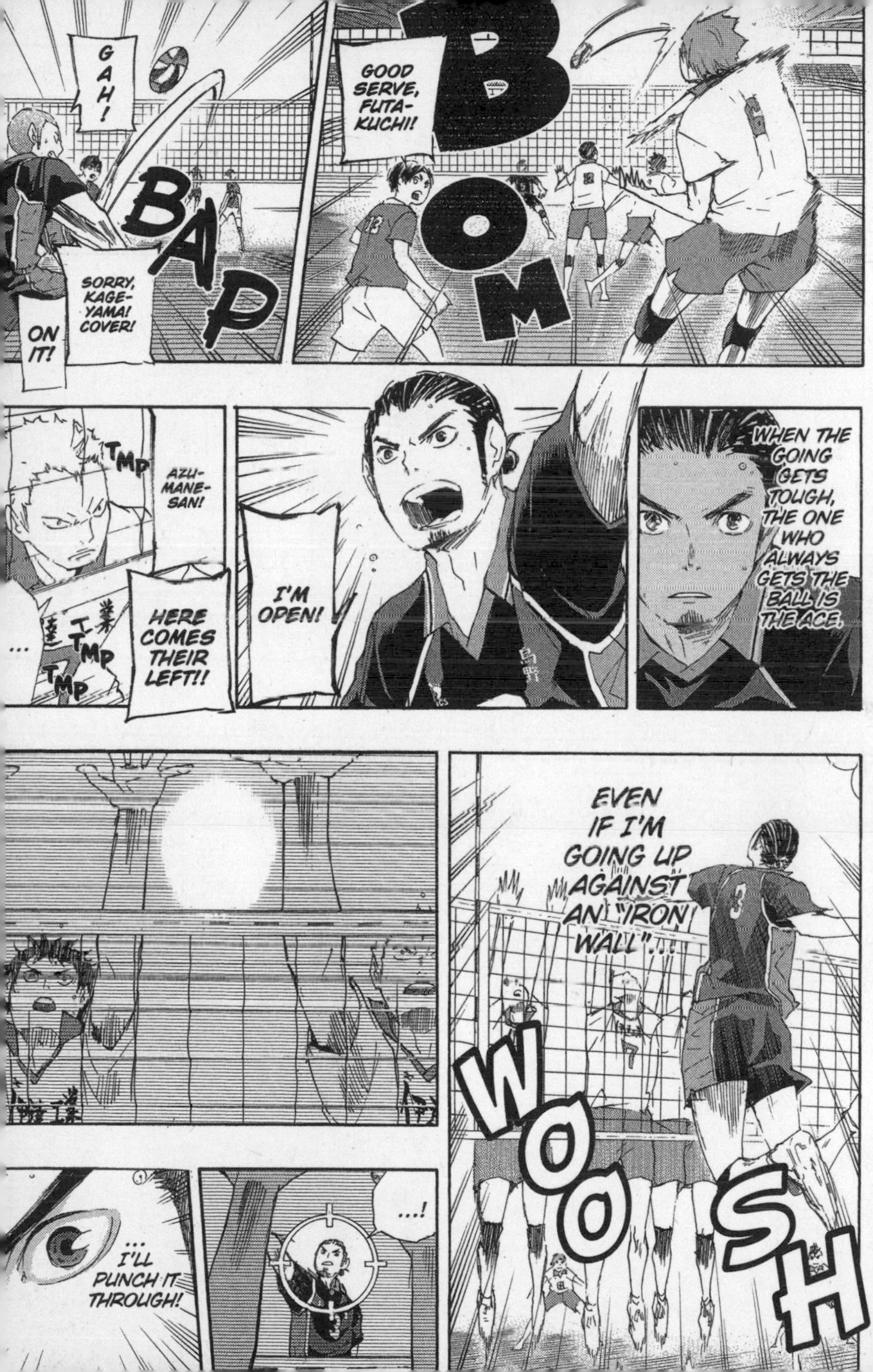
GOOD SERVE, FUTAKUCHI!
BOOM
GAH!
BAP
SORRY, KAGEYAMA! COVER!
ON IT!
WHEN THE GOING GETS TOUGH, THE ONE WHO ALWAYS GETS THE BALL IS THE ACE.
I'M OPEN!
TMP
AZUMANE-SAN!
HERE COMES THEIR LEFT!!
...
TMP
TMP
EVEN IF I'M GOING UP AGAINST AN "IRON WALL"...
WOOSH
...!
... I'LL PUNCH IT THROUGH!

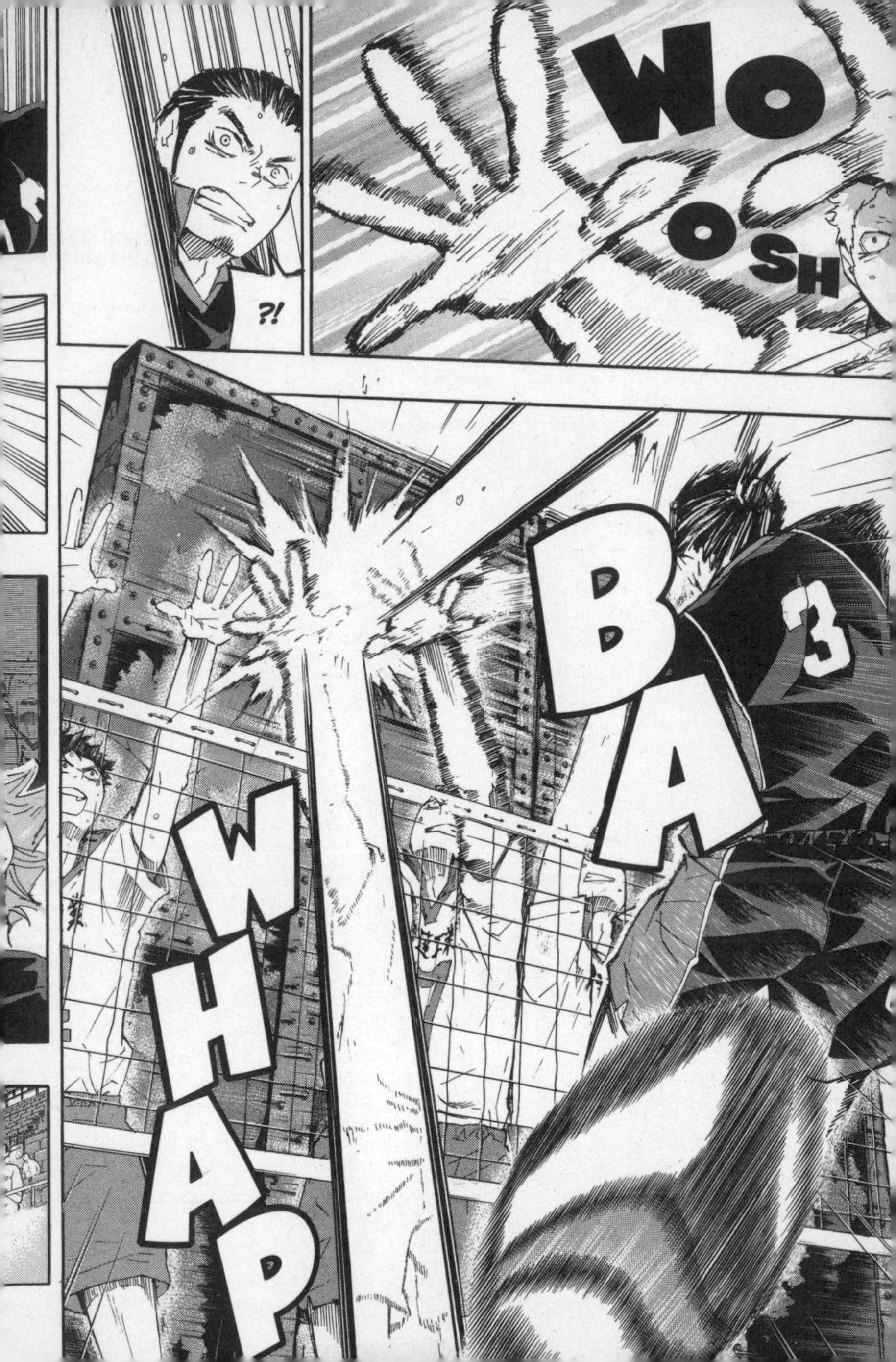
WOOSH
?!
BA
WHAP

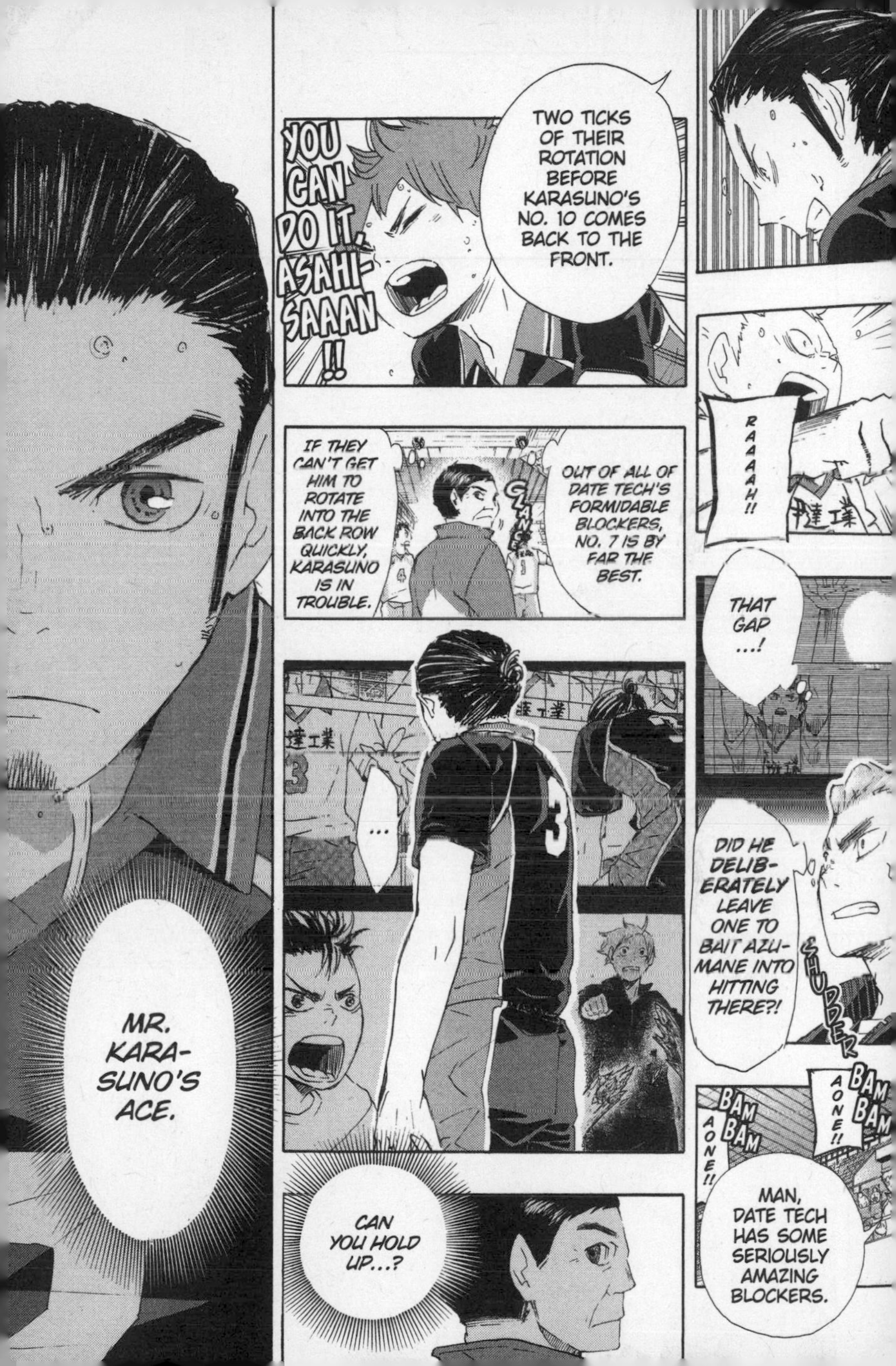

RAAAAAH!!
THAT GAP ...!
DID HE DELIBERATELY LEAVE ONE TO BAIT AZUMANE INTO HITTING THERE?!
SHUDDER
BAM BAM
AONE!!
BAM BAM
AONE!!
MAN, DATE TECH HAS SOME SERIOUSLY AMAZING BLOCKERS.
TWO TICKS OF THEIR ROTATION BEFORE KARASUNO'S NO. 10 COMES BACK TO THE FRONT.
YOU CAN DO IT, ASAHI-SAAAN!!
OUT OF ALL OF DATE TECH'S FORMIDABLE BLOCKERS, NO. 7 IS BY FAR THE BEST.
GLANCE
IF THEY CAN'T GET HIM TO ROTATE INTO THE BACK ROW QUICKLY, KARASUNO IS IN TROUBLE.
...
CAN YOU HOLD UP...?
MR. KARASUNO'S ACE.

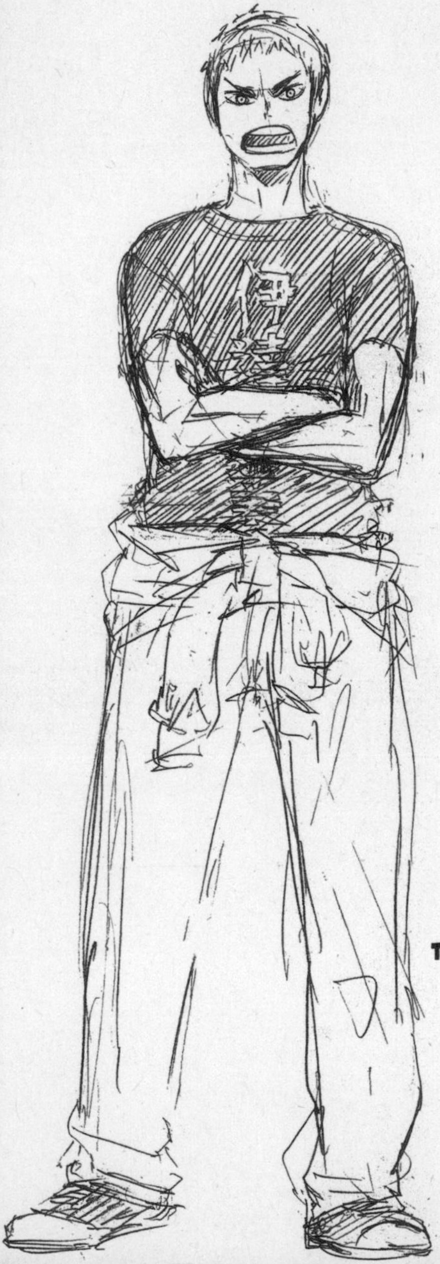

YASUSHI KAMASAKI

DATE TECHNICAL HIGH SCHOOL
CLASS 3-A

POSITION:
MIDDLE BLOCKER

HEIGHT: 6'1"

WEIGHT: 181 LBS.
(AS OF APRIL, 3RD YEAR
OF HIGH SCHOOL)

BIRTHDAY: NOVEMBER 8

FAVORITE FOOD:
MONAKA (SWEET
WHITE BEAN PASTE
FILLING) CAKES

CURRENT WORRY:
HOW MUCH MORE RIPPED
CAN HE GET?!

ABILITY PARAMETERS
(5-POINT SCALE)

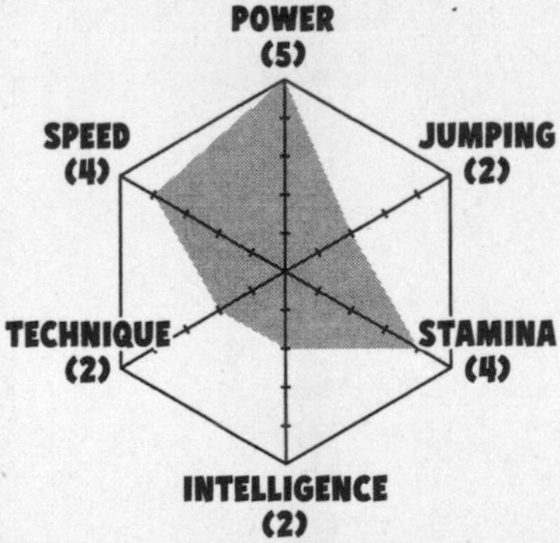
POWER (5)
JUMPING (2)
STAMINA (4)
INTELLIGENCE (2)
TECHNIQUE (2)
SPEED (4)

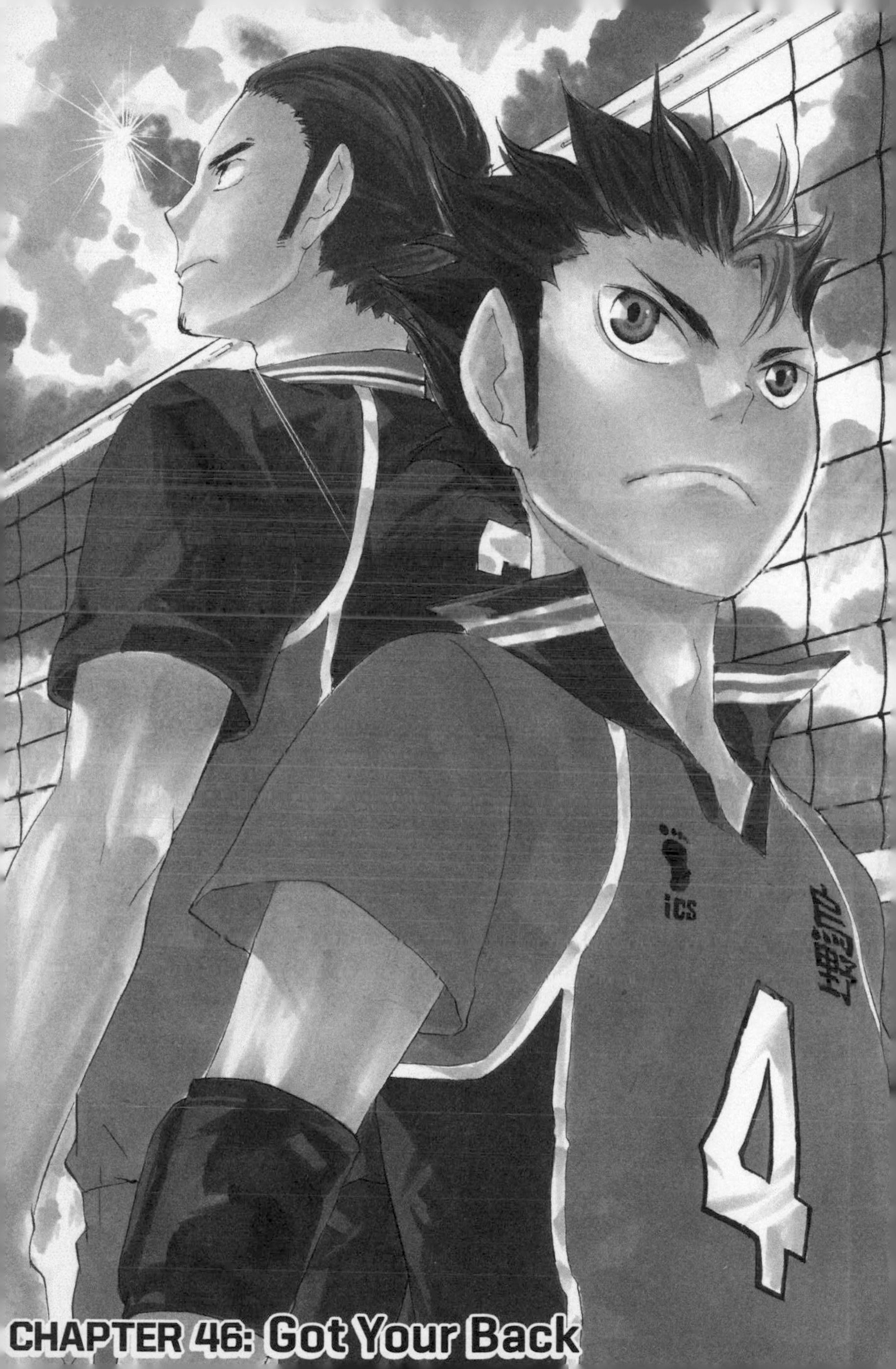

CHAPTER 46: Got Your Back

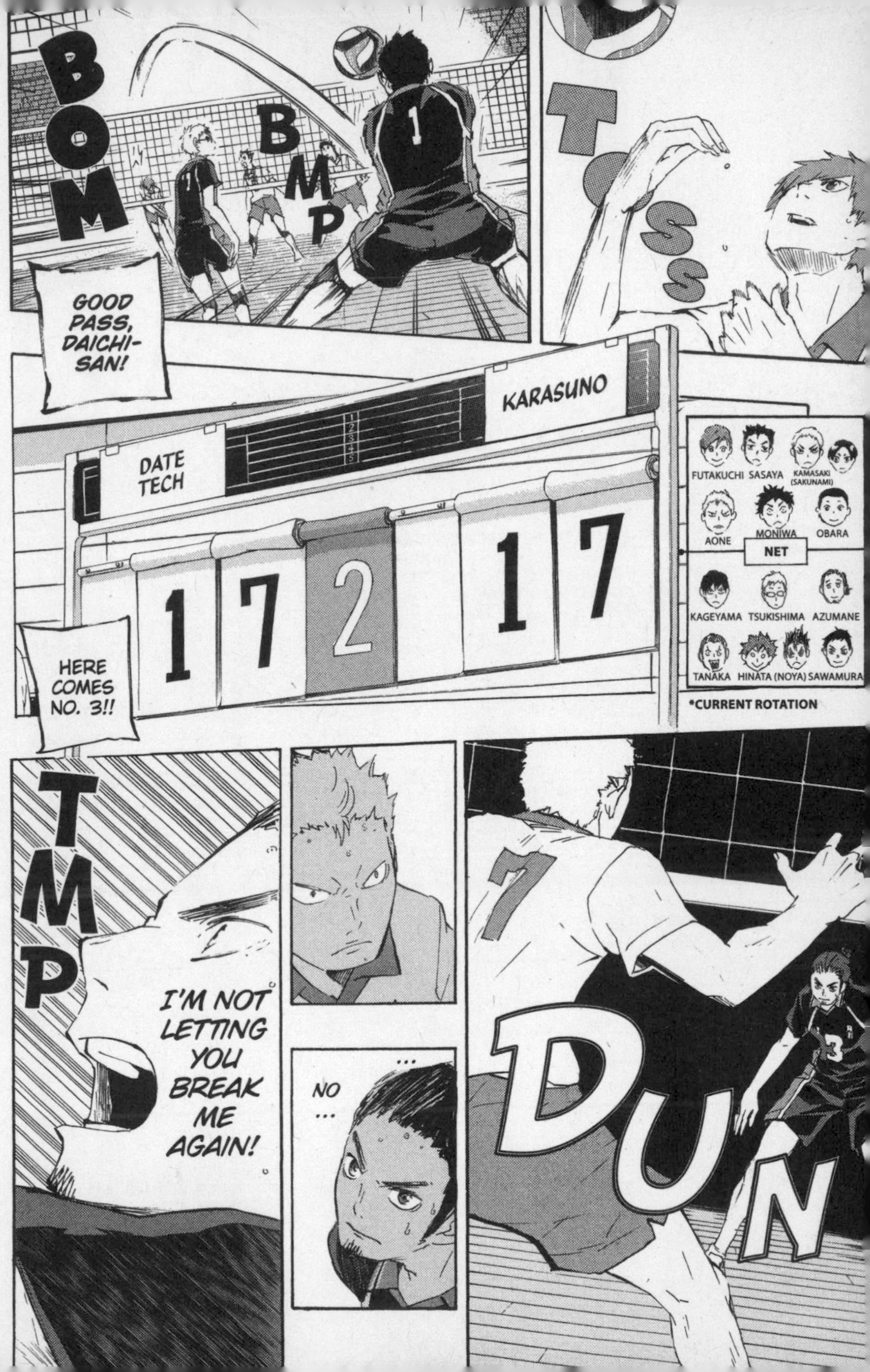

TOSS
BOM
BMP
GOOD PASS, DAICHI-SAN!
KARASUNO
DATE TECH
1 2 3 4 5
17
2
17
FUTAKUCHI
SASAYA
KAMASAKI (SAKUNAMI)
AONE
MONIWA
OBARA
NET
KAGEYAMA
TSUKISHIMA
AZUMANE
TANAKA
HINATA (NOYA)
SAWAMURA
*CURRENT ROTATION
HERE COMES NO. 3!!
DUN
...
NO ...
TMP
I'M NOT LETTING YOU BREAK ME AGAIN!

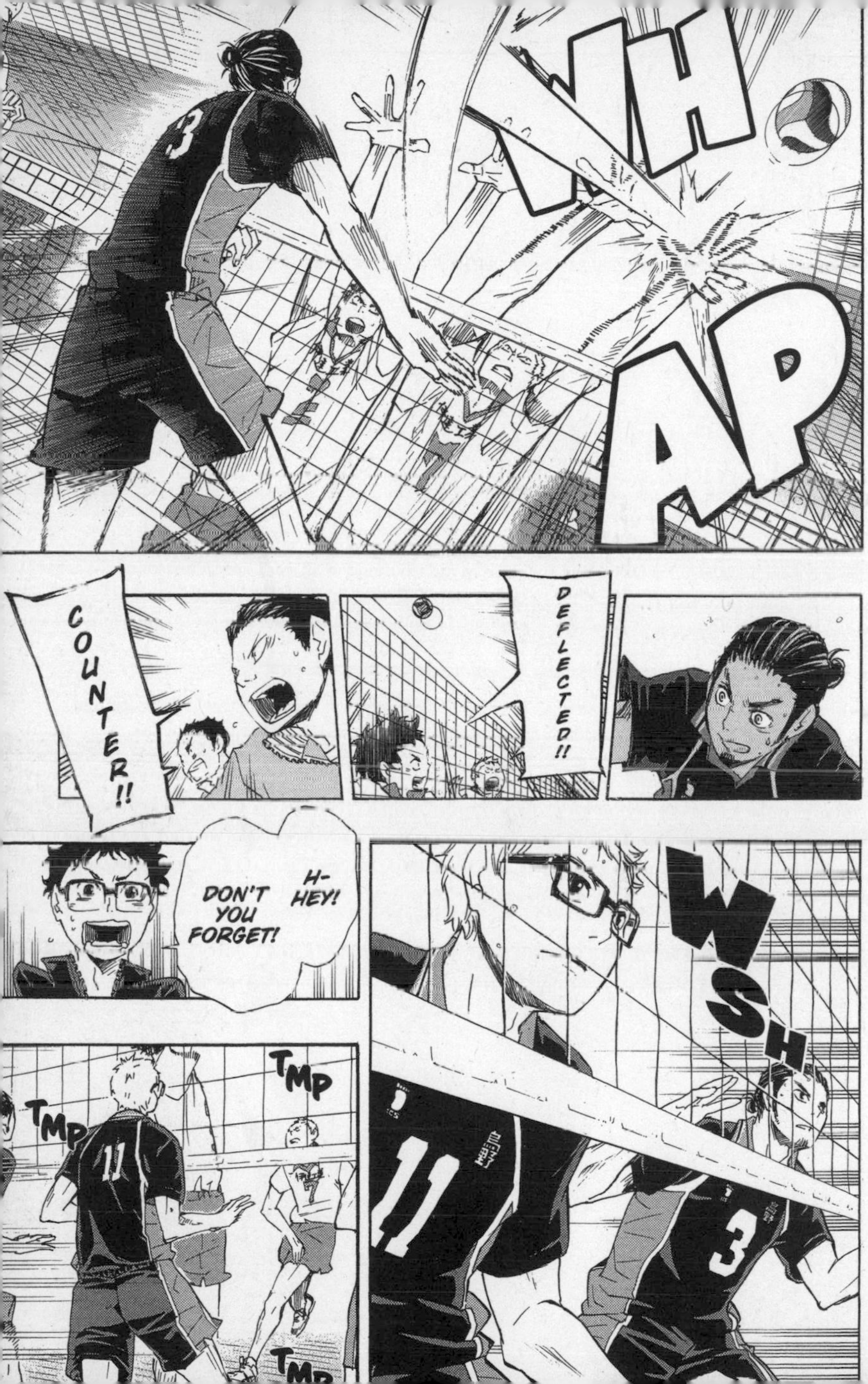
WHAP
DEFLECTED!!
COUNTER!!
WSH
H-HEY!
DON'T YOU FORGET!
TMP
TMP
TMP

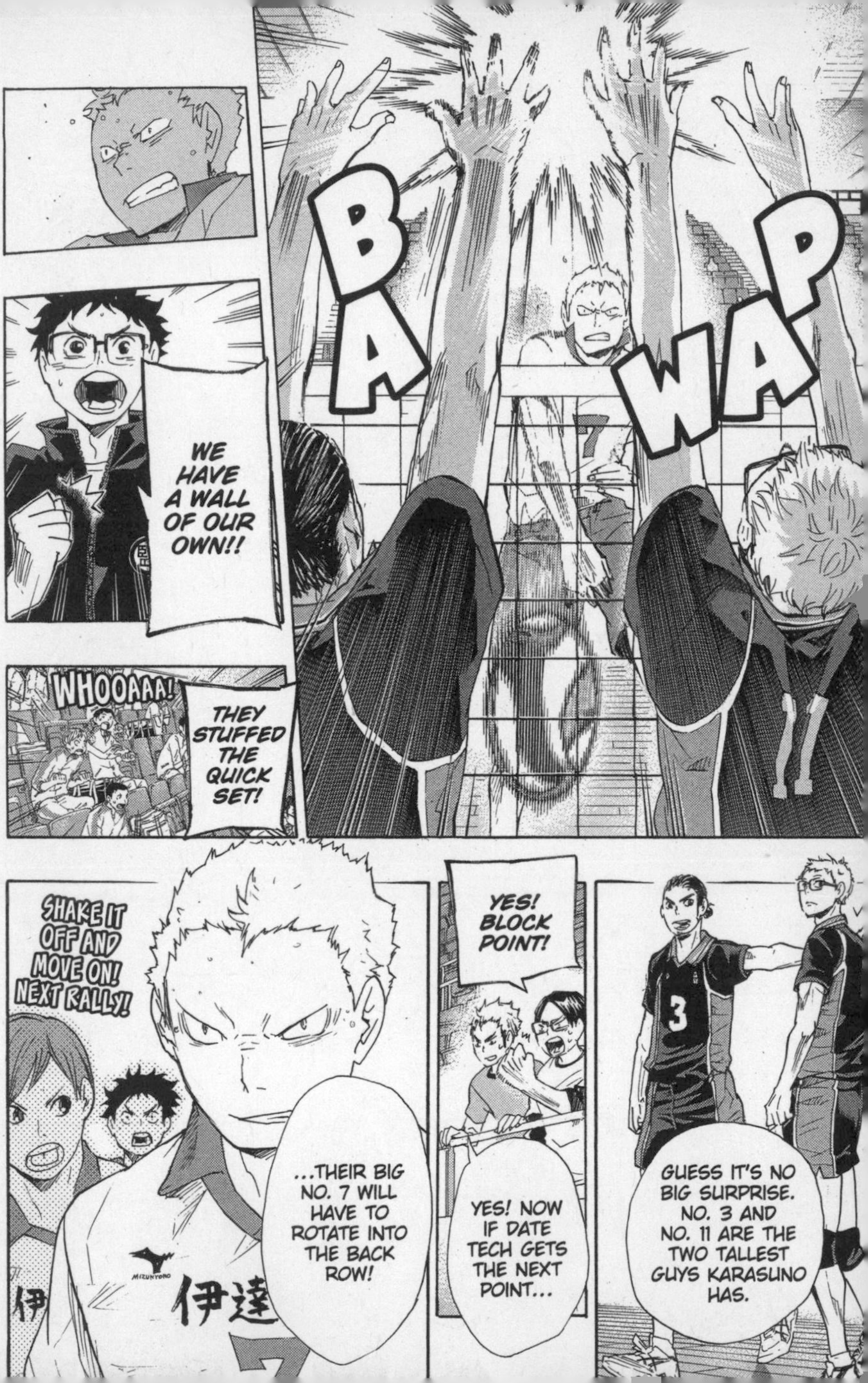
BAWAP
WE HAVE A WALL OF OUR OWN!!
WHOOAAA!
THEY STUFFED THE QUICK SET!
GUESS IT'S NO BIG SURPRISE. NO. 3 AND NO. 11 ARE THE TWO TALLEST GUYS KARASUNO HAS.
YES! BLOCK POINT!
YES! NOW IF DATE TECH GETS THE NEXT POINT...
...THEIR BIG NO. 7 WILL HAVE TO ROTATE INTO THE BACK ROW!
SHAKE IT OFF AND MOVE ON! NEXT RALLY!

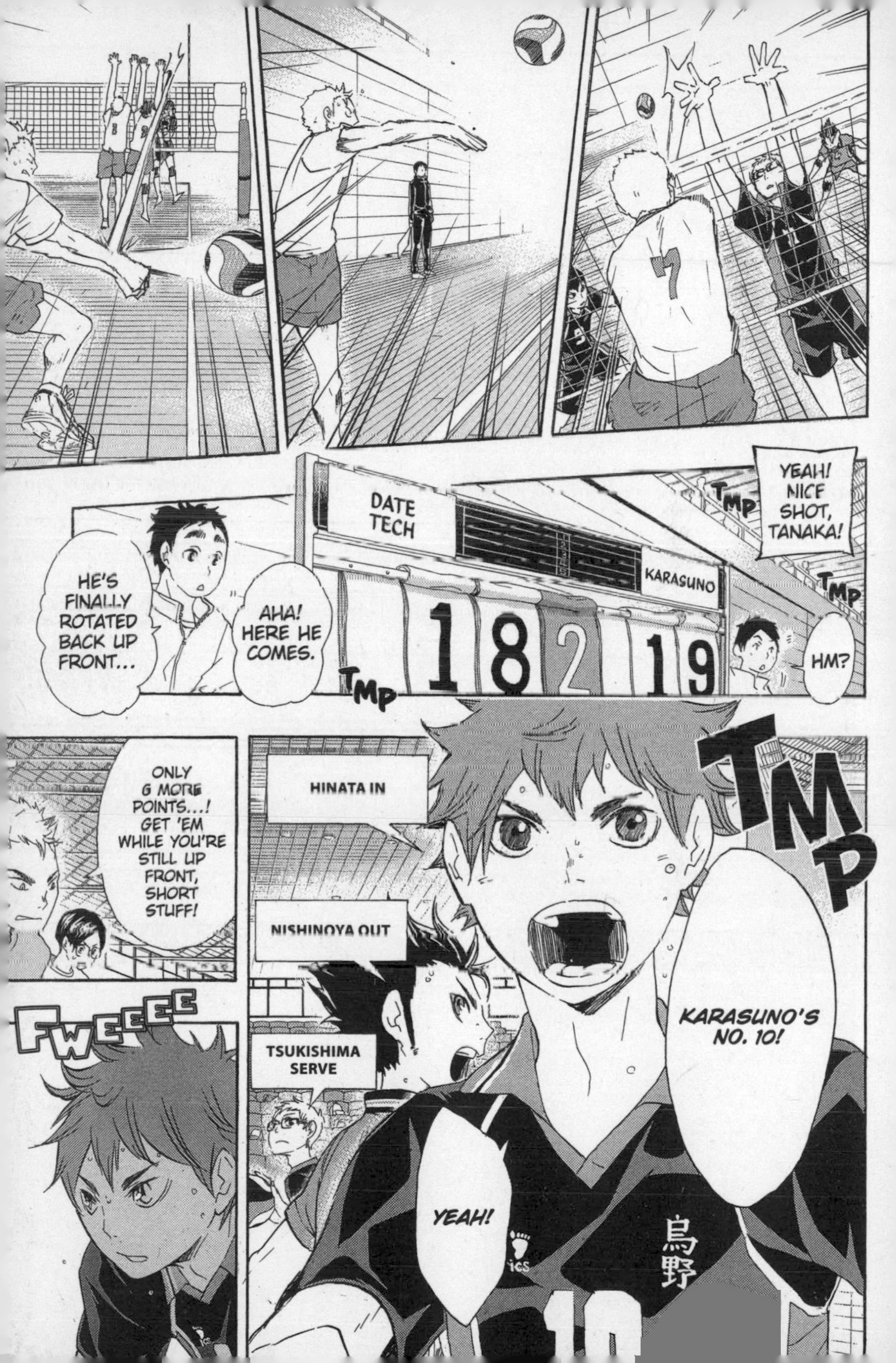
YEAH! NICE SHOT, TANAKA!
TMP
TMP
HM?
KARASUNO
DATE TECH
18 2 19
TMP
AHA! HERE HE COMES.
HE'S FINALLY ROTATED BACK UP FRONT...
TMP
KARASUNO'S NO. 10!
HINATA IN
NISHINOYA OUT
TSUKISHIMA SERVE
YEAH!
ONLY 6 MORE POINTS...! GET 'EM WHILE YOU'RE STILL UP FRONT, SHORT STUFF!
FWEEEE

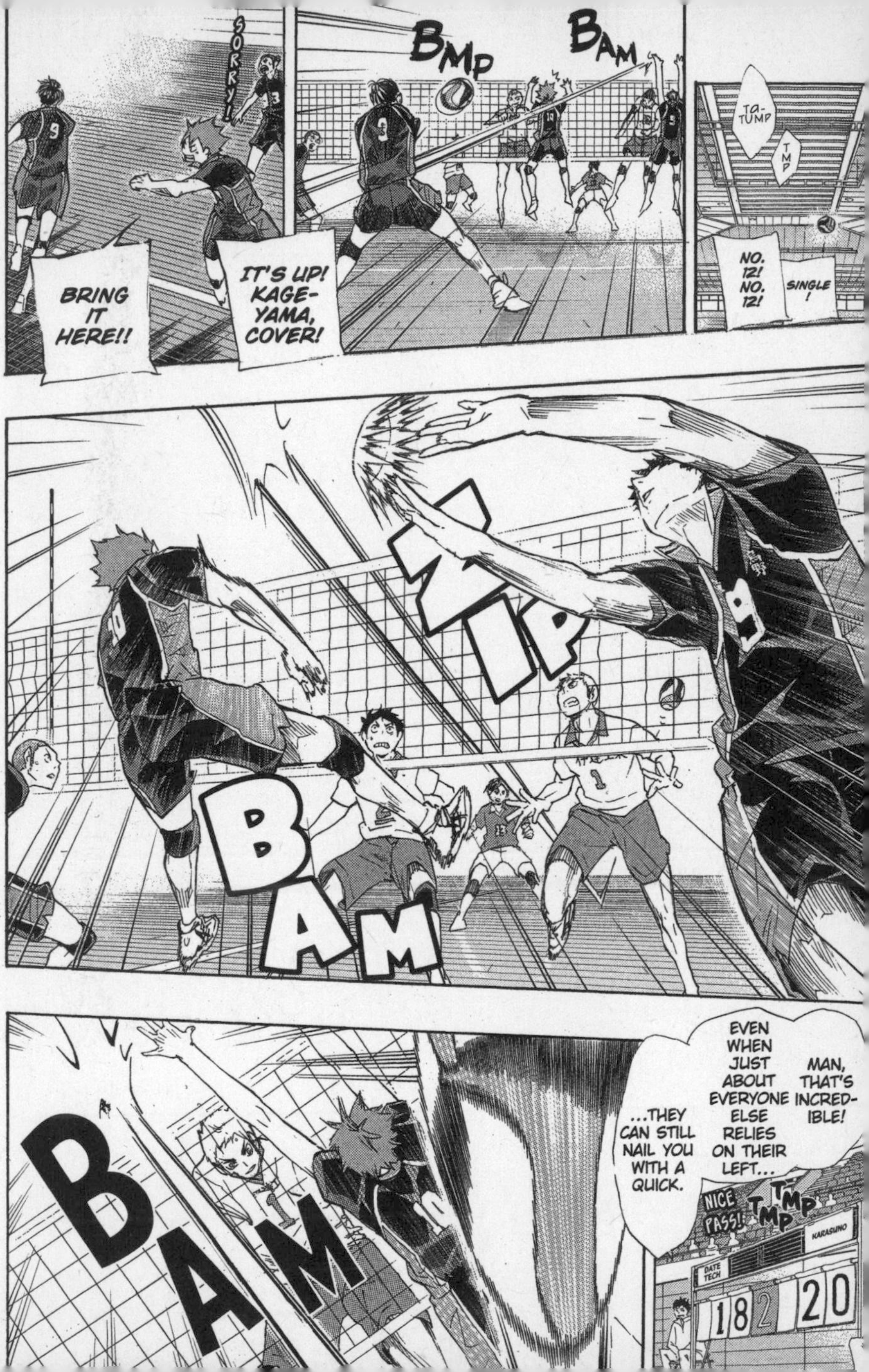

ta-TUMP
TMP
SINGLE!
NO. 12! NO. 12!
BAM
BMP
IT'S UP! KAGEYAMA, COVER!
SORRY!
BRING IT HERE!!
ZIP
BAM
MAN, THAT'S INCREDIBLE!
EVEN WHEN JUST ABOUT EVERYONE ELSE RELIES ON THEIR LEFT...
...THEY CAN STILL NAIL YOU WITH A QUICK.
TMP TMP
NICE PASS!
KARASUNO
DATE TECH
18 2 20
BAM

WHOA! DATE TECH HAS GOT A REAL SHARP QUICK SET TOO!

WE WON'T LET YOU HAVE IT THAT EASY!!

YEAH! GREAT ONE, KAMA-CHI!

BRING IT ON!

SERVER UP!

TMP TMP

BA

BAM BAM

KAMAGAKI!!

KAMASAKI!!

EASY NOW... STEADY AS SHE GOES...

SASAYA!

TMP

DATE TECH	KARASUNO
20	22

DATE TECH	KARASUNO
20	21

DATE TECH	KARASUNO
19	21

YEAH!! NICE DEFLECTION, ASAHI-SAN!!

FREE BALL!!

BMP

WHAP

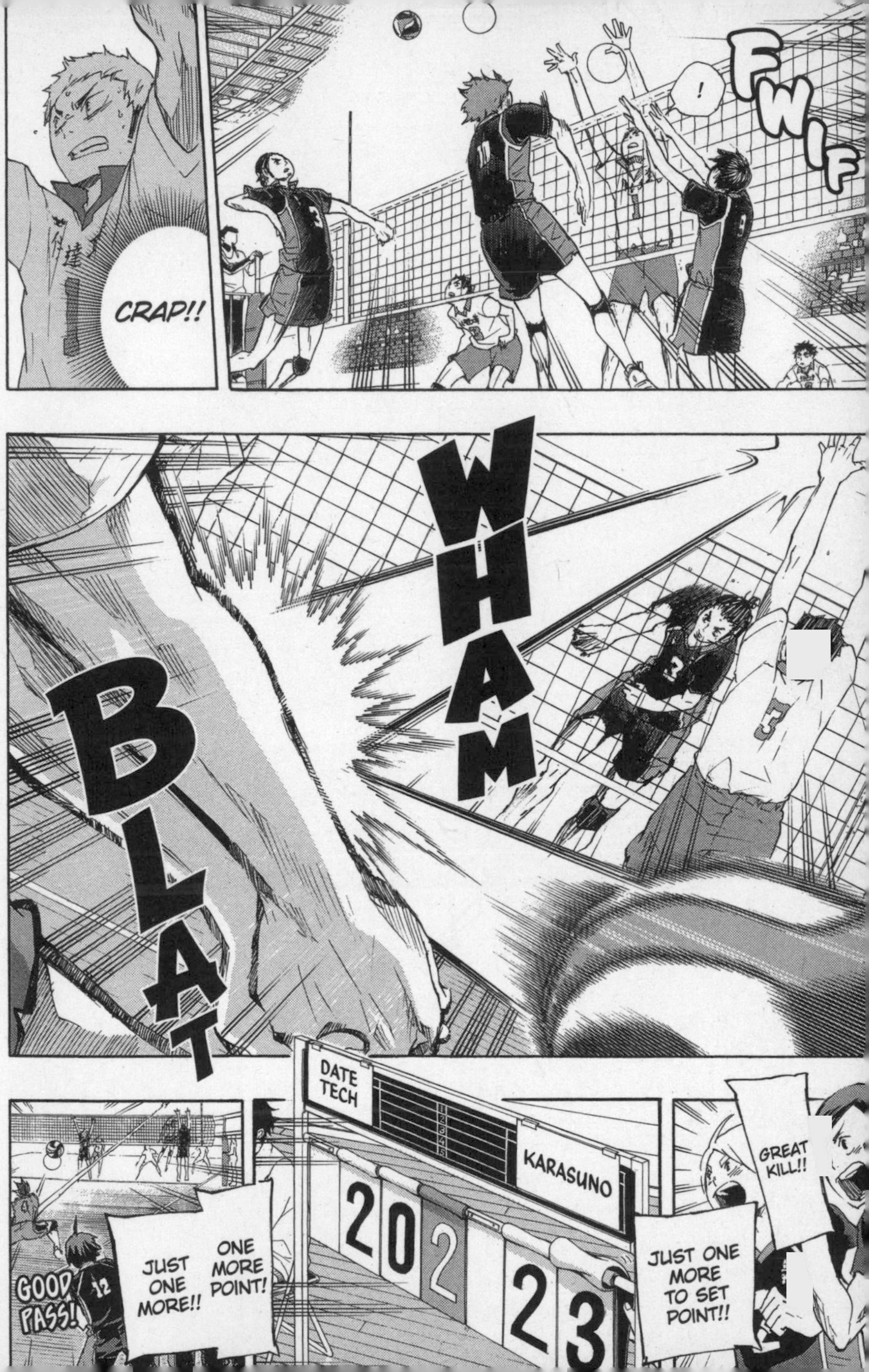
FWIF
!
CRAP!!
WHAM
BLAT
GREAT KILL!!
JUST ONE MORE TO SET POINT!!
DATE TECH
KARASUNO
20
23
ONE MORE POINT!
JUST ONE MORE!!
GOOD PASS!

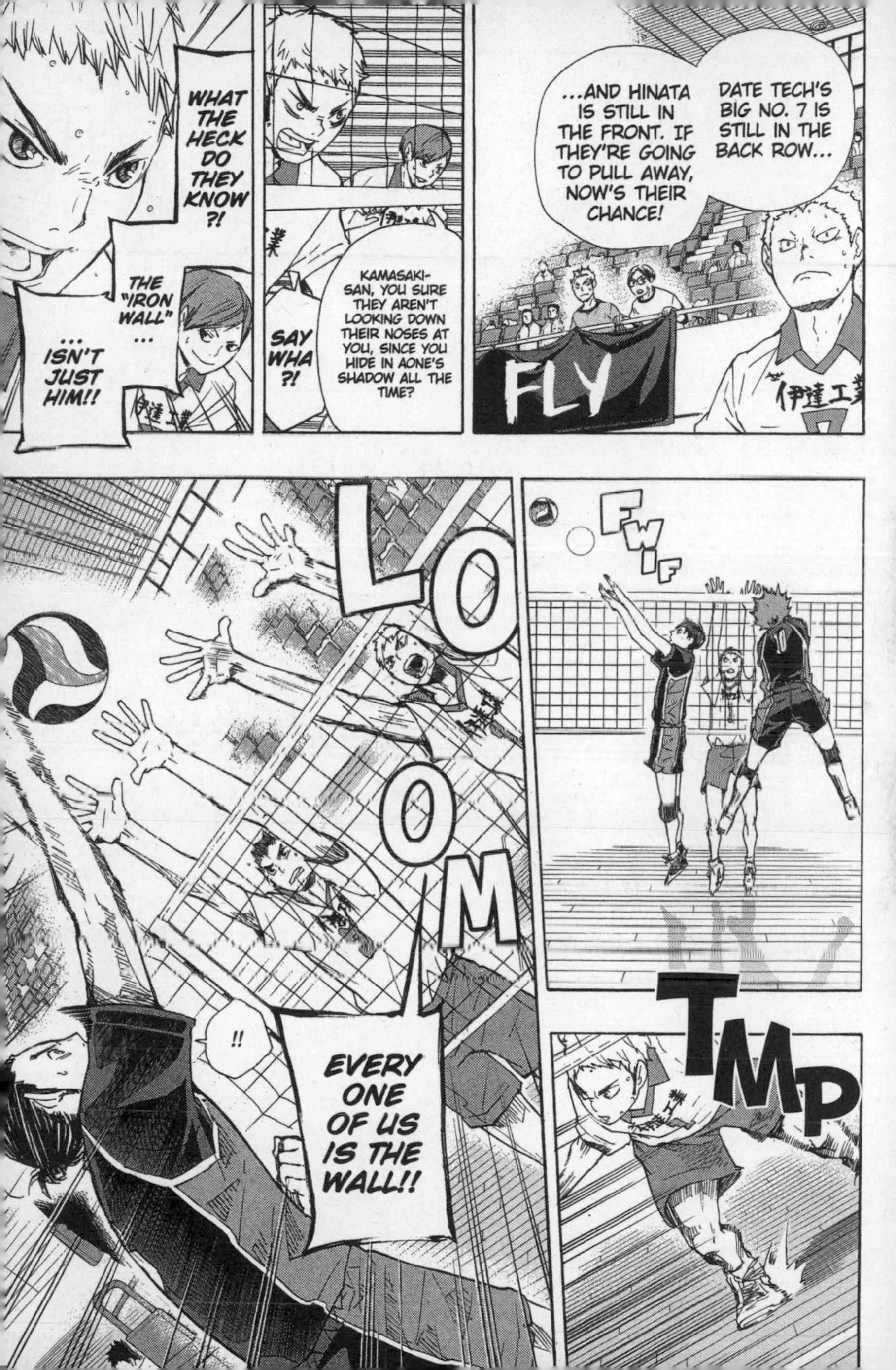

DATE TECH'S BIG NO. 7 IS STILL IN THE BACK ROW...
...AND HINATA IS STILL IN THE FRONT. IF THEY'RE GOING TO PULL AWAY, NOW'S THEIR CHANCE!
FLY
KAMASAKI-SAN, YOU SURE THEY AREN'T LOOKING DOWN THEIR NOSES AT YOU, SINCE YOU HIDE IN AONE'S SHADOW ALL THE TIME?
SAY WHA?!
WHAT THE HECK DO THEY KNOW?!
THE "IRON WALL"...
...ISN'T JUST HIM!!
FWIF
TMP
LOOM
!!
EVERY ONE OF US IS THE WALL!!

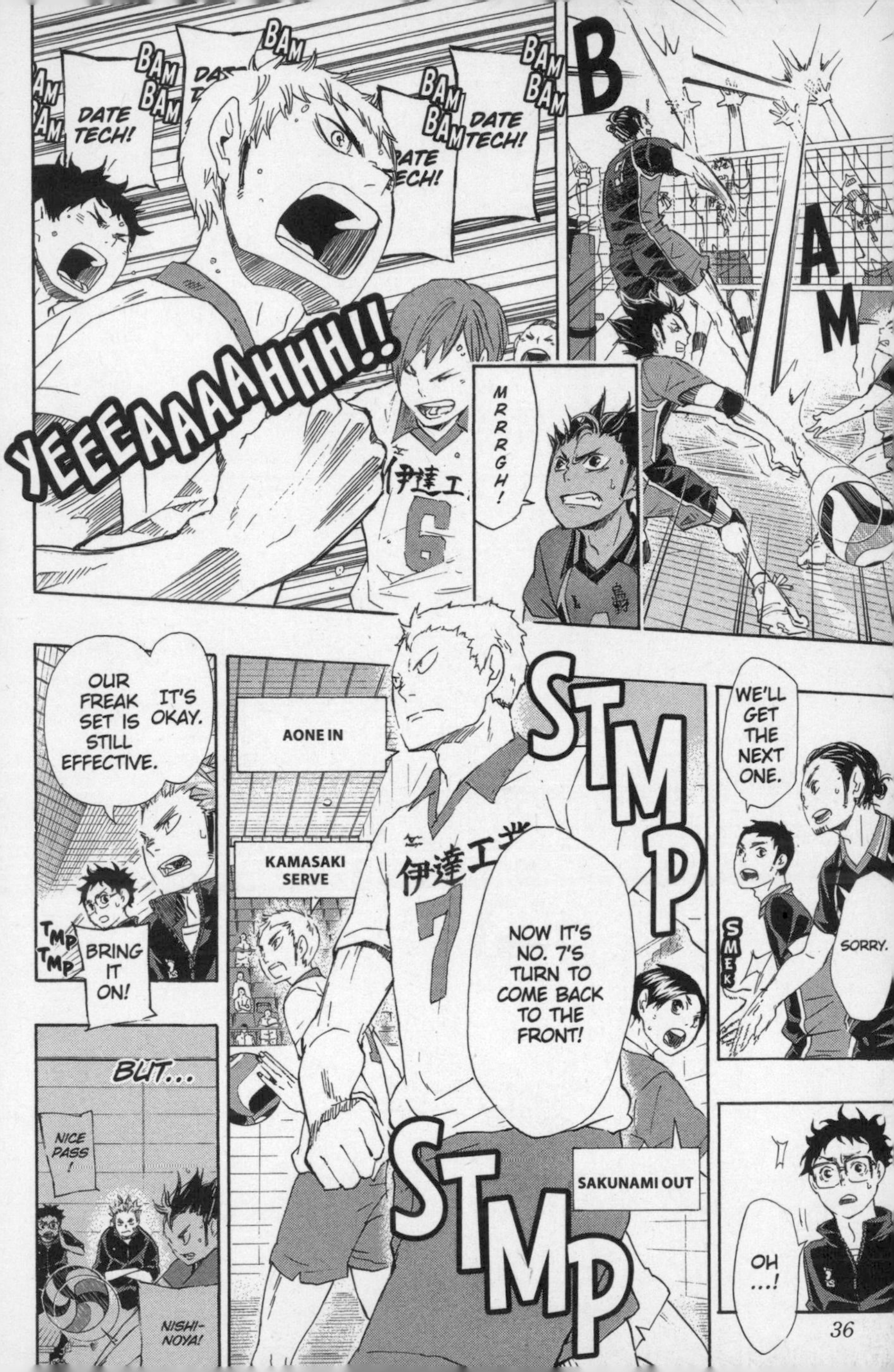
B
A
M
MRRRGH!
BAM BAM
DATE TECH!
BAM BAM
DATE TECH!
BAM BAM
DATE TECH!
BAM
DATE TECH!
BAM BAM
YEEEAAAAHHH!!
WE'LL GET THE NEXT ONE.
SMEK
SORRY.
OH ...!
STMP
AONE IN
KAMASAKI SERVE
NOW IT'S NO. 7'S TURN TO COME BACK TO THE FRONT!
SAKUNAMI OUT
STMP
IT'S OKAY.
OUR FREAK SET IS STILL EFFECTIVE.
TMP TMP
BRING IT ON!
BUT...
NICE PASS!
NISHI-NOYA!

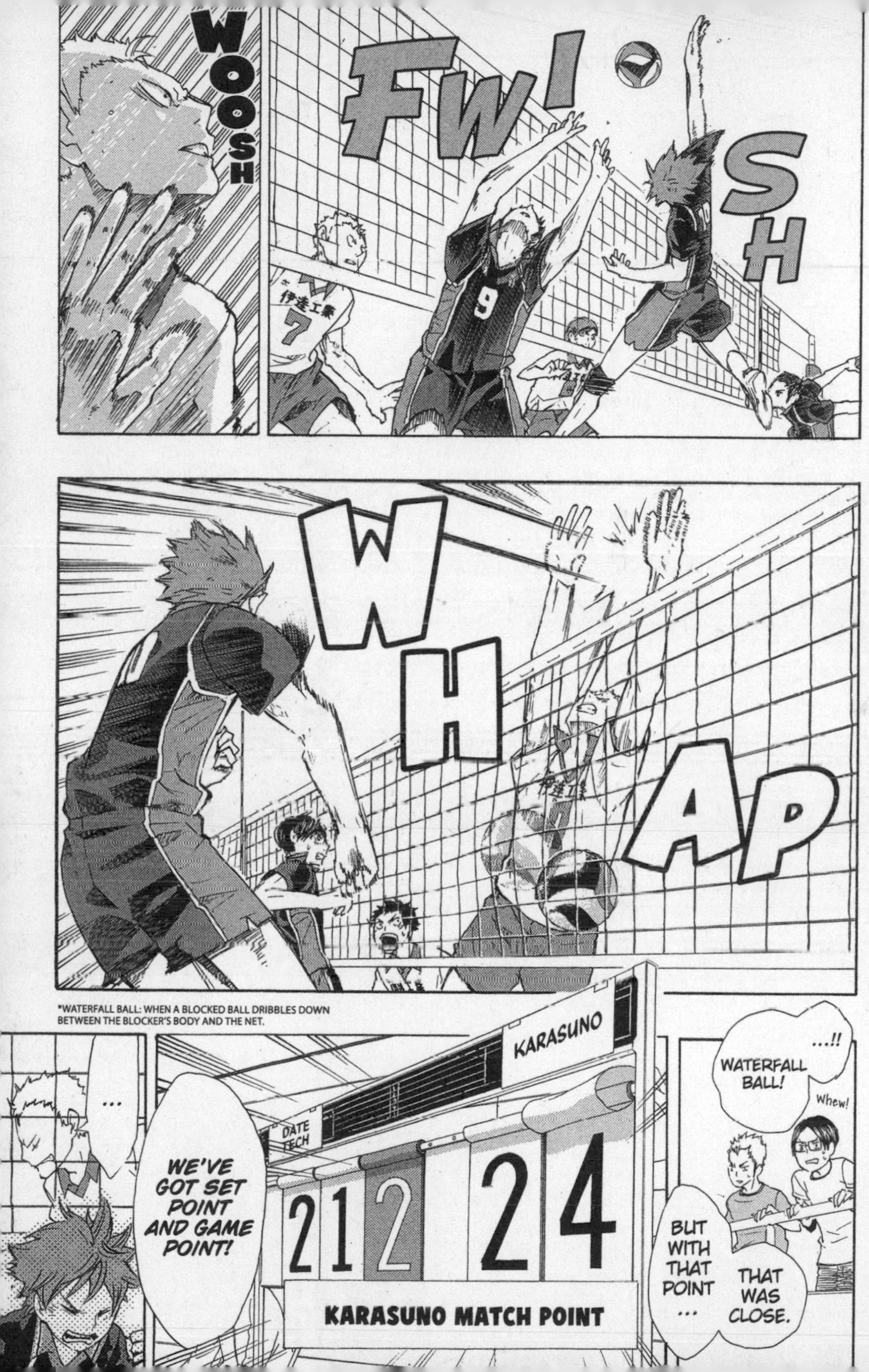
FWISH
WOOSH
WHAP
...!!
WATERFALL BALL!
Whew!
THAT WAS CLOSE.
BUT WITH THAT POINT...
KARASUNO
DATE TECH
21
24
KARASUNO MATCH POINT
WE'VE GOT SET POINT AND GAME POINT!
...

*WATERFALL BALL: WHEN A BLOCKED BALL DRIBBLES DOWN BETWEEN THE BLOCKER'S BODY AND THE NET.

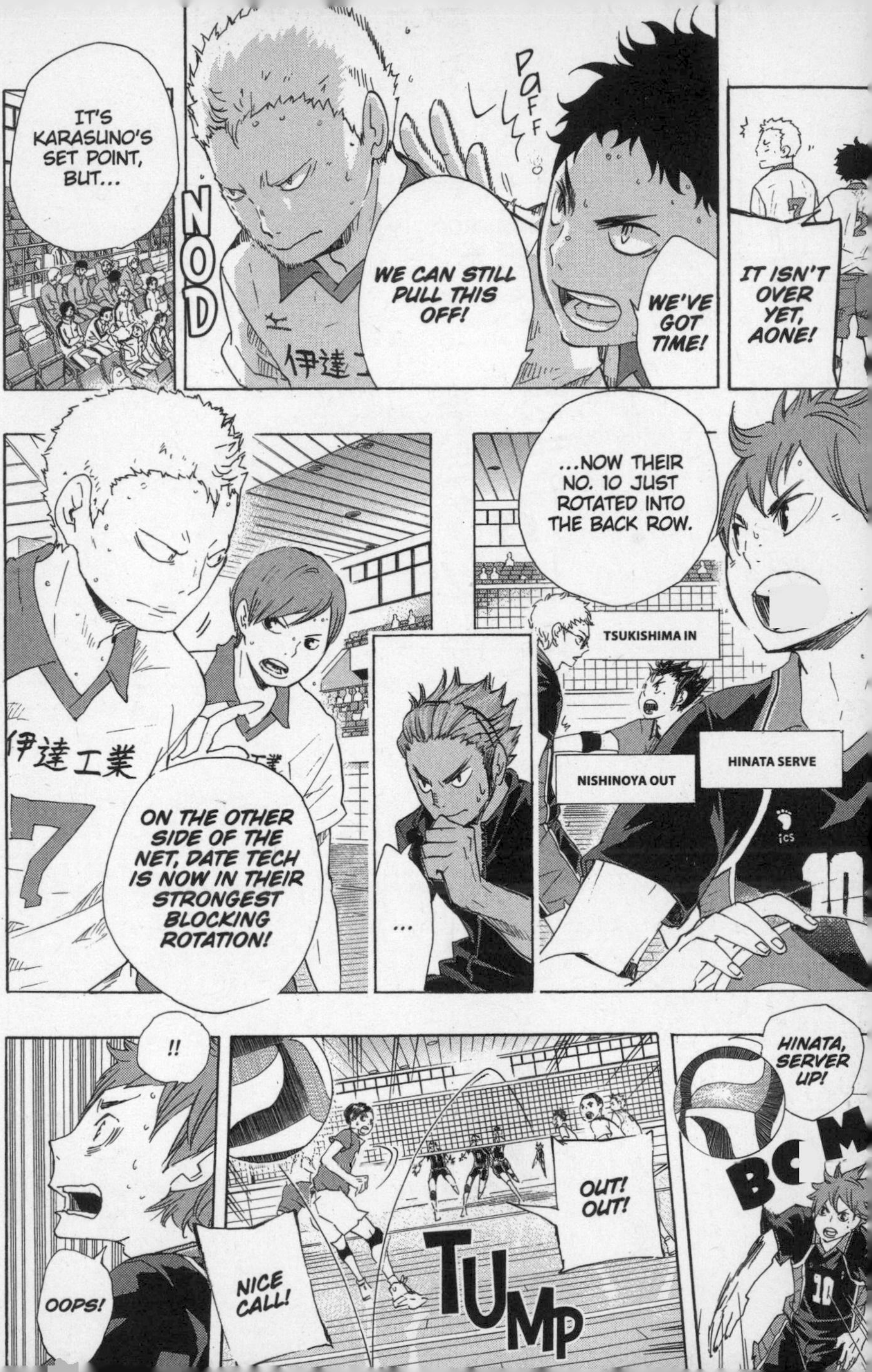
IT ISN'T OVER YET, AONE!
WE'VE GOT TIME!
PaFF
WE CAN STILL PULL THIS OFF!
NOD
伊達工
IT'S KARASUNO'S SET POINT, BUT...
...NOW THEIR NO. 10 JUST ROTATED INTO THE BACK ROW.
TSUKISHIMA IN
HINATA SERVE
NISHINOYA OUT
...
ON THE OTHER SIDE OF THE NET, DATE TECH IS NOW IN THEIR STRONGEST BLOCKING ROTATION!
伊達工業
HINATA, SERVER UP!
BOM
OUT! OUT!
TUMP
NICE CALL!
!!
OOPS!

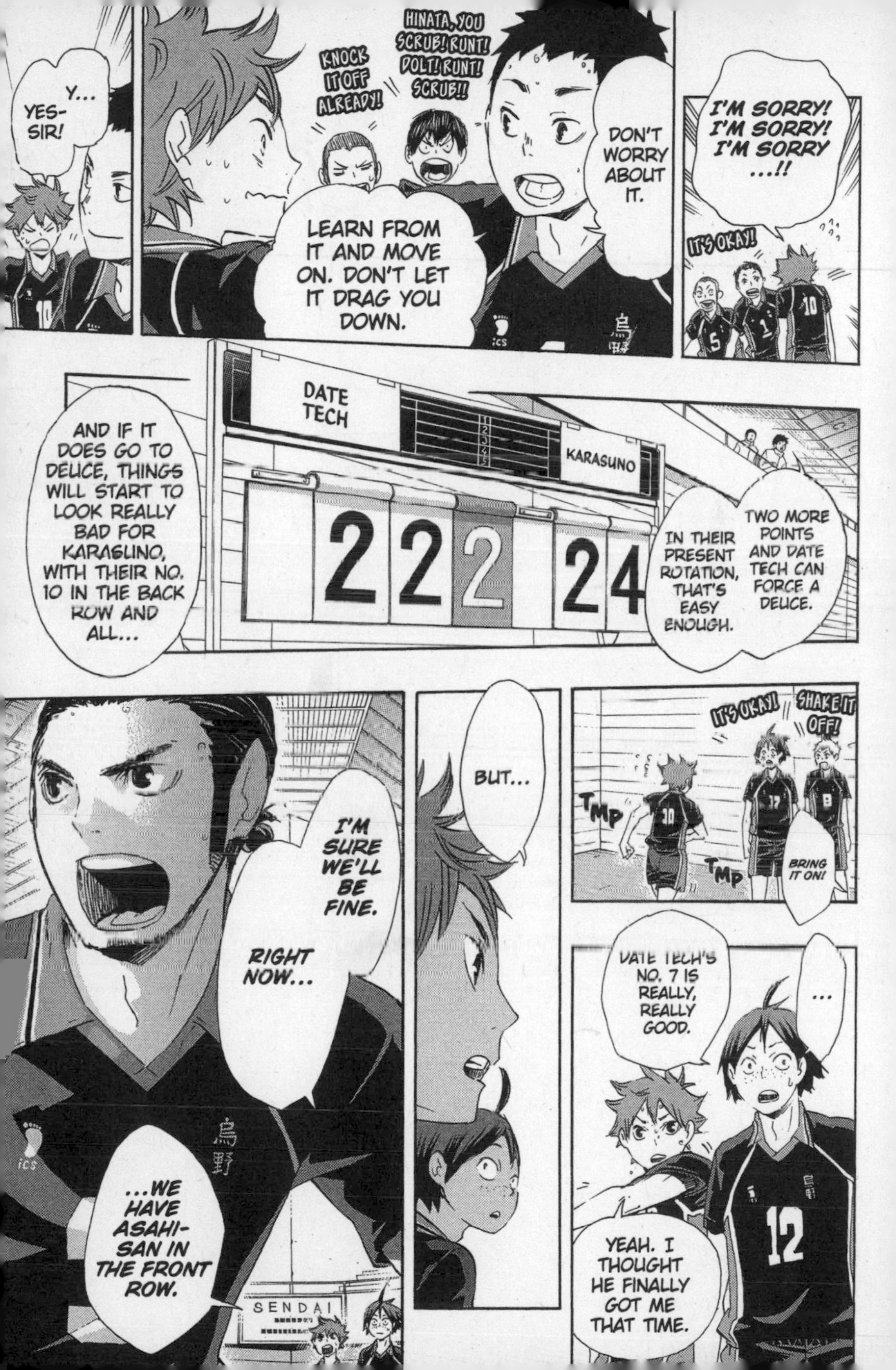
I'M SORRY! I'M SORRY! I'M SORRY ...!!
IT'S OKAY!
HINATA, YOU SCRUB! RUNT! DOLT! RUNT! SCRUB!!
DON'T WORRY ABOUT IT.
KNOCK IT OFF ALREADY!
LEARN FROM IT AND MOVE ON. DON'T LET IT DRAG YOU DOWN.
Y... YES-SIR!
TWO MORE POINTS AND DATE TECH CAN FORCE A DEUCE.
IN THEIR PRESENT ROTATION, THAT'S EASY ENOUGH.
KARASUNO
24
2
22
DATE TECH
AND IF IT DOES GO TO DEUCE, THINGS WILL START TO LOOK REALLY BAD FOR KARASUNO, WITH THEIR NO. 10 IN THE BACK ROW AND ALL...
SHAKE IT OFF!
IT'S OKAY!
BRING IT ON!
TMP
TMP
...
DATE TECH'S NO. 7 IS REALLY, REALLY GOOD.
YEAH. I THOUGHT HE FINALLY GOT ME THAT TIME.
BUT...
I'M SURE WE'LL BE FINE.
RIGHT NOW...
...WE HAVE ASAHI-SAN IN THE FRONT ROW.
SENDAI

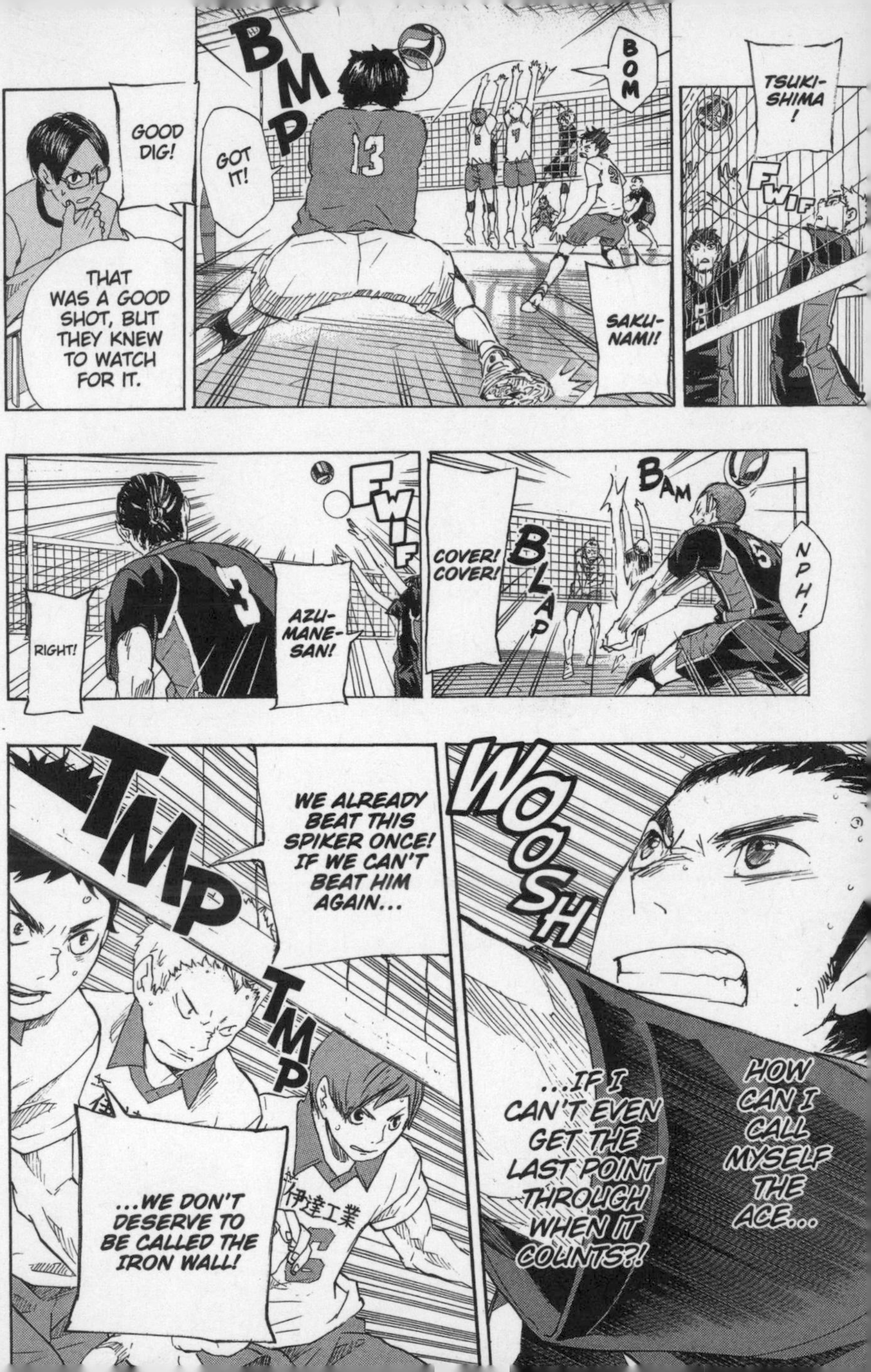
TSUKISHIMA!
FWIF
BOM
SAKUNAMI!
BMP
GOT IT!
GOOD DIG!
THAT WAS A GOOD SHOT, BUT THEY KNEW TO WATCH FOR IT.
BAM
NPH!
COVER! COVER!
BLAP
FWIF
AZUMANE-SAN!
RIGHT!
WOOSH
HOW CAN I CALL MYSELF THE ACE...
...IF I CAN'T EVEN GET THE LAST POINT THROUGH WHEN IT COUNTS?!
TMP
WE ALREADY BEAT THIS SPIKER ONCE! IF WE CAN'T BEAT HIM AGAIN...
TMP
伊達工業
...WE DON'T DESERVE TO BE CALLED THE IRON WALL!

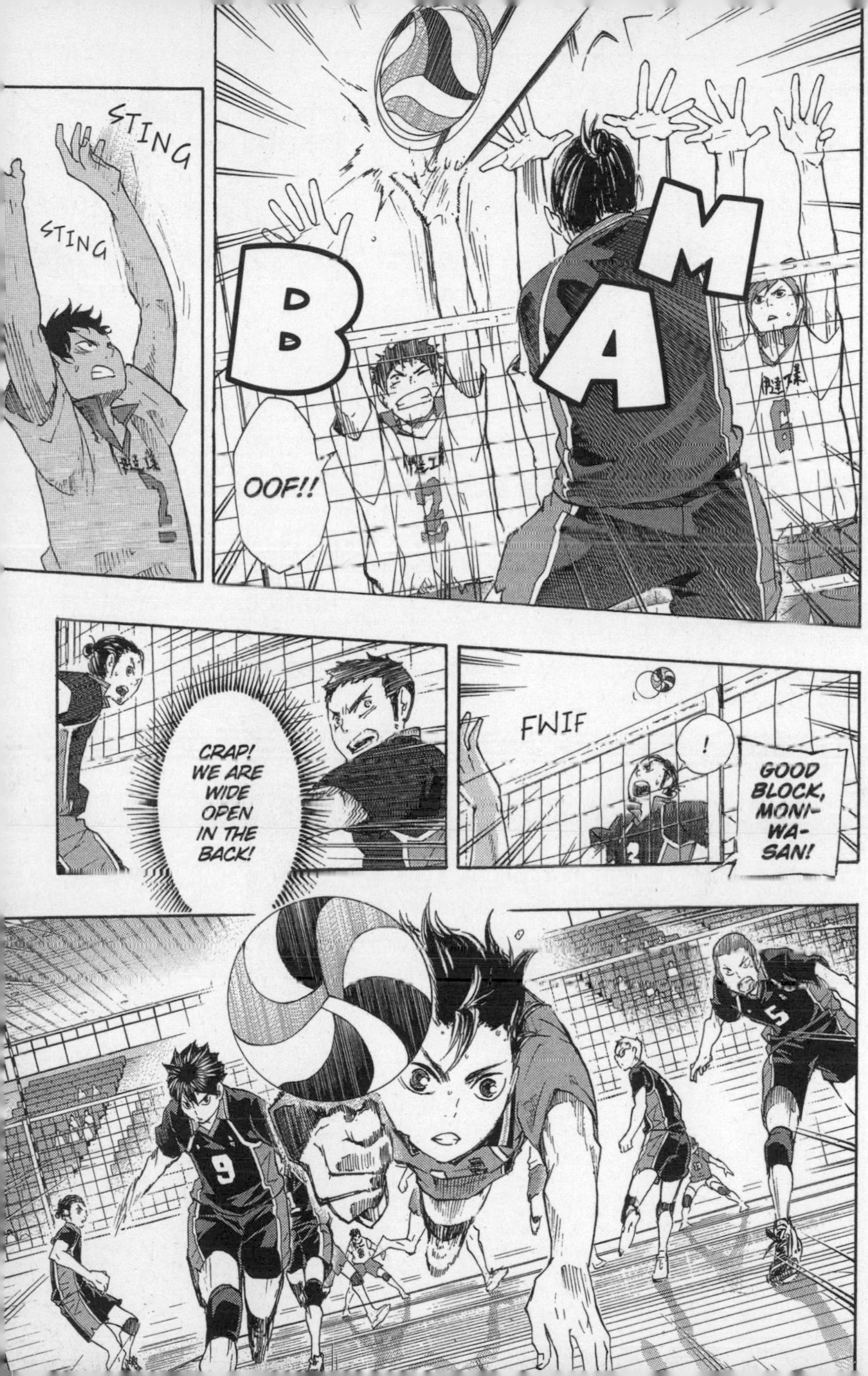
BAM
OOF!!
STING
STING
FWIF
!
GOOD BLOCK, MONI-WA-SAN!
CRAP! WE ARE WIDE OPEN IN THE BACK!

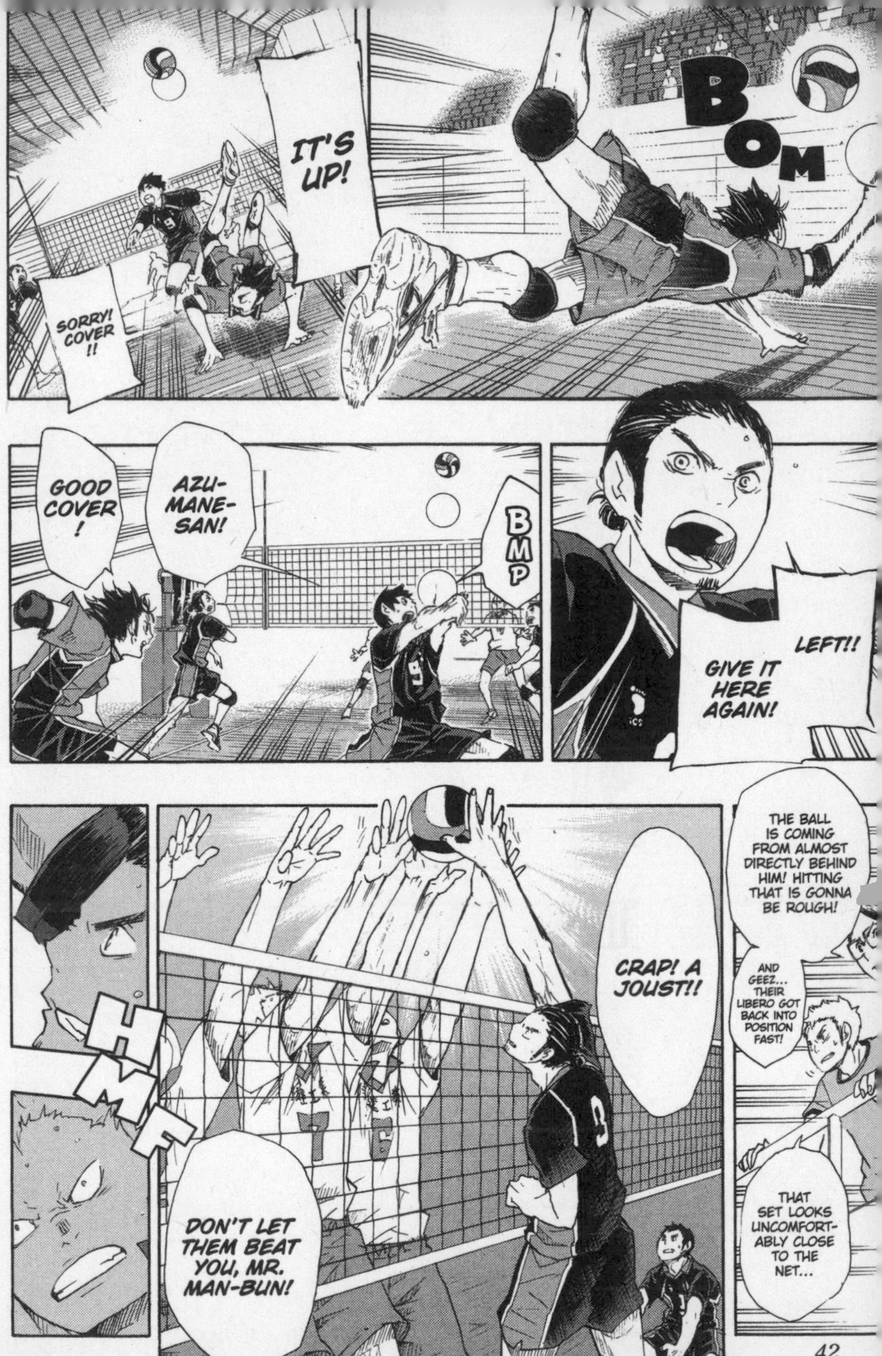

BOM
IT'S UP!
SORRY! COVER !!
GIVE IT HERE AGAIN!
LEFT!!
BMP
AZU-MANE-SAN!
GOOD COVER !
THE BALL IS COMING FROM ALMOST DIRECTLY BEHIND HIM! HITTING THAT IS GONNA BE ROUGH!
AND GEEZ... THEIR LIBERO GOT BACK INTO POSITION FAST!
THAT SET LOOKS UNCOMFORT-ABLY CLOSE TO THE NET...
CRAP! A JOUST!!
DON'T LET THEM BEAT YOU, MR. MAN-BUN!
HMF

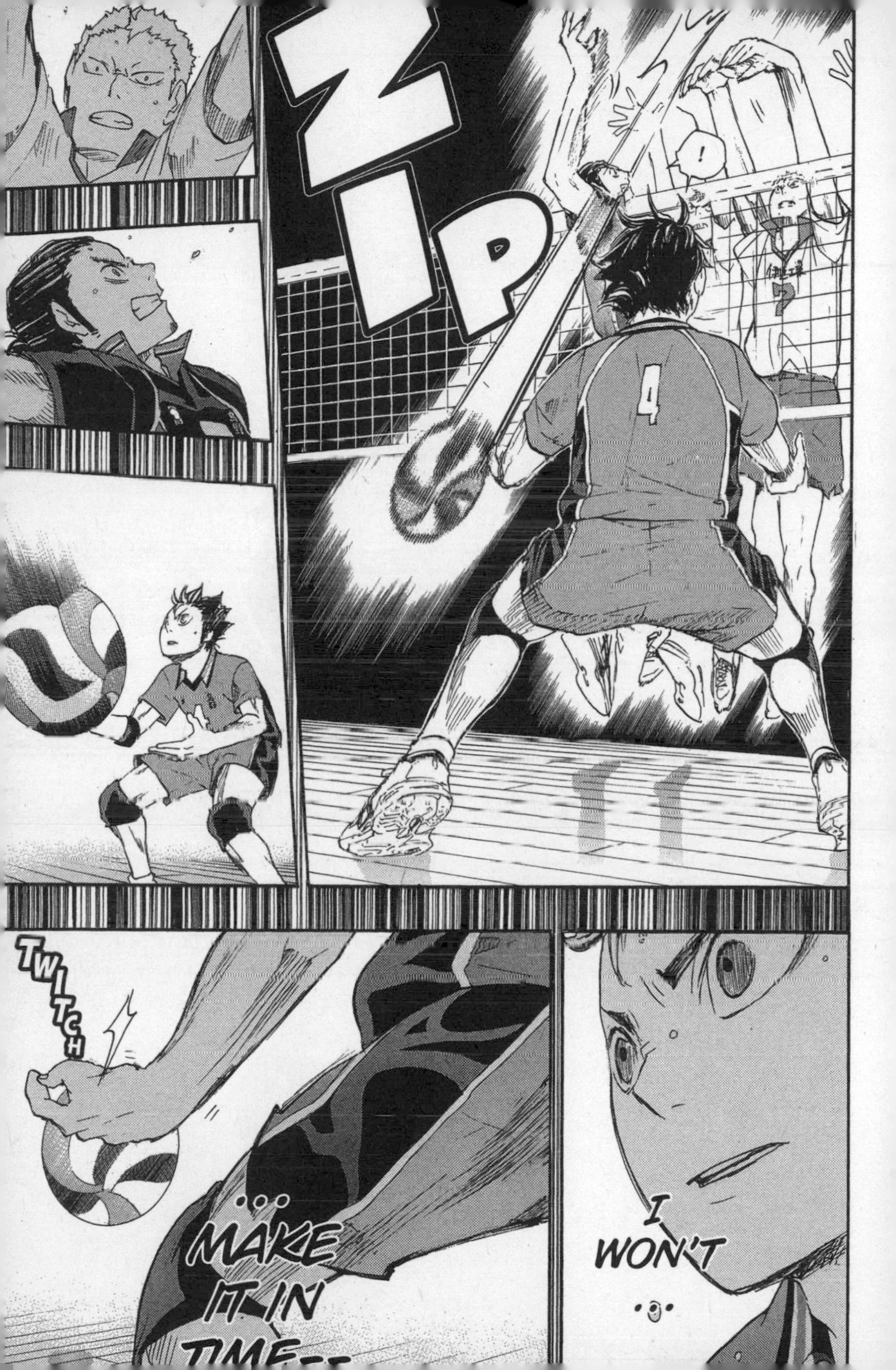
!
ZIP
I WON'T
...
TWITCH
...MAKE IT IN TIME--

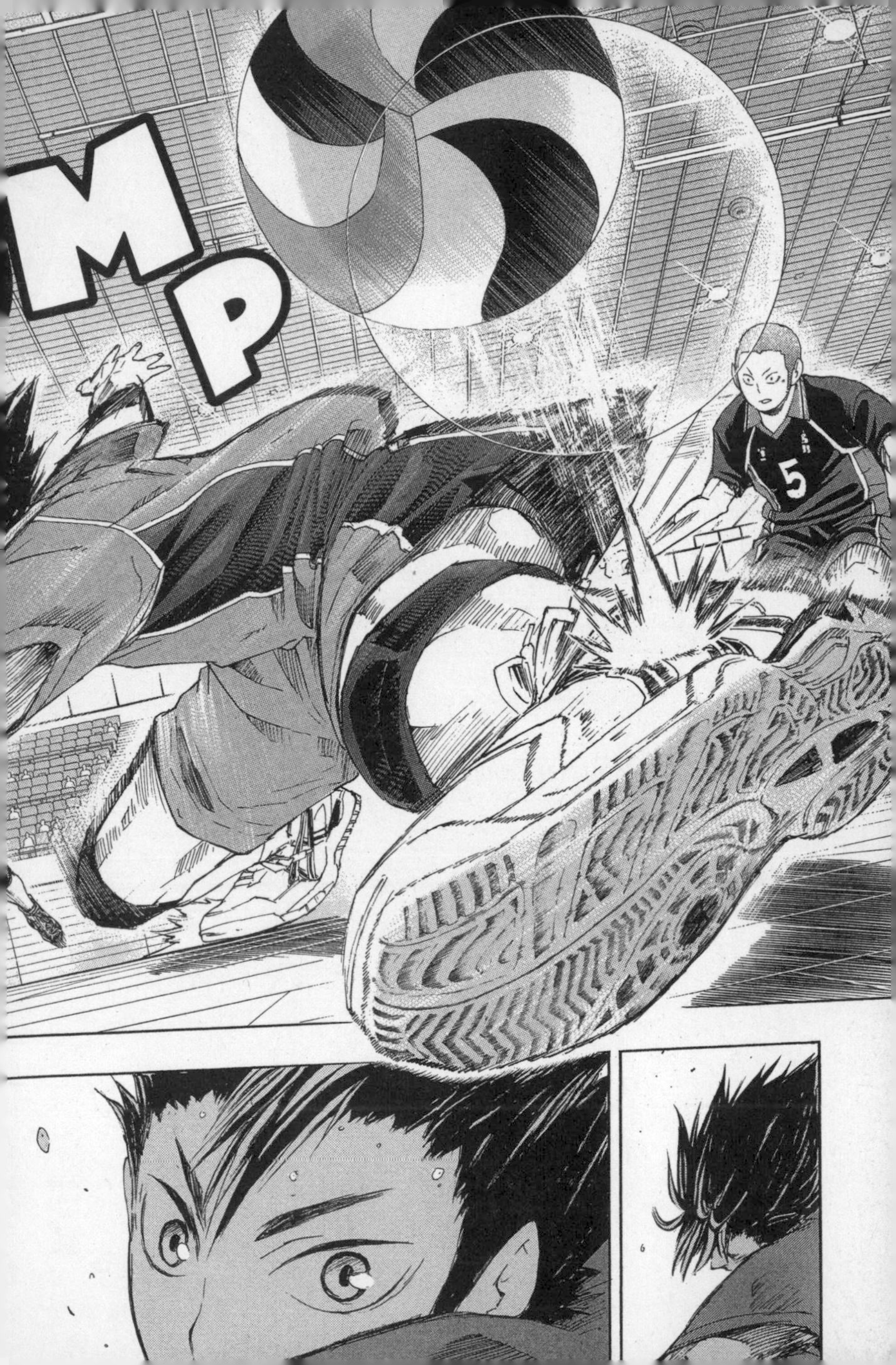
MP

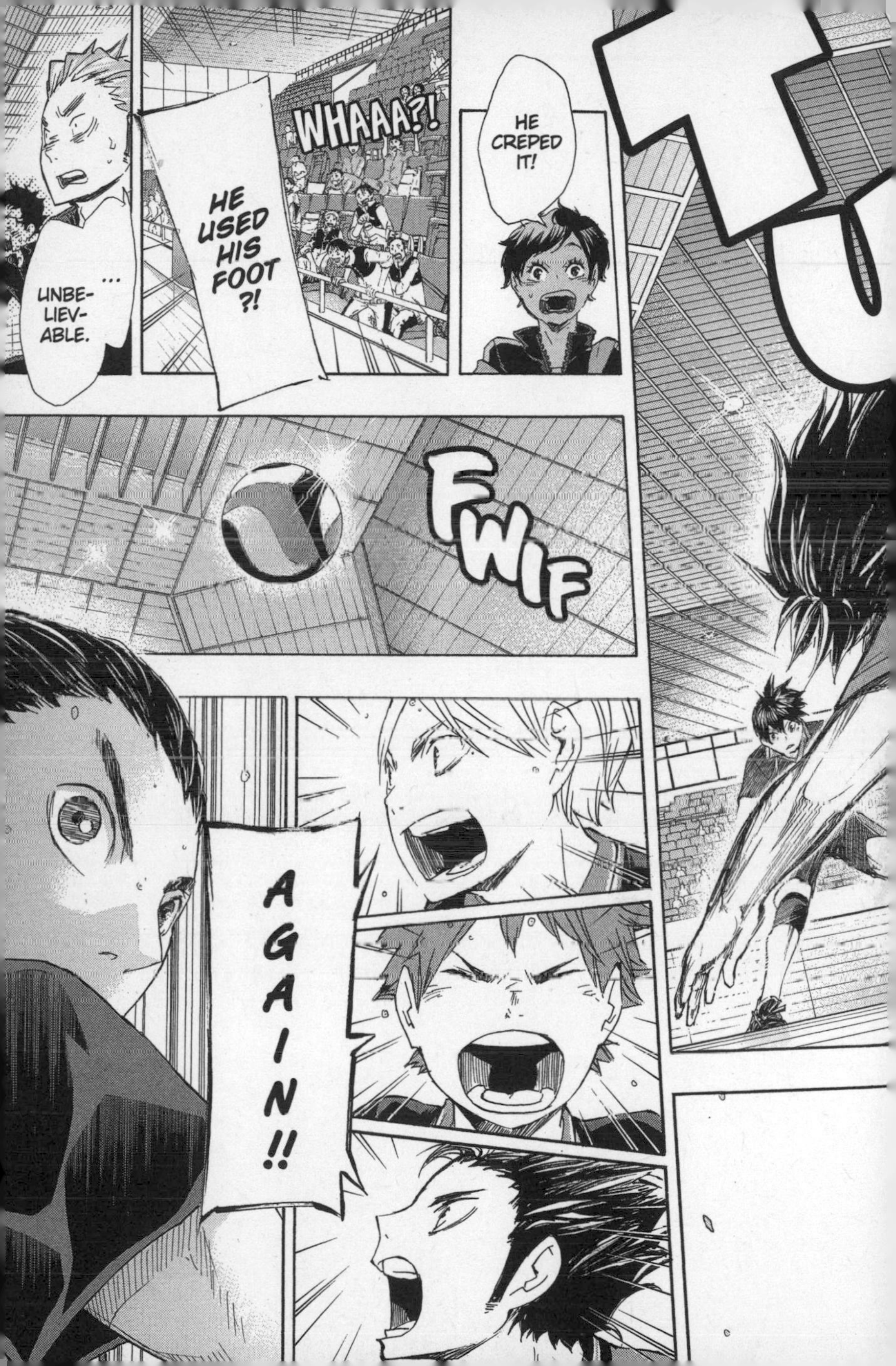
HE CREPED IT!
WHAAA?!
HE USED HIS FOOT?!
... UNBE-LIEV-ABLE.
FWIF
AGAIN!!

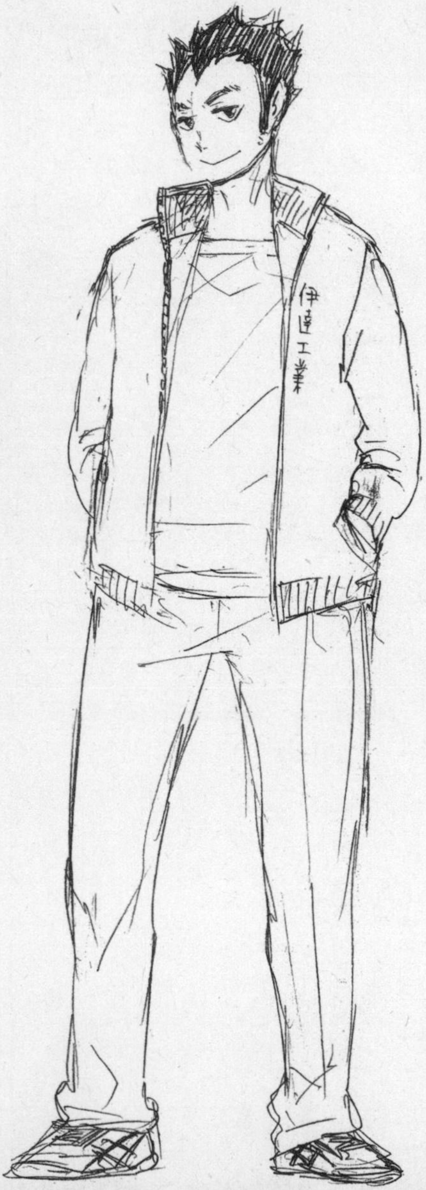
伊達工業

TAKEHITO SASAYA

DATE TECHNICAL HIGH SCHOOL
CLASS 3-C

POSITION:
WING SPIKER

HEIGHT: 5'9"

WEIGHT: 150 LBS.
(AS OF APRIL, 3RD YEAR
OF HIGH SCHOOL)

BIRTHDAY: FEBRUARY 10

FAVORITE FOOD:
SASA-KAMABOKO
(TOASTED FISH CAKES)

CURRENT WORRY:
PEOPLE TELL HIM HE
ACTS LIKE AN OLD MAN.

ABILITY PARAMETERS
(5-POINT SCALE)

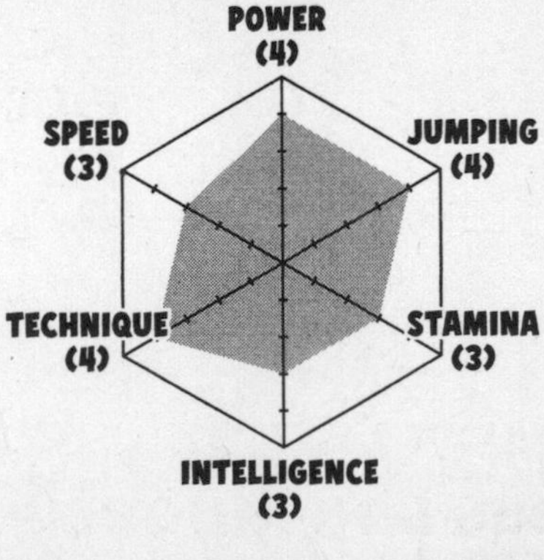
POWER
(4)
JUMPING
(4)
STAMINA
(3)
INTELLIGENCE
(3)
TECHNIQUE
(4)
SPEED
(3)

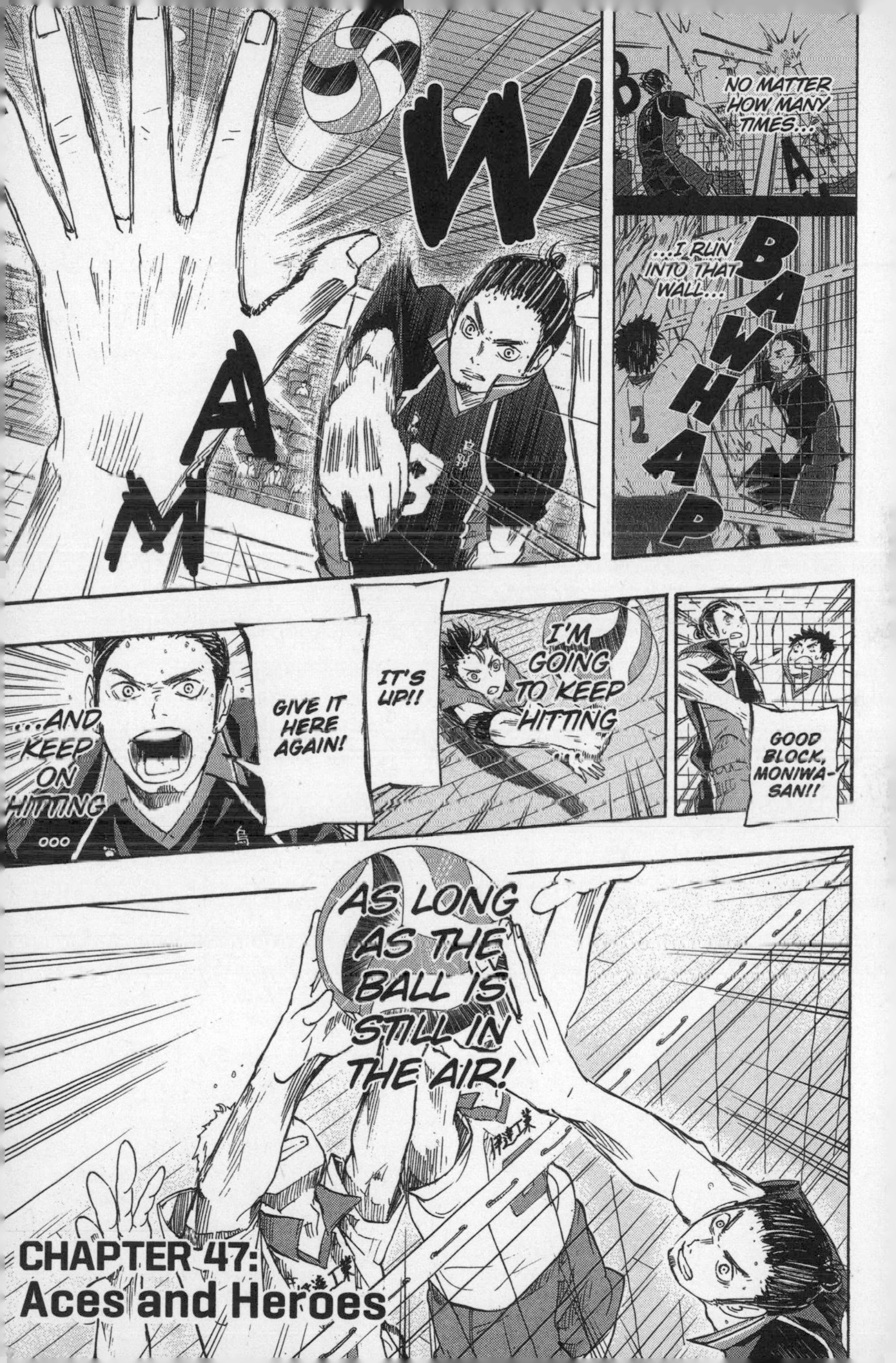
NO MATTER HOW MANY TIMES...
...I RUN INTO THAT WALL...
BAWHAP
WHAM
GOOD BLOCK, MONIWA-SAN!!
I'M GOING TO KEEP HITTING
IT'S UP!!
GIVE IT HERE AGAIN!
...AND KEEP ON HITTING
ooo
AS LONG AS THE BALL IS STILL IN THE AIR!

CHAPTER 47: Aces and Heroes

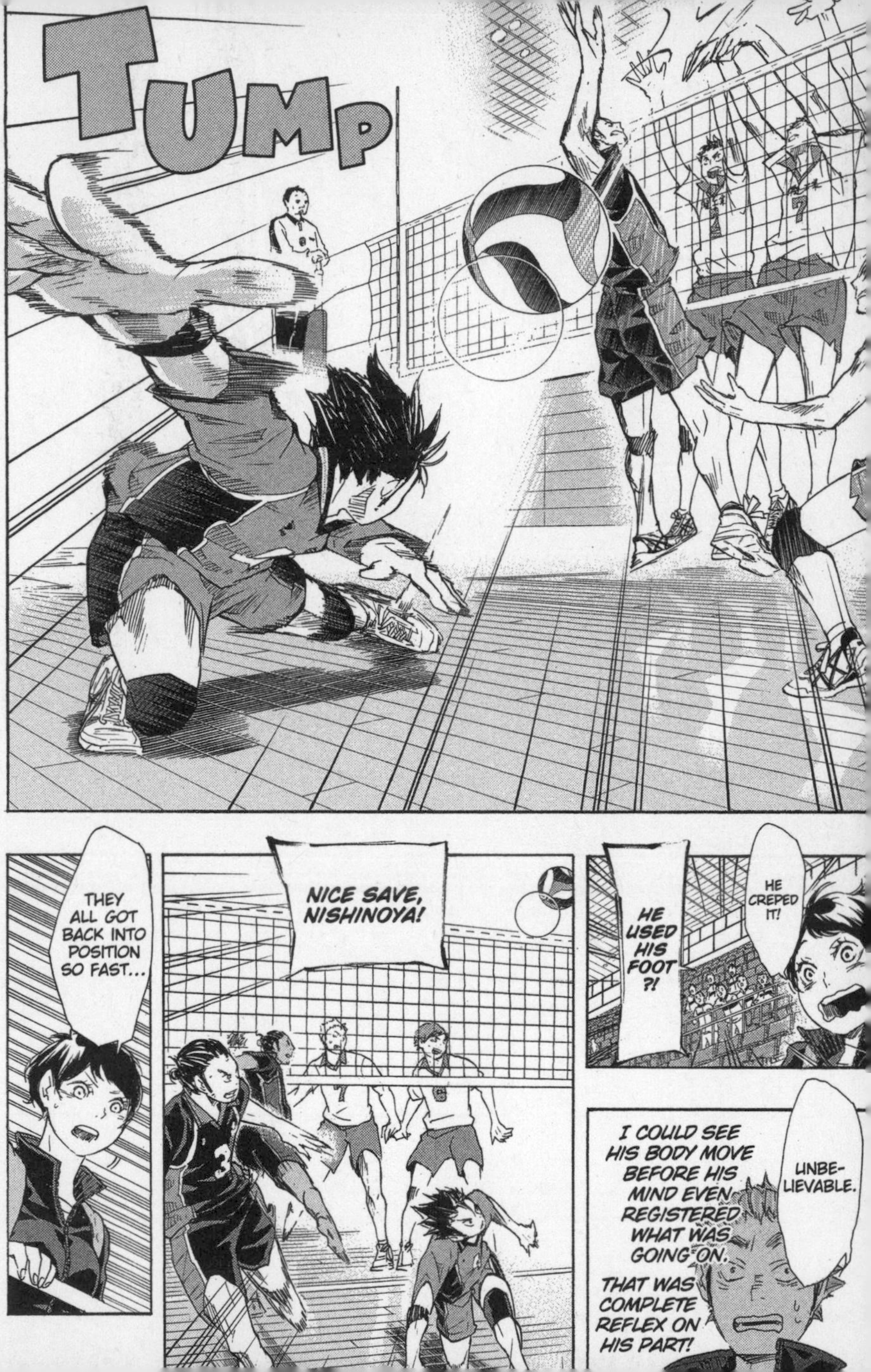
TUMP
HE CREPED IT!
HE USED HIS FOOT?!
UNBE-LIEVABLE.
I COULD SEE HIS BODY MOVE BEFORE HIS MIND EVEN REGISTERED WHAT WAS GOING ON.
THAT WAS COMPLETE REFLEX ON HIS PART!
NICE SAVE, NISHINOYA!
THEY ALL GOT BACK INTO POSITION SO FAST...

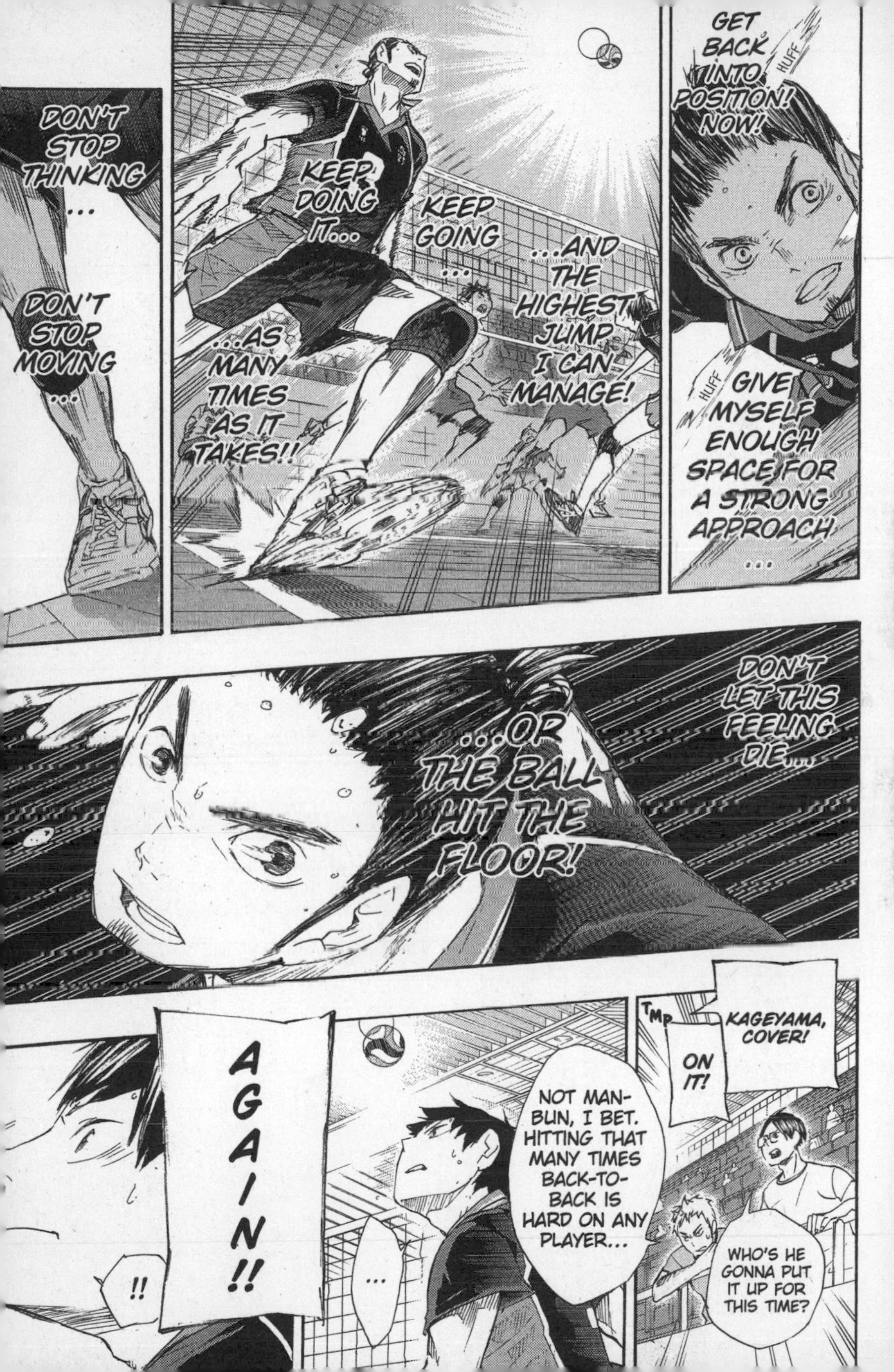
GET BACK INTO POSITION! NOW!
HUFF
HUFF
GIVE MYSELF ENOUGH SPACE FOR A STRONG APPROACH...
KEEP GOING...
...AND THE HIGHEST JUMP I CAN MANAGE!
KEEP DOING IT...
...AS MANY TIMES AS IT TAKES!!
DON'T STOP THINKING...
DON'T STOP MOVING...
DON'T LET THIS FEELING DIE...
...OR THE BALL HIT THE FLOOR!
KAGEYAMA, COVER!
TMP
ON IT!
WHO'S HE GONNA PUT IT UP FOR THIS TIME?
NOT MAN-BUN, I BET. HITTING THAT MANY TIMES BACK-TO-BACK IS HARD ON ANY PLAYER...
...
AGAIN!!
!!

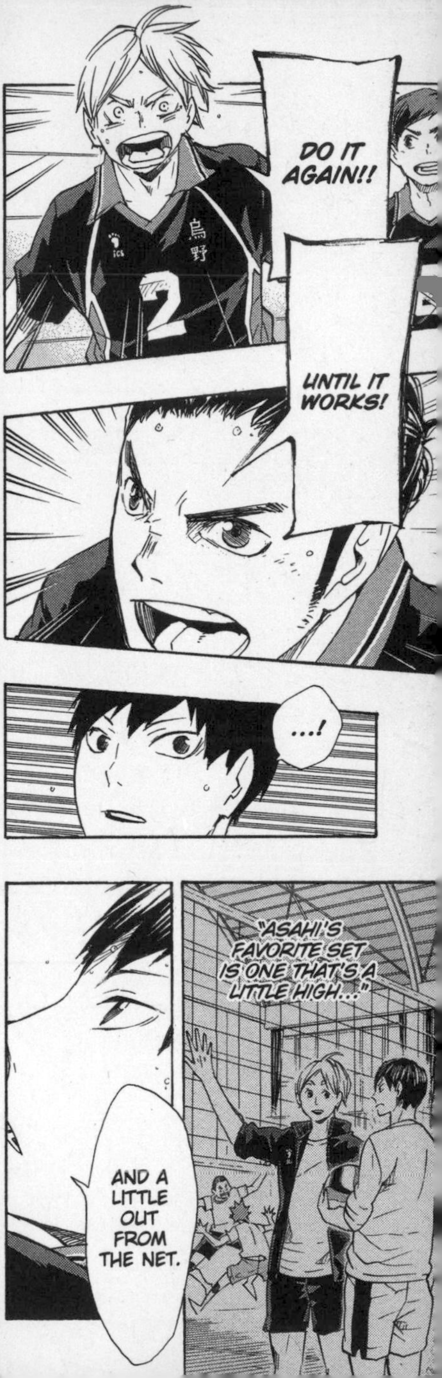
DO IT AGAIN!!
UNTIL IT WORKS!
...!
"ASAHI'S FAVORITE SET IS ONE THAT'S A LITTLE HIGH..."
AND A LITTLE OUT FROM THE NET.

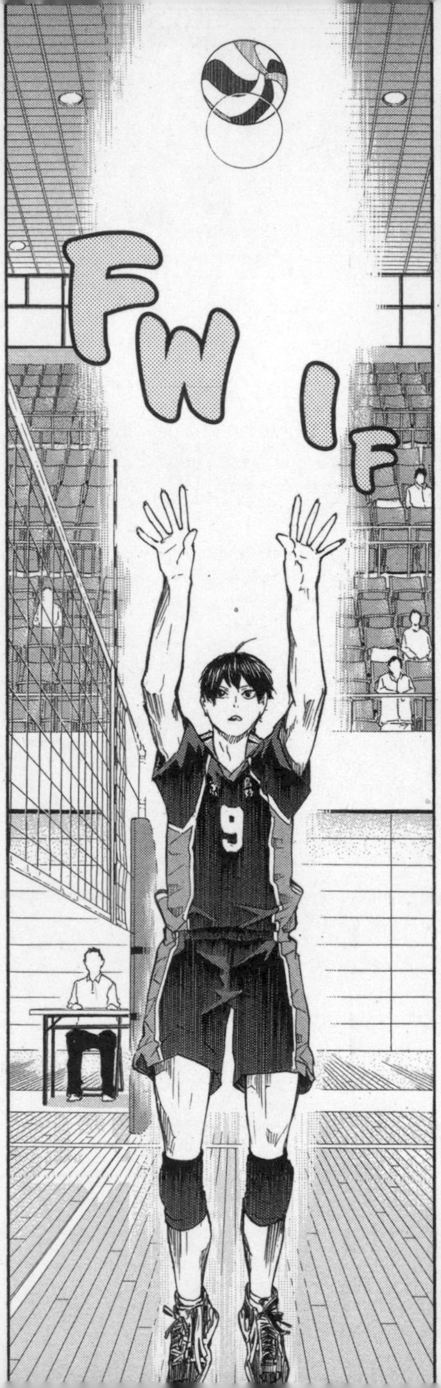
FWIF

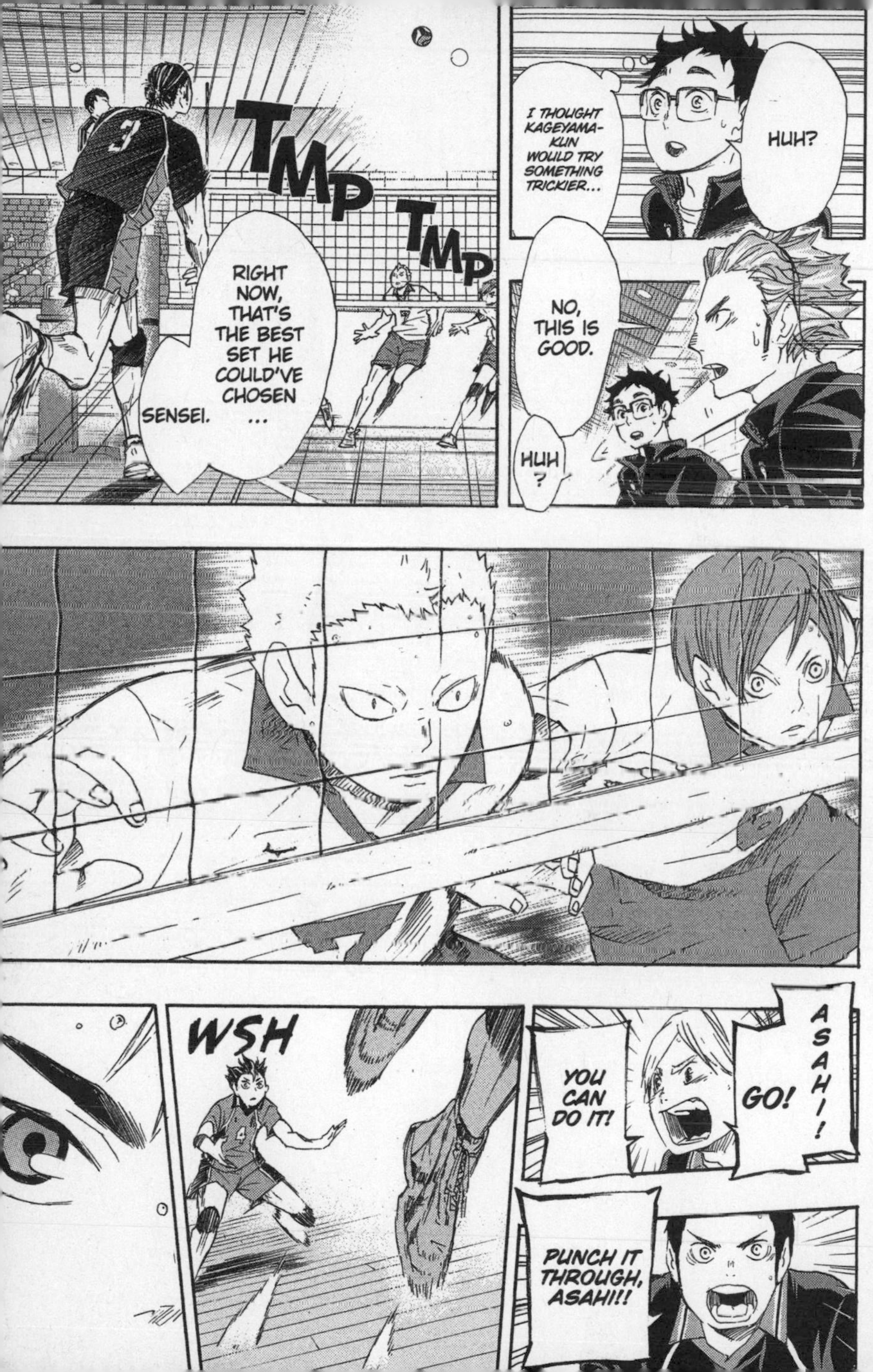
HUH?
I THOUGHT KAGEYAMA-KUN WOULD TRY SOMETHING TRICKIER...
NO, THIS IS GOOD.
HUH?
TMP TMP
RIGHT NOW, THAT'S THE BEST SET HE COULD'VE CHOSEN...
SENSEI.
ASAHI!
GO!
YOU CAN DO IT!
PUNCH IT THROUGH, ASAHI!!
WSH

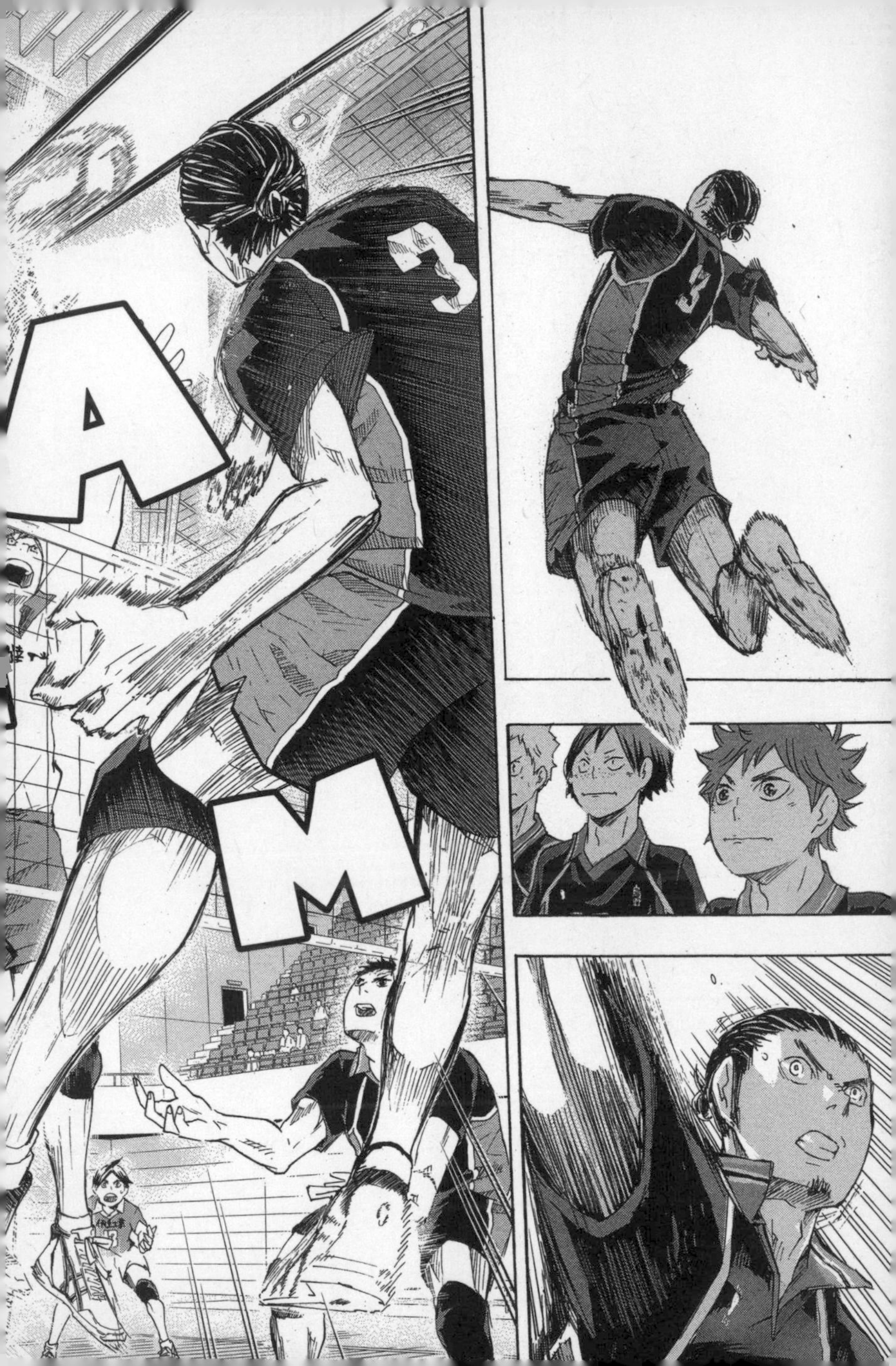
AM

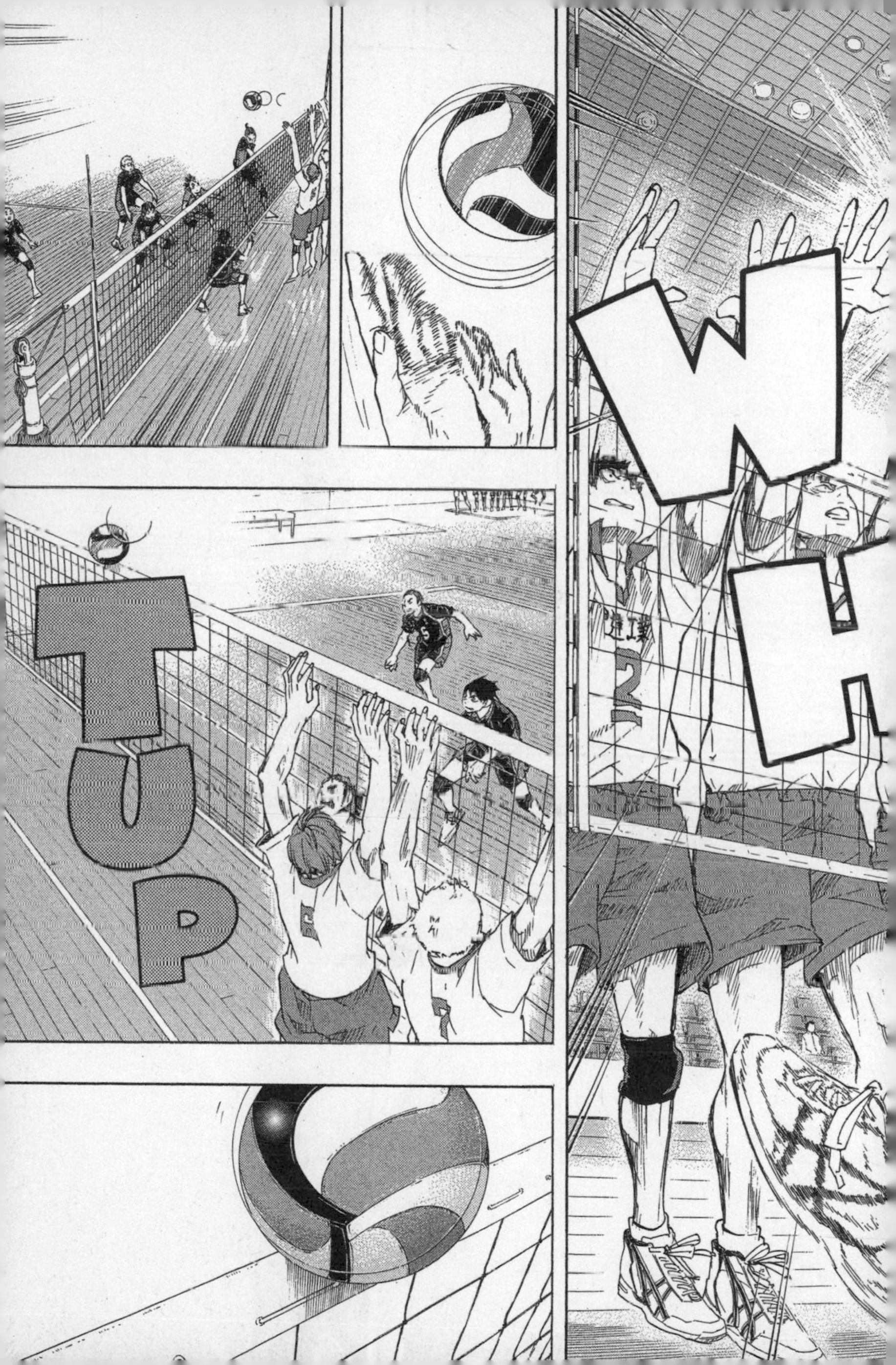
WH
TUP

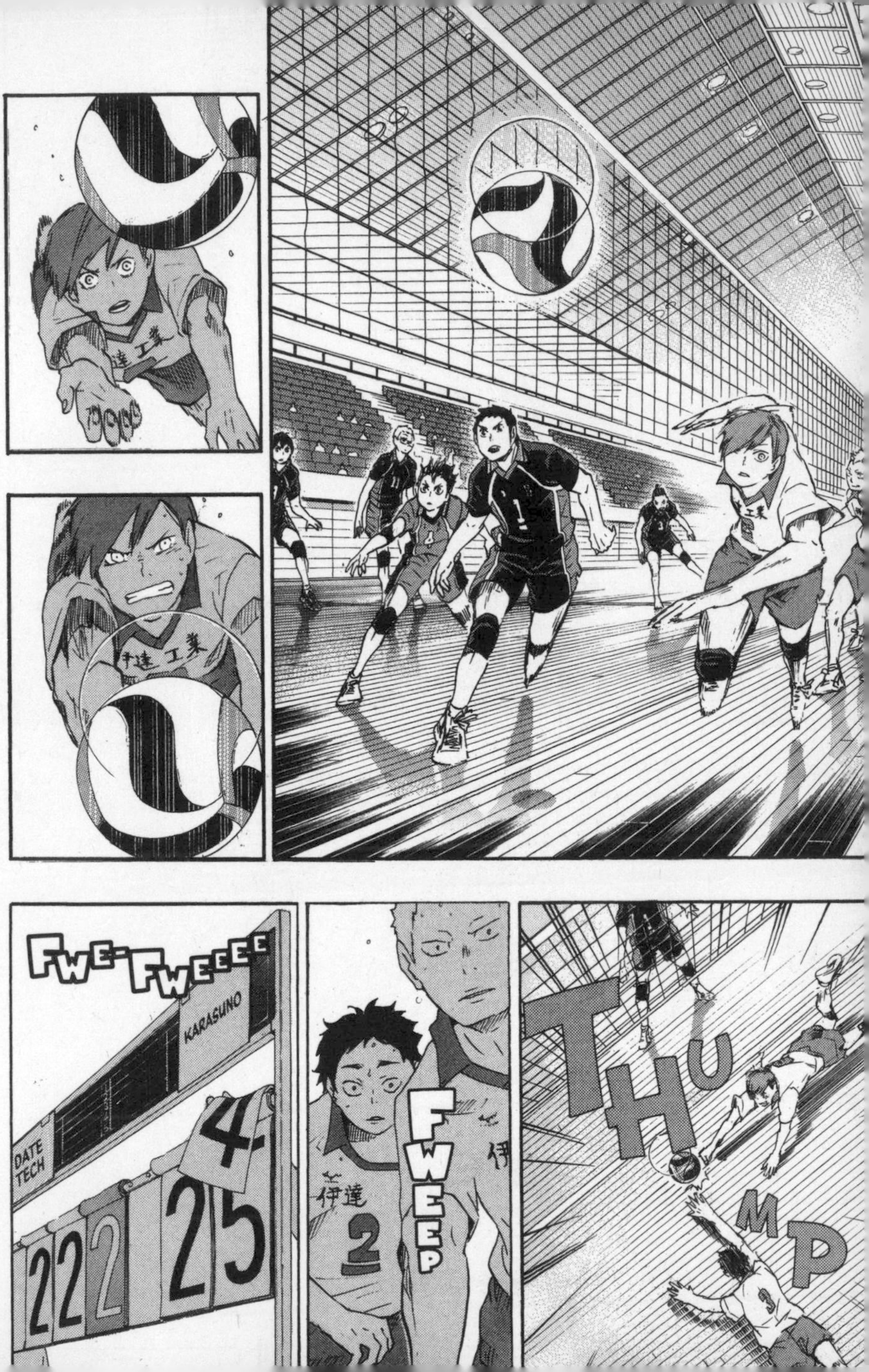
THUMP
FWEEP
FWE-FWEEEE
KARASUNO
DATE TECH
4
22
25

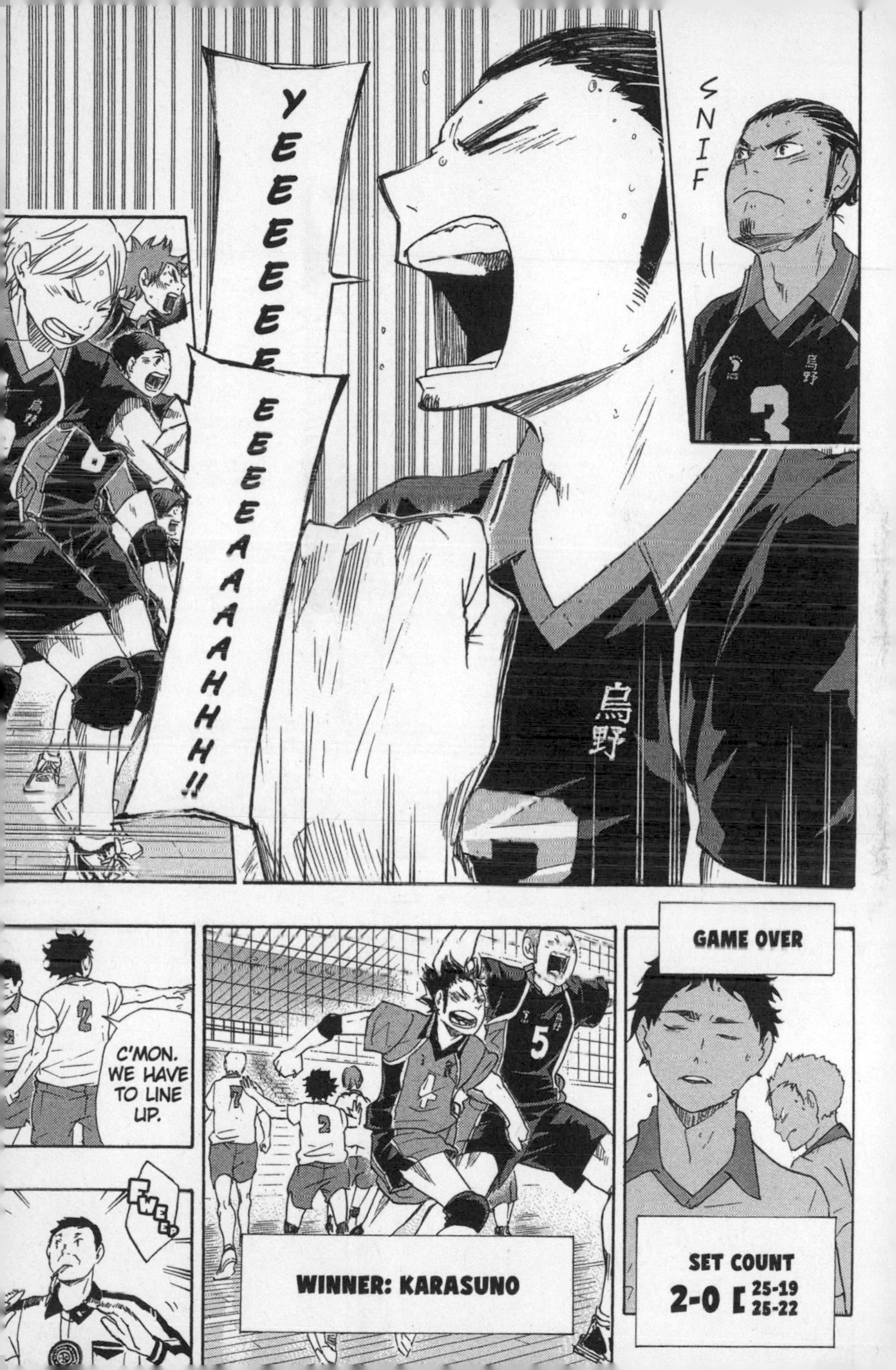
SNIF
YEEEEEEEEEEAAAAAHHHH!!
GAME OVER
SET COUNT
2-0 [25-19 25-22
WINNER: KARASUNO
C'MON. WE HAVE TO LINE UP.
FWEEP

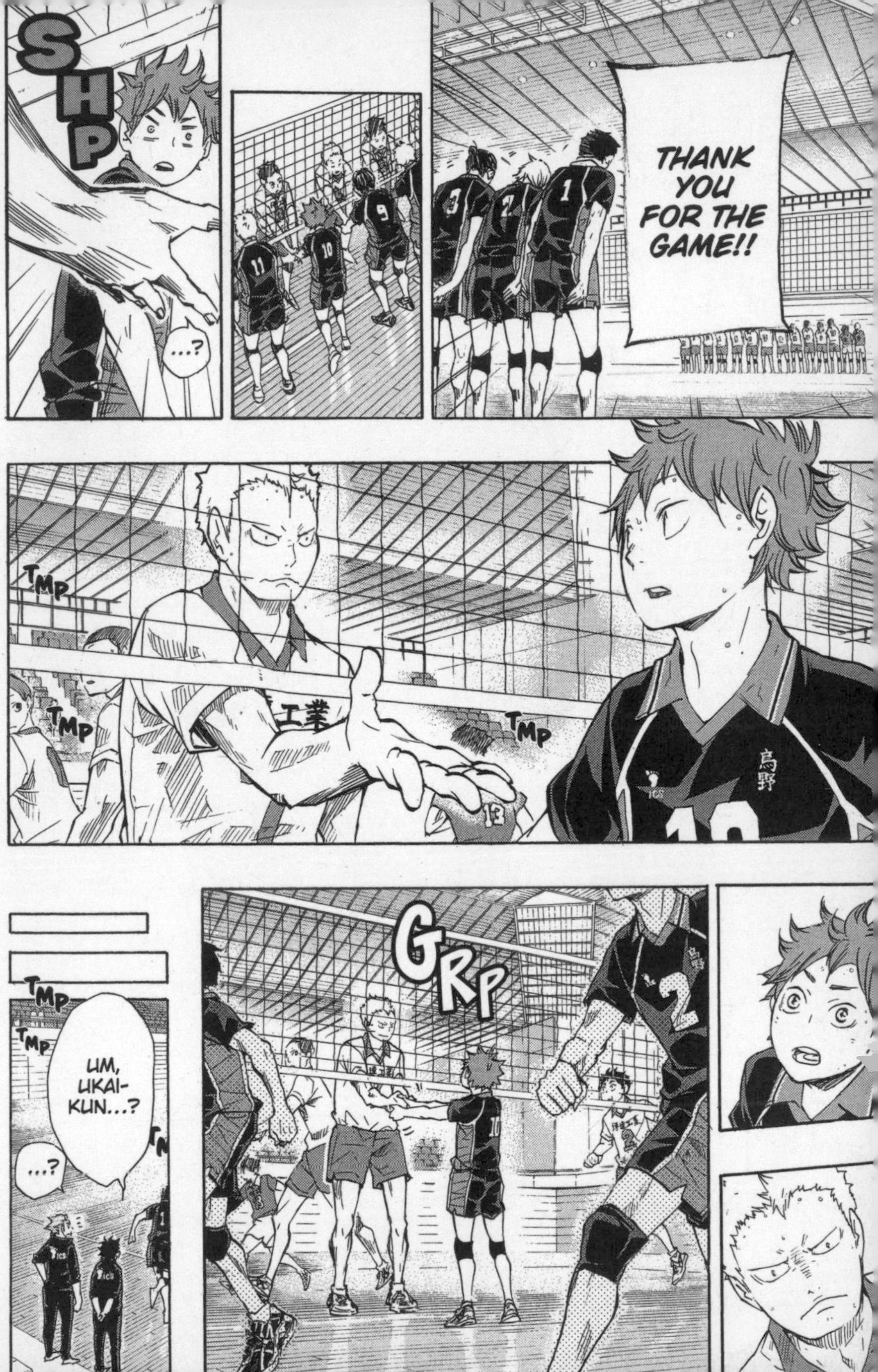
THANK YOU FOR THE GAME!!
SHP
...?
TMP
TMP
TMP
GRP
TMP
TMP
UM, UKAI-KUN...?
...?

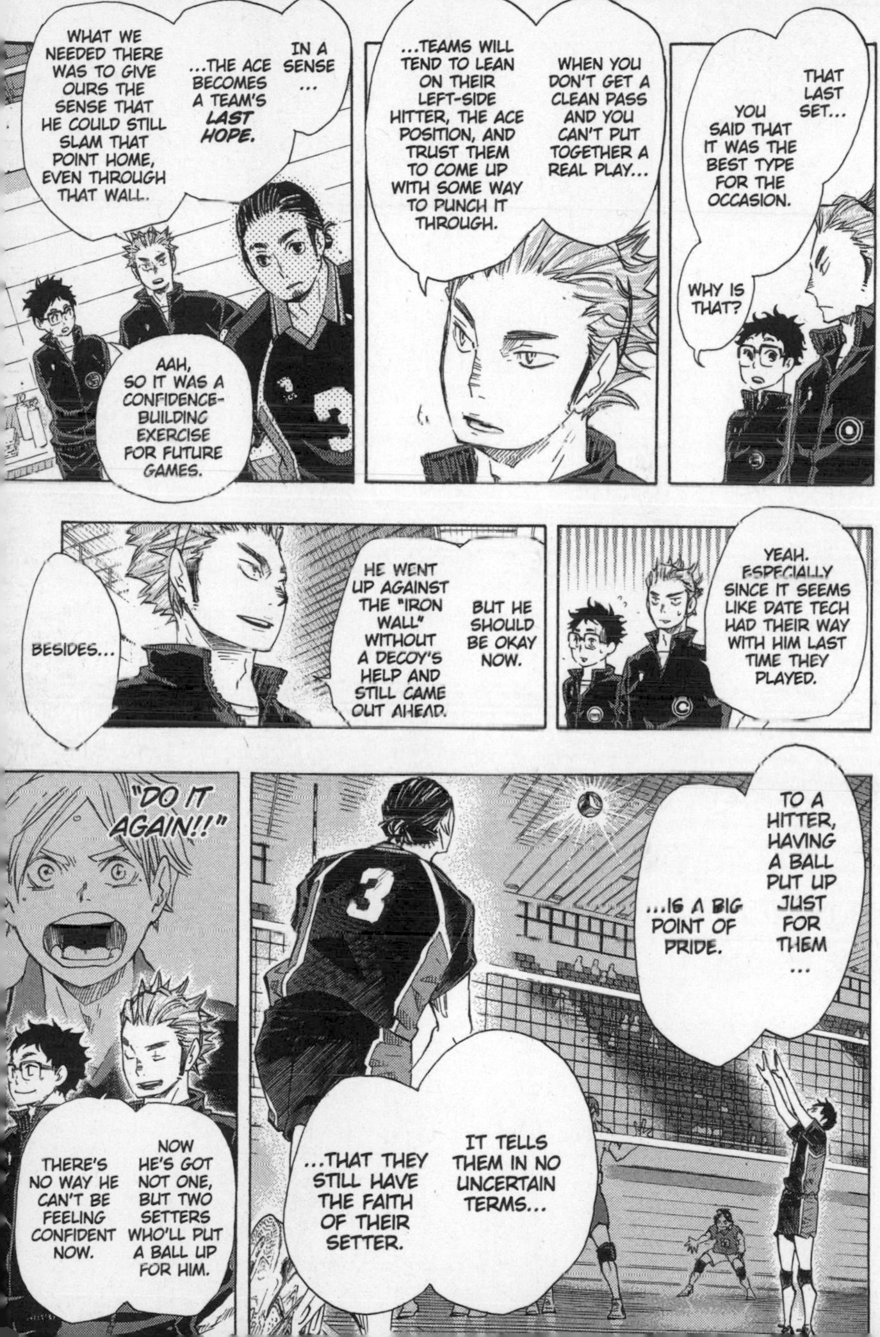
THAT LAST SET...
YOU SAID THAT IT WAS THE BEST TYPE FOR THE OCCASION.
WHY IS THAT?
WHEN YOU DON'T GET A CLEAN PASS AND YOU CAN'T PUT TOGETHER A REAL PLAY...
...TEAMS WILL TEND TO LEAN ON THEIR LEFT-SIDE HITTER, THE ACE POSITION, AND TRUST THEM TO COME UP WITH SOME WAY TO PUNCH IT THROUGH.
IN A SENSE...
...THE ACE BECOMES A TEAM'S *LAST HOPE.*
WHAT WE NEEDED THERE WAS TO GIVE OURS THE SENSE THAT HE COULD STILL SLAM THAT POINT HOME, EVEN THROUGH THAT WALL.
AAH, SO IT WAS A CONFIDENCE-BUILDING EXERCISE FOR FUTURE GAMES.
YEAH. ESPECIALLY SINCE IT SEEMS LIKE DATE TECH HAD THEIR WAY WITH HIM LAST TIME THEY PLAYED.
BUT HE SHOULD BE OKAY NOW.
HE WENT UP AGAINST THE "IRON WALL" WITHOUT A DECOY'S HELP AND STILL CAME OUT AHEAD.
BESIDES...
TO A HITTER, HAVING A BALL PUT UP JUST FOR THEM...
...IS A BIG POINT OF PRIDE.
IT TELLS THEM IN NO UNCERTAIN TERMS...
...THAT THEY STILL HAVE THE FAITH OF THEIR SETTER.
"DO IT AGAIN!!"
NOW HE'S GOT NOT ONE, BUT TWO SETTERS WHO'LL PUT A BALL UP FOR HIM.
THERE'S NO WAY HE CAN'T BE FEELING CONFIDENT NOW.

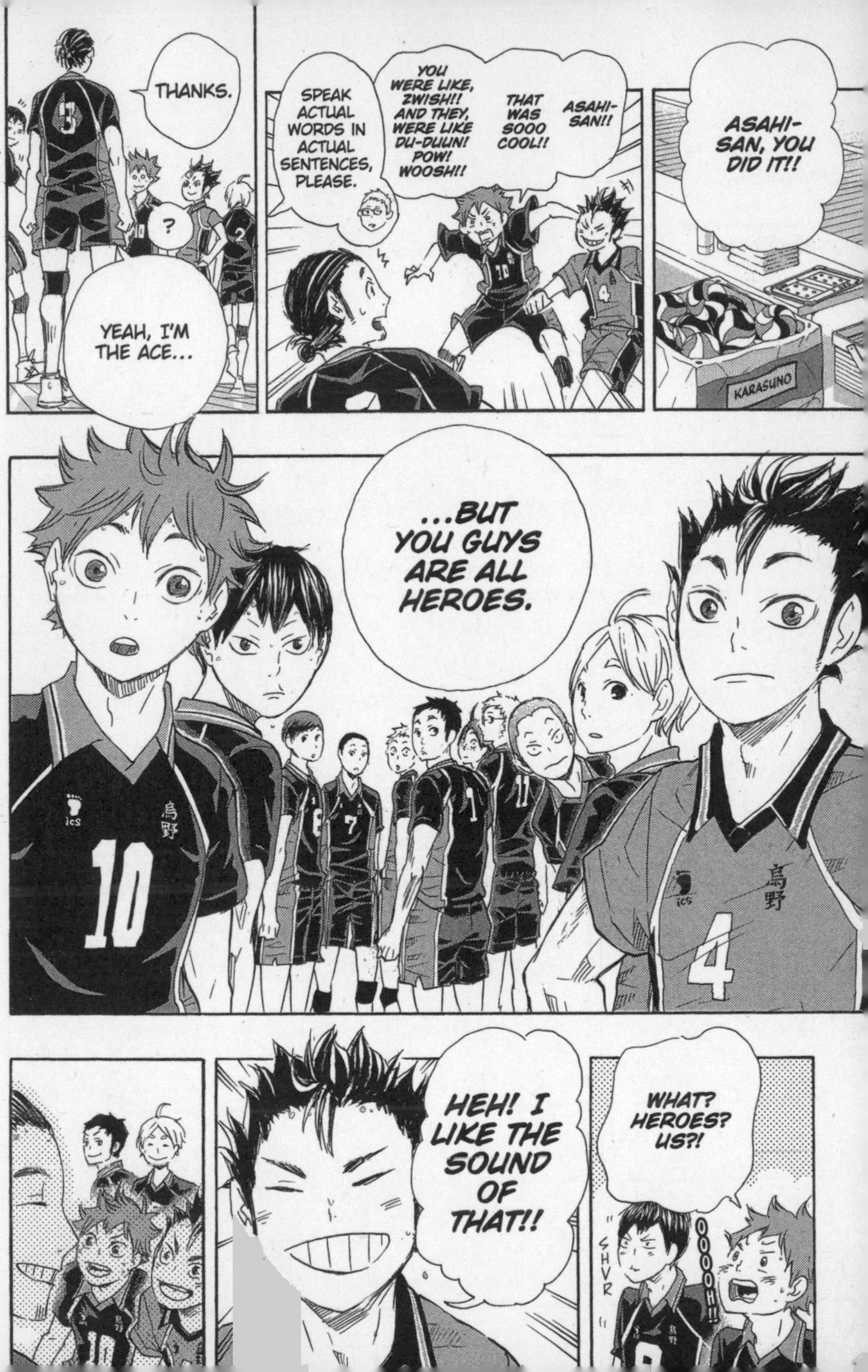
ASAHI-SAN, YOU DID IT!!
KARASUNO
ASAHI-SAN!!
THAT WAS SOOO COOL!!
YOU WERE LIKE, ZWISH!! AND THEY, WERE LIKE DU-DUUN! POW! WOOSH!!
SPEAK ACTUAL WORDS IN ACTUAL SENTENCES, PLEASE.
THANKS.
?
YEAH, I'M THE ACE...
...BUT YOU GUYS ARE ALL HEROES.
WHAT? HEROES? US?!
SHVR
OOOOH!!
HEH! I LIKE THE SOUND OF THAT!!

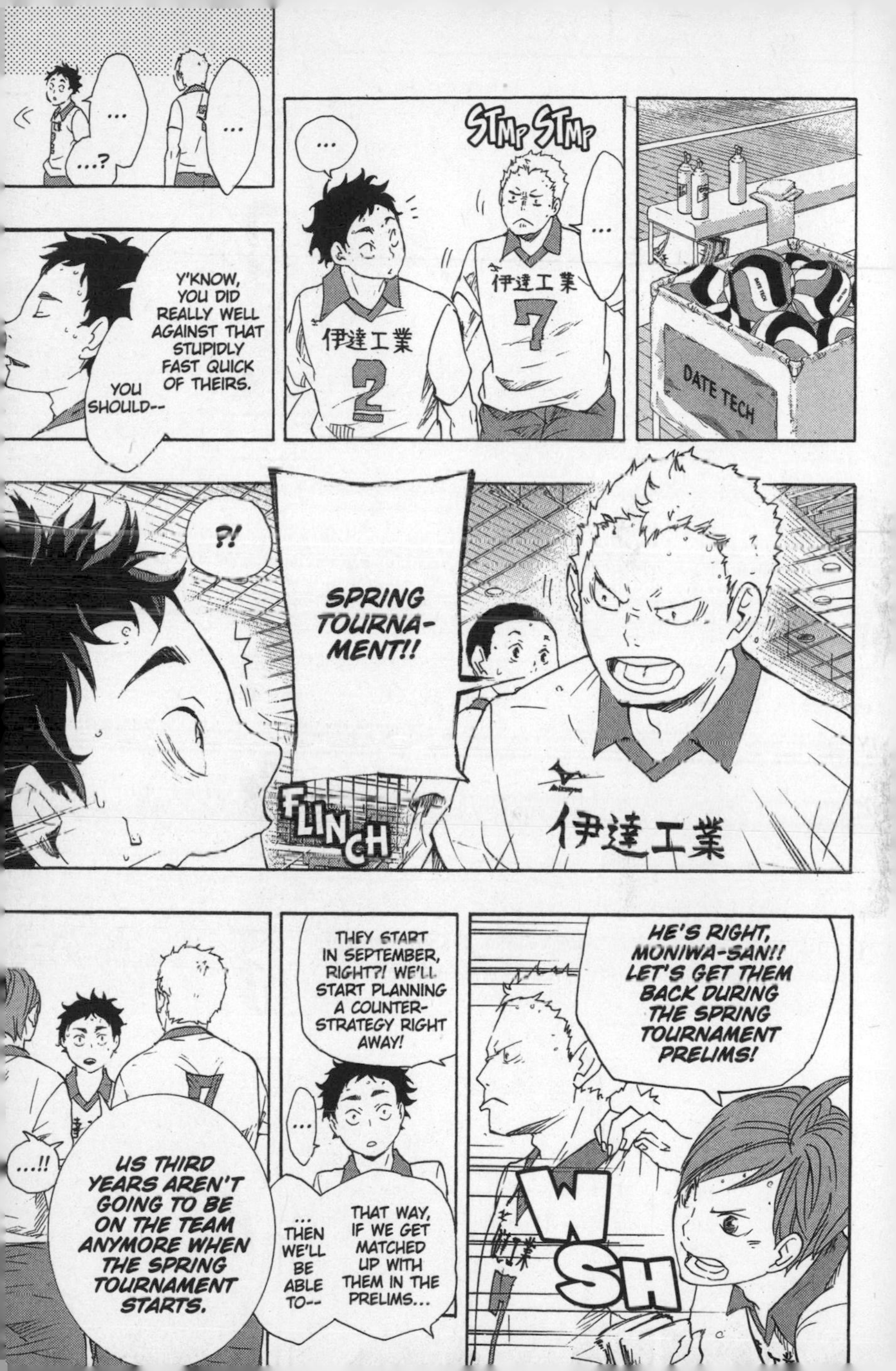
...
...
...?
DATE TECH
STMP STMP
...
...
Y'KNOW, YOU DID REALLY WELL AGAINST THAT STUPIDLY FAST QUICK OF THEIRS.
YOU SHOULD--
SPRING TOURNAMENT!!
FLINCH
?!
HE'S RIGHT, MONIWA-SAN!! LET'S GET THEM BACK DURING THE SPRING TOURNAMENT PRELIMS!
WSH
THEY START IN SEPTEMBER, RIGHT?! WE'LL START PLANNING A COUNTER-STRATEGY RIGHT AWAY!
...
THAT WAY, IF WE GET MATCHED UP WITH THEM IN THE PRELIMS...
... THEN WE'LL BE ABLE TO--
US THIRD YEARS AREN'T GOING TO BE ON THE TEAM ANYMORE WHEN THE SPRING TOURNAMENT STARTS.
...!!

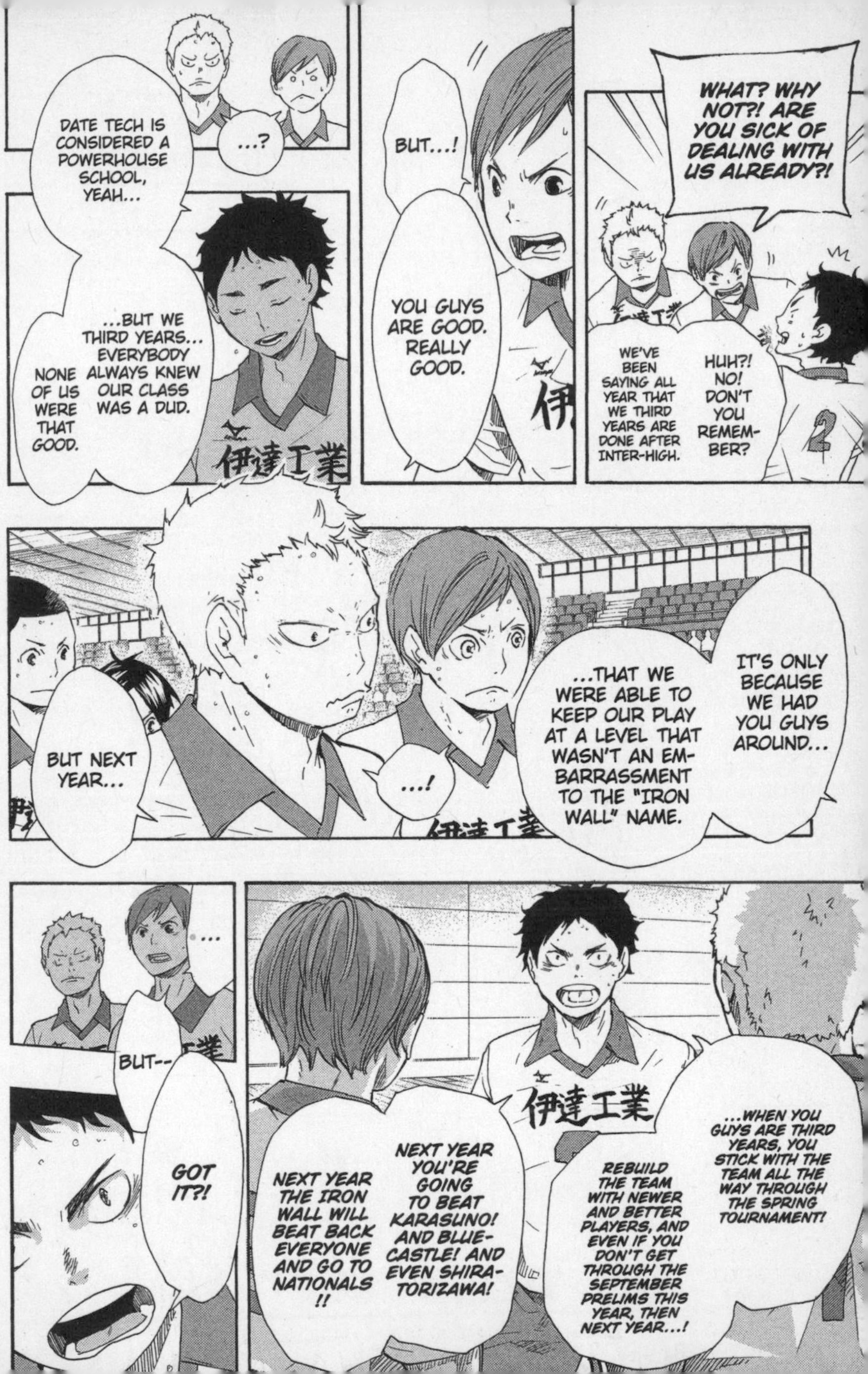
WHAT? WHY NOT?! ARE YOU SICK OF DEALING WITH US ALREADY?!
HUH?! NO! DON'T YOU REMEMBER?
WE'VE BEEN SAYING ALL YEAR THAT WE THIRD YEARS ARE DONE AFTER INTER-HIGH.
BUT...!
YOU GUYS ARE GOOD. REALLY GOOD.
DATE TECH IS CONSIDERED A POWERHOUSE SCHOOL, YEAH...
...?
...BUT WE THIRD YEARS... EVERYBODY ALWAYS KNEW OUR CLASS WAS A DUD.
NONE OF US WERE THAT GOOD.
伊達工業
IT'S ONLY BECAUSE WE HAD YOU GUYS AROUND...
...THAT WE WERE ABLE TO KEEP OUR PLAY AT A LEVEL THAT WASN'T AN EMBARRASSMENT TO THE "IRON WALL" NAME.
...!
BUT NEXT YEAR...
...WHEN YOU GUYS ARE THIRD YEARS, YOU STICK WITH THE TEAM ALL THE WAY THROUGH THE SPRING TOURNAMENT!
REBUILD THE TEAM WITH NEWER AND BETTER PLAYERS, AND EVEN IF YOU DON'T GET THROUGH THE SEPTEMBER PRELIMS THIS YEAR, THEN NEXT YEAR...!
NEXT YEAR YOU'RE GOING TO BEAT KARASUNO! AND BLUE-CASTLE! AND EVEN SHIRATORIZAWA!
NEXT YEAR THE IRON WALL WILL BEAT BACK EVERYONE AND GO TO NATIONALS!!
...
BUT--
GOT IT?!

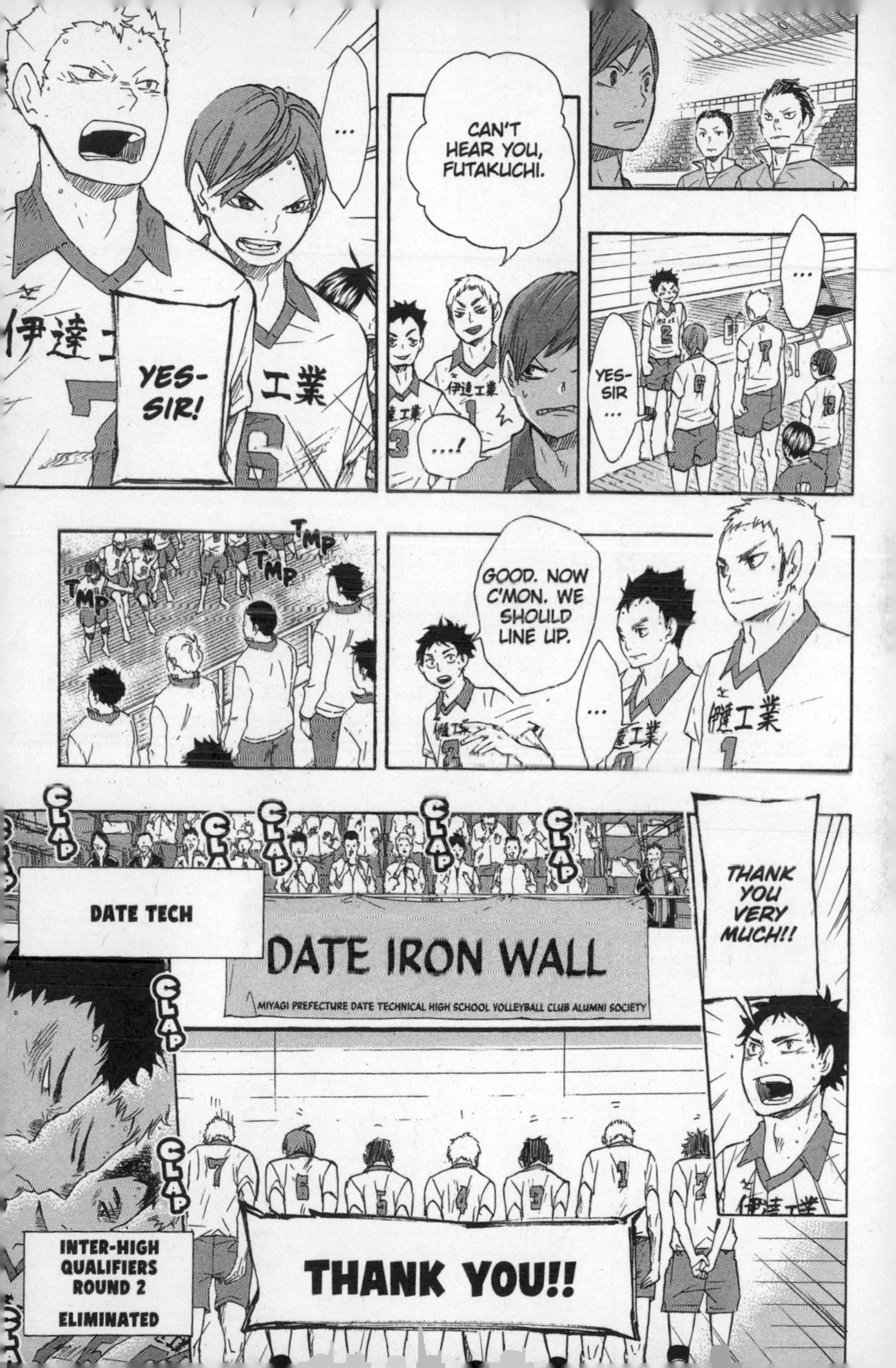
...
YES-SIR ...
CAN'T HEAR YOU, FUTAKUCHI.
....!
...
YES-SIR!
GOOD. NOW C'MON. WE SHOULD LINE UP.
...
TMP
TMP
TMP
THANK YOU VERY MUCH!!
CLAP
CLAP
CLAP
CLAP
CLAP
DATE TECH
DATE IRON WALL
MIYAGI PREFECTURE DATE TECHNICAL HIGH SCHOOL VOLLEYBALL CLUB ALUMNI SOCIETY
CLAP
CLAP
THANK YOU!!
INTER-HIGH QUALIFIERS ROUND 2
ELIMINATED

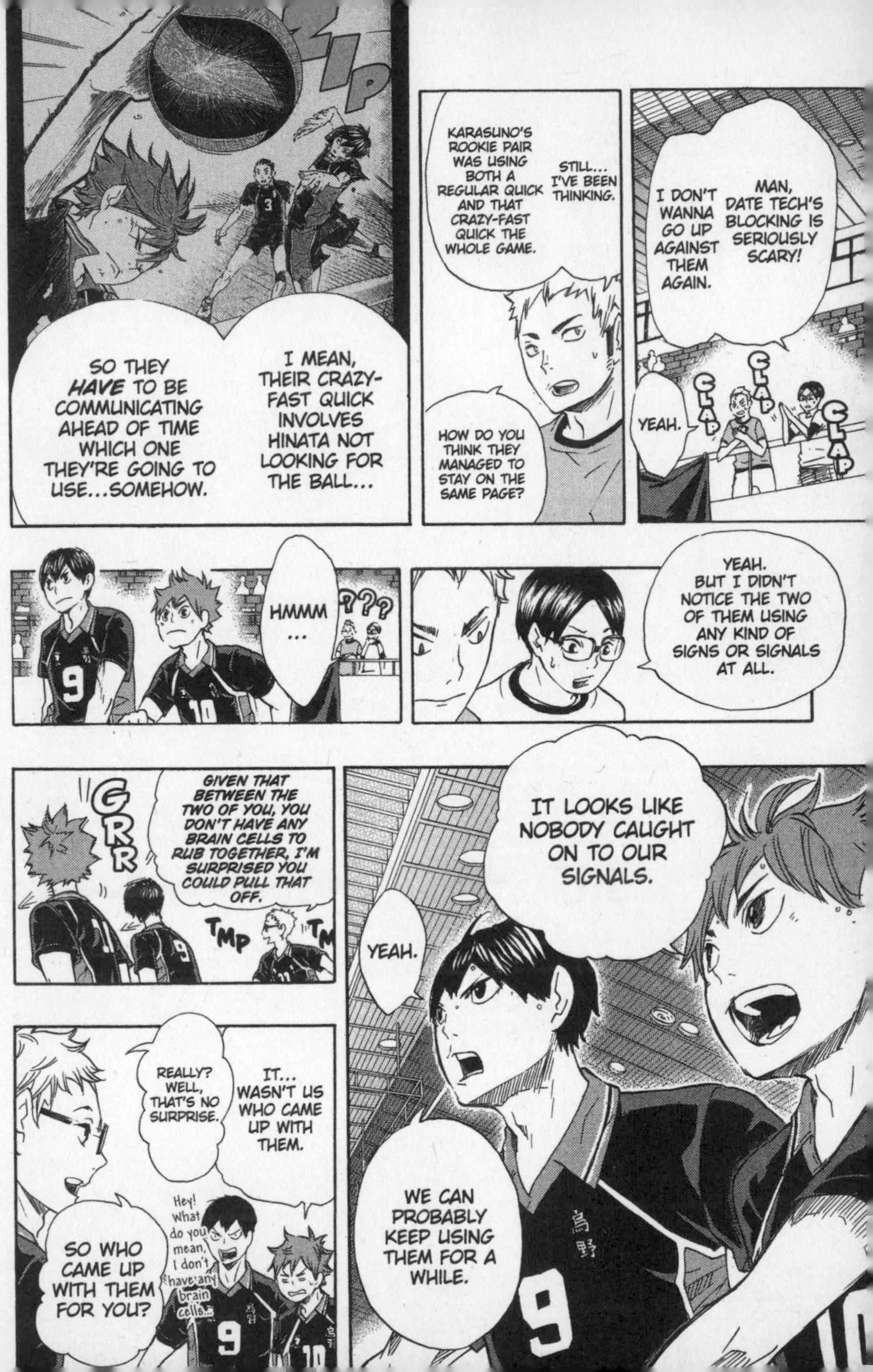
MAN, DATE TECH'S BLOCKING IS SERIOUSLY SCARY!
I DON'T WANNA GO UP AGAINST THEM AGAIN.
CLAP
CLAP
CLAP
YEAH.
STILL... I'VE BEEN THINKING.
KARASUNO'S ROOKIE PAIR WAS USING BOTH A REGULAR QUICK AND THAT CRAZY-FAST QUICK THE WHOLE GAME.
HOW DO YOU THINK THEY MANAGED TO STAY ON THE SAME PAGE?
I MEAN, THEIR CRAZY-FAST QUICK INVOLVES HINATA NOT LOOKING FOR THE BALL...
SO THEY *HAVE* TO BE COMMUNICATING AHEAD OF TIME WHICH ONE THEY'RE GOING TO USE...SOMEHOW.
YEAH. BUT I DIDN'T NOTICE THE TWO OF THEM USING ANY KIND OF SIGNS OR SIGNALS AT ALL.
???
HMMM ...
IT LOOKS LIKE NOBODY CAUGHT ON TO OUR SIGNALS.
YEAH.
WE CAN PROBABLY KEEP USING THEM FOR A WHILE.
GIVEN THAT BETWEEN THE TWO OF YOU, YOU DON'T HAVE ANY BRAIN CELLS TO RUB TOGETHER, I'M SURPRISED YOU COULD PULL THAT OFF.
GRR
TMP
TMP
IT... WASN'T US WHO CAME UP WITH THEM.
REALLY? WELL, THAT'S NO SURPRISE.
Hey! What do you mean, I don't have any brain cells...
SO WHO CAME UP WITH THEM FOR YOU?

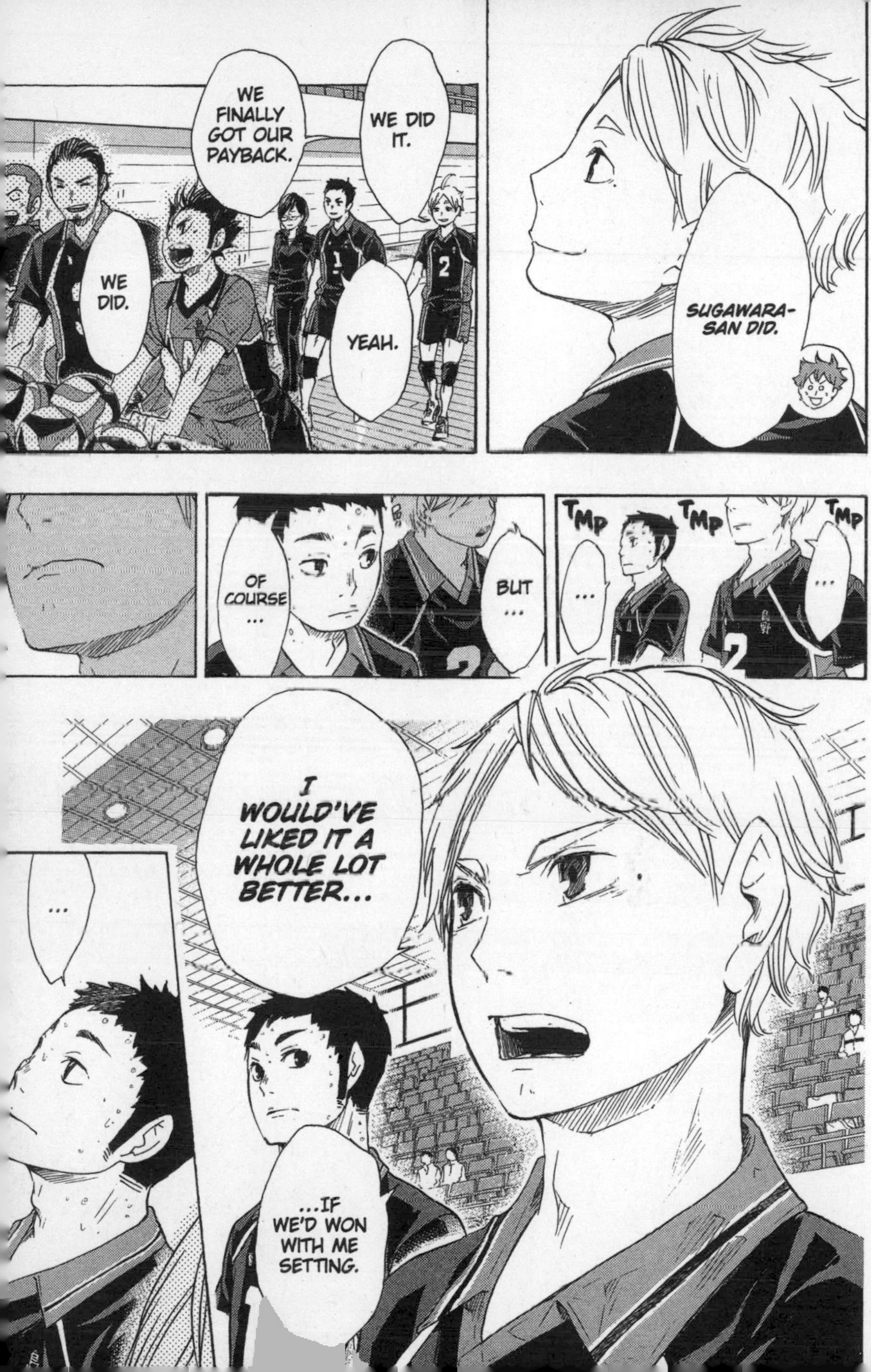
SUGAWARA-SAN DID.
WE DID IT.
WE FINALLY GOT OUR PAYBACK.
YEAH.
WE DID.
TMP TMP TMP
...
...
BUT ...
OF COURSE ...
I WOULD'VE LIKED IT A WHOLE LOT BETTER...
...
...IF WE'D WON WITH ME SETTING.

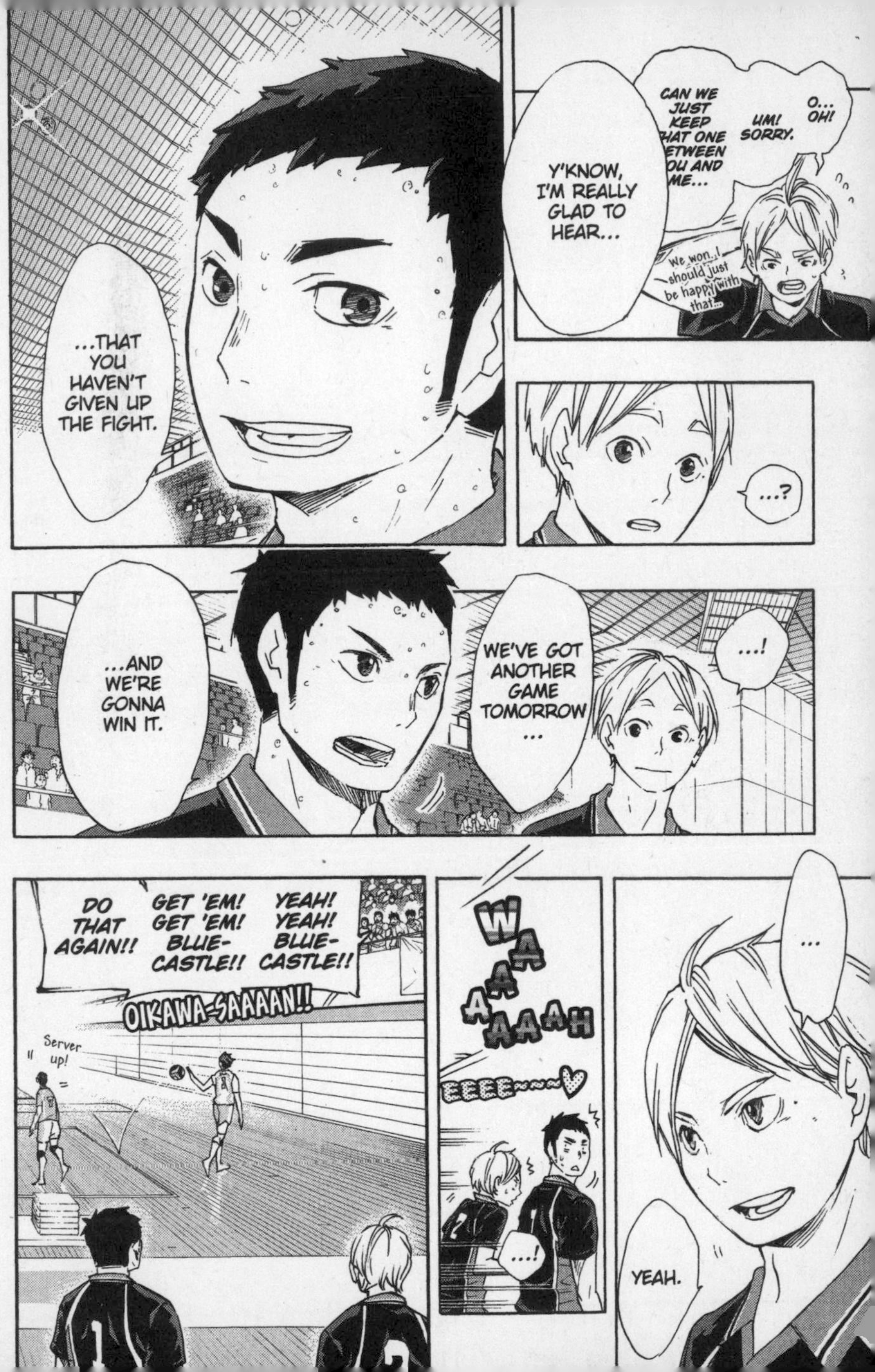
O... OH!
UM! SORRY.
CAN WE JUST KEEP THAT ONE BETWEEN YOU AND ME...
We won. I should just be happy with that...
Y'KNOW, I'M REALLY GLAD TO HEAR...
...?
...THAT YOU HAVEN'T GIVEN UP THE FIGHT.
...!
WE'VE GOT ANOTHER GAME TOMORROW...
...AND WE'RE GONNA WIN IT.
...
YEAH.
WAAAAAAAH
EEEE~~~♥
...!
YEAH! YEAH! BLUE-CASTLE!!
GET 'EM! GET 'EM! BLUE-CASTLE!!
DO THAT AGAIN!!
OIKAWA-SAAAAN!!
Server up!

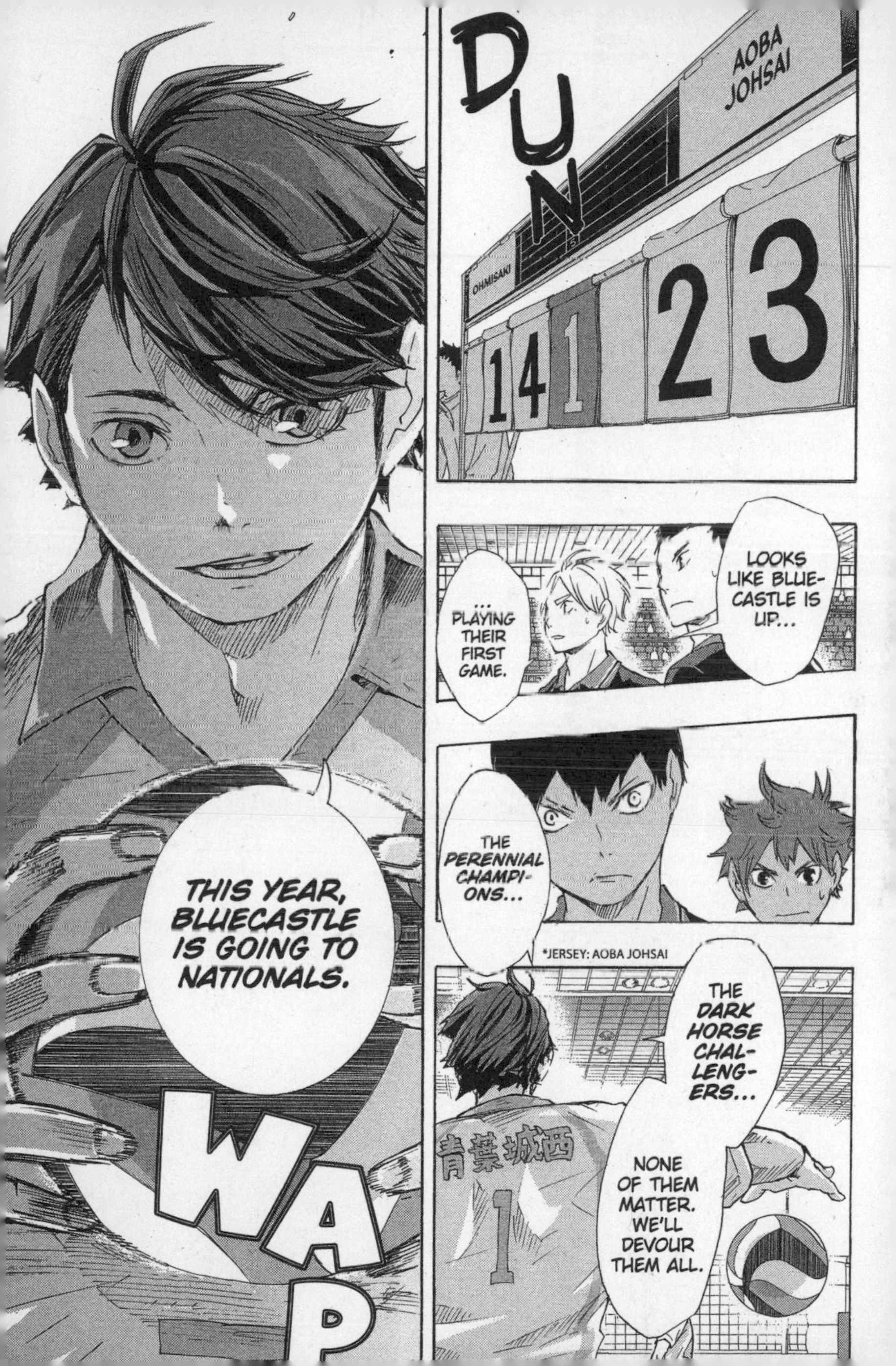
DUN
AOBA JOHSAI
OHMISAKI
14
1
2
3
LOOKS LIKE BLUE-CASTLE IS UP...
...PLAYING THEIR FIRST GAME.
THE PERENNIAL CHAMPI-ONS...
*JERSEY: AOBA JOHSAI
THE DARK HORSE CHAL-LENG-ERS...
NONE OF THEM MATTER. WE'LL DEVOUR THEM ALL.
青葉城西
1
THIS YEAR, BLUECASTLE IS GOING TO NATIONALS.
WAP

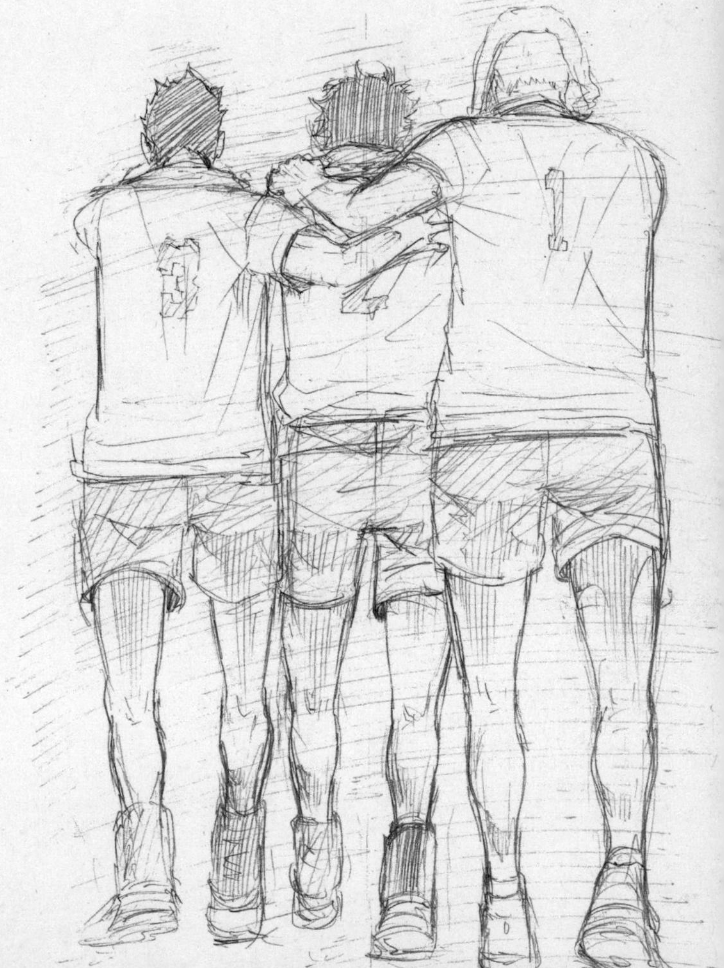

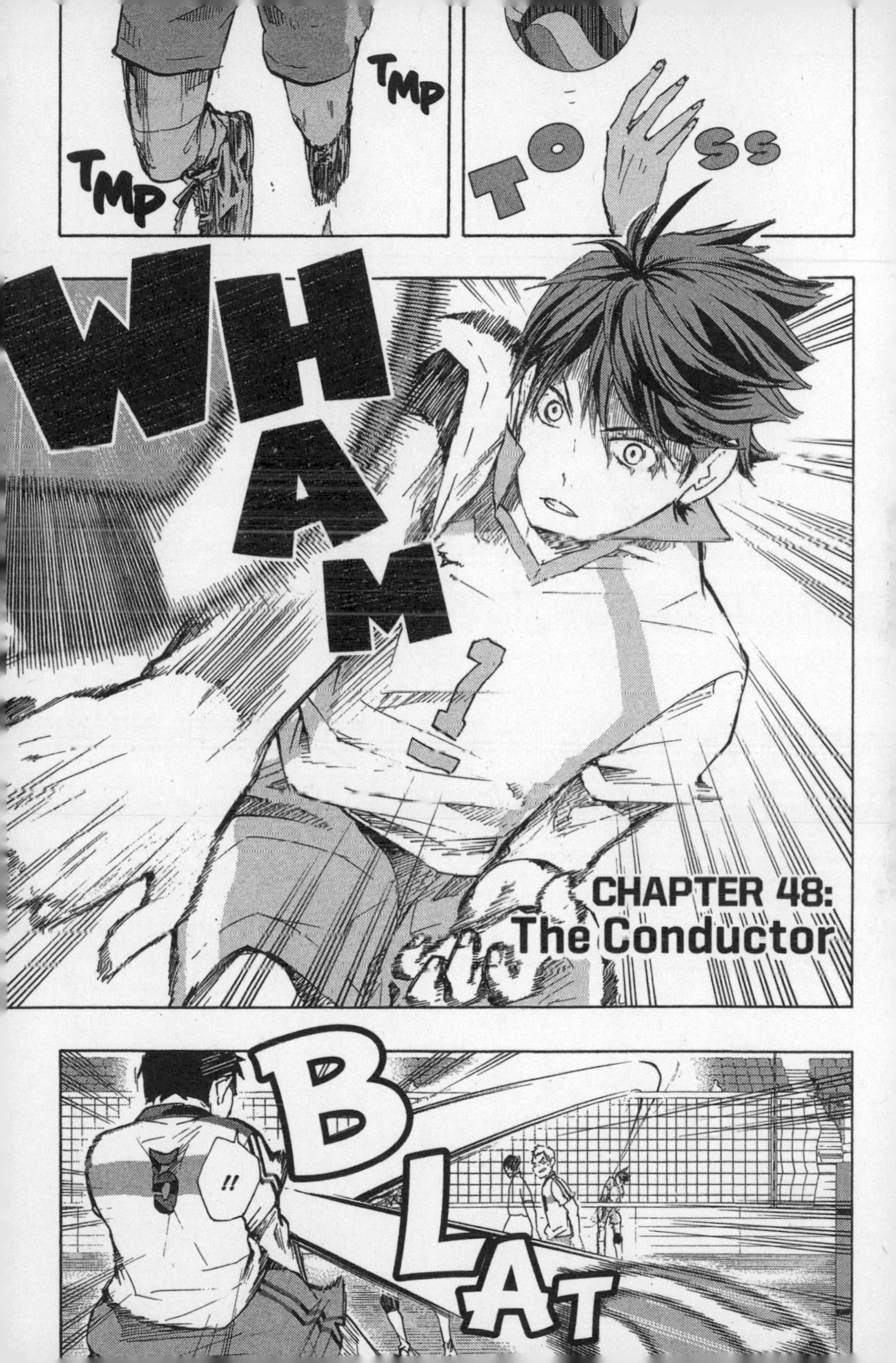
TOSS
TMP
TMP
WHAM!
CHAPTER 48:
The Conductor
!!
BLAT

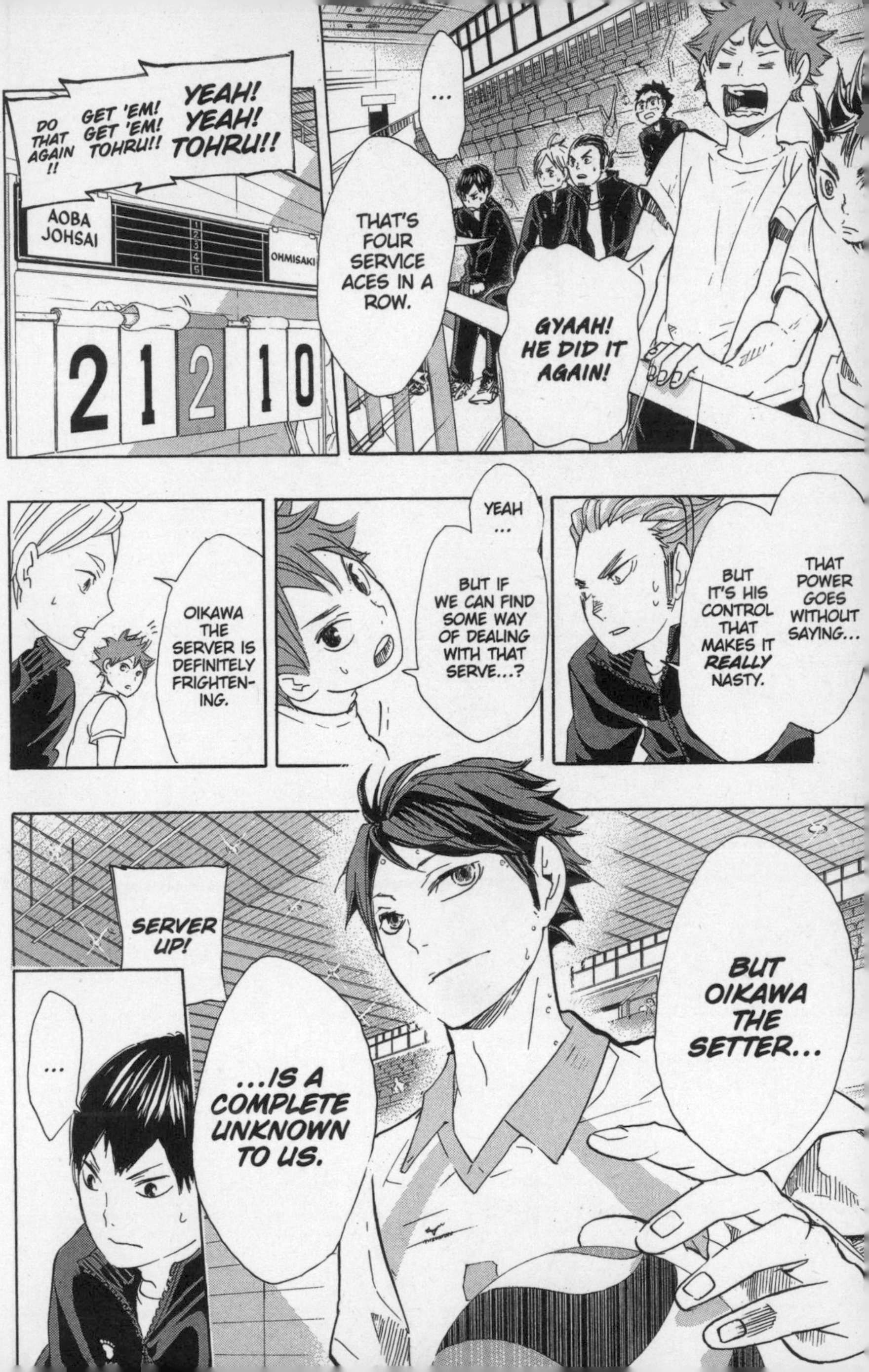
GYAAH! HE DID IT AGAIN!
...
THAT'S FOUR SERVICE ACES IN A ROW.
YEAH! YEAH! TOHRU!!
GET 'EM! GET 'EM! TOHRU!!
DO THAT AGAIN !!
AOBA JOHSAI
OHMISAKI
21
2
10
THAT POWER GOES WITHOUT SAYING...
BUT IT'S HIS CONTROL THAT MAKES IT REALLY NASTY.
YEAH ...
BUT IF WE CAN FIND SOME WAY OF DEALING WITH THAT SERVE...?
OIKAWA THE SERVER IS DEFINITELY FRIGHTEN-ING.
BUT OIKAWA THE SETTER...
SERVER UP!
...IS A COMPLETE UNKNOWN TO US.
...

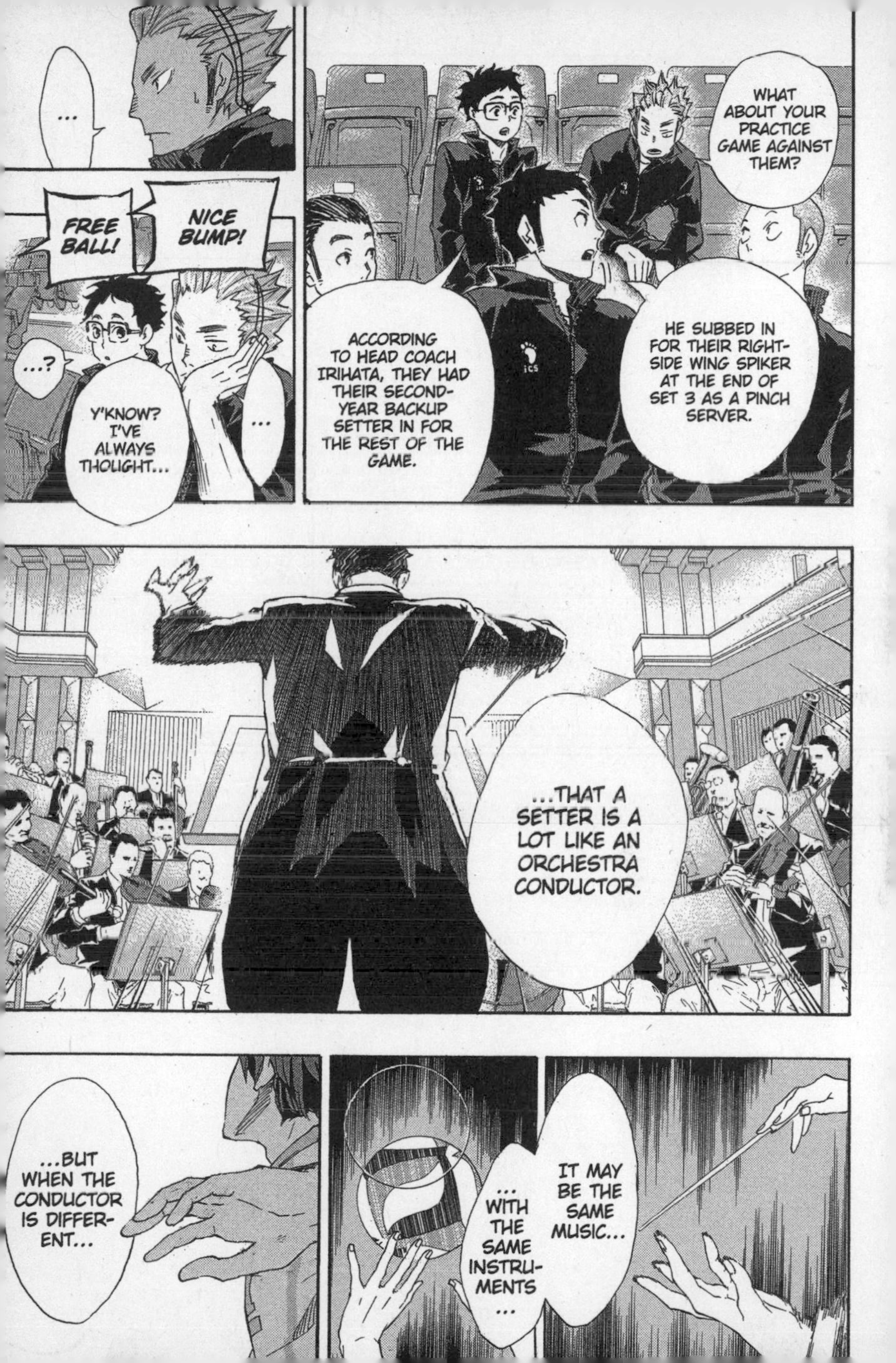
WHAT ABOUT YOUR PRACTICE GAME AGAINST THEM?
HE SUBBED IN FOR THEIR RIGHT-SIDE WING SPIKER AT THE END OF SET 3 AS A PINCH SERVER.
ACCORDING TO HEAD COACH IRIHATA, THEY HAD THEIR SECOND-YEAR BACKUP SETTER IN FOR THE REST OF THE GAME.
...
NICE BUMP!
FREE BALL!
...
...?
Y'KNOW? I'VE ALWAYS THOUGHT...
...THAT A SETTER IS A LOT LIKE AN ORCHESTRA CONDUCTOR.
IT MAY BE THE SAME MUSIC...
... WITH THE SAME INSTRUMENTS ...
...BUT WHEN THE CONDUCTOR IS DIFFER-ENT...

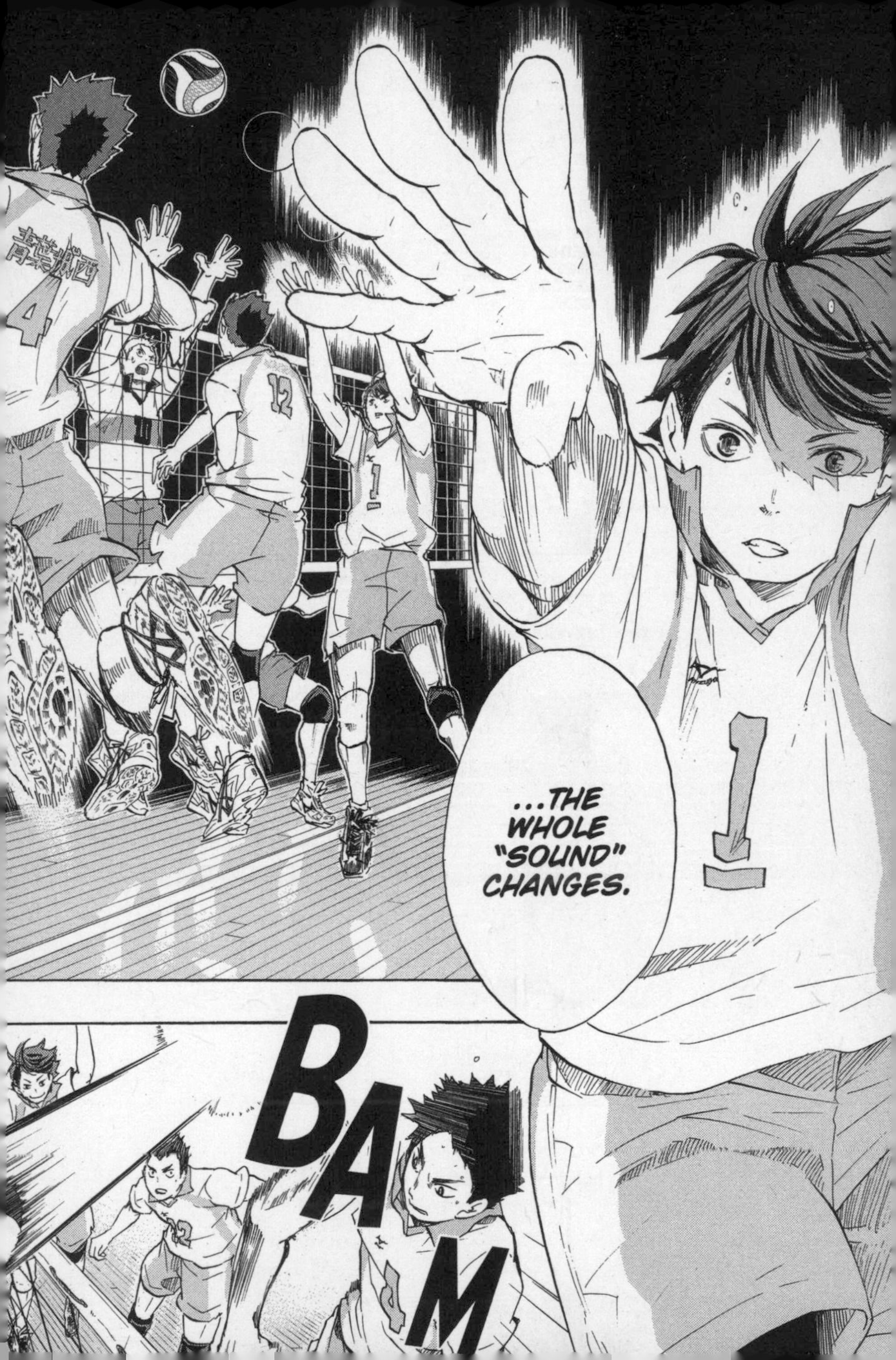
...THE WHOLE "SOUND" CHANGES.
BAM

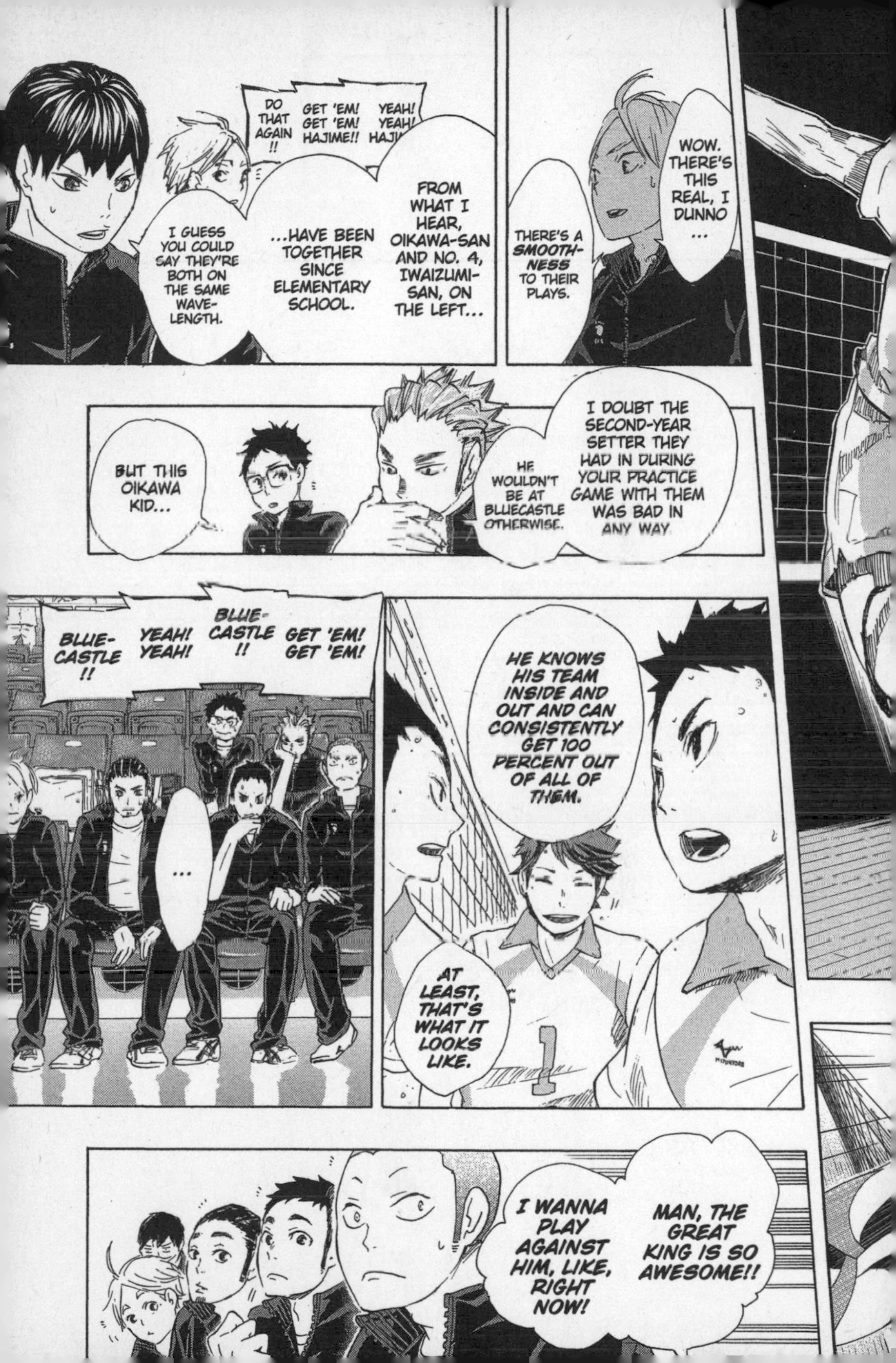
WOW. THERE'S THIS REAL, I DUNNO ...
THERE'S A SMOOTHNESS TO THEIR PLAYS.
YEAH! YEAH!
GET 'EM! GET 'EM! HAJIME!!
DO THAT AGAIN !!
FROM WHAT I HEAR, OIKAWA-SAN AND NO. 4, IWAIZUMI-SAN, ON THE LEFT...
...HAVE BEEN TOGETHER SINCE ELEMENTARY SCHOOL.
I GUESS YOU COULD SAY THEY'RE BOTH ON THE SAME WAVE-LENGTH.
I DOUBT THE SECOND-YEAR SETTER THEY HAD IN DURING YOUR PRACTICE GAME WITH THEM WAS BAD IN ANY WAY.
HE WOULDN'T BE AT BLUECASTLE OTHERWISE.
BUT THIS OIKAWA KID...
HE KNOWS HIS TEAM INSIDE AND OUT AND CAN CONSISTENTLY GET 100 PERCENT OUT OF ALL OF THEM.
AT LEAST, THAT'S WHAT IT LOOKS LIKE.
GET 'EM! GET 'EM!
BLUE-CASTLE !!
YEAH! YEAH!
BLUE-CASTLE !!
...
MAN, THE GREAT KING IS SO AWESOME!!
I WANNA PLAY AGAINST HIM, LIKE, RIGHT NOW!

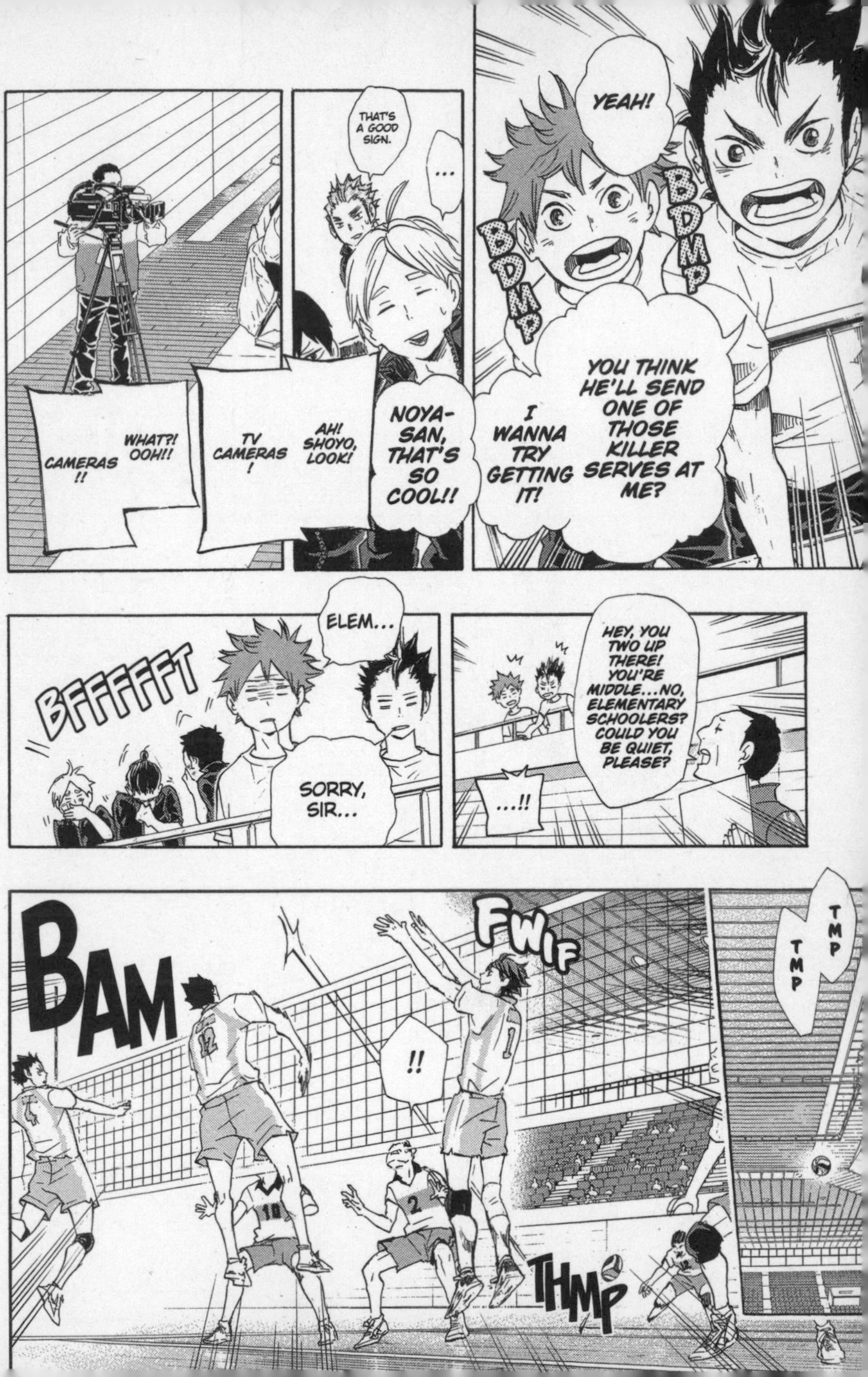
YEAH!
BDMP
BDMP
YOU THINK HE'LL SEND ONE OF THOSE KILLER SERVES AT ME?
I WANNA TRY GETTING IT!
THAT'S A GOOD SIGN.
...
NOYA-SAN, THAT'S SO COOL!!
AH! SHOYO, LOOK!
TV CAMERAS!
WHAT?! OOH!!
CAMERAS!!
HEY, YOU TWO UP THERE! YOU'RE MIDDLE...NO, ELEMENTARY SCHOOLERS? COULD YOU BE QUIET, PLEASE?
...!!
ELEM...
SORRY, SIR...
BFFFFFT
TMP
TMP
FWIF
BAM
!!
THMP

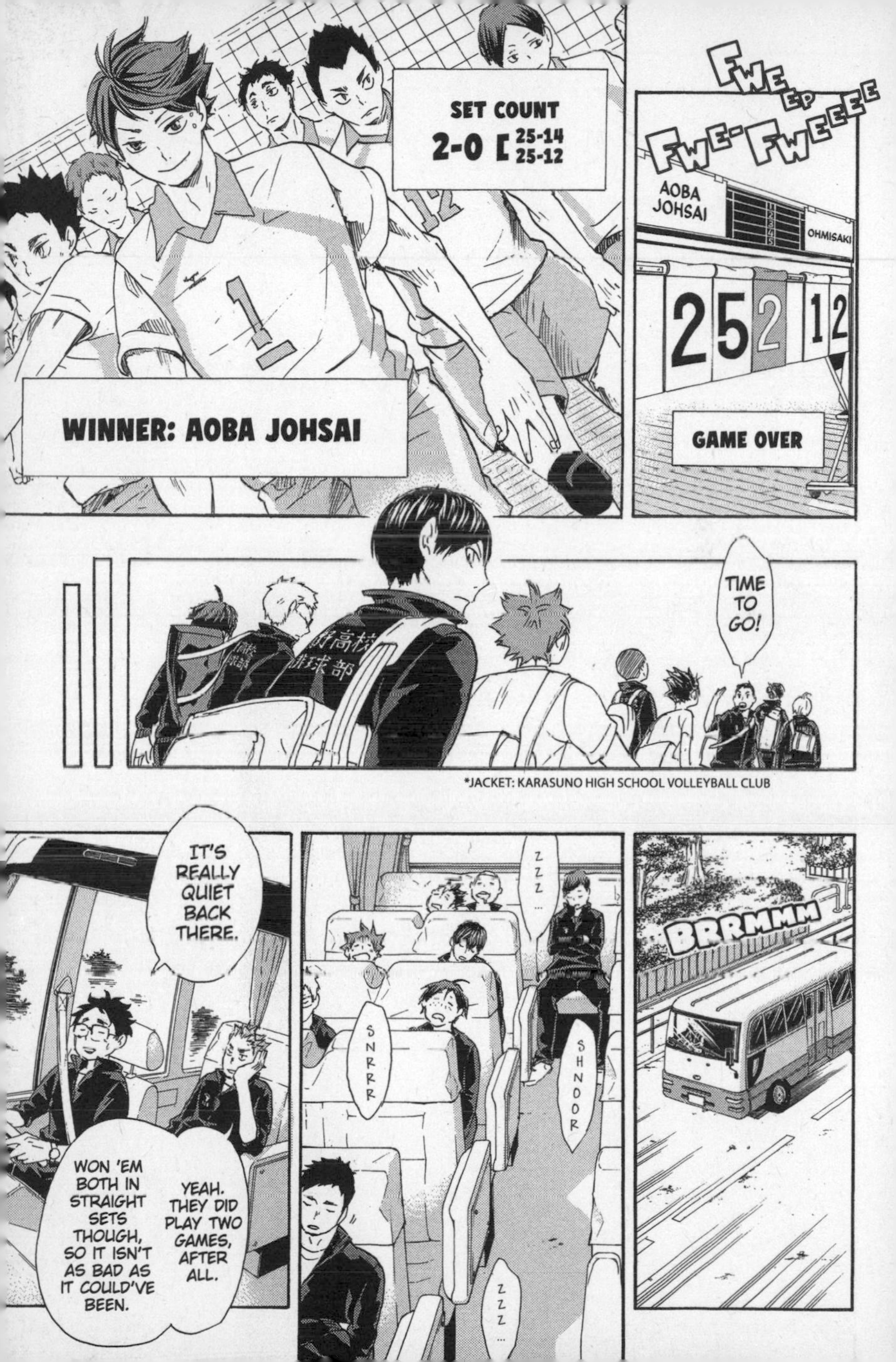

FWEEP
FWE-FWEEEE
AOBA JOHSAI
OHMISAKI
25 2 12
GAME OVER
SET COUNT
2-0 [25-14 25-12
WINNER: AOBA JOHSAI
TIME TO GO!
*JACKET: KARASUNO HIGH SCHOOL VOLLEYBALL CLUB
BRRMMM
ZZZ...
SHNOOR
SNRRR
ZZZ...
IT'S REALLY QUIET BACK THERE.
YEAH. THEY DID PLAY TWO GAMES, AFTER ALL.
WON 'EM BOTH IN STRAIGHT SETS THOUGH, SO IT ISN'T AS BAD AS IT COULD'VE BEEN.

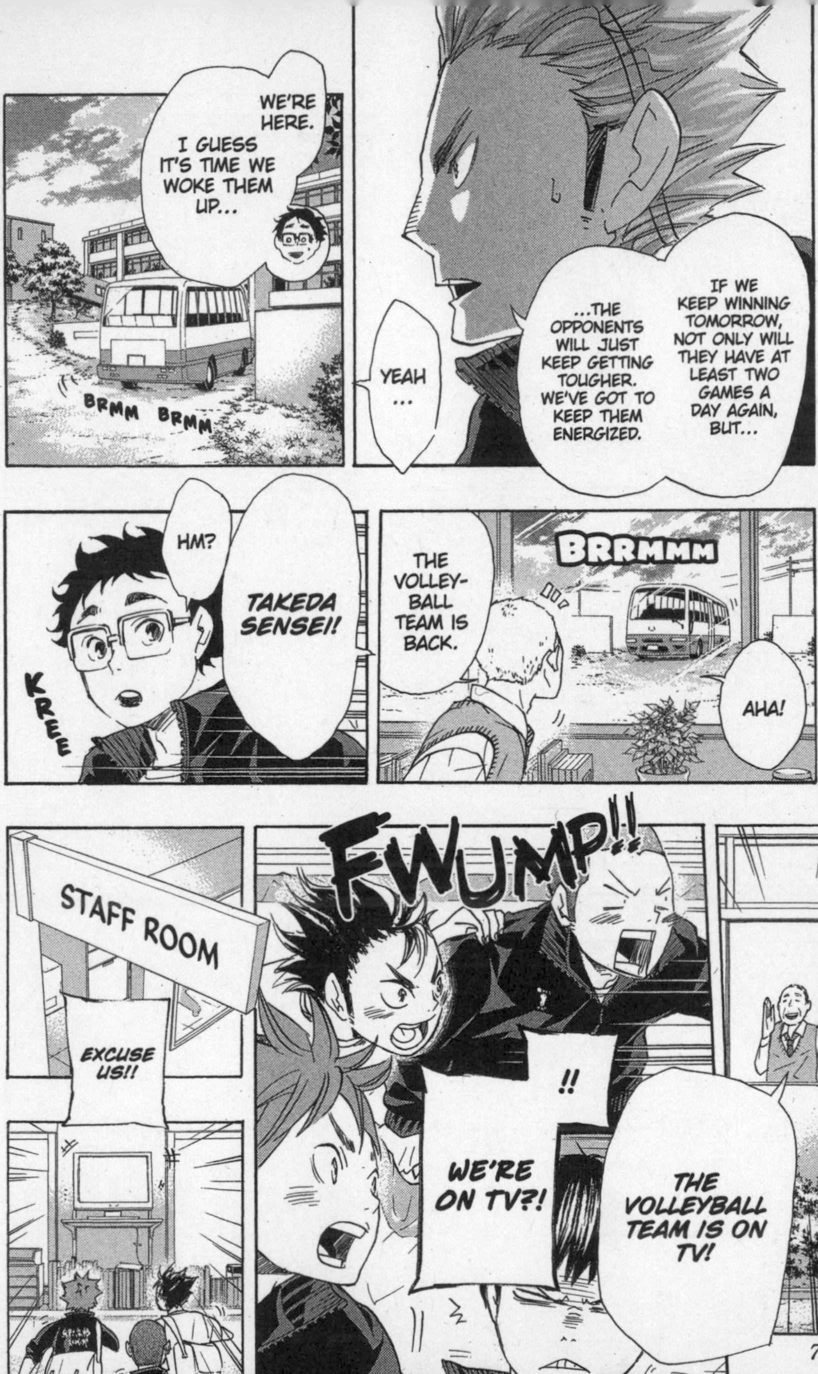
IF WE KEEP WINNING TOMORROW, NOT ONLY WILL THEY HAVE AT LEAST TWO GAMES A DAY AGAIN, BUT...
...THE OPPONENTS WILL JUST KEEP GETTING TOUGHER. WE'VE GOT TO KEEP THEM ENERGIZED.
YEAH ...
WE'RE HERE.
I GUESS IT'S TIME WE WOKE THEM UP...
BRMM BRMM
BRRMMM
THE VOLLEY-BALL TEAM IS BACK.
AHA!
TAKEDA SENSEI!!
HM?
KREE
FWUMP!!
THE VOLLEYBALL TEAM IS ON TV!
!!
WE'RE ON TV?!
STAFF ROOM
EXCUSE US!!

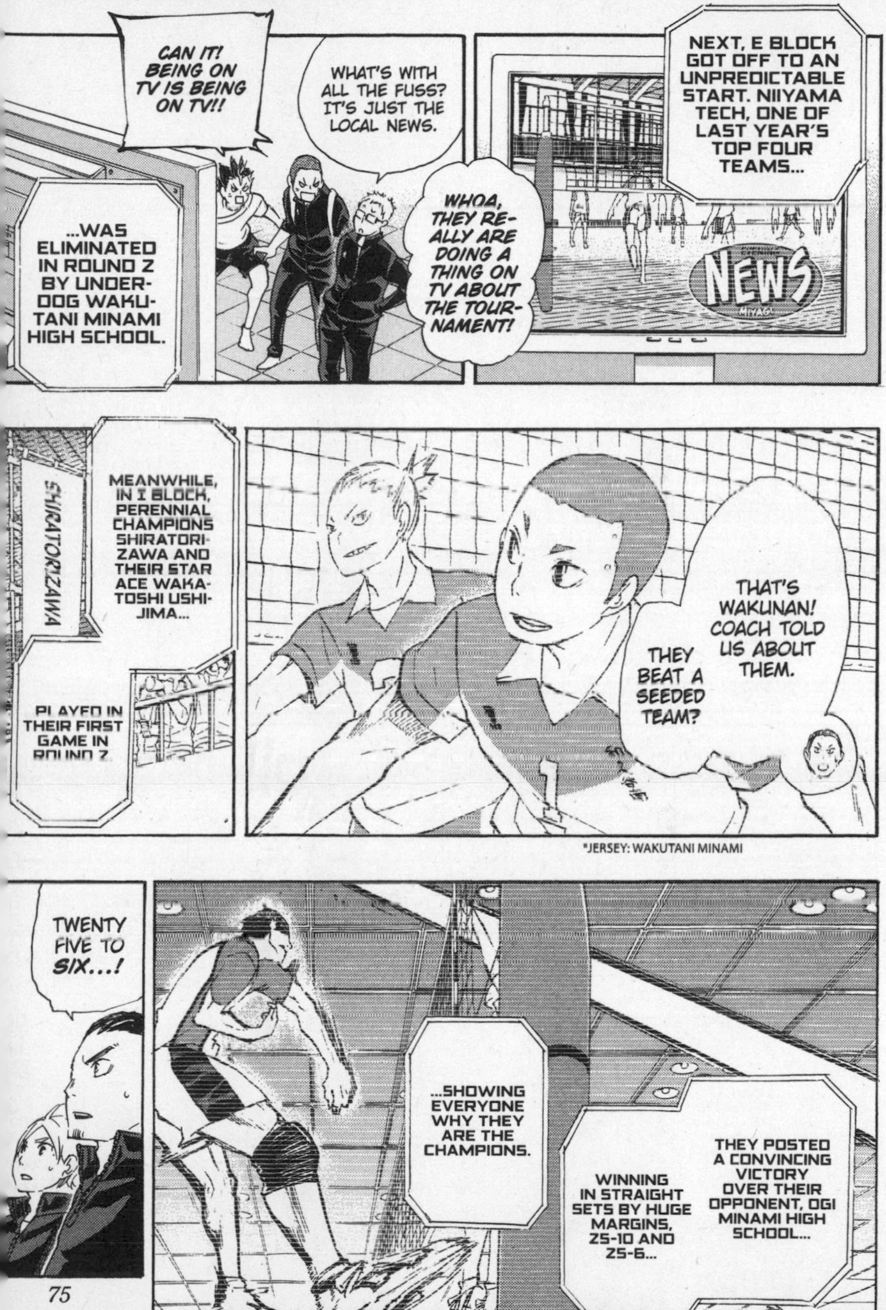
NEXT, E BLOCK GOT OFF TO AN UNPREDICTABLE START. NIIYAMA TECH, ONE OF LAST YEAR'S TOP FOUR TEAMS...
NEWS
MIYAGI
WHOA, THEY REALLY ARE DOING A THING ON TV ABOUT THE TOURNAMENT!
WHAT'S WITH ALL THE FUSS? IT'S JUST THE LOCAL NEWS.
CAN IT! BEING ON TV IS BEING ON TV!!
...WAS ELIMINATED IN ROUND 2 BY UNDERDOG WAKUTANI MINAMI HIGH SCHOOL.
THAT'S WAKUNAN! COACH TOLD US ABOUT THEM.
THEY BEAT A SEEDED TEAM?
*JERSEY: WAKUTANI MINAMI
SHIRATORIZAWA
MEANWHILE, IN I BLOCK, PERENNIAL CHAMPIONS SHIRATORIZAWA AND THEIR STAR ACE WAKATOSHI USHIJIMA...
PLAYED IN THEIR FIRST GAME IN ROUND 2.
THEY POSTED A CONVINCING VICTORY OVER THEIR OPPONENT, OGI MINAMI HIGH SCHOOL...
WINNING IN STRAIGHT SETS BY HUGE MARGINS, 25-10 AND 25-6...
...SHOWING EVERYONE WHY THEY ARE THE CHAMPIONS.
TWENTY FIVE TO SIX...!

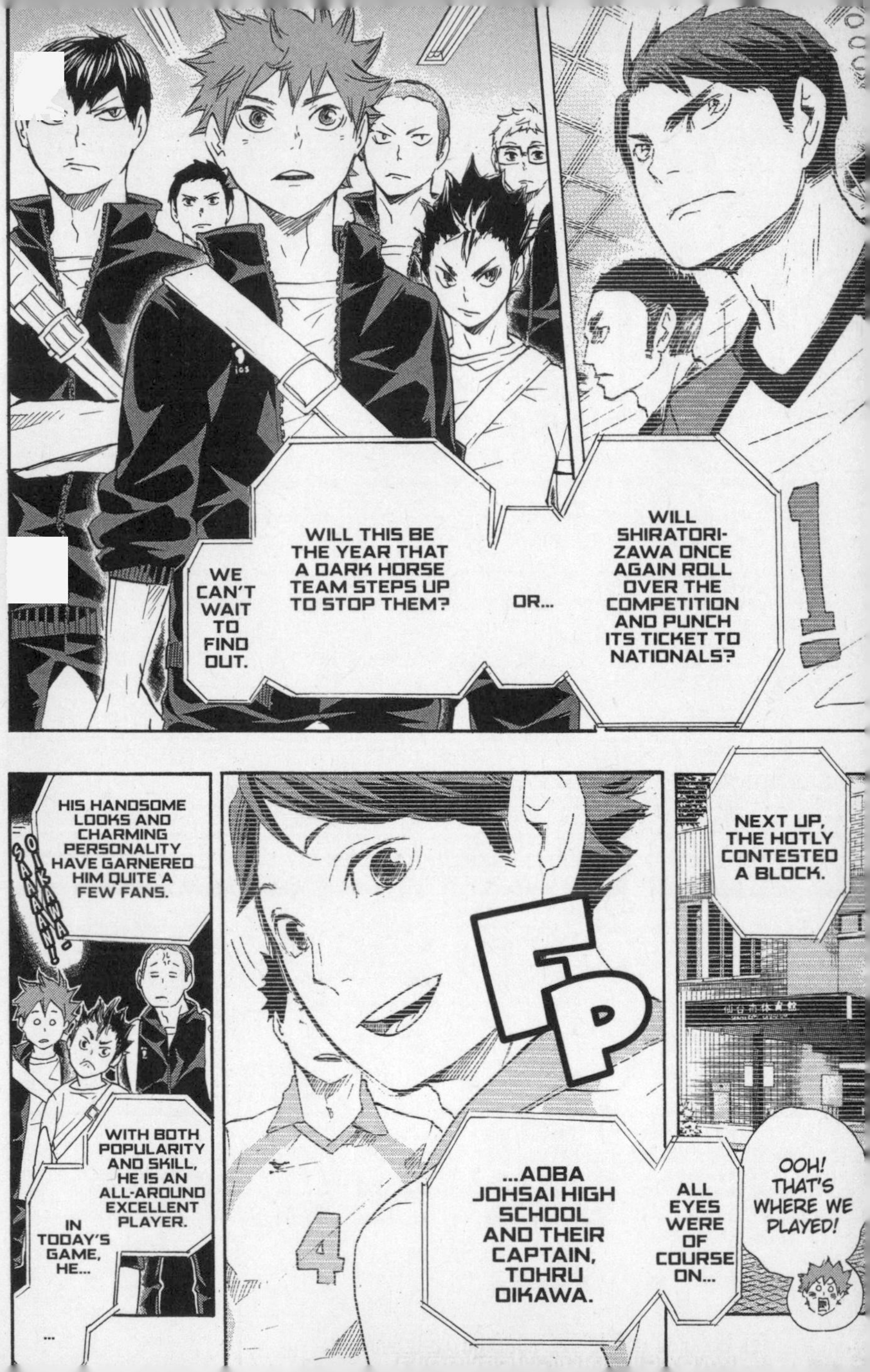
WILL SHIRATORIZAWA ONCE AGAIN ROLL OVER THE COMPETITION AND PUNCH ITS TICKET TO NATIONALS?
OR...
WILL THIS BE THE YEAR THAT A DARK HORSE TEAM STEPS UP TO STOP THEM?
WE CAN'T WAIT TO FIND OUT.
NEXT UP, THE HOTLY CONTESTED A BLOCK.
OOH! THAT'S WHERE WE PLAYED!
ALL EYES WERE OF COURSE ON...
...AOBA JOHSAI HIGH SCHOOL AND THEIR CAPTAIN, TOHRU OIKAWA.
FP
HIS HANDSOME LOOKS AND CHARMING PERSONALITY HAVE GARNERED HIM QUITE A FEW FANS.
OIKAWA-SAAAAAN!
WITH BOTH POPULARITY AND SKILL, HE IS AN ALL-AROUND EXCELLENT PLAYER.
IN TODAY'S GAME, HE...
...

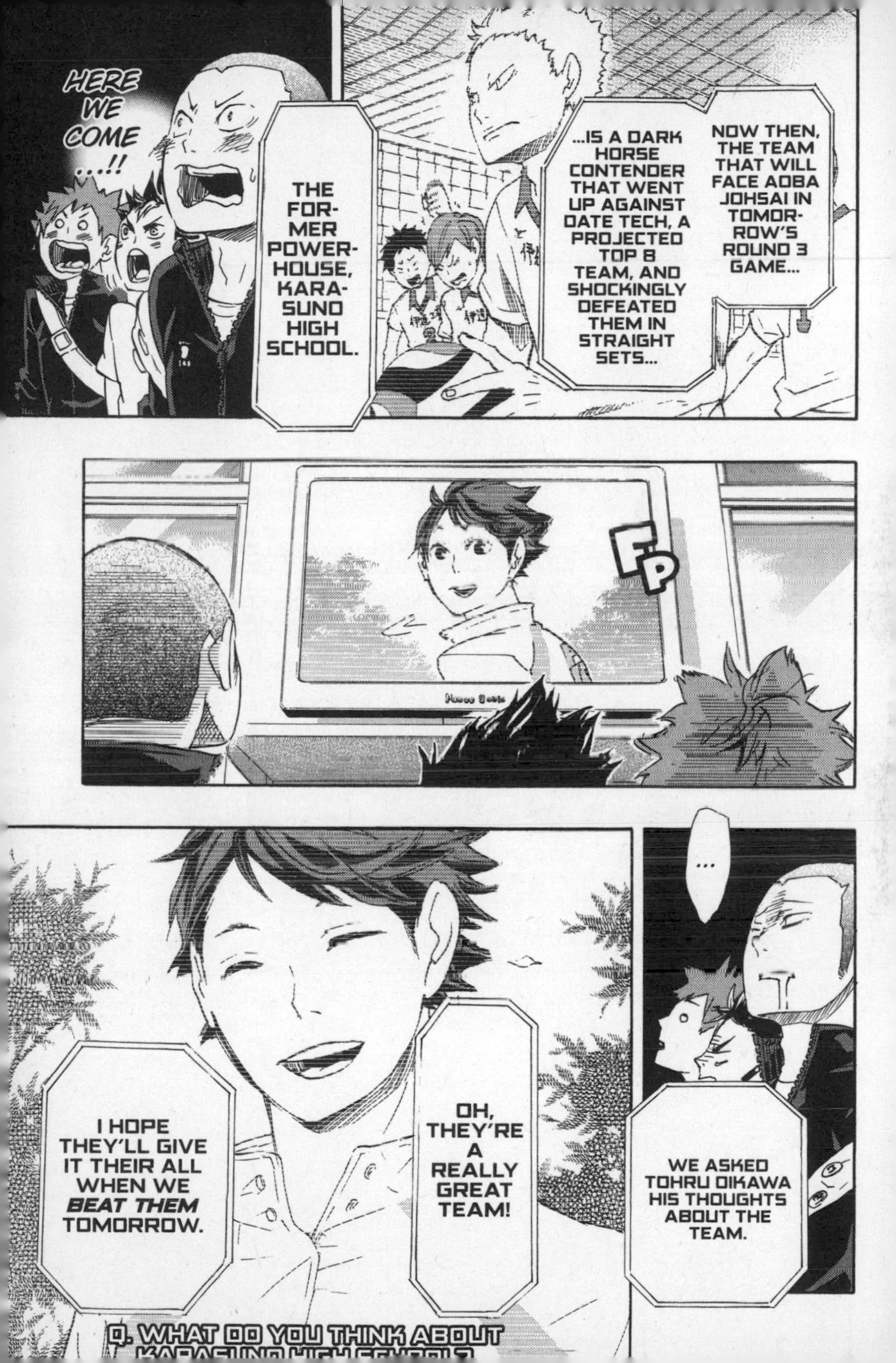
NOW THEN, THE TEAM THAT WILL FACE AOBA JOHSAI IN TOMORROW'S ROUND 3 GAME...
...IS A DARK HORSE CONTENDER THAT WENT UP AGAINST DATE TECH, A PROJECTED TOP 8 TEAM, AND SHOCKINGLY DEFEATED THEM IN STRAIGHT SETS...
THE FORMER POWERHOUSE, KARASUNO HIGH SCHOOL.
HERE WE COME ...!!
FP
...
WE ASKED TOHRU OIKAWA HIS THOUGHTS ABOUT THE TEAM.
OH, THEY'RE A REALLY GREAT TEAM!
I HOPE THEY'LL GIVE IT THEIR ALL WHEN WE *BEAT THEM* TOMORROW.
Q. WHAT DO YOU THINK ABOUT

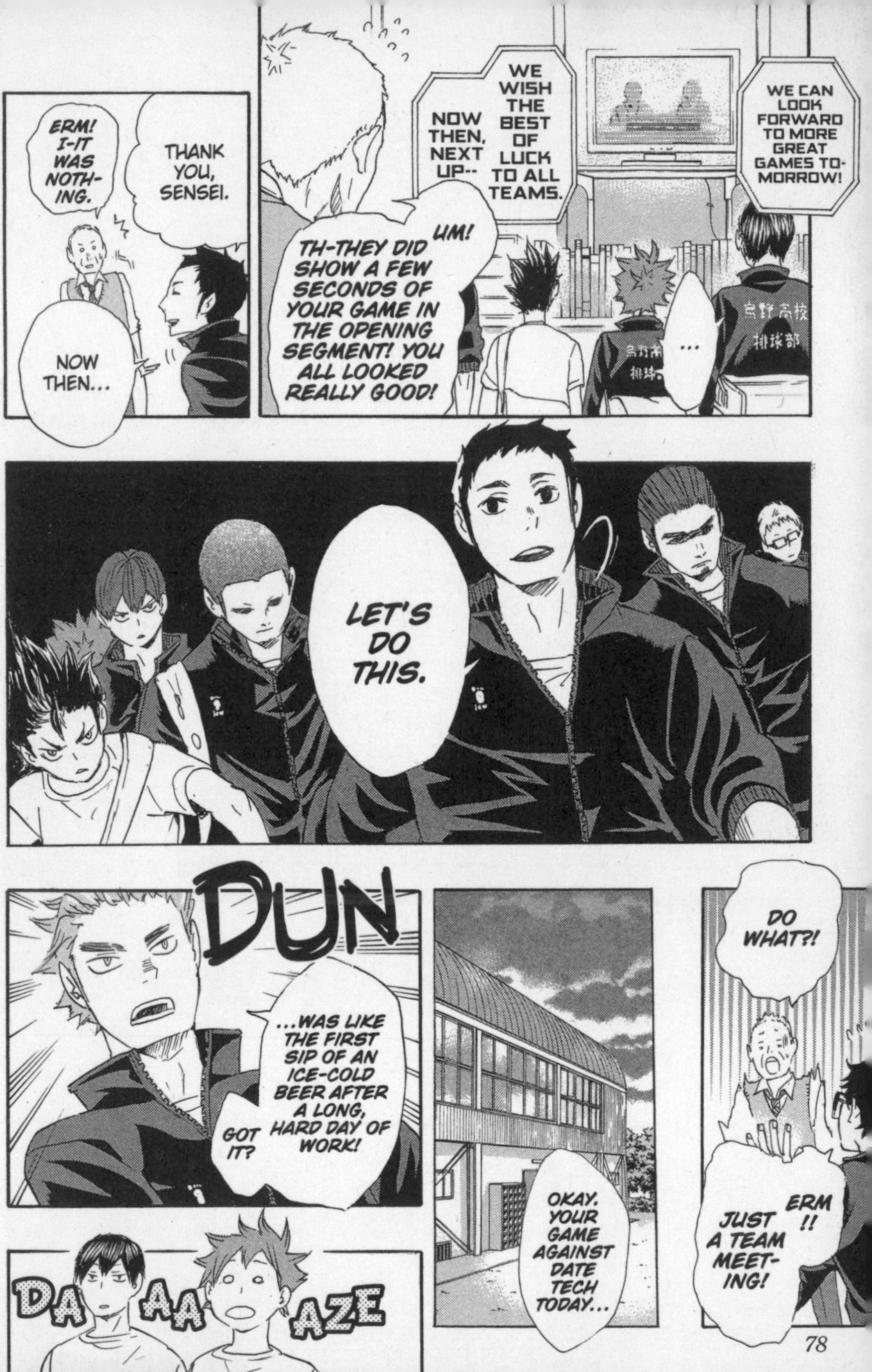

WE CAN LOOK FORWARD TO MORE GREAT GAMES TO-MORROW!
WE WISH THE BEST OF LUCK TO ALL TEAMS.
NOW THEN, NEXT UP--
UM!
TH-THEY DID SHOW A FEW SECONDS OF YOUR GAME IN THE OPENING SEGMENT! YOU ALL LOOKED REALLY GOOD!
...
THANK YOU, SENSEI.
ERM! I-IT WAS NOTH-ING.
NOW THEN...
LET'S DO THIS.
DO WHAT?!
ERM !!
JUST A TEAM MEET-ING!
OKAY. YOUR GAME AGAINST DATE TECH TODAY...
DUN
...WAS LIKE THE FIRST SIP OF AN ICE-COLD BEER AFTER A LONG, HARD DAY OF WORK!
GOT IT?
DA AA AZE

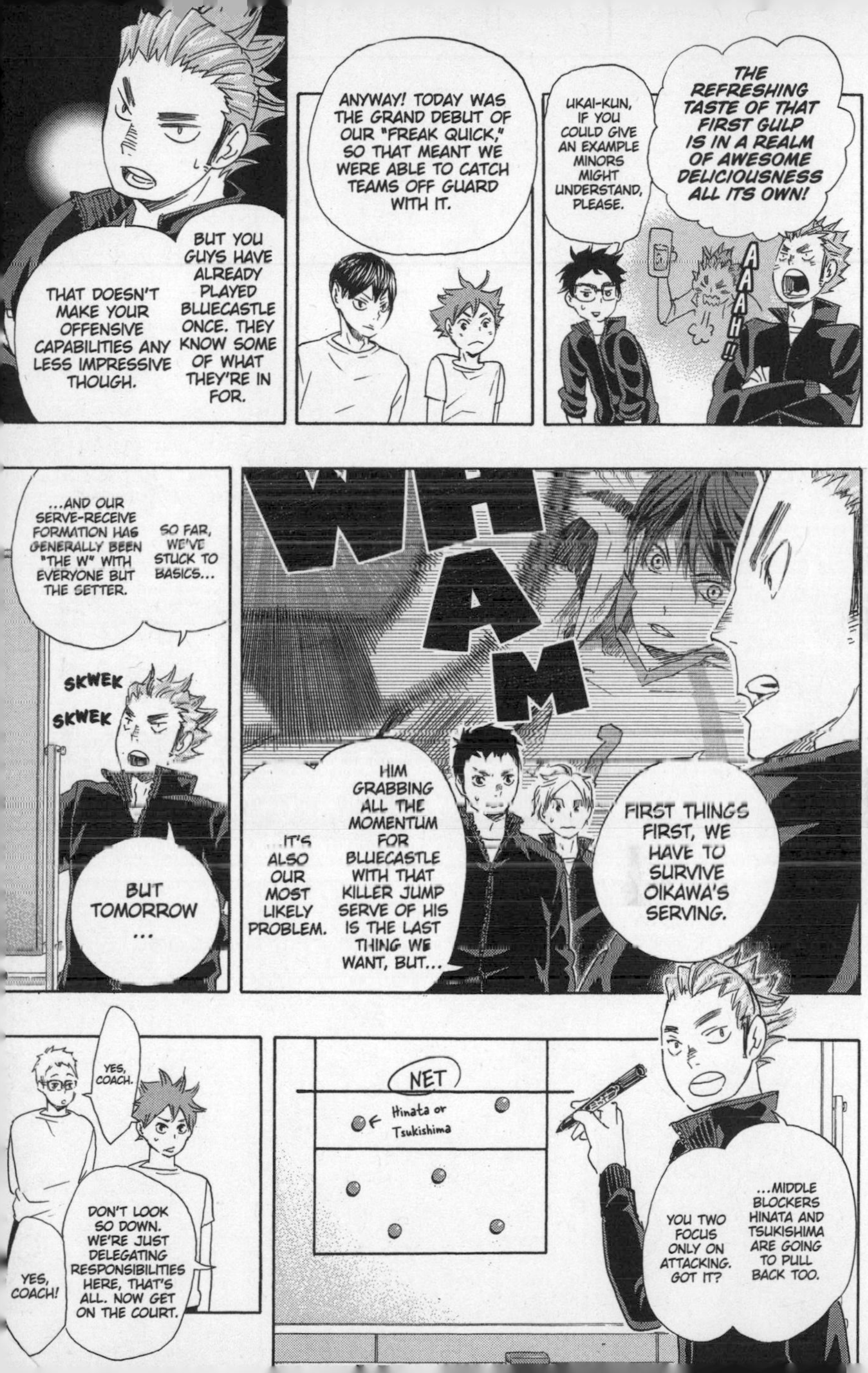
THE REFRESHING TASTE OF THAT FIRST GULP IS IN A REALM OF AWESOME DELICIOUSNESS ALL ITS OWN!
UKAI-KUN, IF YOU COULD GIVE AN EXAMPLE MINORS MIGHT UNDERSTAND, PLEASE.
AAAAH!!
ANYWAY! TODAY WAS THE GRAND DEBUT OF OUR "FREAK QUICK," SO THAT MEANT WE WERE ABLE TO CATCH TEAMS OFF GUARD WITH IT.
BUT YOU GUYS HAVE ALREADY PLAYED BLUECASTLE ONCE. THEY KNOW SOME OF WHAT THEY'RE IN FOR.
THAT DOESN'T MAKE YOUR OFFENSIVE CAPABILITIES ANY LESS IMPRESSIVE THOUGH.
WHAM
FIRST THINGS FIRST, WE HAVE TO SURVIVE OIKAWA'S SERVING.
HIM GRABBING ALL THE MOMENTUM FOR BLUECASTLE WITH THAT KILLER JUMP SERVE OF HIS IS THE LAST THING WE WANT, BUT...
...IT'S ALSO OUR MOST LIKELY PROBLEM.
SO FAR, WE'VE STUCK TO BASICS...
...AND OUR SERVE-RECEIVE FORMATION HAS GENERALLY BEEN "THE W" WITH EVERYONE BUT THE SETTER.
SKWEK
SKWEK
BUT TOMORROW ...
...MIDDLE BLOCKERS HINATA AND TSUKISHIMA ARE GOING TO PULL BACK TOO.
YOU TWO FOCUS ONLY ON ATTACKING. GOT IT?
NET
Hinata or Tsukishima
YES, COACH.
DON'T LOOK SO DOWN. WE'RE JUST DELEGATING RESPONSIBILITIES HERE, THAT'S ALL. NOW GET ON THE COURT.
YES, COACH!

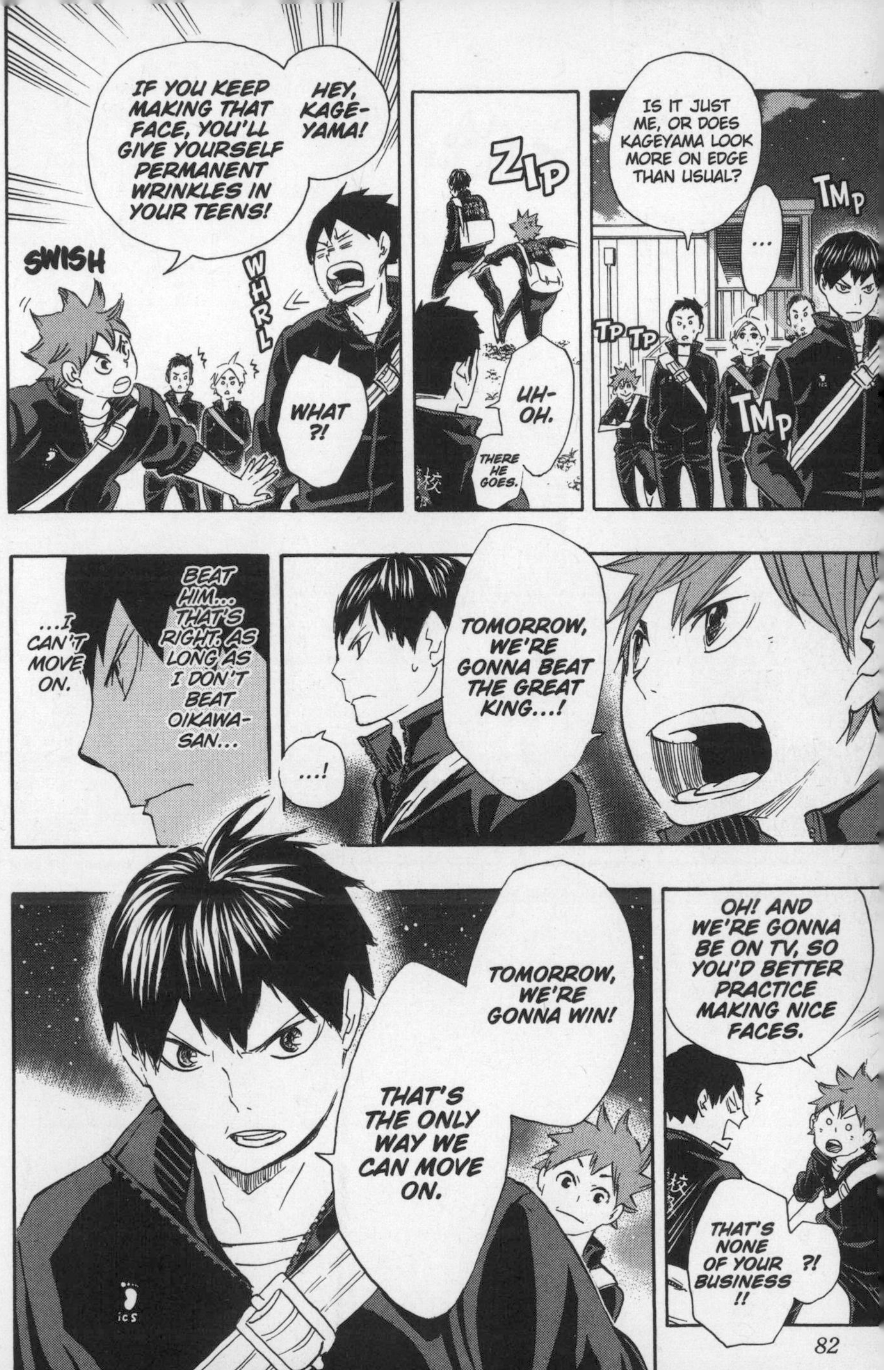

IS IT JUST ME, OR DOES KAGEYAMA LOOK MORE ON EDGE THAN USUAL?
...
TMP
TP TP
TMP
ZIP
UH-OH.
THERE HE GOES.
HEY, KAGE-YAMA!
IF YOU KEEP MAKING THAT FACE, YOU'LL GIVE YOURSELF PERMANENT WRINKLES IN YOUR TEENS!
SWISH
WHRL
WHAT?!
TOMORROW, WE'RE GONNA BEAT THE GREAT KING...!
...!
BEAT HIM... THAT'S RIGHT. AS LONG AS I DON'T BEAT OIKAWA-SAN...
...I CAN'T MOVE ON.
OH! AND WE'RE GONNA BE ON TV, SO YOU'D BETTER PRACTICE MAKING NICE FACES.
THAT'S NONE OF YOUR BUSINESS!!
?!
TOMORROW, WE'RE GONNA WIN!
THAT'S THE ONLY WAY WE CAN MOVE ON.

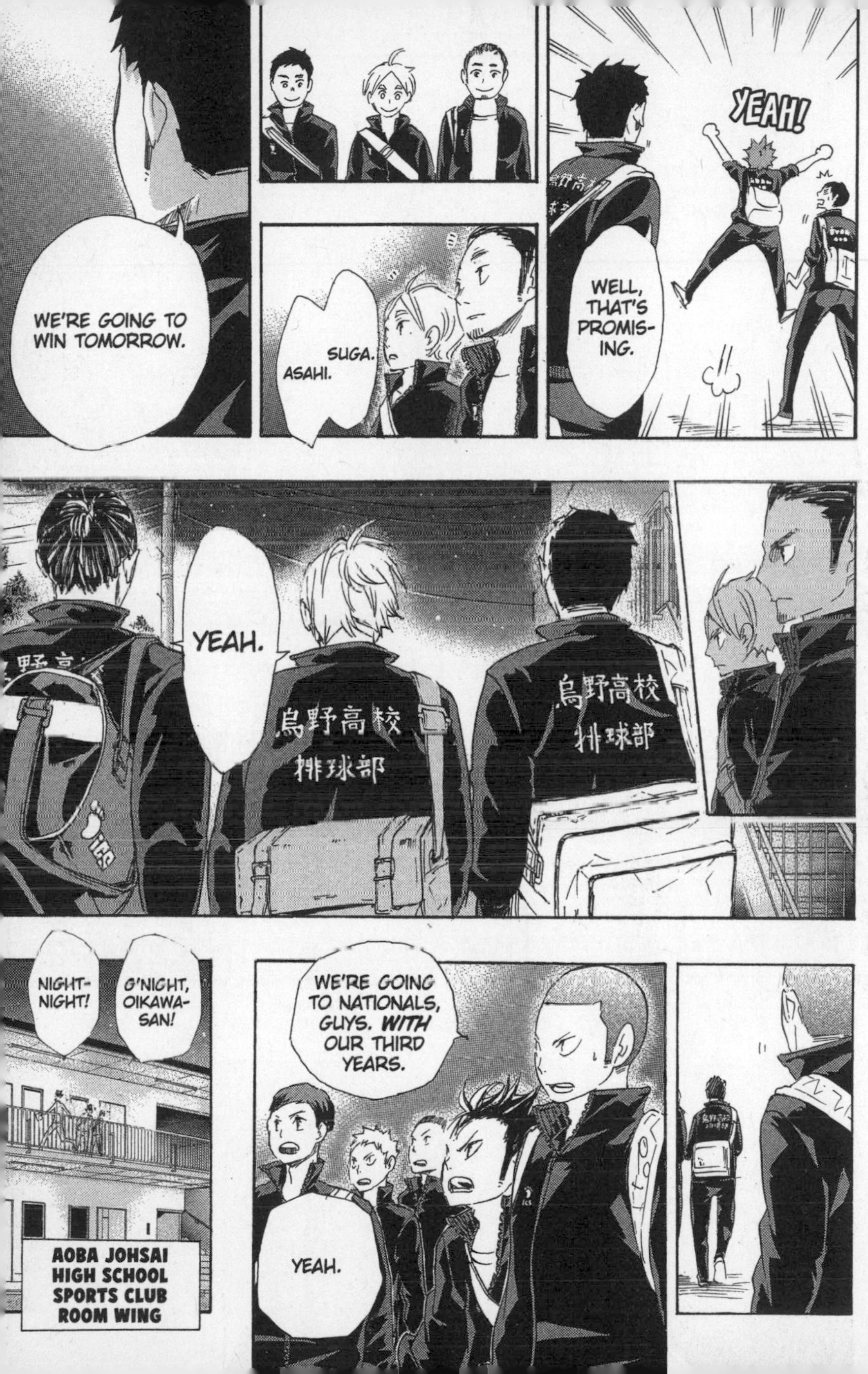
YEAH!
WELL, THAT'S PROMIS-ING.
SUGA. ASAHI.
WE'RE GOING TO WIN TOMORROW.
YEAH.
WE'RE GOING TO NATIONALS, GUYS. *WITH* OUR THIRD YEARS.
YEAH.
G'NIGHT, OIKAWA-SAN!
NIGHT-NIGHT!
AOBA JOHSAI HIGH SCHOOL SPORTS CLUB ROOM WING

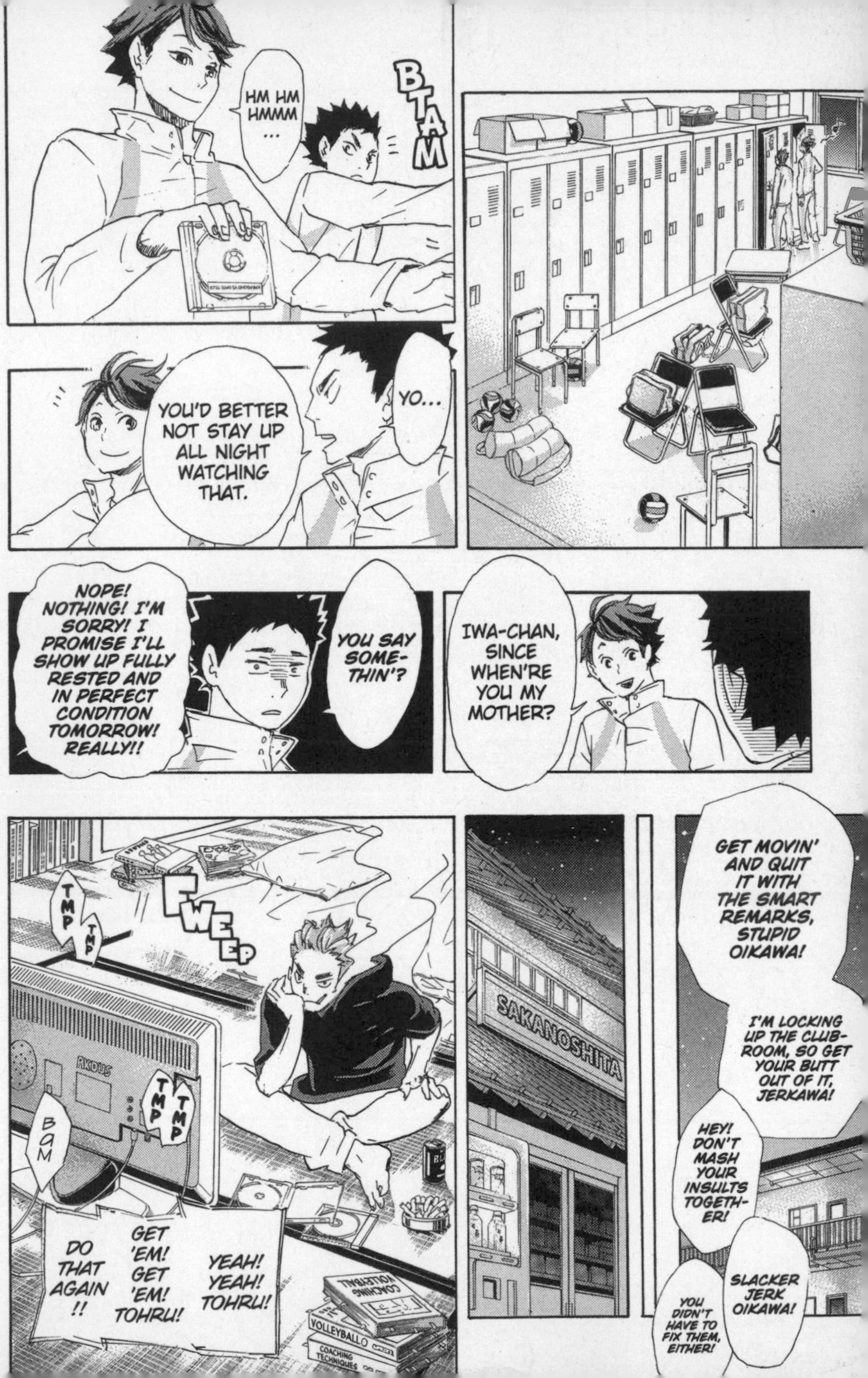
BTAM
HM HM HMMM...
YO...
YOU'D BETTER NOT STAY UP ALL NIGHT WATCHING THAT.
IWA-CHAN, SINCE WHEN'RE YOU MY MOTHER?
YOU SAY SOMETHIN'?
NOPE! NOTHING! I'M SORRY! I PROMISE I'LL SHOW UP FULLY RESTED AND IN PERFECT CONDITION TOMORROW! REALLY!!
GET MOVIN' AND QUIT IT WITH THE SMART REMARKS, STUPID OIKAWA!
I'M LOCKING UP THE CLUB-ROOM, SO GET YOUR BUTT OUT OF IT, JERKAWA!
HEY! DON'T MASH YOUR INSULTS TOGETH-ER!
SLACKER JERK OIKAWA!
YOU DIDN'T HAVE TO FIX THEM, EITHER!
SAKANOSHITA
FWEEP
TMP
TMP
BAM
TMP
TMP
YEAH! YEAH! TOHRU!
GET 'EM! GET 'EM! TOHRU!
DO THAT AGAIN!!
COACHING VOLLEYBALL
VOLLEYBALL
COACHING TECHNIQUES

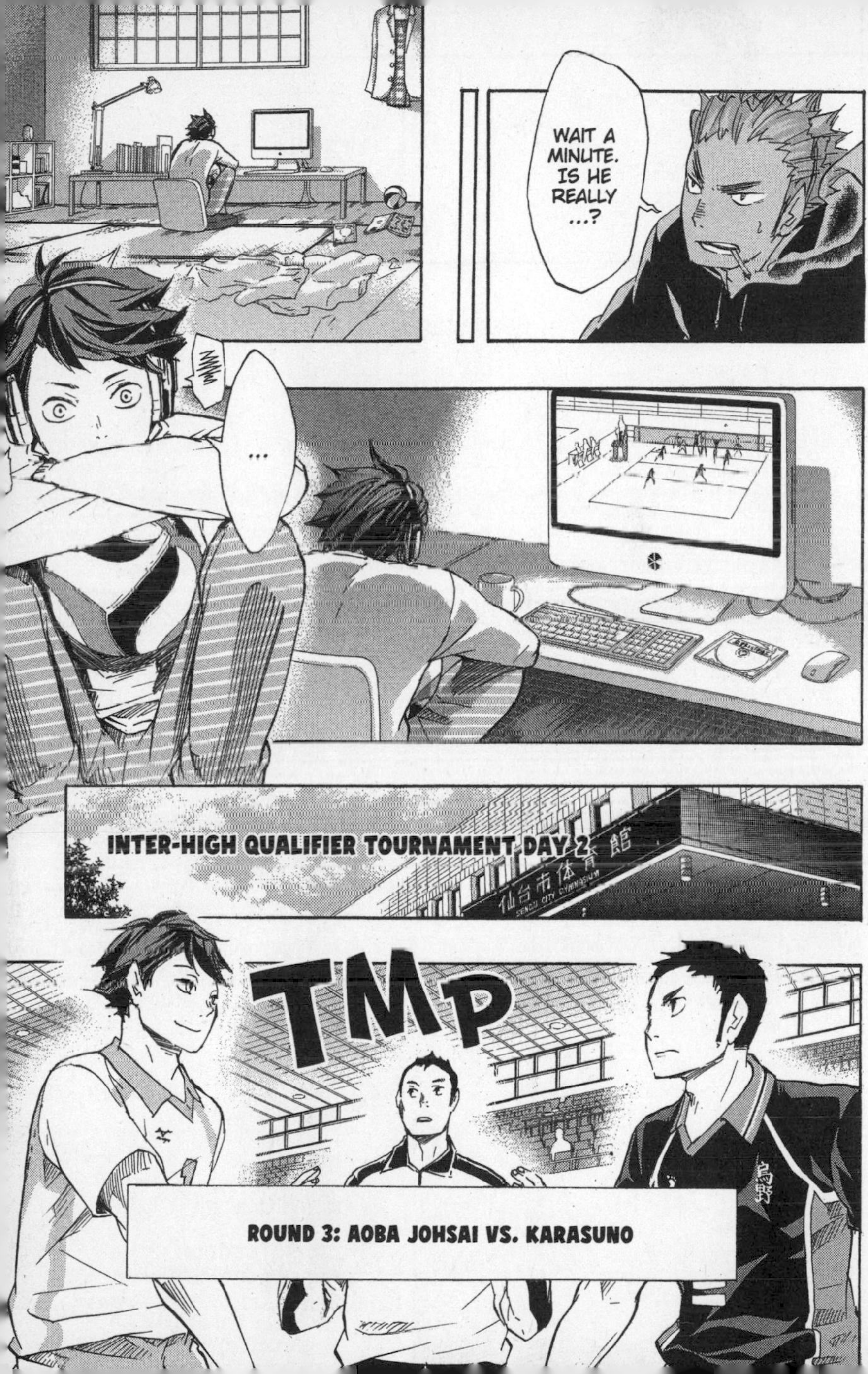
WAIT A MINUTE. IS HE REALLY ...?
...
INTER-HIGH QUALIFIER TOURNAMENT DAY 2
仙台市体育館
TMP
ROUND 3: AOBA JOHSAI VS. KARASUNO

YUTAKA OBARA

DATE TECHNICAL HIGH SCHOOL
CLASS 2-B

POSITION:
WING SPIKER

HEIGHT: 6'1"

WEIGHT: 183 LBS.
(AS OF APRIL, 2ND YEAR
OF HIGH SCHOOL)

BIRTHDAY: DECEMBER 15

FAVORITE FOOD:
TERIYAKI CHICKEN

CURRENT WORRY:
IT FEELS LIKE HE FADES INTO
THE BACKGROUND COMPARED
TO THE OTHER SECOND YEARS.

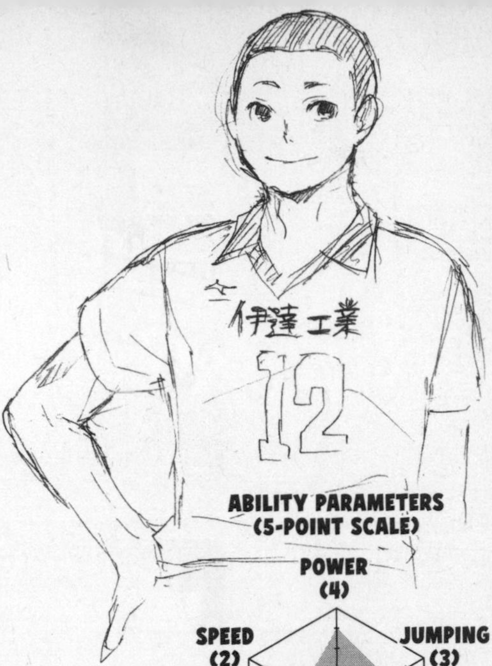
伊達工業
12

ABILITY PARAMETERS
(5-POINT SCALE)

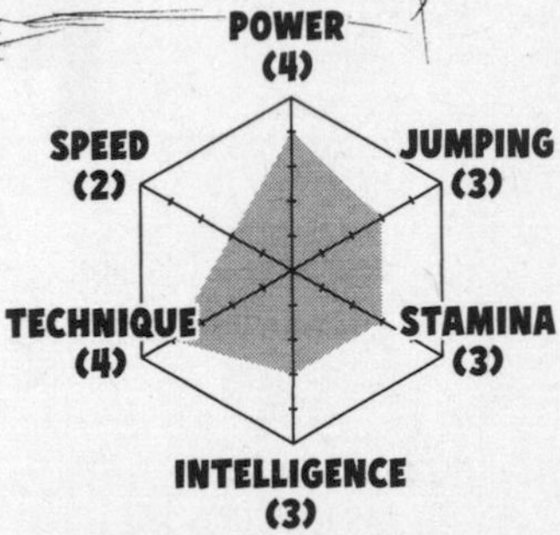
POWER
(4)
JUMPING
(3)
STAMINA
(3)
INTELLIGENCE
(3)
TECHNIQUE
(4)
SPEED
(2)

KOSUKE SAKUNAMI

DATE TECHNICAL HIGH SCHOOL
CLASS 1-A

POSITION:
LIBERO

HEIGHT: 5'5"

WEIGHT: 131 LBS.
(AS OF APRIL, 1ST YEAR
OF HIGH SCHOOL)

BIRTHDAY: AUGUST 30

FAVORITE FOOD:
KAKI-PI CRACKERS

CURRENT WORRY:
IT WOULD BE NICE IF HE COULD
GROW ANOTHER INCH OR TWO

ABILITY PARAMETERS
(5-POINT SCALE)

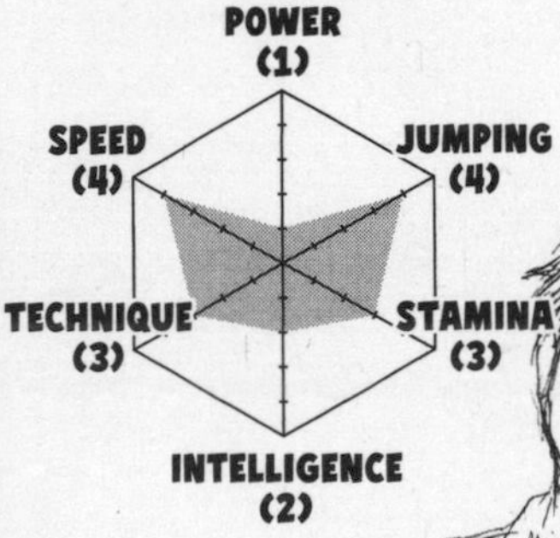
POWER
(1)
JUMPING
(4)
STAMINA
(3)
INTELLIGENCE
(2)
TECHNIQUE
(3)
SPEED
(4)

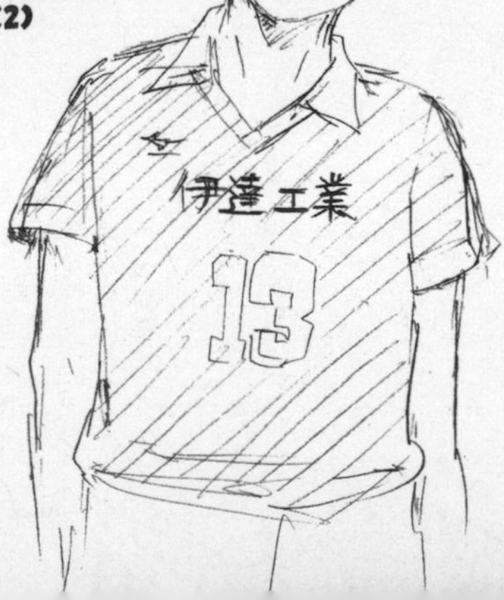
伊達工業
13

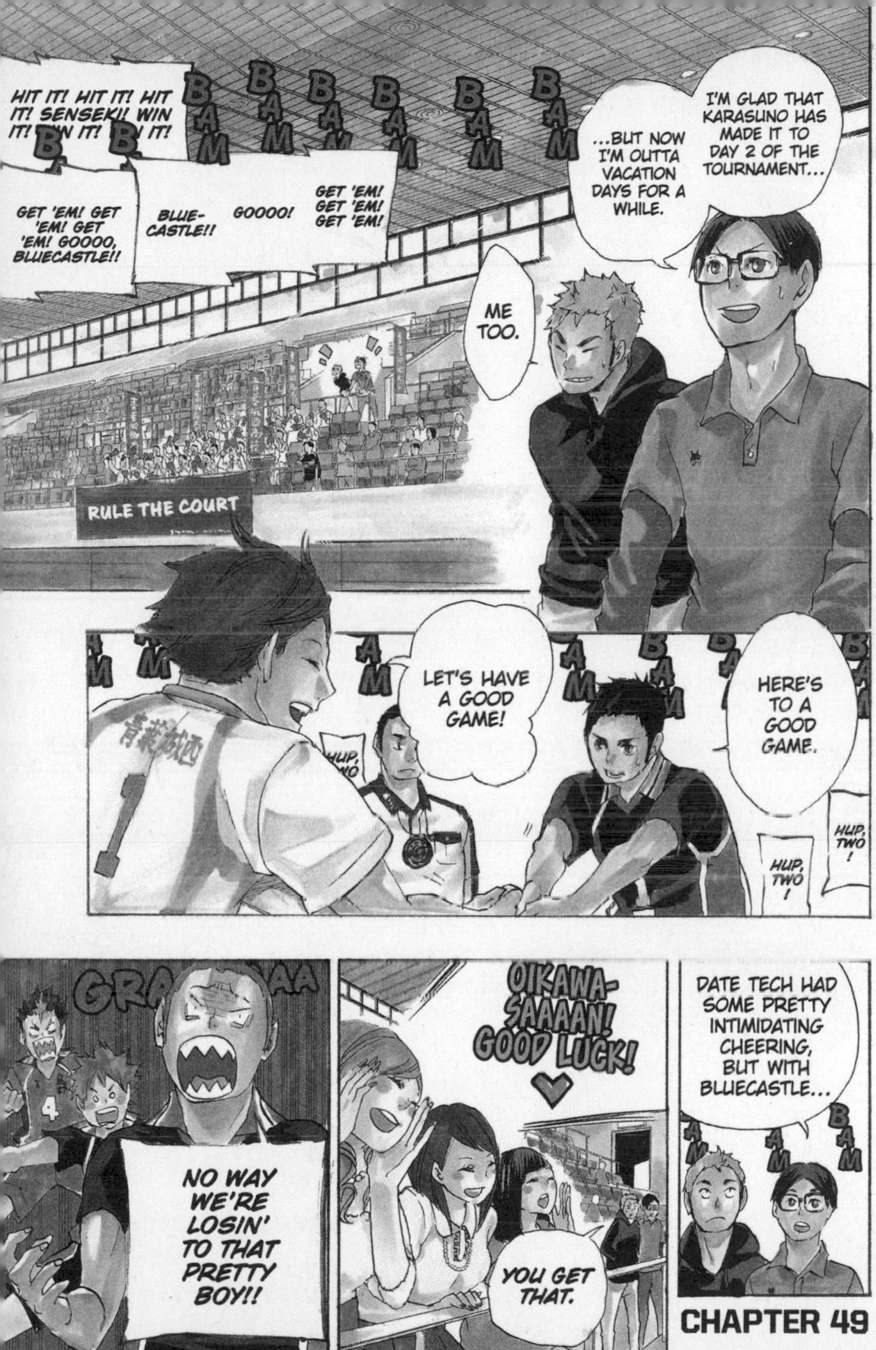

I'M GLAD THAT KARASUNO HAS MADE IT TO DAY 2 OF THE TOURNAMENT...
...BUT NOW I'M OUTTA VACATION DAYS FOR A WHILE.
ME TOO.
BAM BAM BAM BAM BAM BAM
GET 'EM! GET 'EM! GET 'EM!
GOOOO!
BLUE-CASTLE!!
GET 'EM! GET 'EM! GET 'EM! GOOOO, BLUECASTLE!!
HIT IT! HIT IT! HIT IT! SENSEKI!! WIN IT!
RULE THE COURT
HERE'S TO A GOOD GAME.
HUP, TWO!
HUP, TWO!
LET'S HAVE A GOOD GAME!
DATE TECH HAD SOME PRETTY INTIMIDATING CHEERING, BUT WITH BLUECASTLE...
BAM
OIKAWA-SAAAAN! GOOD LUCK!
YOU GET THAT.
NO WAY WE'RE LOSIN' TO THAT PRETTY BOY!!

CHAPTER 49

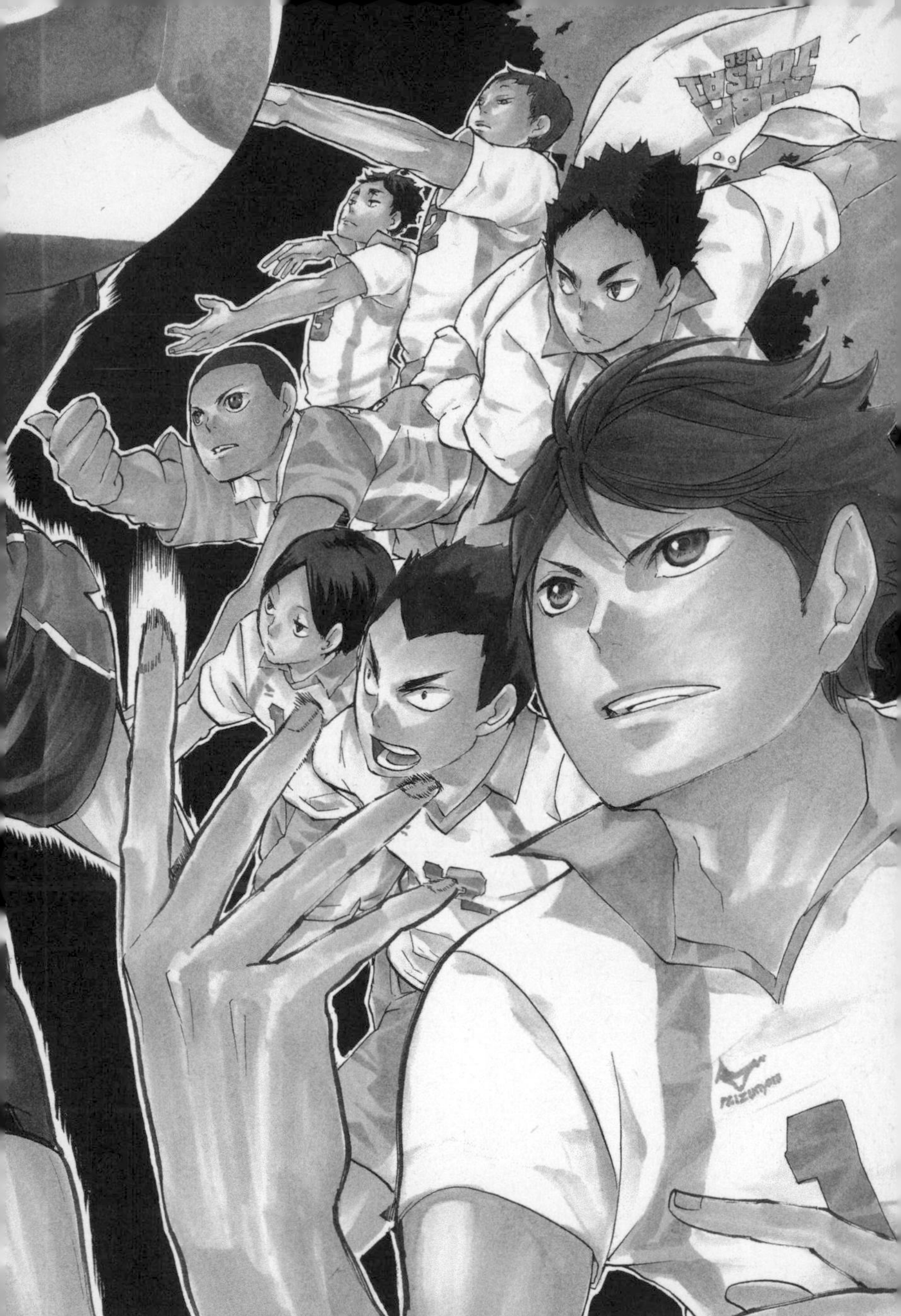

CHAPTER 49: Vs. the Great King: Part 2

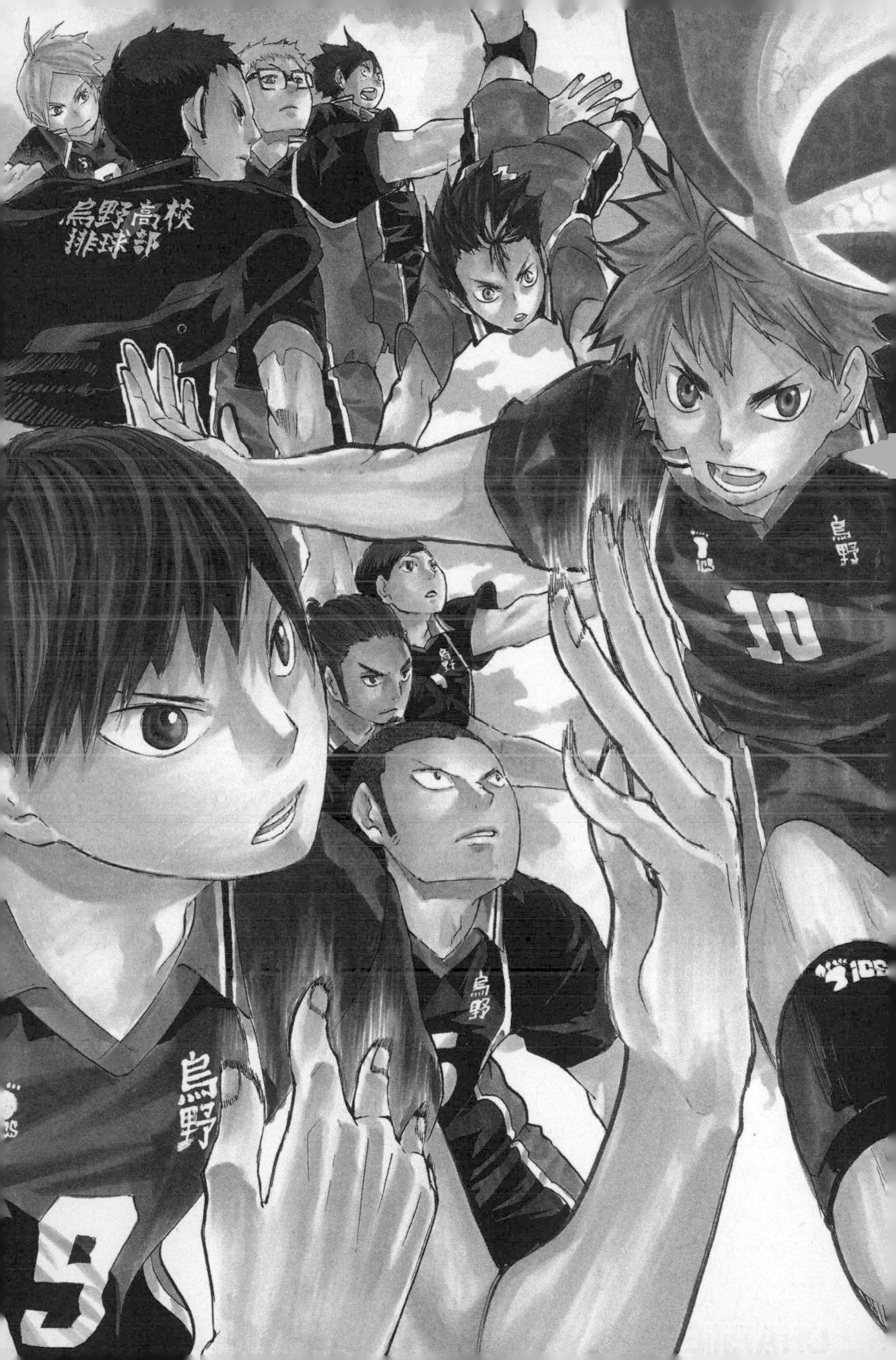
烏野高校
排球部
烏野
10
烏野
烏野
5

HAIKYU!!

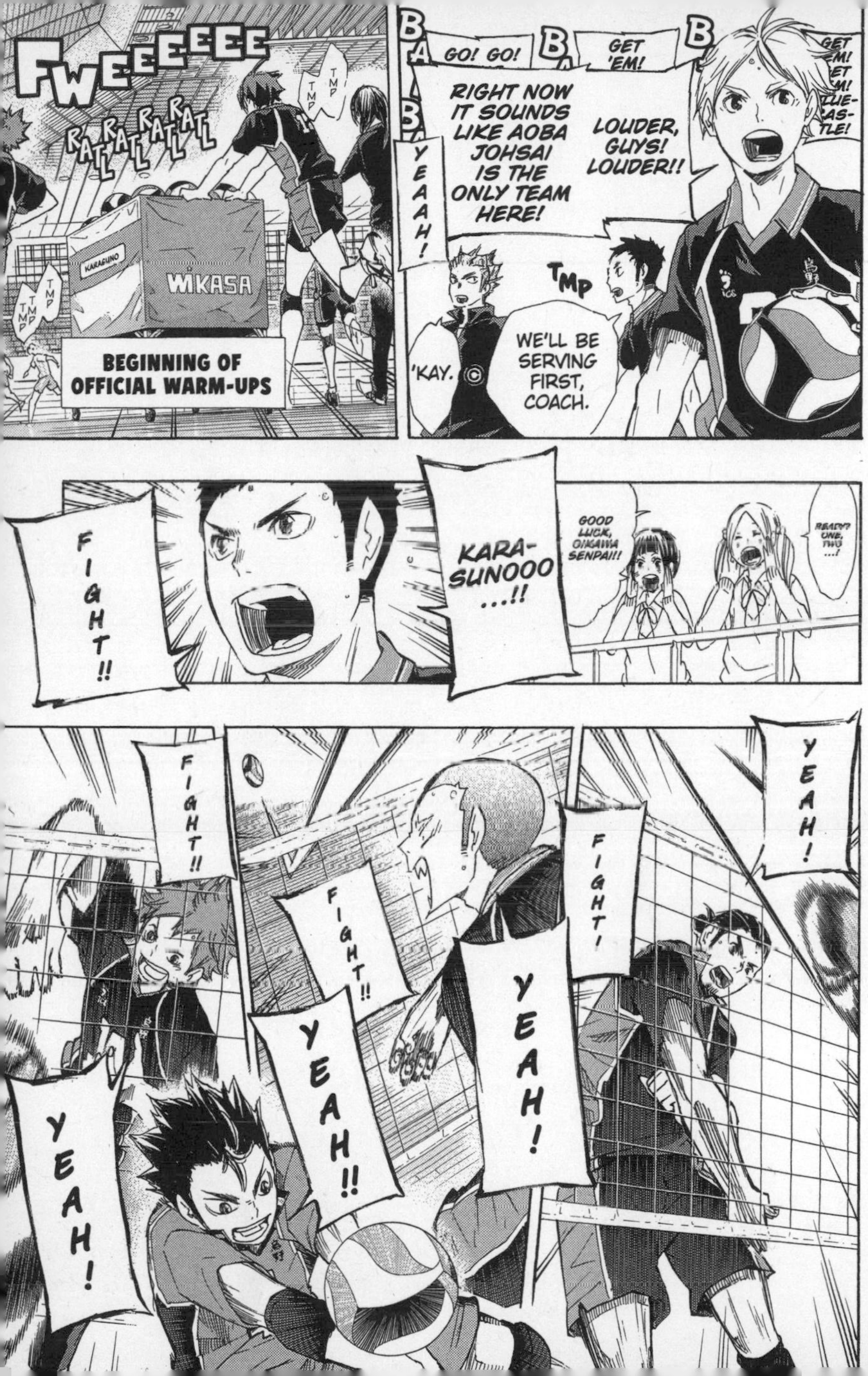
GO! GO!
GET 'EM!
LOUDER, GUYS! LOUDER!!
RIGHT NOW IT SOUNDS LIKE AOBA JOHSAI IS THE ONLY TEAM HERE!
YEAAAH!
TMP
WE'LL BE SERVING FIRST, COACH.
'KAY.
FWEEEEEE
TMP TMP
RATTLE RATTLE RATTLE
TMP TMP TMP
WIKASA
BEGINNING OF OFFICIAL WARM-UPS
READY? ONE, TWO …!
GOOD LUCK, OIKAWA SENPAI!!
KARA-SUNOOO …!!
FIGHT!!
YEAH!
FIGHT!
YEAH!
FIGHT!!
YEAH!!
FIGHT!!
YEAH!

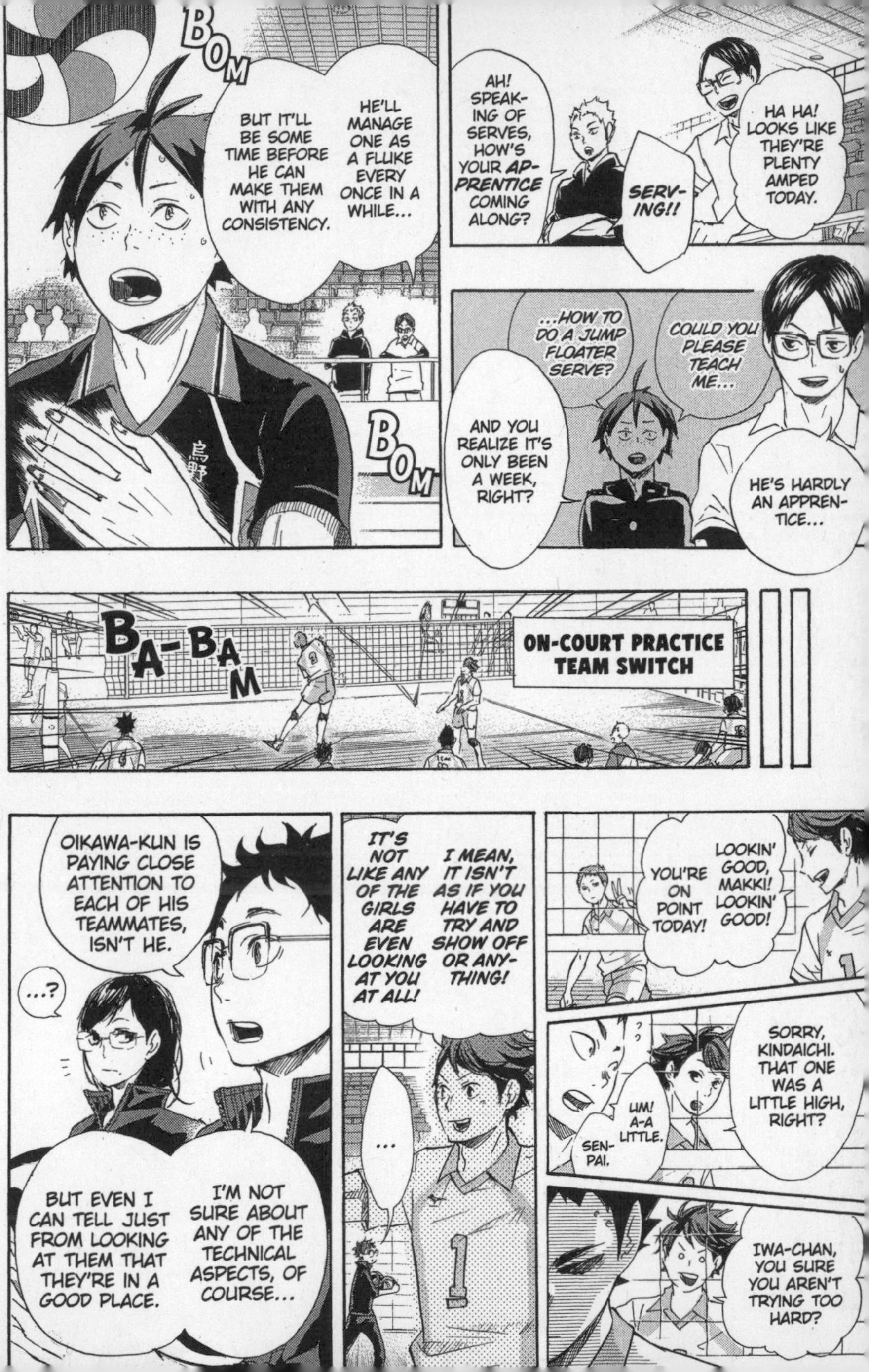

HA HA! LOOKS LIKE THEY'RE PLENTY AMPED TODAY.
SERV-ING!!
AH! SPEAKING OF SERVES, HOW'S YOUR APPRENTICE COMING ALONG?
HE'S HARDLY AN APPREN-TICE...
COULD YOU PLEASE TEACH ME...
...HOW TO DO A JUMP FLOATER SERVE?
AND YOU REALIZE IT'S ONLY BEEN A WEEK, RIGHT?
BOM
HE'LL MANAGE ONE AS A FLUKE EVERY ONCE IN A WHILE...
BUT IT'LL BE SOME TIME BEFORE HE CAN MAKE THEM WITH ANY CONSISTENCY.
BOM
ON-COURT PRACTICE TEAM SWITCH
BA-BAM
LOOKIN' GOOD, MAKKI! LOOKIN' GOOD!
YOU'RE ON POINT TODAY!
SORRY, KINDAICHI. THAT ONE WAS A LITTLE HIGH, RIGHT?
UM! A-A LITTLE.
SEN-PAI.
IWA-CHAN, YOU SURE YOU AREN'T TRYING TOO HARD?
I MEAN, IT ISN'T AS IF YOU HAVE TO TRY AND SHOW OFF OR ANY-THING!
IT'S NOT LIKE ANY OF THE GIRLS ARE EVEN LOOKING AT YOU AT ALL!
...
OIKAWA-KUN IS PAYING CLOSE ATTENTION TO EACH OF HIS TEAMMATES, ISN'T HE.
...?
I'M NOT SURE ABOUT ANY OF THE TECHNICAL ASPECTS, OF COURSE...
BUT EVEN I CAN TELL JUST FROM LOOKING AT THEM THAT THEY'RE IN A GOOD PLACE.

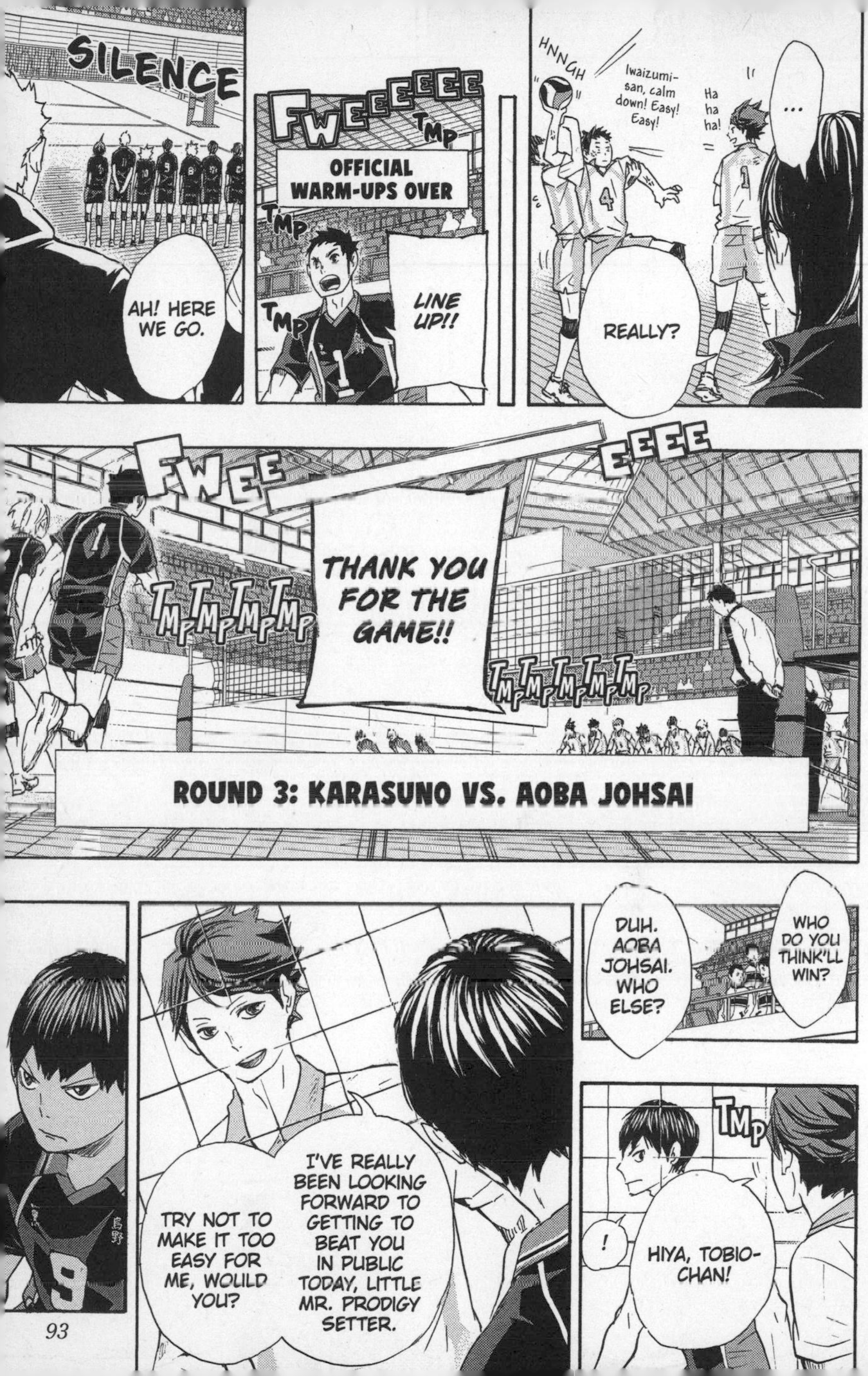
HNNGH
Iwaizumi-san, calm down! Easy! Easy!
Ha ha ha!
...
REALLY?
FWEEEEEE
TMP
OFFICIAL WARM-UPS OVER
TMP
LINE UP!!
TMP
SILENCE
AH! HERE WE GO.
FWEEEEEE
THANK YOU FOR THE GAME!!
TMP TMP TMP TMP TMP
TMP TMP TMP TMP
ROUND 3: KARASUNO VS. AOBA JOHSAI
WHO DO YOU THINK'LL WIN?
DUH. AOBA JOHSAI. WHO ELSE?
TMP
!
HIYA, TOBIO-CHAN!
I'VE REALLY BEEN LOOKING FORWARD TO GETTING TO BEAT YOU IN PUBLIC TODAY, LITTLE MR. PRODIGY SETTER.
TRY NOT TO MAKE IT TOO EASY FOR ME, WOULD YOU?

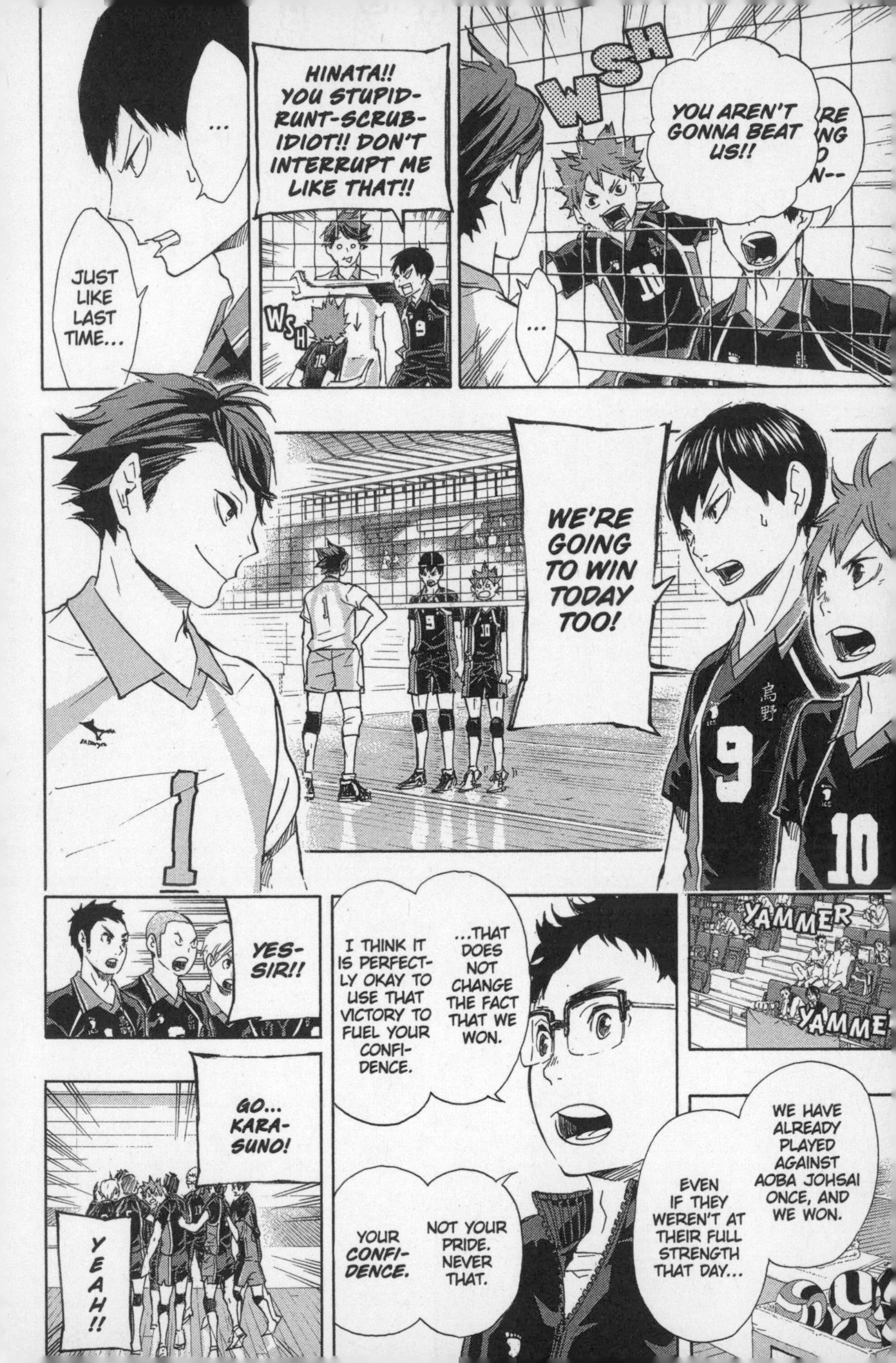
WSH
YOU AREN'T GONNA BEAT US!!
...
HINATA!! YOU STUPID-RUNT-SCRUB-IDIOT!! DON'T INTERRUPT ME LIKE THAT!!
WSH
...
JUST LIKE LAST TIME...
WE'RE GOING TO WIN TODAY TOO!
YAMMER
YAMME
WE HAVE ALREADY PLAYED AGAINST AOBA JOHSAI ONCE, AND WE WON.
EVEN IF THEY WEREN'T AT THEIR FULL STRENGTH THAT DAY...
...THAT DOES NOT CHANGE THE FACT THAT WE WON.
I THINK IT IS PERFECTLY OKAY TO USE THAT VICTORY TO FUEL YOUR CONFIDENCE.
NOT YOUR PRIDE. NEVER THAT.
YOUR CONFIDENCE.
YES-SIR!!
GO... KARASUNO!
YEAH!!

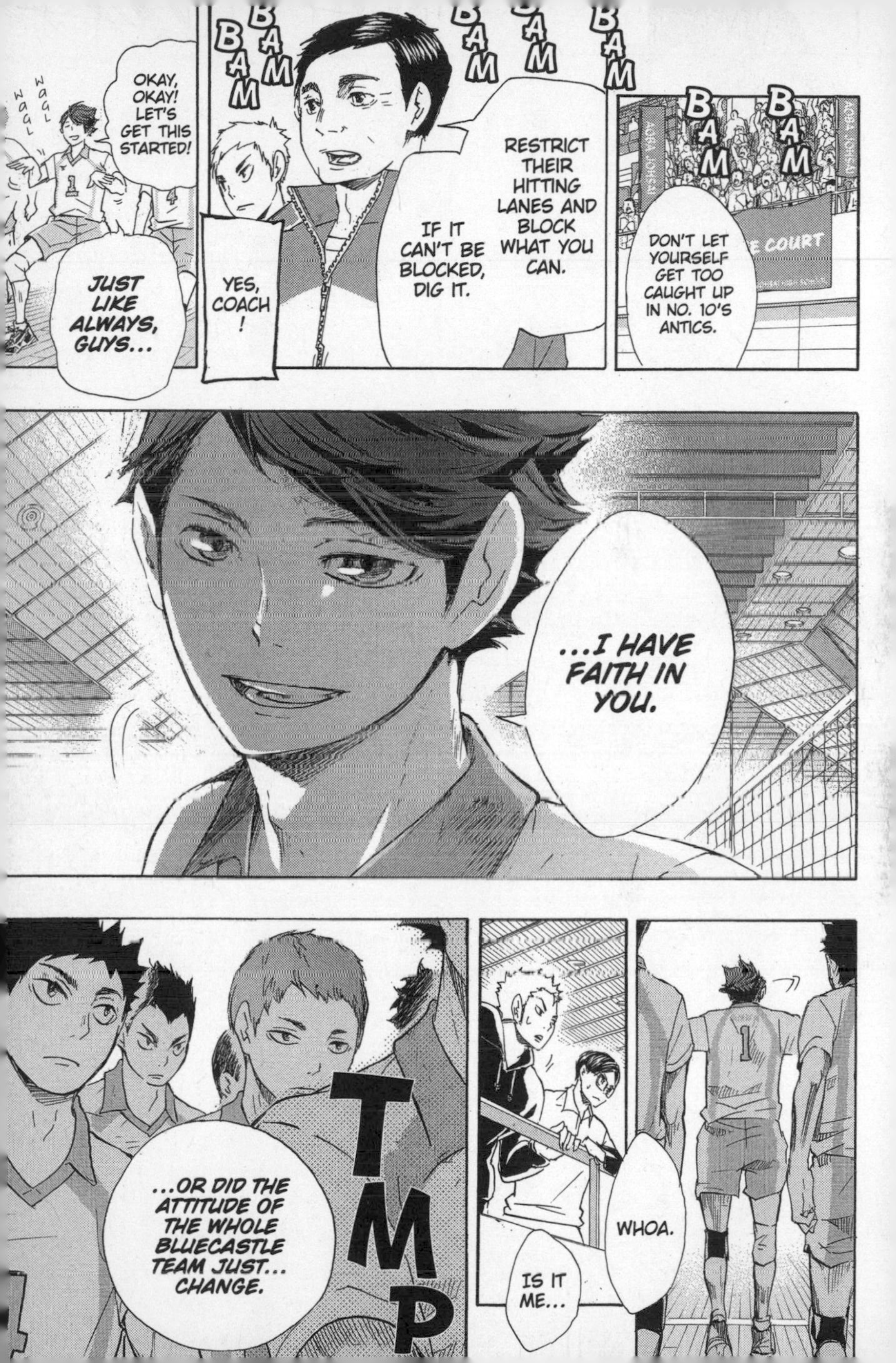

BAM BAM
DON'T LET YOURSELF GET TOO CAUGHT UP IN NO. 10'S ANTICS.
BAM BAM BAM
RESTRICT THEIR HITTING LANES AND BLOCK WHAT YOU CAN.
IF IT CAN'T BE BLOCKED, DIG IT.
YES, COACH!
BAM BAM
OKAY, OKAY! LET'S GET THIS STARTED!
JUST LIKE ALWAYS, GUYS...
...I HAVE FAITH IN YOU.
WHOA.
IS IT ME...
...OR DID THE ATTITUDE OF THE WHOLE BLUECASTLE TEAM JUST... CHANGE.
TMP

KUNIMI
1ST YEAR / WS
6'0"

KINDAICHI
1ST YEAR / MB
6'2"

OIKAWA
3RD YEAR / S
6'1"

WATARI
2ND YEAR / L
5'7"

AOBA JOHSAI

HANANAKI	KUNIMI	KINDAICHI (WATARI)
MATSUKAWA	OIKAWA	IWAIZUMI

Order

KARASUNO

HINATA	TANAKA	KAGEYAMA
SAWAMURA	AZUMANE	TSUKISHIMA (NOYA)

TSUKISHIMA
1ST YEAR / MB
6'2"

SAWAMURA
3RD YEAR / WS
5'9"

NISHINOYA
2ND YEAR / L
5'3"

HINATA
1ST YEAR / MB
5'4"

OIKAWA SAYS THAT BEFORE EVERY GAME.

GIVEN HIS USUALLY FLIPPANT ATTITUDE, SOME PEOPLE MIGHT TAKE THAT FOR A JOKE, OR EVEN A THREAT.

BUT EVERY PLAYER ON THIS TEAM KNOWS THAT IT IS THE UNVARNISHED TRUTH.

AND AS HE HAS FAITH IN THEM, THEY TOO HAVE COMPLETE FAITH IN HIM.

LET'S GO.

YEAH!

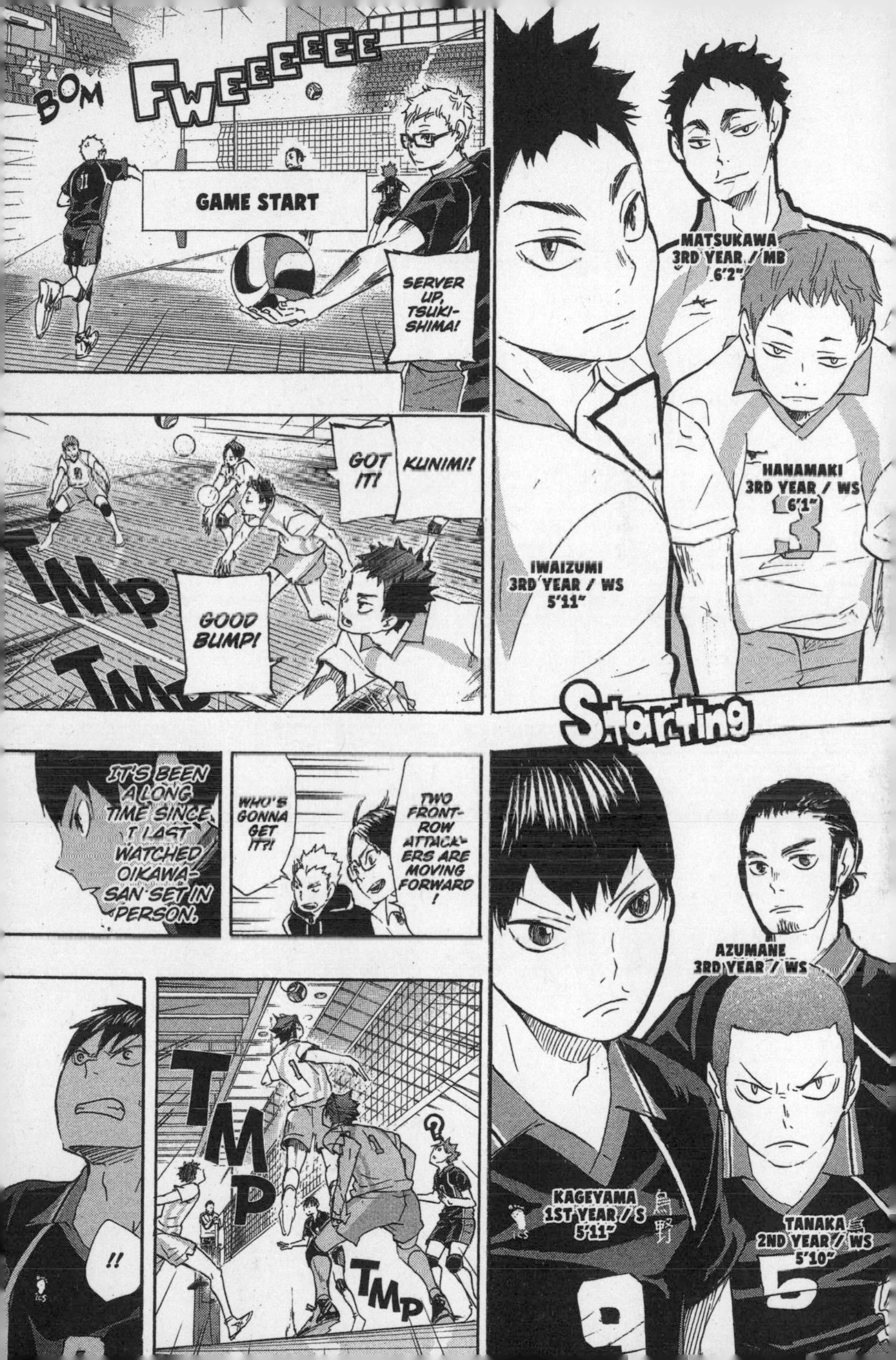
MATSUKAWA
3RD YEAR / MB
6'2"
HANAMAKI
3RD YEAR / WS
6'1"
IWAIZUMI
3RD YEAR / WS
5'11"
SERVER UP, TSUKI-SHIMA!
FWEEEEEEE
BOM
GAME START
KUNIMI!
GOT IT!
GOOD BUMP!
TMP
TMP
Starting
AZUMANE
3RD YEAR / WS
TANAKA
2ND YEAR / WS
5'10"
KAGEYAMA
1ST YEAR / S
5'11"
TWO FRONT-ROW ATTACKERS ARE MOVING FORWARD!
WHO'S GONNA GET IT?!
IT'S BEEN A LONG TIME SINCE I LAST WATCHED OIKAWA-SAN SET IN PERSON.
TMP
TMP
!!

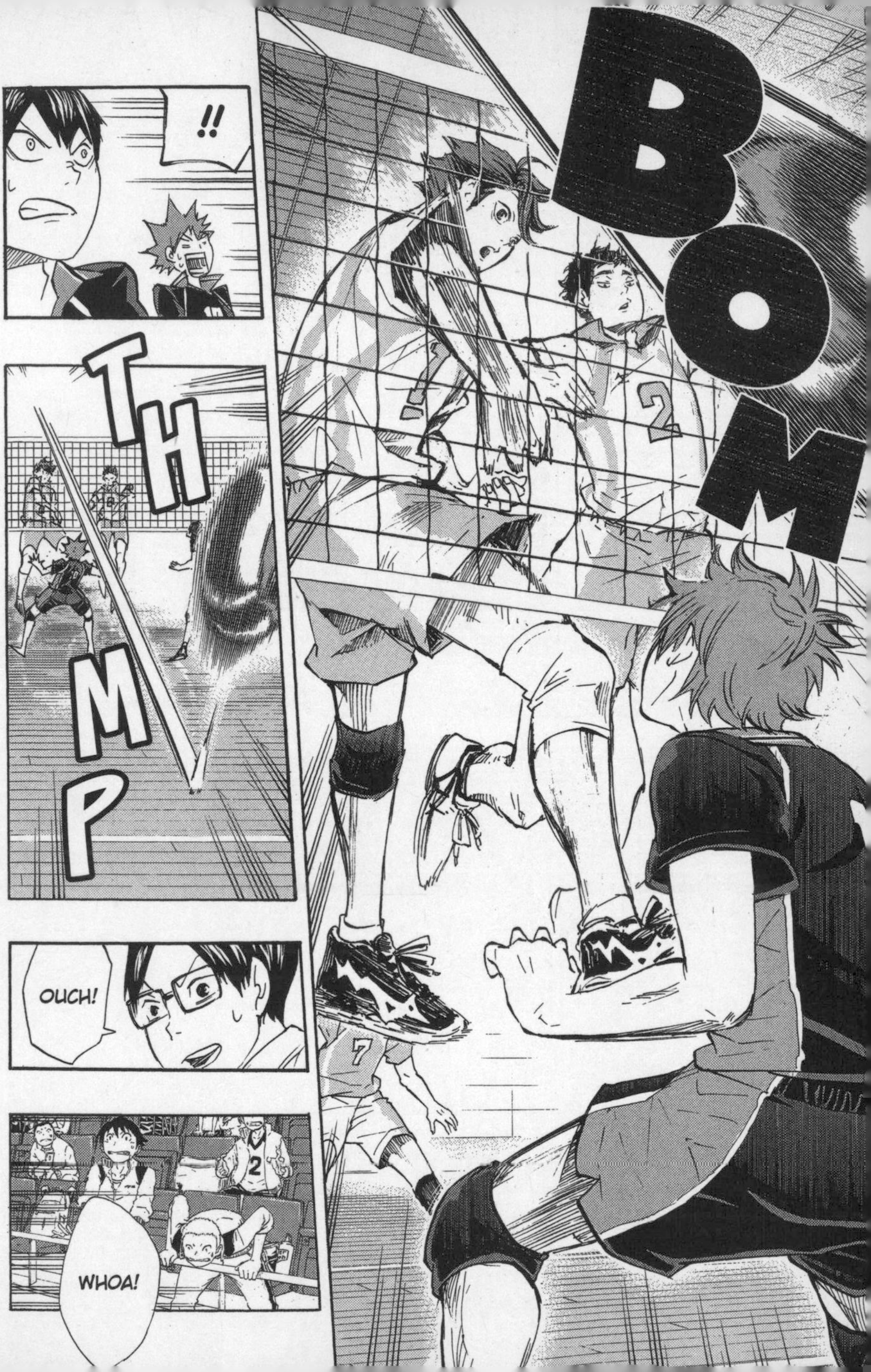
BOOM
!!
THUMP
OUCH!
WHOA!

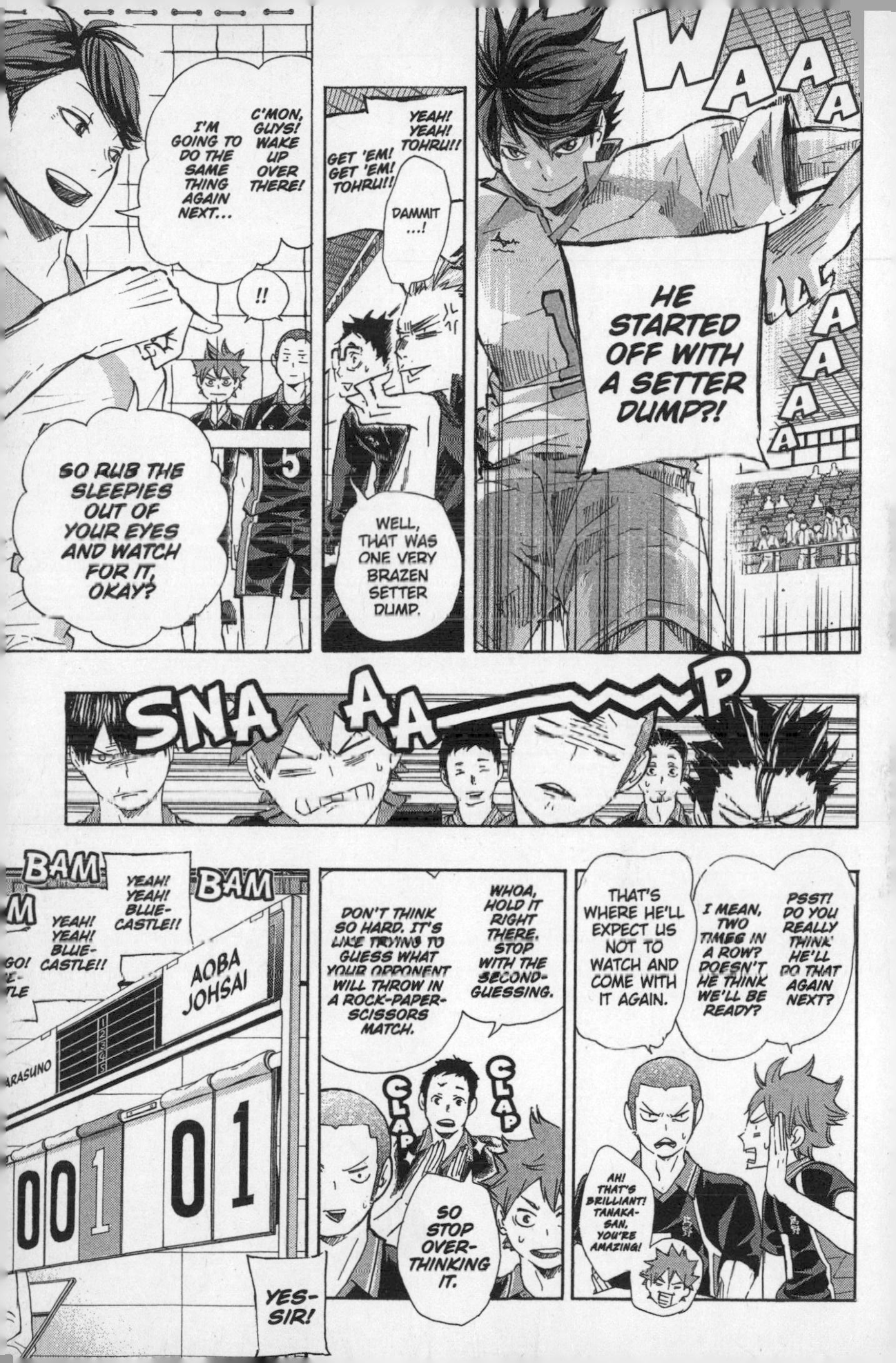

WAAAA
AAAAA
HE STARTED OFF WITH A SETTER DUMP?!
YEAH! YEAH! TOHRU!!
GET 'EM! GET 'EM! TOHRU!!
DAMMIT ...!
WELL, THAT WAS ONE VERY BRAZEN SETTER DUMP.
C'MON, GUYS! WAKE UP OVER THERE!
I'M GOING TO DO THE SAME THING AGAIN NEXT...
!!
SO RUB THE SLEEPIES OUT OF YOUR EYES AND WATCH FOR IT, OKAY?
SNAAAP
PSST! DO YOU REALLY THINK HE'LL DO THAT AGAIN NEXT?
I MEAN, TWO TIMES IN A ROW? DOESN'T HE THINK WE'LL BE READY?
THAT'S WHERE HE'LL EXPECT US NOT TO WATCH AND COME WITH IT AGAIN.
AH! THAT'S BRILLIANT! TANAKA-SAN, YOU'RE AMAZING!
WHOA, HOLD IT RIGHT THERE. STOP WITH THE SECOND-GUESSING.
DON'T THINK SO HARD. IT'S LIKE TRYING TO GUESS WHAT YOUR OPPONENT WILL THROW IN A ROCK-PAPER-SCISSORS MATCH.
CLAP
CLAP
SO STOP OVER-THINKING IT.
BAM
BAM
YEAH! YEAH! BLUE-CASTLE!!
YEAH! YEAH! BLUE-CASTLE!!
AOBA JOHSAI
00 1 01
YES-SIR!

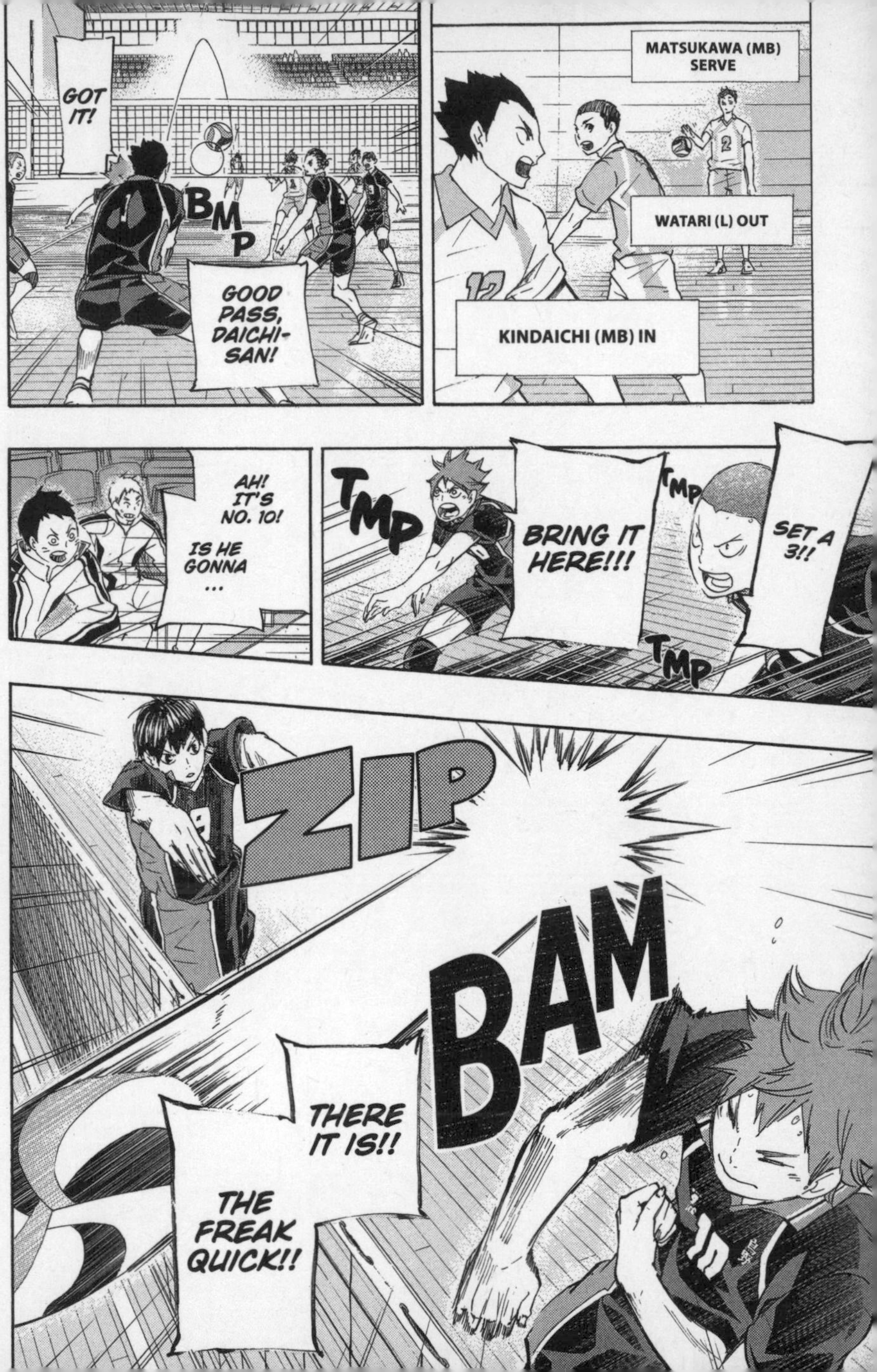
MATSUKAWA (MB) SERVE
WATARI (L) OUT
KINDAICHI (MB) IN
GOT IT!
BMP
GOOD PASS, DAICHI-SAN!
SET A 3!!
TMP
BRING IT HERE!!!
TMP
TMP
AH! IT'S NO. 10!
IS HE GONNA ...
ZIP
BAM
THERE IT IS!!
THE FREAK QUICK!!

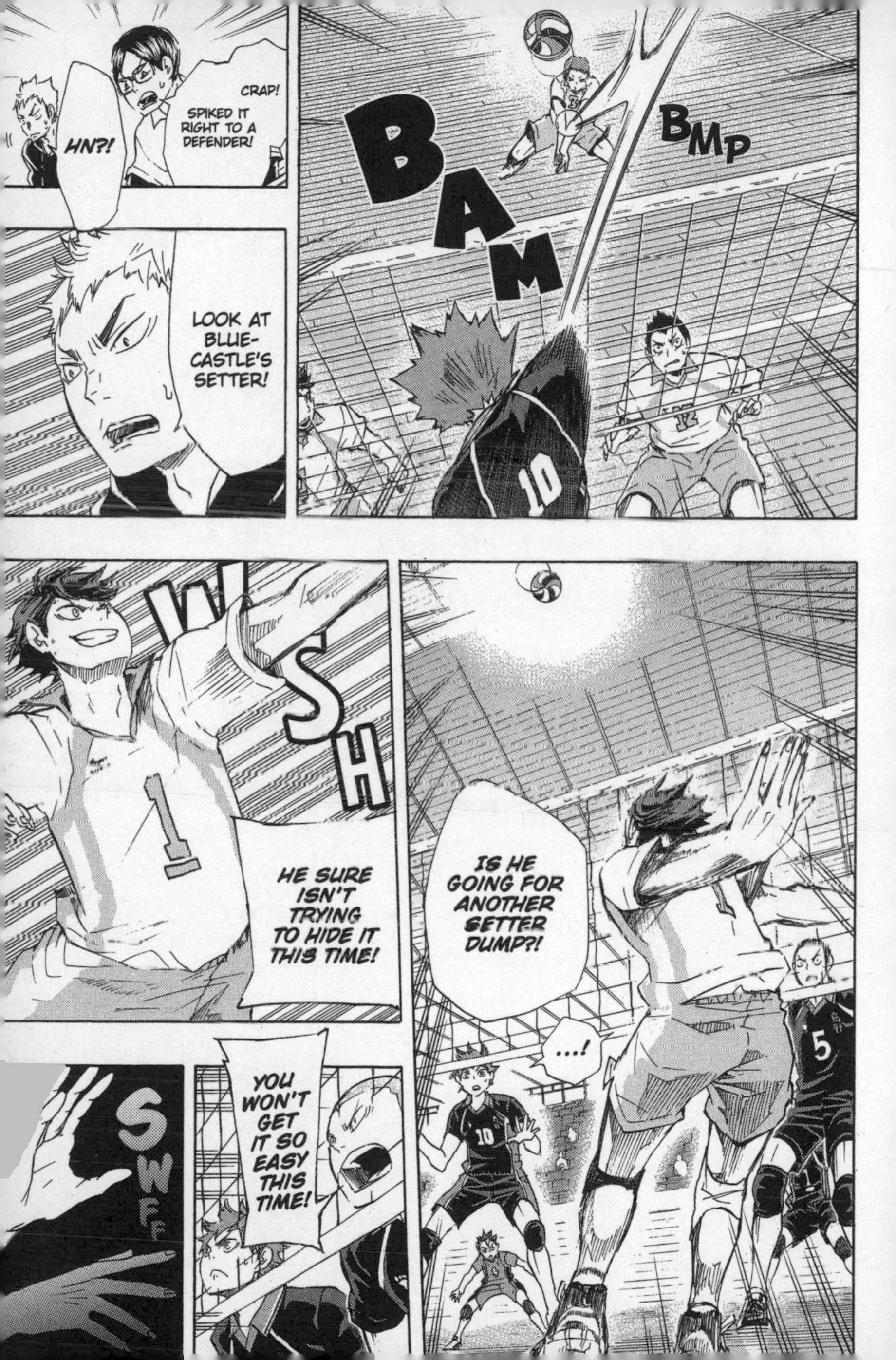
BAM
BMP
CRAP! SPIKED IT RIGHT TO A DEFENDER!
HN?!
LOOK AT BLUE-CASTLE'S SETTER!
IS HE GOING FOR ANOTHER SETTER DUMP?!
...!
WSH
HE SURE ISN'T TRYING TO HIDE IT THIS TIME!
YOU WON'T GET IT SO EASY THIS TIME!
SWFF

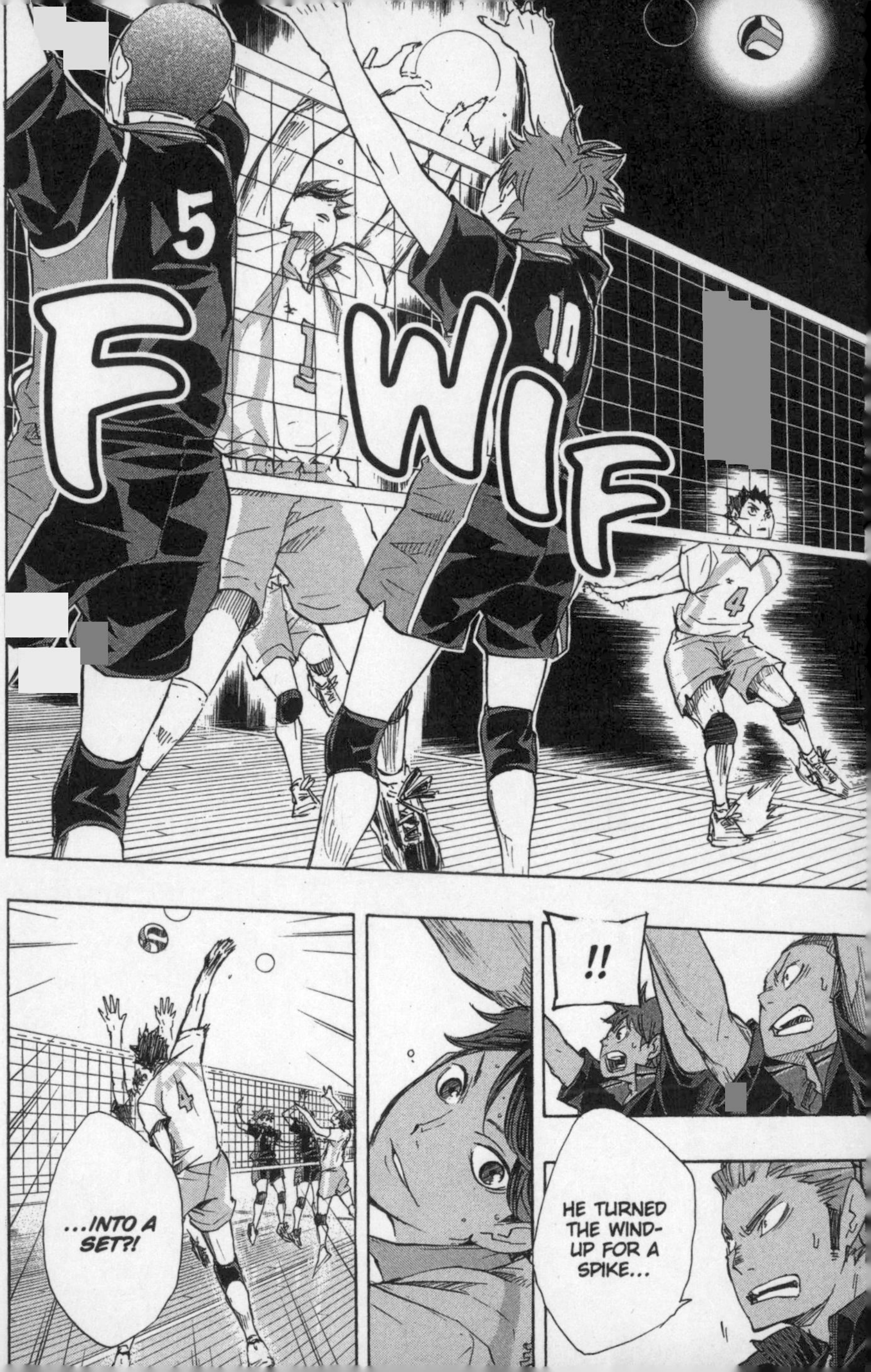
FWIF
!!
HE TURNED THE WIND-UP FOR A SPIKE...
...INTO A SET?!

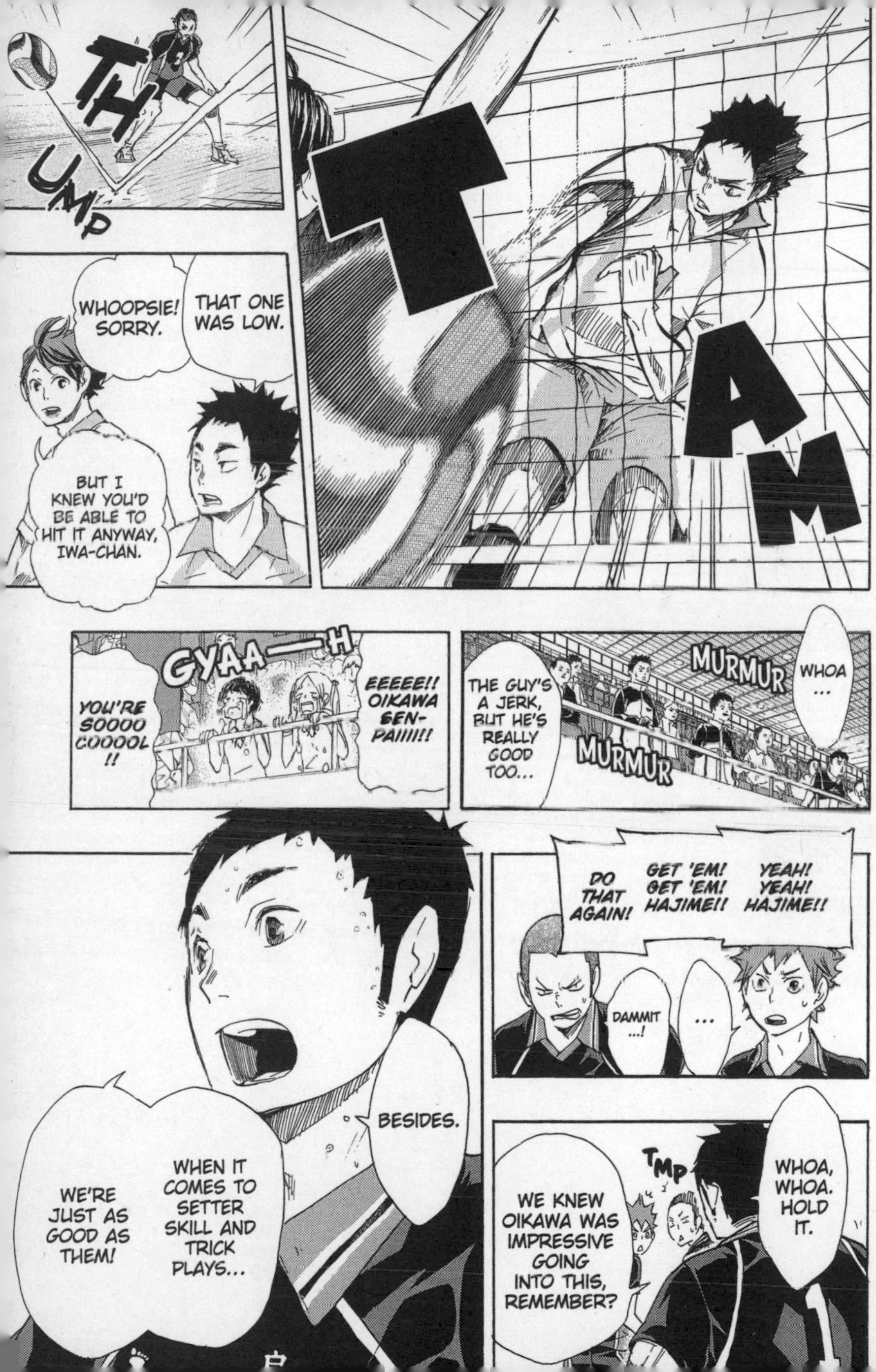

TAM
THUMP
THAT ONE WAS LOW.
WHOOPSIE! SORRY.
BUT I KNEW YOU'D BE ABLE TO HIT IT ANYWAY, IWA-CHAN.
WHOA ...
MURMUR
THE GUY'S A JERK, BUT HE'S REALLY GOOD TOO...
MURMUR
EEEEE!! OIKAWA SEN-PAI!!!!!!
GYAA—H
YOU'RE SOOOO COOOOL!!
YEAH! YEAH! HAJIME!!
GET 'EM! GET 'EM! HAJIME!!
DO THAT AGAIN!
...
DAMMIT ...!
WHOA, WHOA. HOLD IT.
TMP
WE KNEW OIKAWA WAS IMPRESSIVE GOING INTO THIS, REMEMBER?
BESIDES.
WHEN IT COMES TO SETTER SKILL AND TRICK PLAYS...
WE'RE JUST AS GOOD AS THEM!

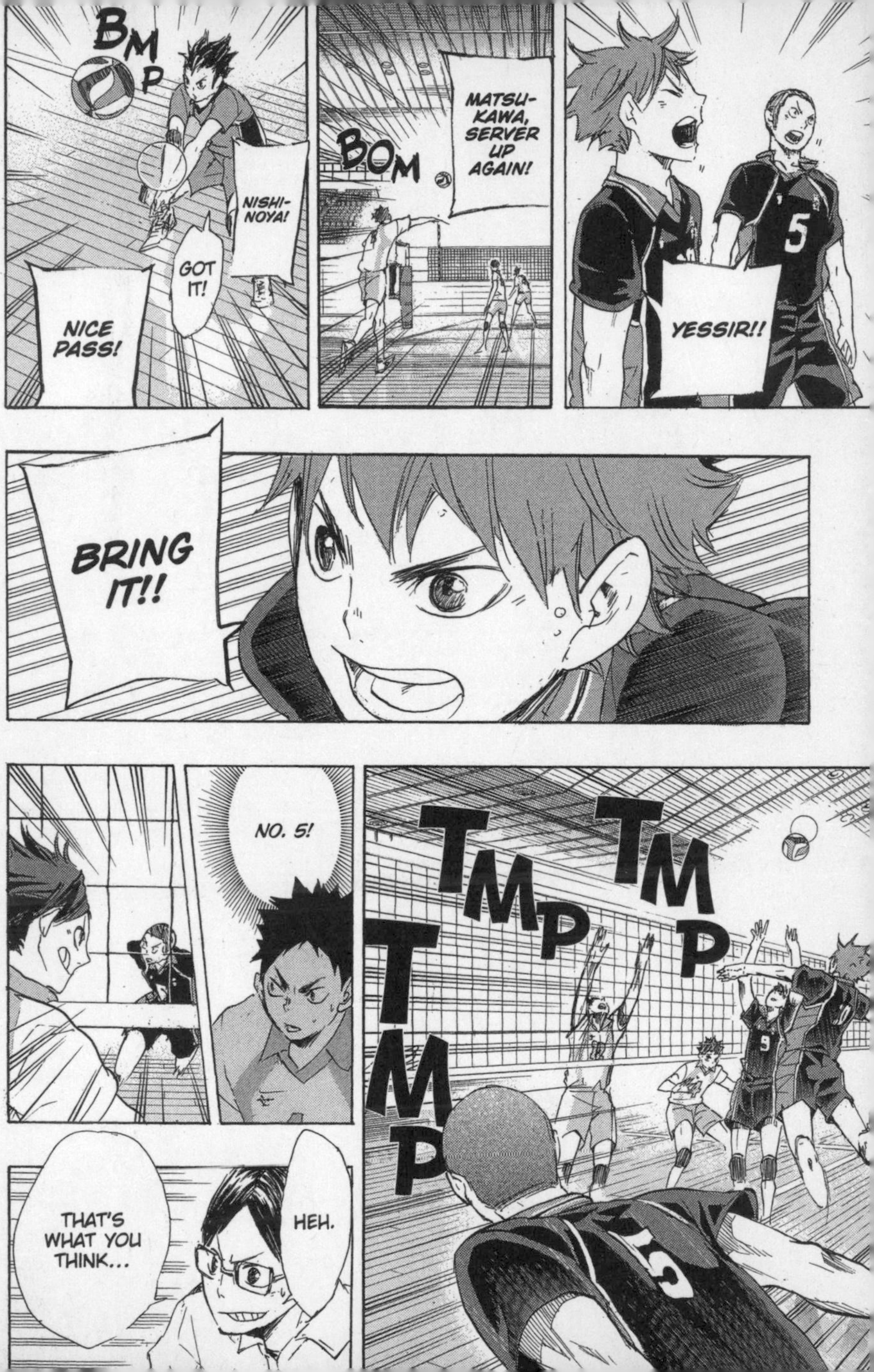
YESSIR!!
BOM
MATSU-KAWA, SERVER UP AGAIN!
BMP
NISHI-NOYA!
GOT IT!
NICE PASS!
BRING IT!!
TMP
TMP
TMP
NO. 5!
HEH.
THAT'S WHAT YOU THINK...

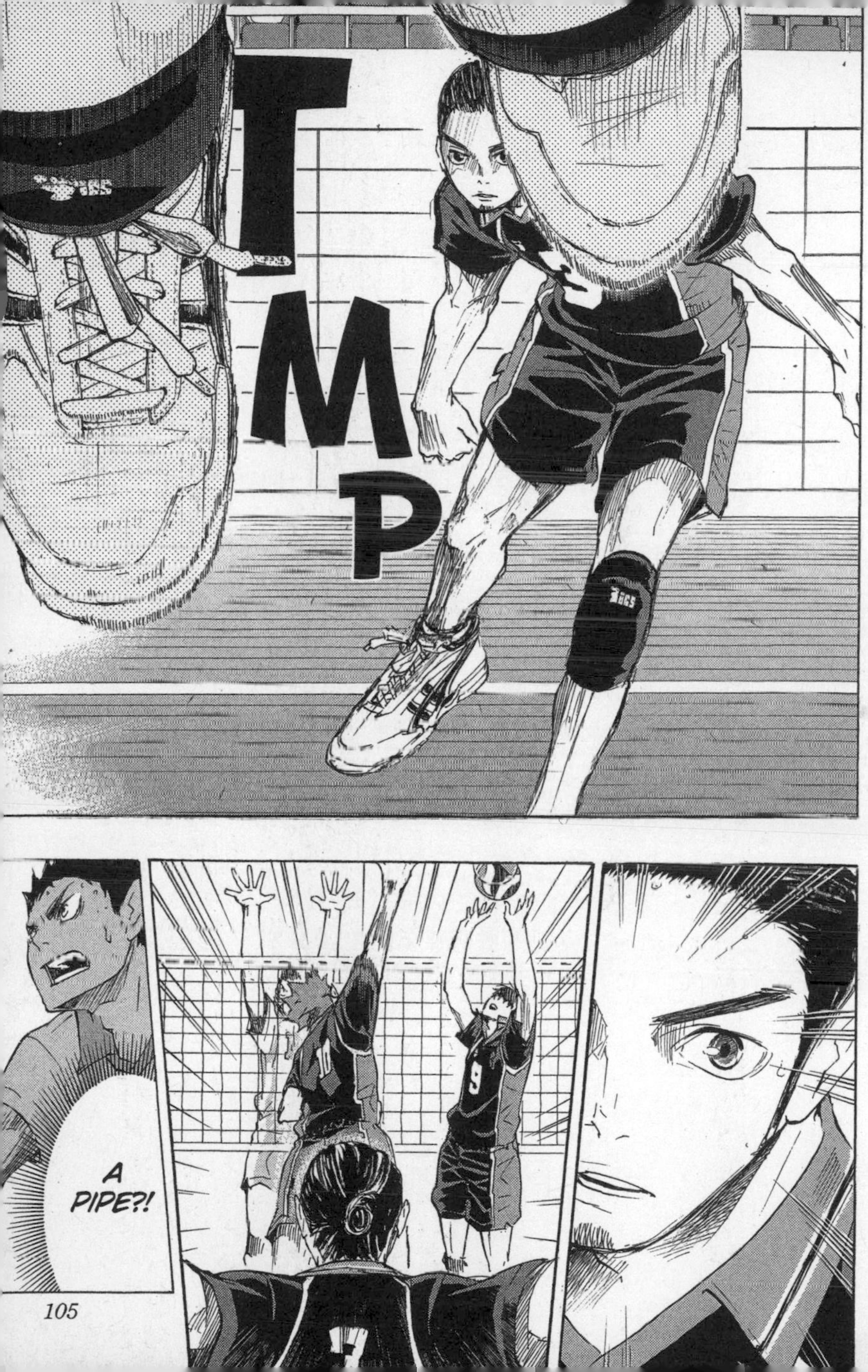
TMP
A PIPE?!

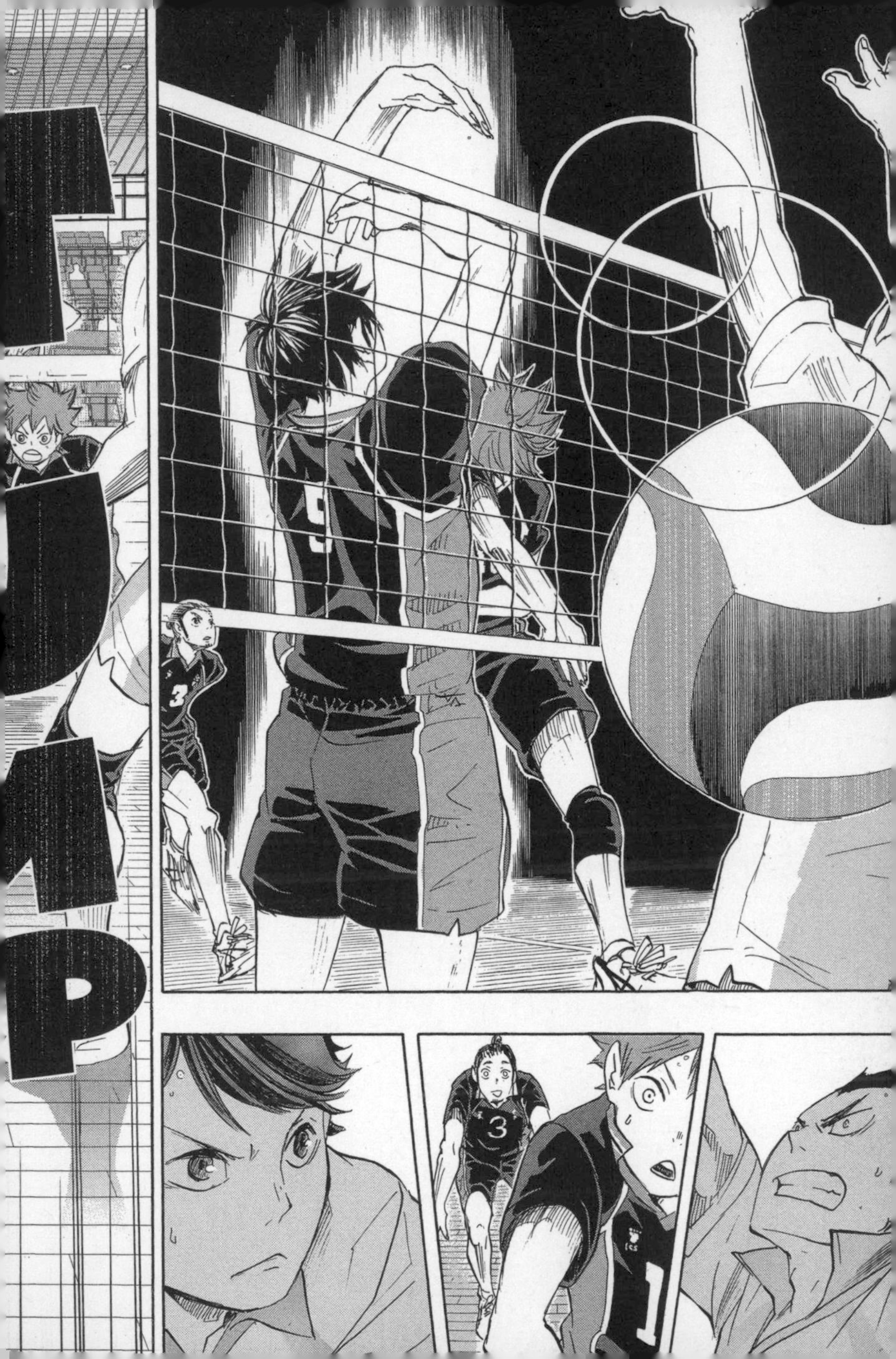

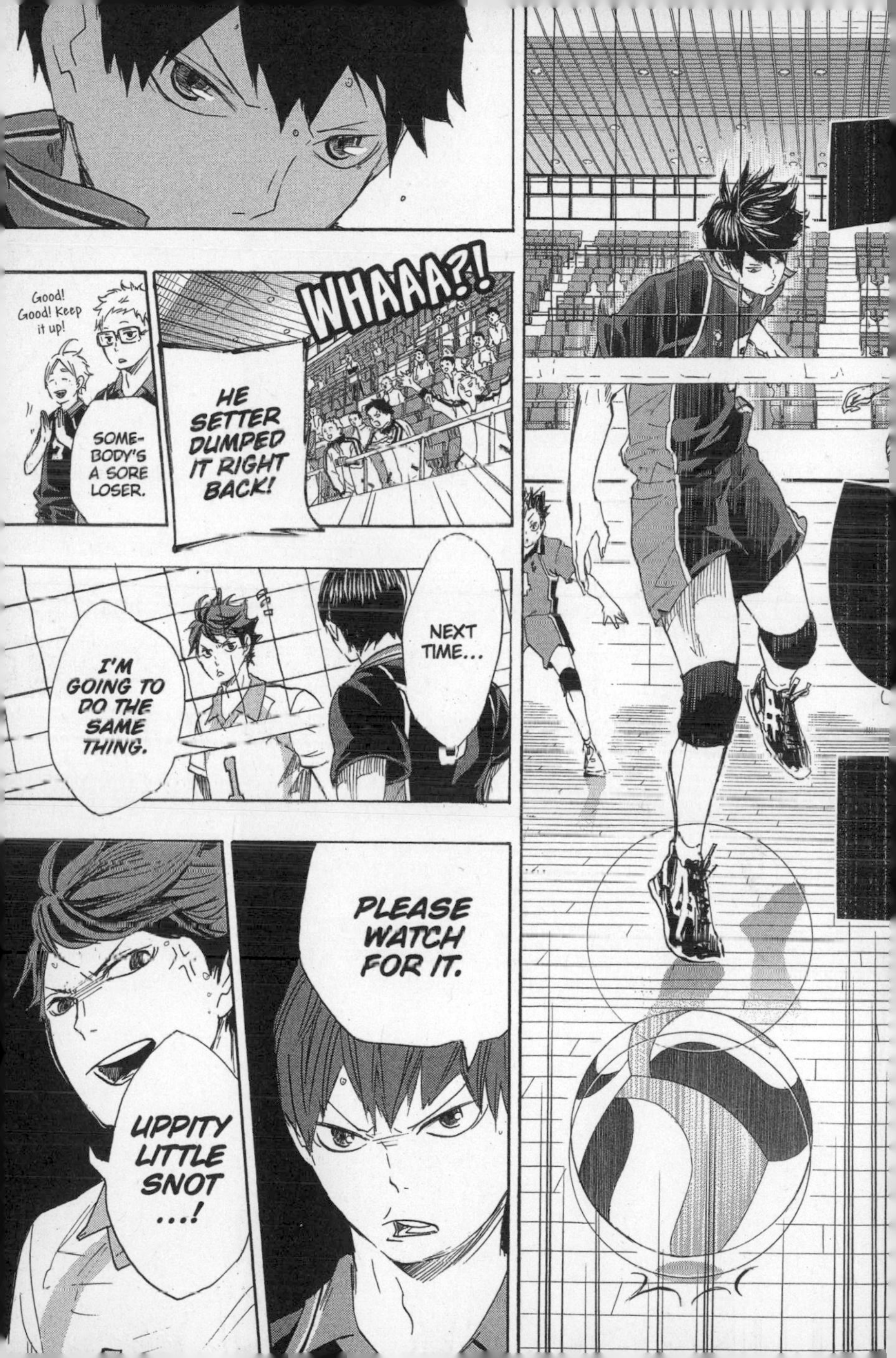
WHAAA?!
HE SETTER DUMPED IT RIGHT BACK!
Good! Good! Keep it up!
SOME-BODY'S A SORE LOSER.
NEXT TIME...
I'M GOING TO DO THE SAME THING.
PLEASE WATCH FOR IT.
UPPITY LITTLE SNOT ...!

TAKURO OIWAKE

**DATE TECHNICAL
HIGH SCHOOL**

**VOLLEYBALL TEAM
HEAD COACH**

AGE: 46

**CURRENT WORRY: HIS
DAUGHTER SUDDENLY TOLD
HIM SHE DIDN'T WANT HER
CLOTHES WASHED IN THE
SAME LOAD AS HIS CLOTHES
BECAUSE IT WAS GROSS.**

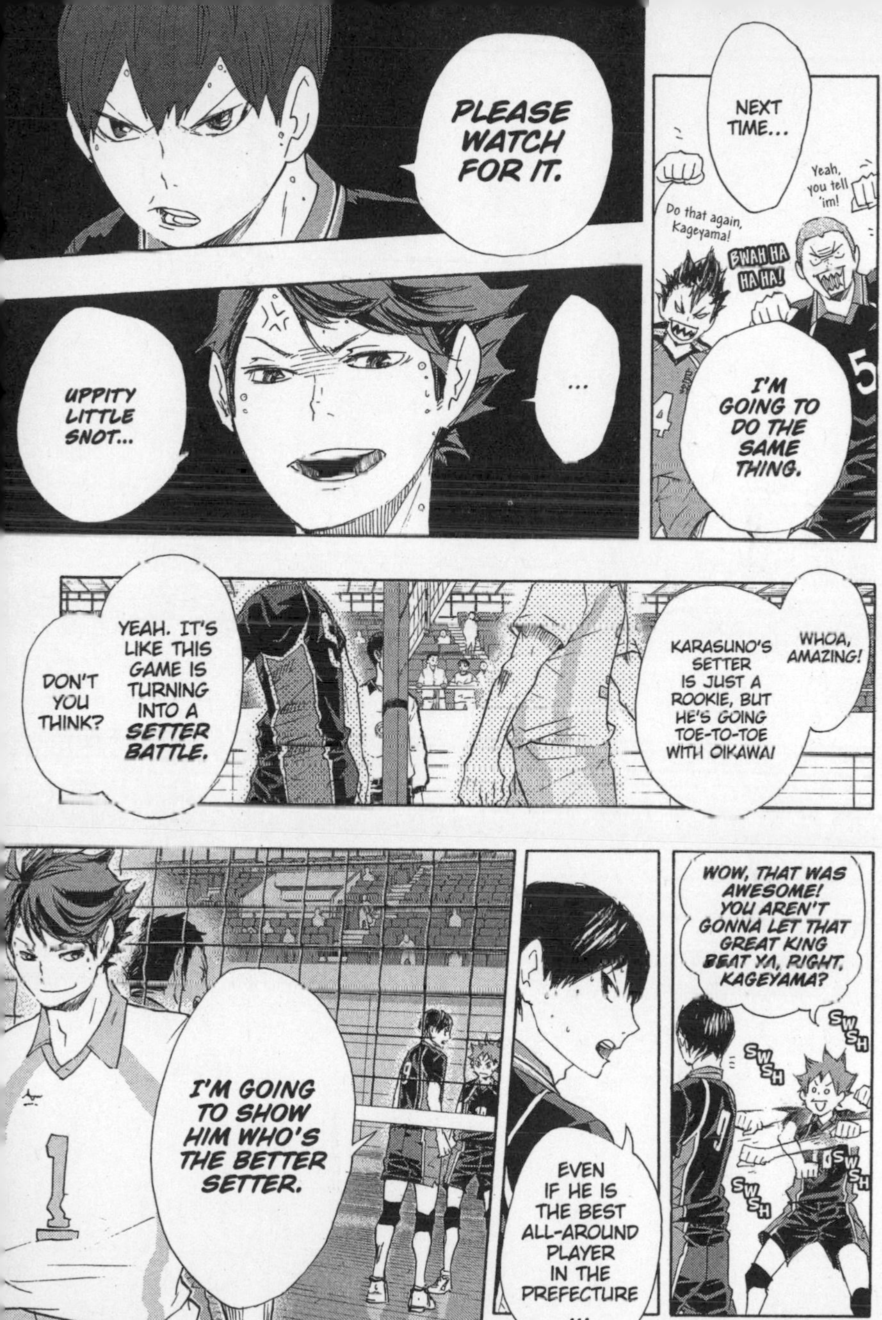
NEXT TIME...
Yeah, you tell 'im!
Do that again, Kageyama!
BWAH HA HA HA!
I'M GOING TO DO THE SAME THING.
PLEASE WATCH FOR IT.
...
UPPITY LITTLE SNOT...
WHOA, AMAZING!
KARASUNO'S SETTER IS JUST A ROOKIE, BUT HE'S GOING TOE-TO-TOE WITH OIKAWA!
YEAH. IT'S LIKE THIS GAME IS TURNING INTO A SETTER BATTLE.
DON'T YOU THINK?
WOW, THAT WAS AWESOME! YOU AREN'T GONNA LET THAT GREAT KING BEAT YA, RIGHT, KAGEYAMA?
SWSH
SWSH
SWSH
SWSH
EVEN IF HE IS THE BEST ALL-AROUND PLAYER IN THE PREFECTURE...
I'M GOING TO SHOW HIM WHO'S THE BETTER SETTER.

CHAPTER 50

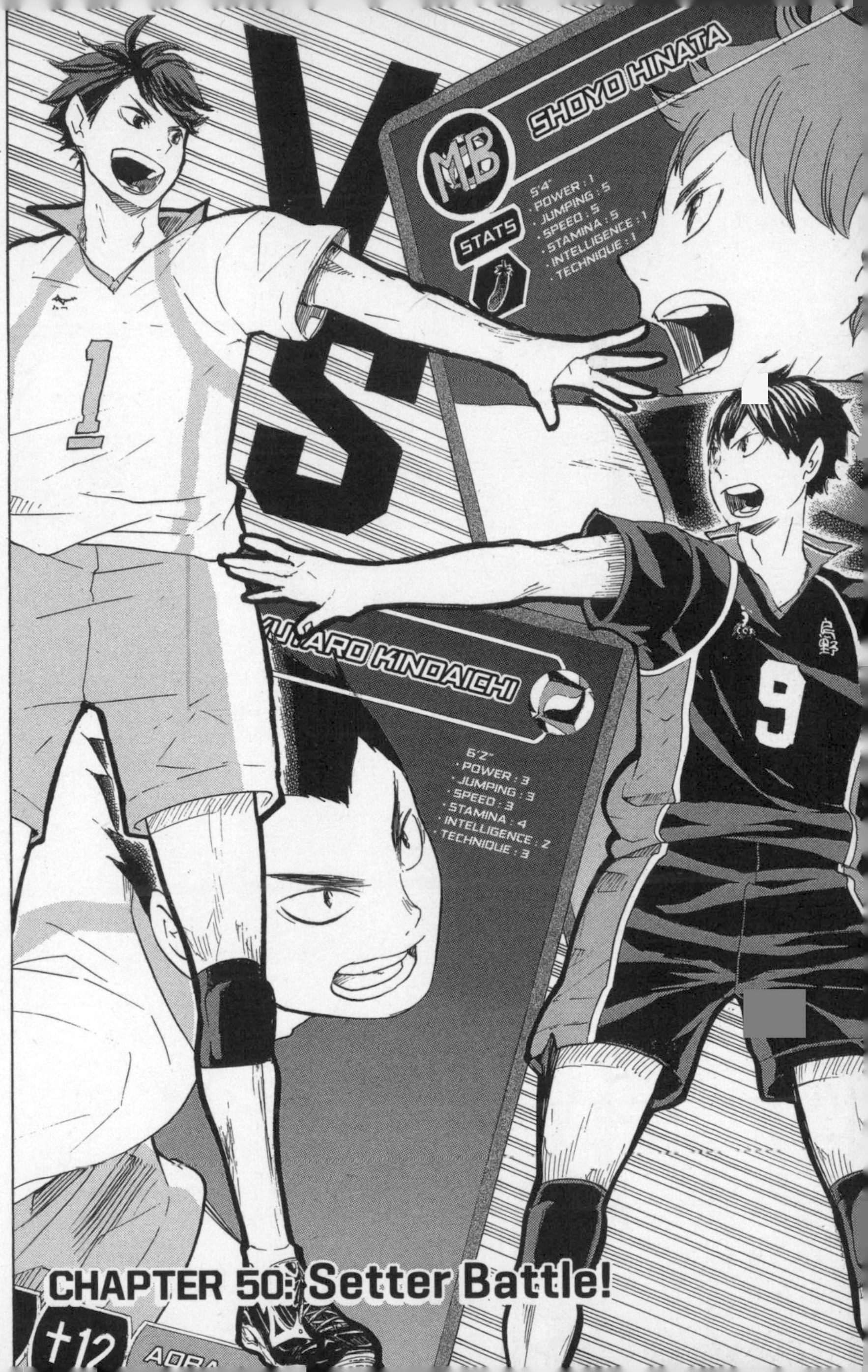
VS
SHOYO HINATA
STATS
5'4"
· POWER : 1
· JUMPING : 5
· SPEED : 5
· STAMINA : 5
· INTELLIGENCE : 1
· TECHNIQUE : 1
KINDAICHI
6'2"
· POWER : 3
· JUMPING : 3
· SPEED : 3
· STAMINA : 4
· INTELLIGENCE : 2
· TECHNIQUE : 3

CHAPTER 50: Setter Battle!

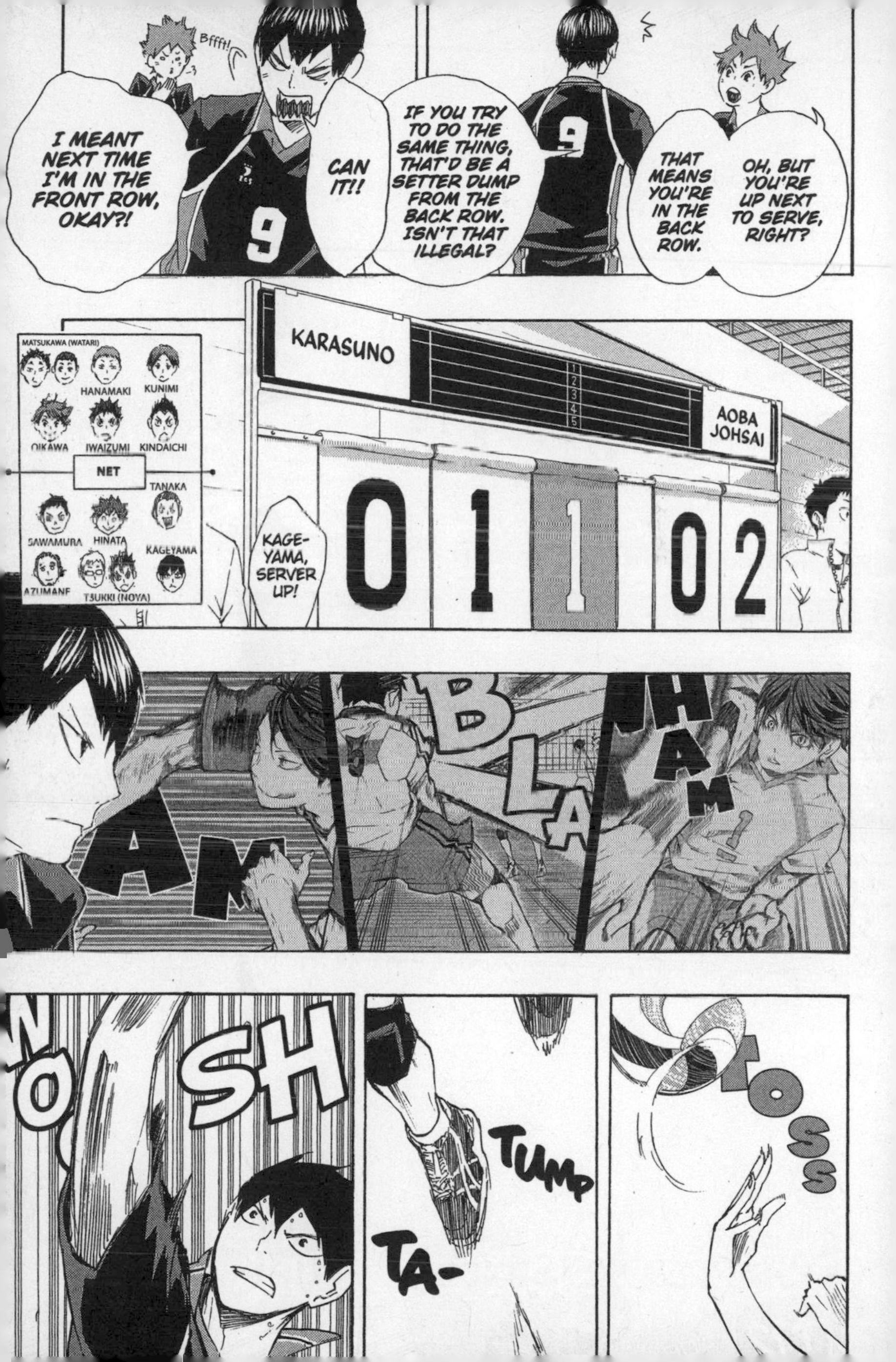
OH, BUT YOU'RE UP NEXT TO SERVE, RIGHT?
THAT MEANS YOU'RE IN THE BACK ROW.
IF YOU TRY TO DO THE SAME THING, THAT'D BE A SETTER DUMP FROM THE BACK ROW. ISN'T THAT ILLEGAL?
CAN IT!!
I MEANT NEXT TIME I'M IN THE FRONT ROW, OKAY?!
Bffff!
KARASUNO
AOBA JOHSAI
1 2 3 4 5
0 1 1 0 2
KAGE-YAMA, SERVER UP!
MATSUKAWA (WATARI)
HANAMAKI
KUNIMI
OIKAWA
IWAIZUMI
KINDAICHI
NET
TANAKA
SAWAMURA
HINATA
KAGEYAMA
AZUMANE
TSUKKI (NOYA)
HAM
BLA
AM
TOSS
TUMP
TA-
SH

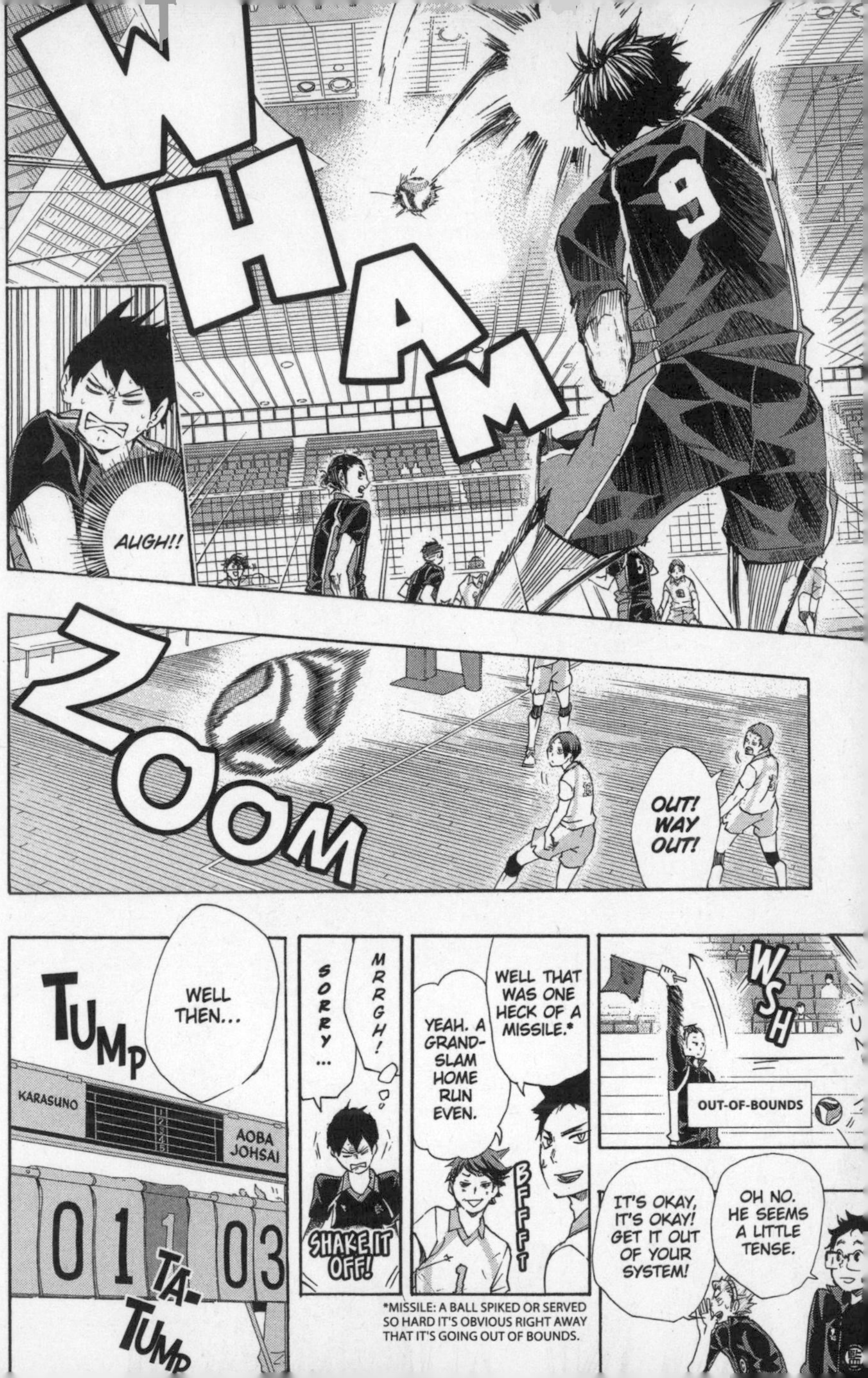
WHAM
AUGH!!
ZOOM
OUT! WAY OUT!
WSH
OUT-OF-BOUNDS
OH NO. HE SEEMS A LITTLE TENSE.
IT'S OKAY, IT'S OKAY! GET IT OUT OF YOUR SYSTEM!
WELL THAT WAS ONE HECK OF A MISSILE.*
YEAH. A GRAND-SLAM HOME RUN EVEN.
BFFFT
MRRGH!
SORRY...
SHAKE IT OFF!
WELL THEN...
TUMP
KARASUNO
AOBA JOHSAI
01 1 03
TA-TUMP

*MISSILE: A BALL SPIKED OR SERVED SO HARD IT'S OBVIOUS RIGHT AWAY THAT IT'S GOING OUT OF BOUNDS.

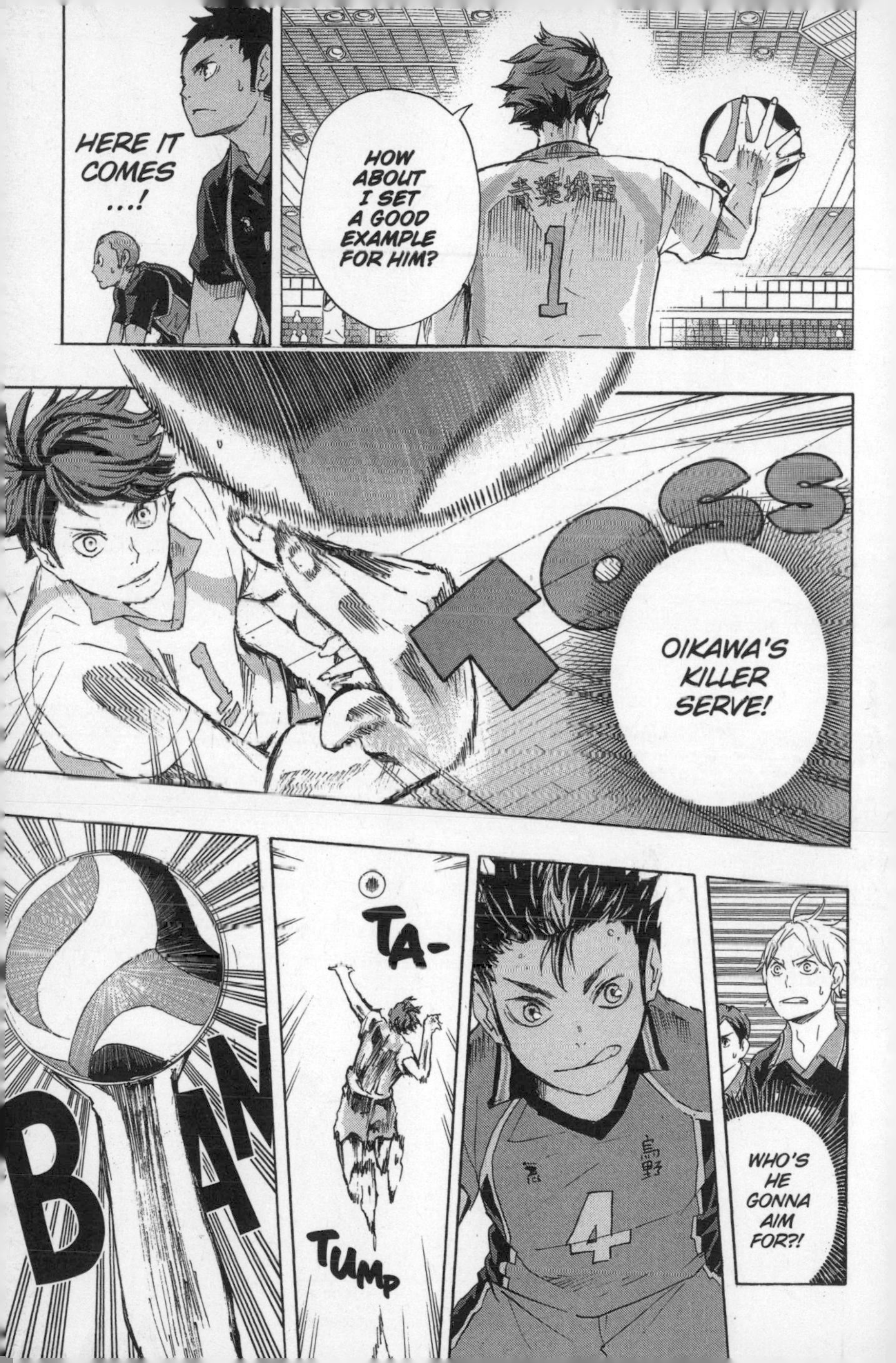
HOW ABOUT I SET A GOOD EXAMPLE FOR HIM?
HERE IT COMES ...!
TOSS
OIKAWA'S KILLER SERVE!
WHO'S HE GONNA AIM FOR?!
TA-
TUMP
BA

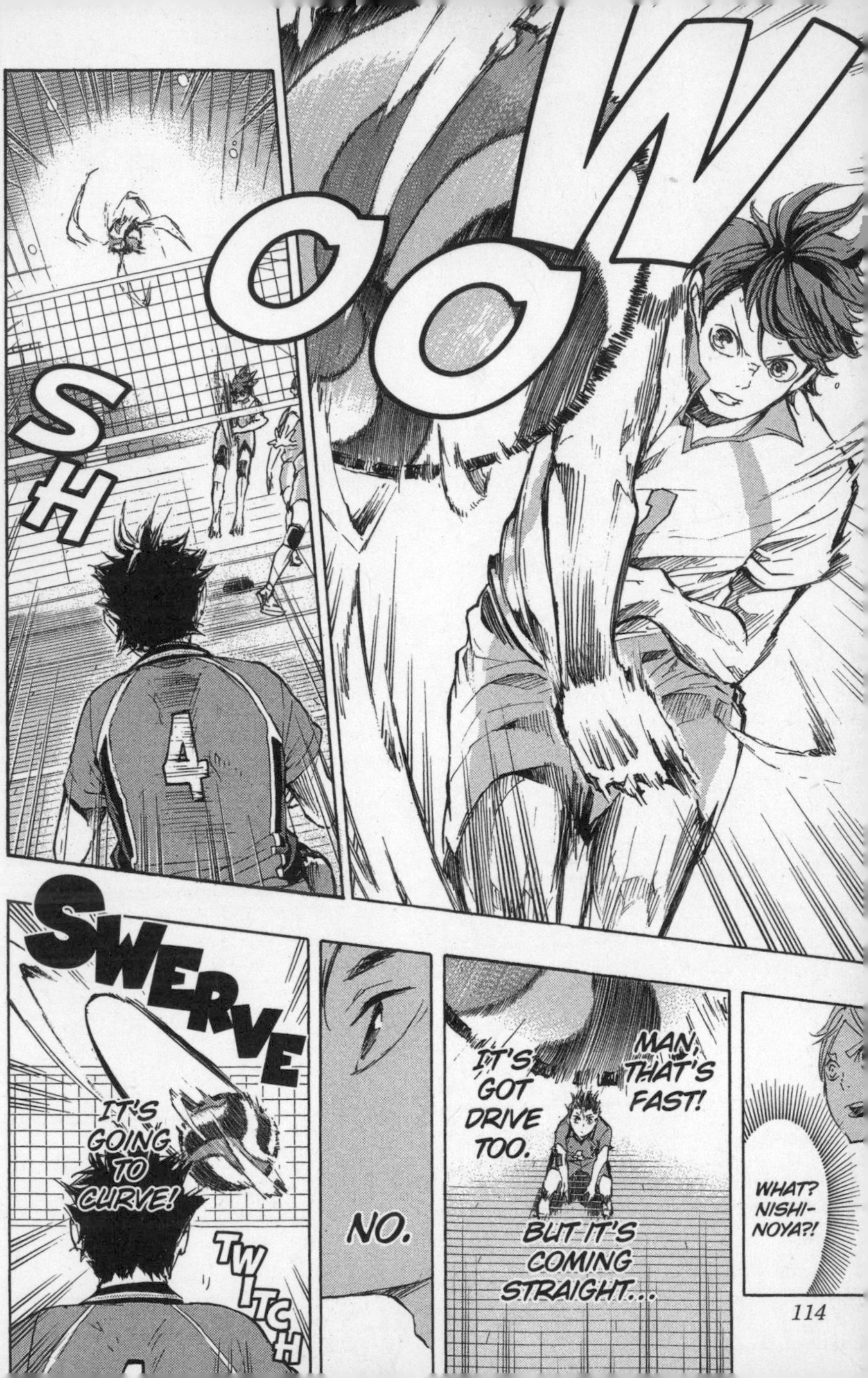
WOOSH
WHAT? NISHI-NOYA?!
MAN, THAT'S FAST!
IT'S GOT DRIVE TOO.
BUT IT'S COMING STRAIGHT...
NO.
SWERVE
IT'S GOING TO CURVE!
TWITCH

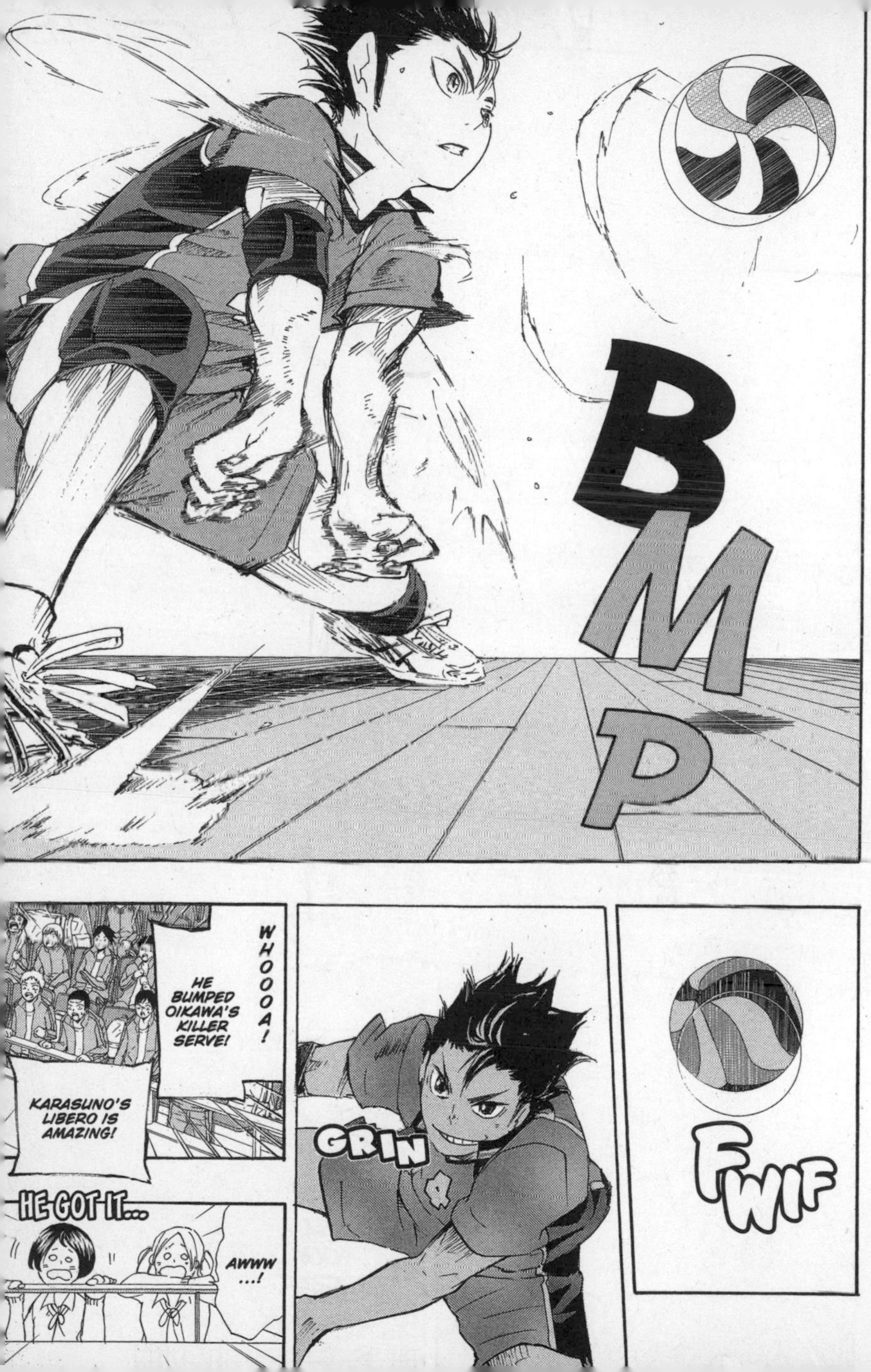
BMP
FWIF
GRIN
WHOOOOA!
HE BUMPED OIKAWA'S KILLER SERVE!
KARASUNO'S LIBERO IS AMAZING!
AWWW ...!
HE GOT IT...

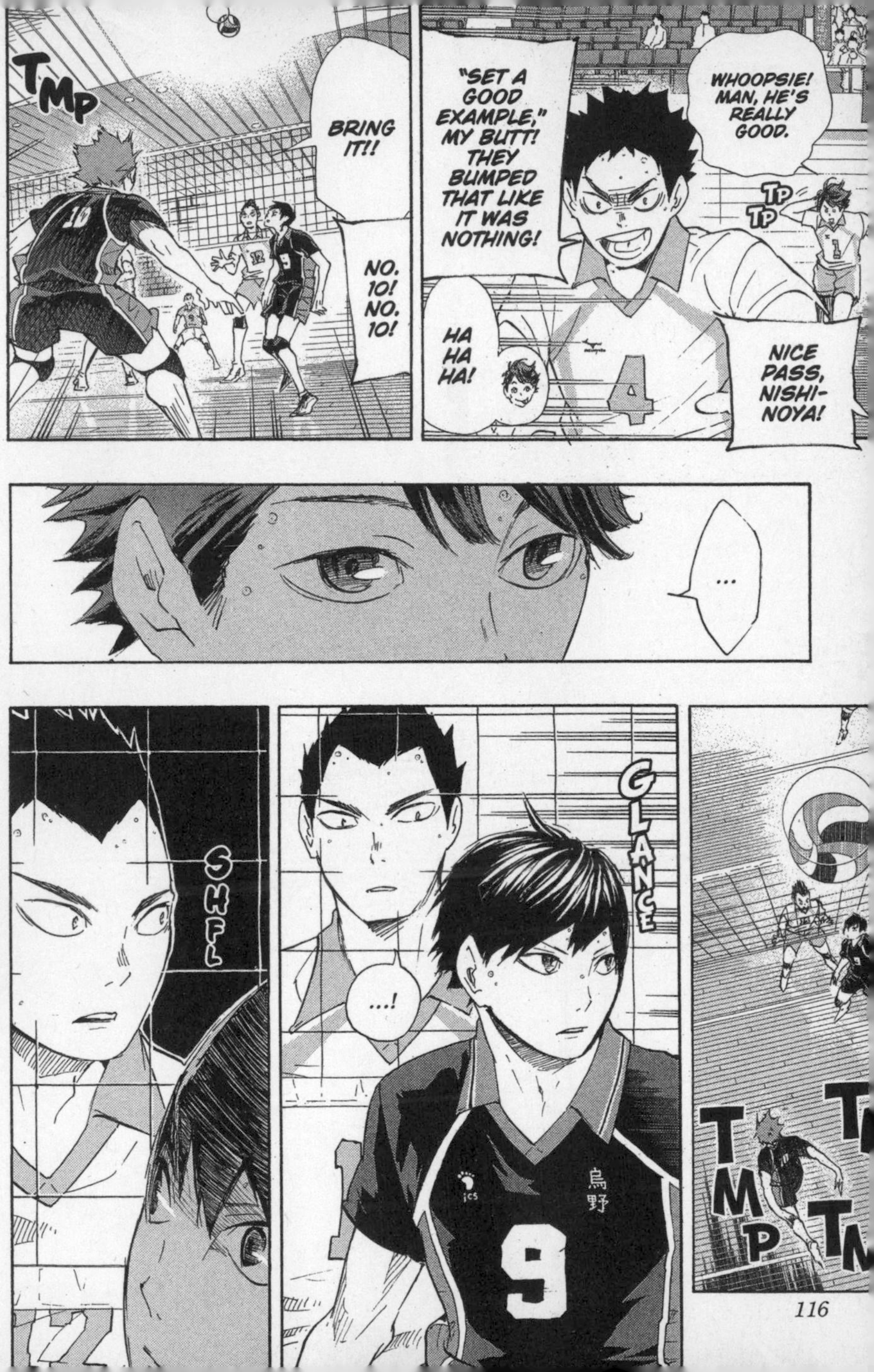
WHOOPSIE! MAN, HE'S REALLY GOOD.
TP TP
"SET A GOOD EXAMPLE," MY BUTT! THEY BUMPED THAT LIKE IT WAS NOTHING!
NICE PASS, NISHI-NOYA!
HA HA HA!
BRING IT!!
TMP
NO. 10! NO. 10!
...
TMP TMP
TMP TMP
GLANCE
...!
SHFL

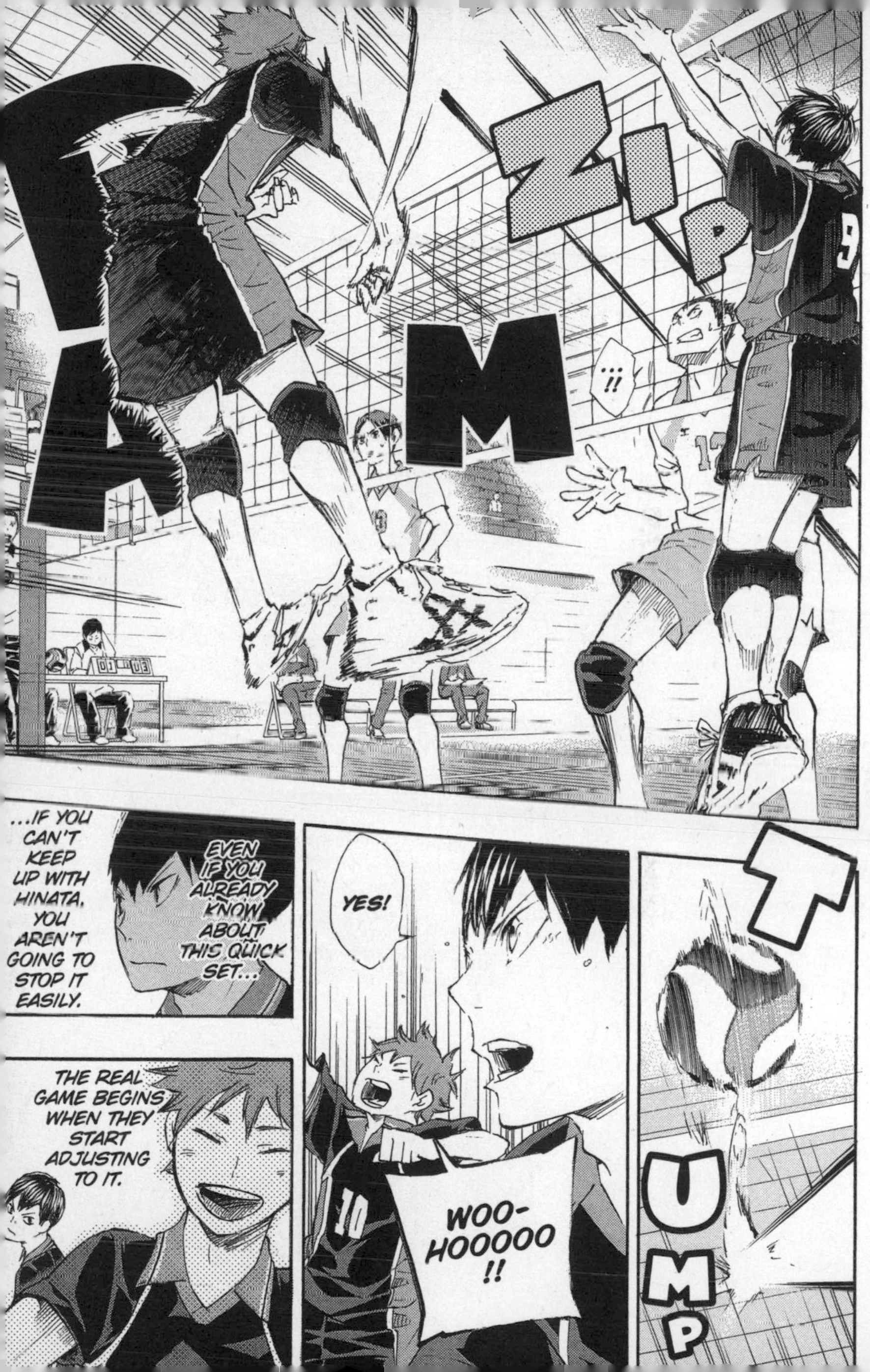
ZIP
...!!
M
T
UMP
YES!
WOO-HOOOOO !!
EVEN IF YOU ALREADY KNOW ABOUT THIS QUICK SET...
...IF YOU CAN'T KEEP UP WITH HINATA, YOU AREN'T GOING TO STOP IT EASILY.
THE REAL GAME BEGINS WHEN THEY START ADJUSTING TO IT.

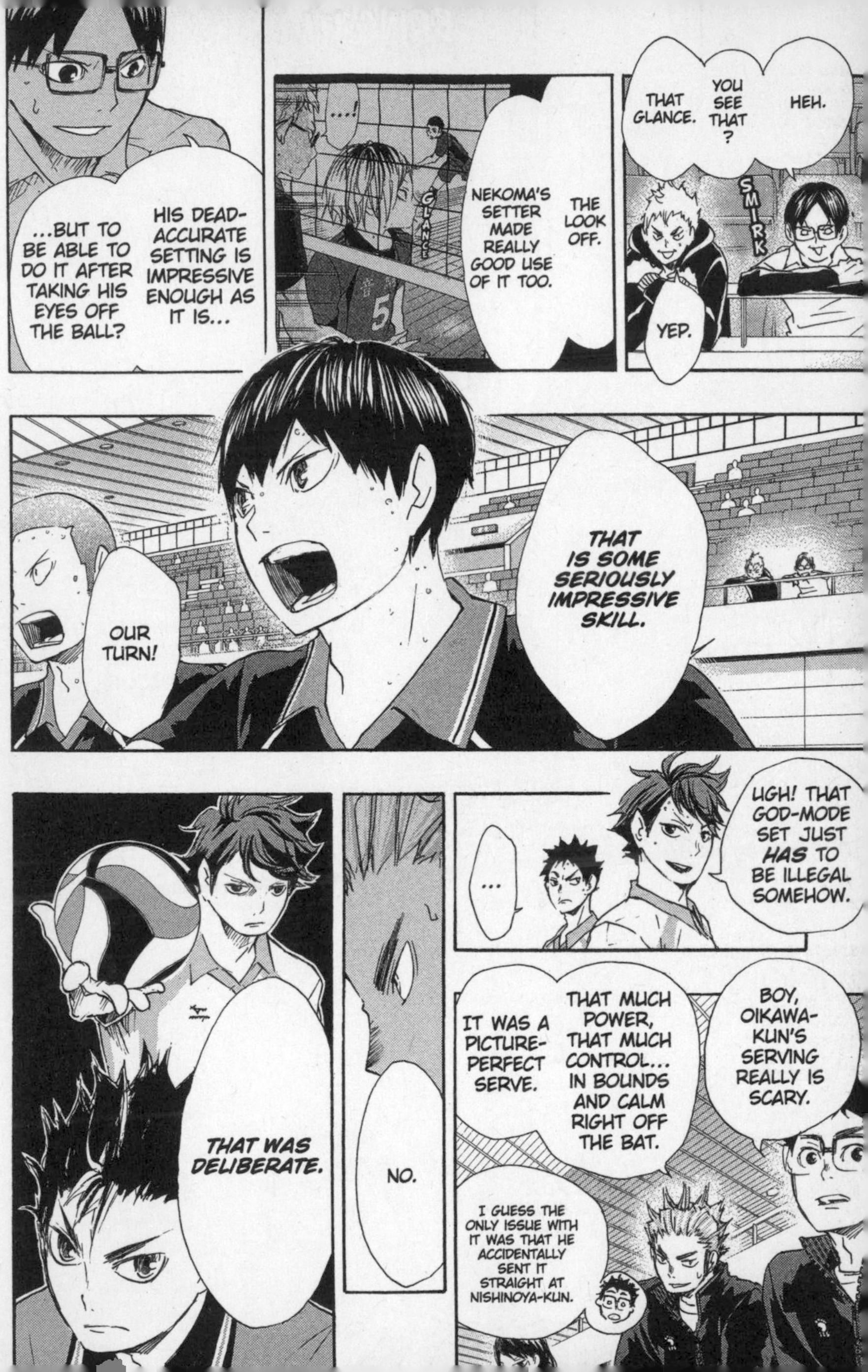
HEH.
YOU SEE THAT?
THAT GLANCE.
SMIRK
YEP.
THE LOOK OFF.
NEKOMA'S SETTER MADE REALLY GOOD USE OF IT TOO.
....!
GLANCE
HIS DEAD-ACCURATE SETTING IS IMPRESSIVE ENOUGH AS IT IS...
...BUT TO BE ABLE TO DO IT AFTER TAKING HIS EYES OFF THE BALL?
THAT IS SOME SERIOUSLY IMPRESSIVE SKILL.
OUR TURN!
UGH! THAT GOD-MODE SET JUST HAS TO BE ILLEGAL SOMEHOW.
...
BOY, OIKAWA-KUN'S SERVING REALLY IS SCARY.
THAT MUCH POWER, THAT MUCH CONTROL... IN BOUNDS AND CALM RIGHT OFF THE BAT.
IT WAS A PICTURE-PERFECT SERVE.
I GUESS THE ONLY ISSUE WITH IT WAS THAT HE ACCIDENTALLY SENT IT STRAIGHT AT NISHINOYA-KUN.
NO.
THAT WAS DELIBERATE.

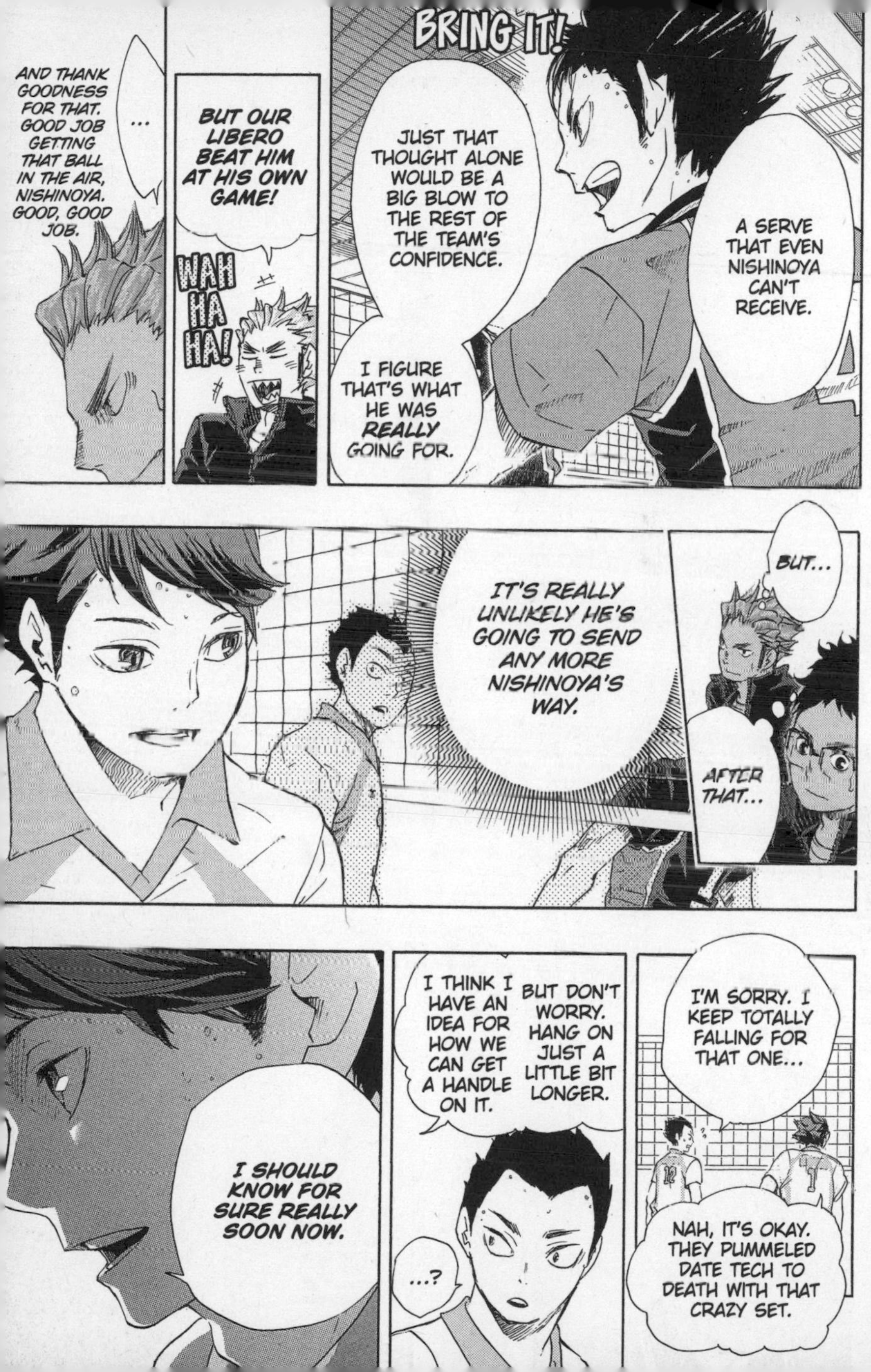
BRING IT!
A SERVE THAT EVEN NISHINOYA CAN'T RECEIVE.
JUST THAT THOUGHT ALONE WOULD BE A BIG BLOW TO THE REST OF THE TEAM'S CONFIDENCE.
I FIGURE THAT'S WHAT HE WAS REALLY GOING FOR.
BUT OUR LIBERO BEAT HIM AT HIS OWN GAME!
WAH HA HA!
...
AND THANK GOODNESS FOR THAT. GOOD JOB GETTING THAT BALL IN THE AIR, NISHINOYA. GOOD, GOOD JOB.
BUT...
AFTER THAT...
IT'S REALLY UNLIKELY HE'S GOING TO SEND ANY MORE NISHINOYA'S WAY.
I'M SORRY. I KEEP TOTALLY FALLING FOR THAT ONE...
NAH, IT'S OKAY. THEY PUMMELED DATE TECH TO DEATH WITH THAT CRAZY SET.
BUT DON'T WORRY. HANG ON JUST A LITTLE BIT LONGER.
I THINK I HAVE AN IDEA FOR HOW WE CAN GET A HANDLE ON IT.
...?
I SHOULD KNOW FOR SURE REALLY SOON NOW.

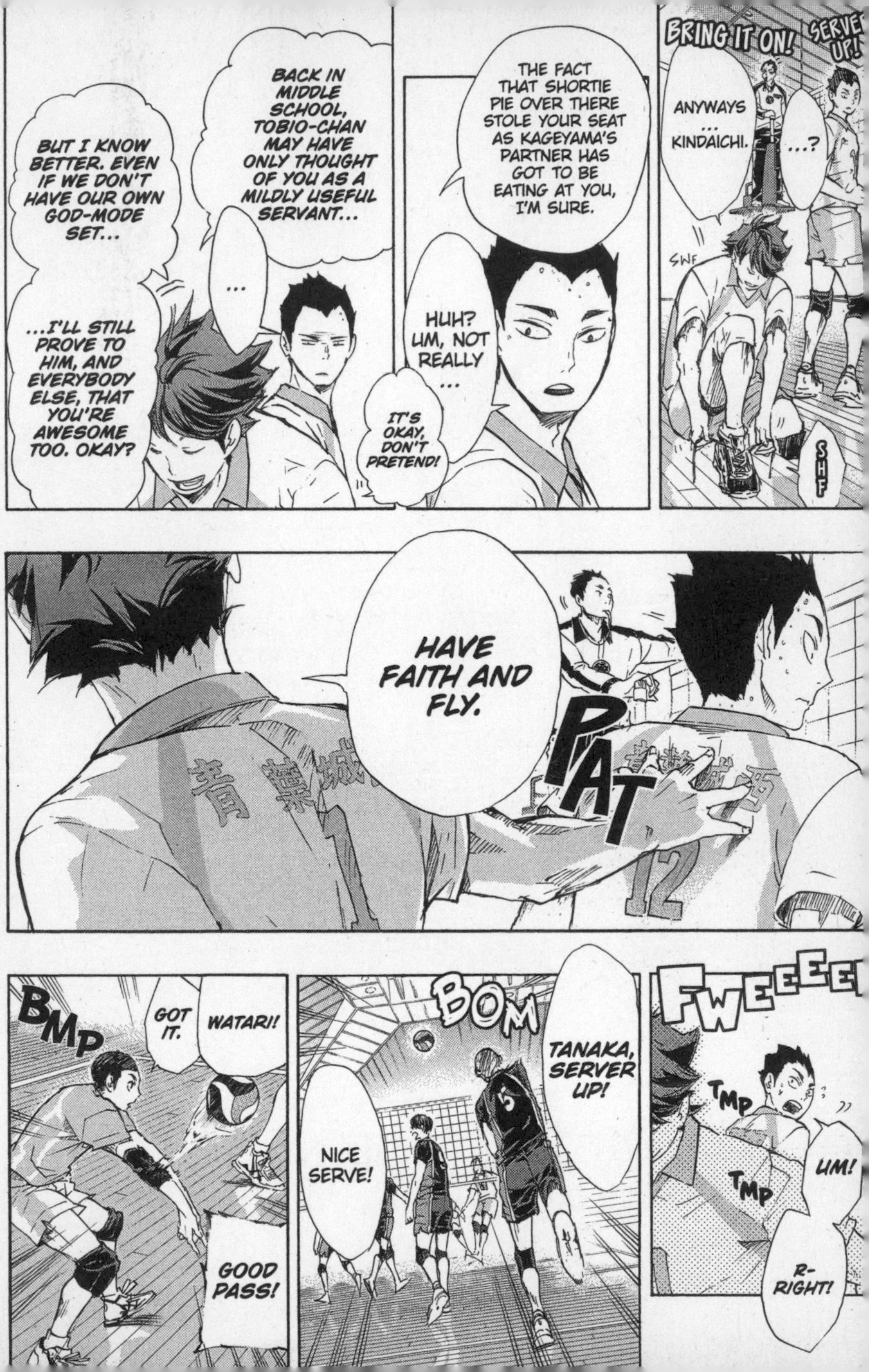
BRING IT ON!
SERVE UP!
ANYWAYS ... KINDAICHI.
...?
SWF
SHF
THE FACT THAT SHORTIE PIE OVER THERE STOLE YOUR SEAT AS KAGEYAMA'S PARTNER HAS GOT TO BE EATING AT YOU, I'M SURE.
HUH? UM, NOT REALLY ...
IT'S OKAY, DON'T PRETEND!
BACK IN MIDDLE SCHOOL, TOBIO-CHAN MAY HAVE ONLY THOUGHT OF YOU AS A MILDLY USEFUL SERVANT...
...
BUT I KNOW BETTER. EVEN IF WE DON'T HAVE OUR OWN GOD-MODE SET...
...I'LL STILL PROVE TO HIM, AND EVERYBODY ELSE, THAT YOU'RE AWESOME TOO. OKAY?
HAVE FAITH AND FLY.
PAT
FWEEEEE
TMP
UM!
TMP
R-RIGHT!
BOM
TANAKA, SERVER UP!
NICE SERVE!
WATARI!
GOT IT.
BMP
GOOD PASS!

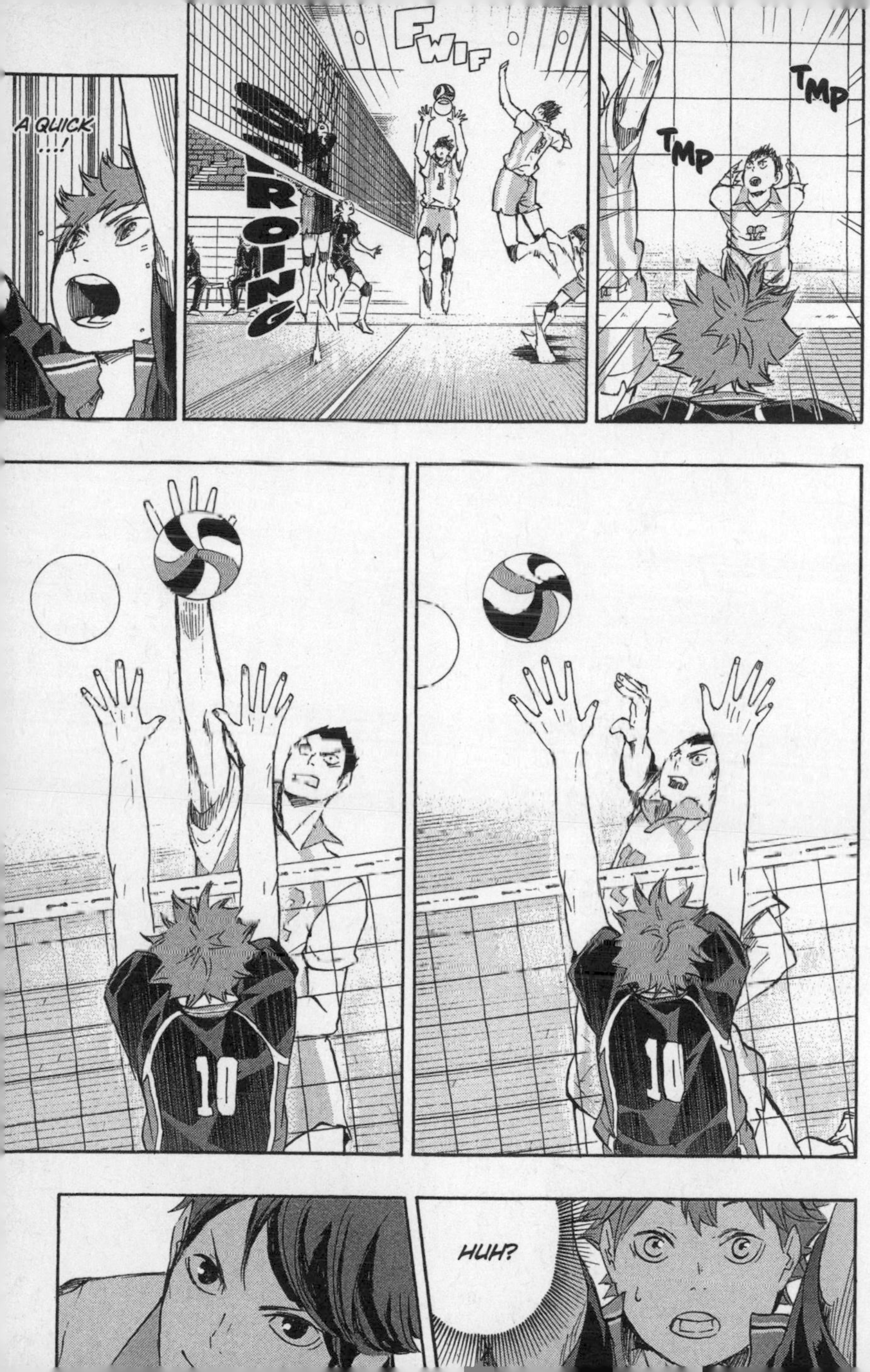
TMP
TMP
FWIF
BOING
A QUICK ...!
HUH?

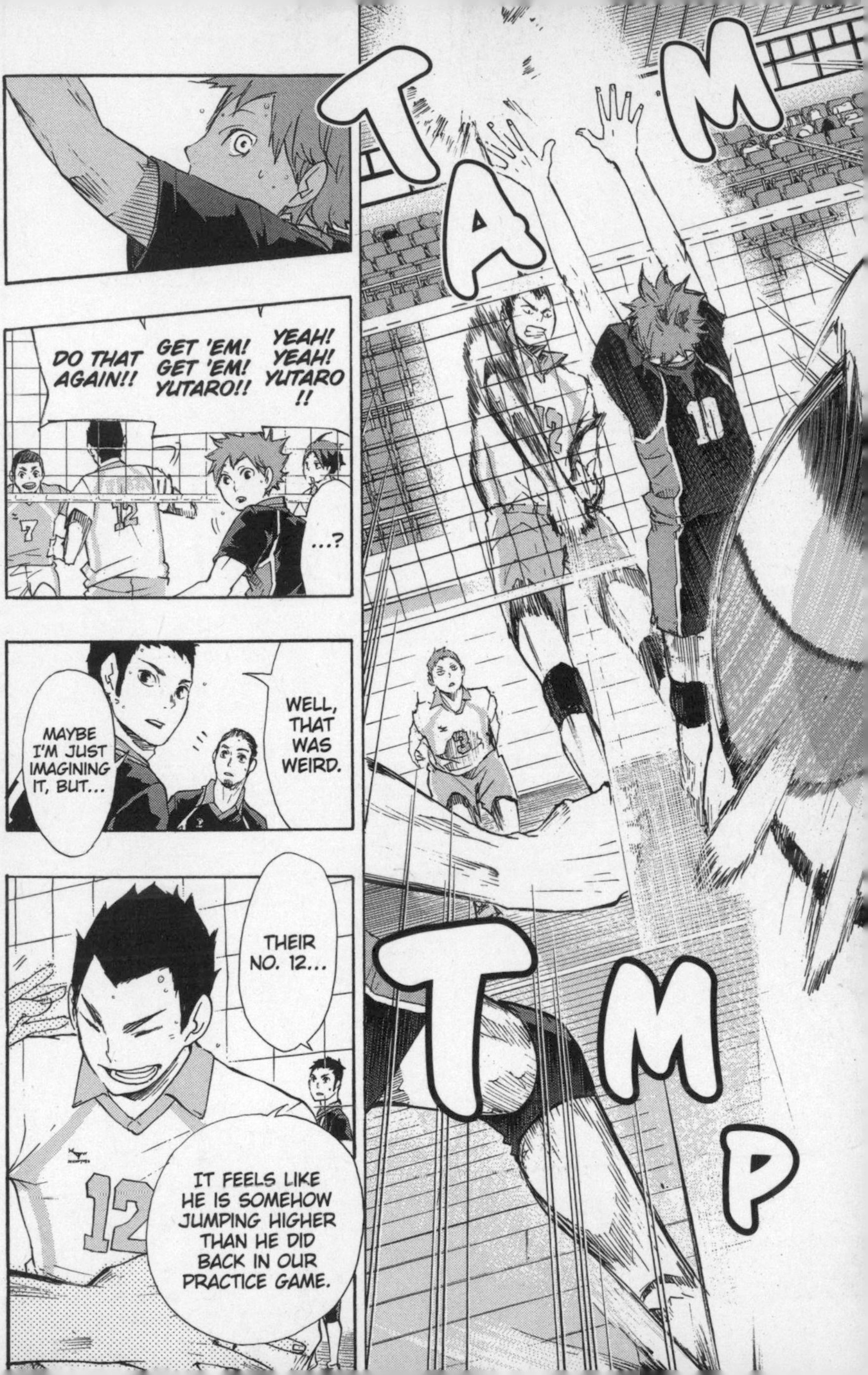
TAM
TMP
YEAH! YEAH! YUTARO!!
GET 'EM! GET 'EM! YUTARO!!
DO THAT AGAIN!!
...?
WELL, THAT WAS WEIRD.
MAYBE I'M JUST IMAGINING IT, BUT...
THEIR NO. 12...
IT FEELS LIKE HE IS SOMEHOW JUMPING HIGHER THAN HE DID BACK IN OUR PRACTICE GAME.

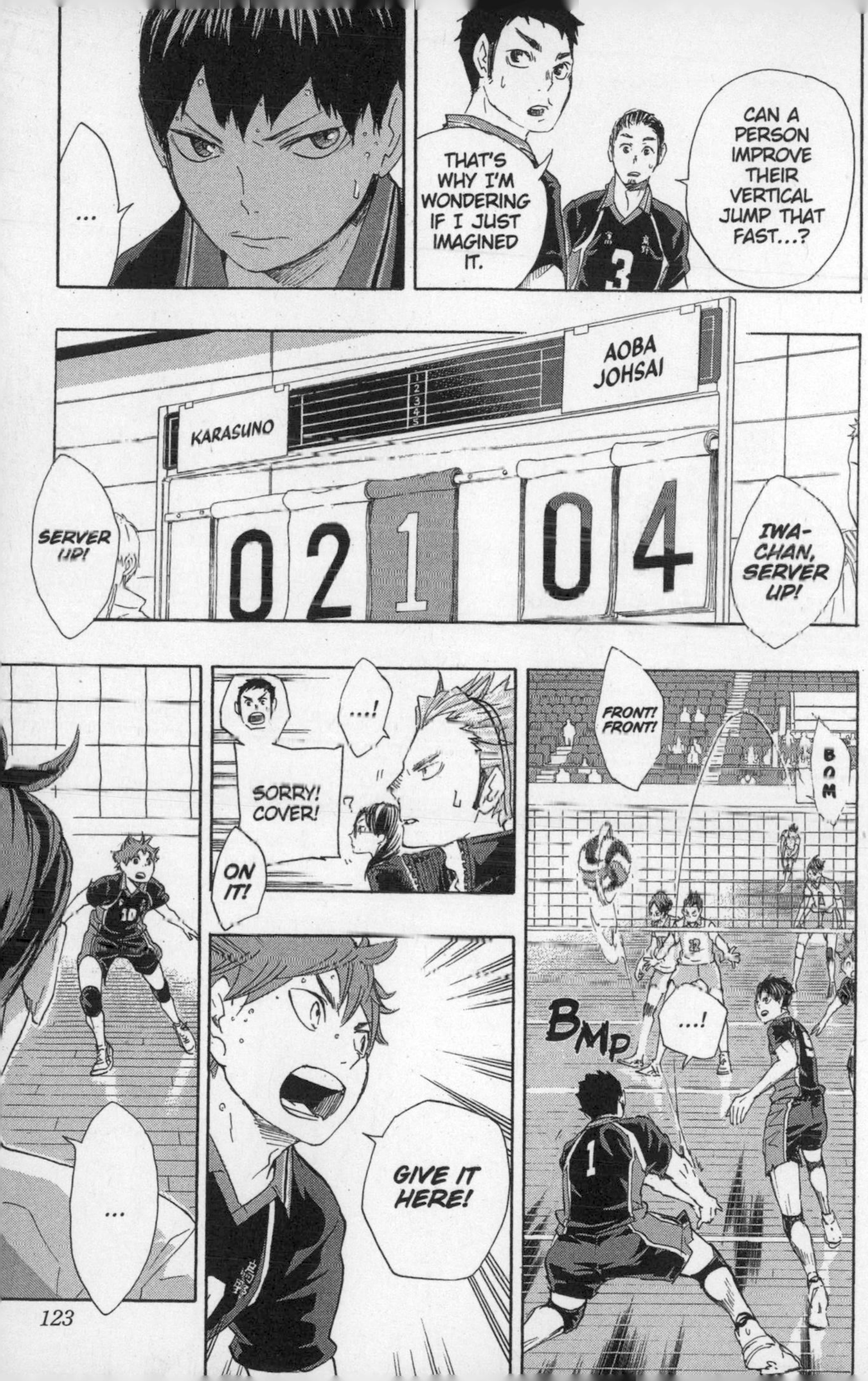
CAN A PERSON IMPROVE THEIR VERTICAL JUMP THAT FAST...?
THAT'S WHY I'M WONDERING IF I JUST IMAGINED IT.
...
AOBA JOHSAI
KARASUNO
02 1 04
IWA-CHAN, SERVER UP!
SERVER UP!
FRONT! FRONT!
BOM
BMP
...!
...!
SORRY! COVER!
ON IT!
GIVE IT HERE!
...

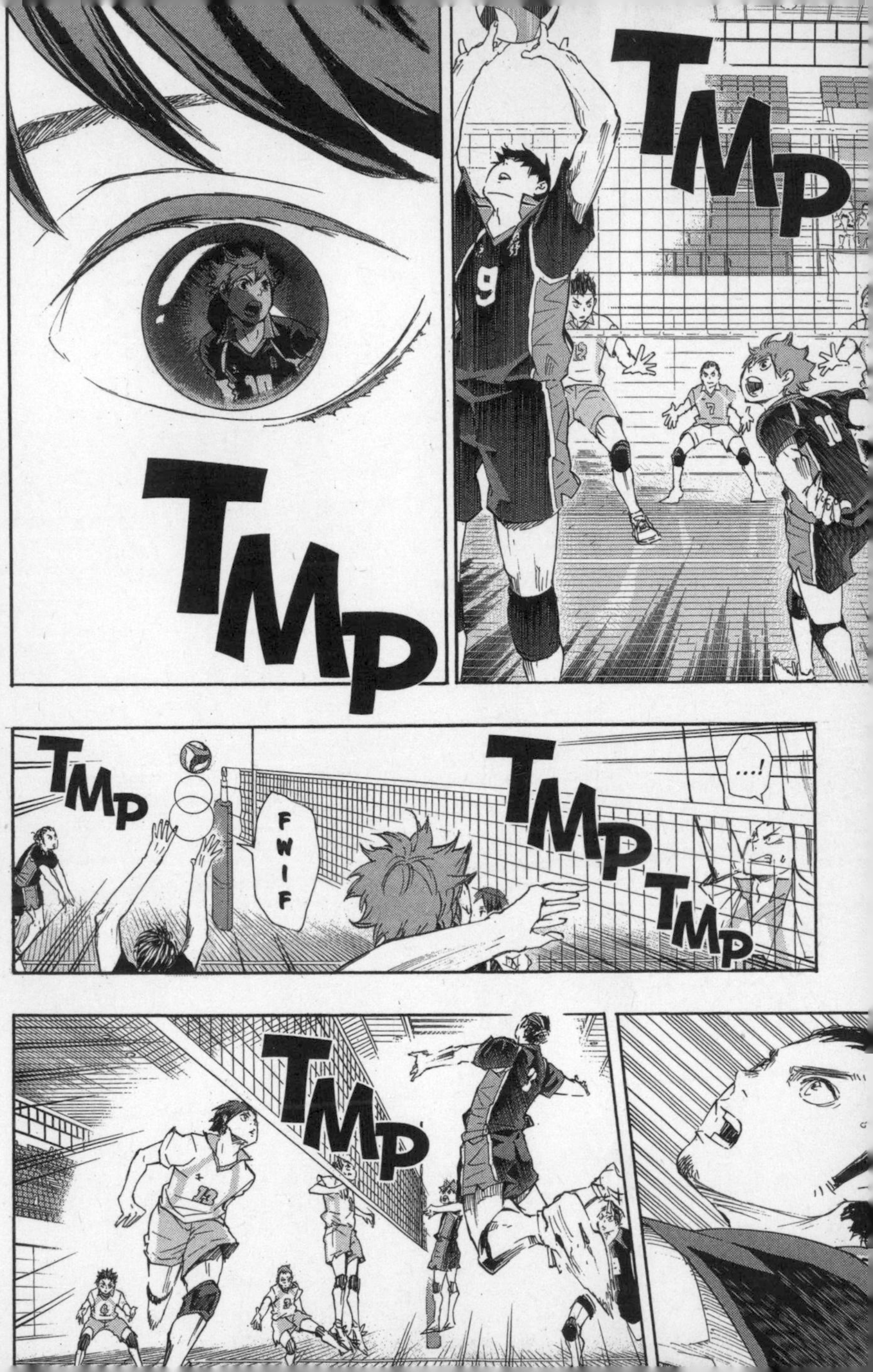

TMP
TMP
...!
TMP
TMP
TMP
TMP
FWIF
TMP

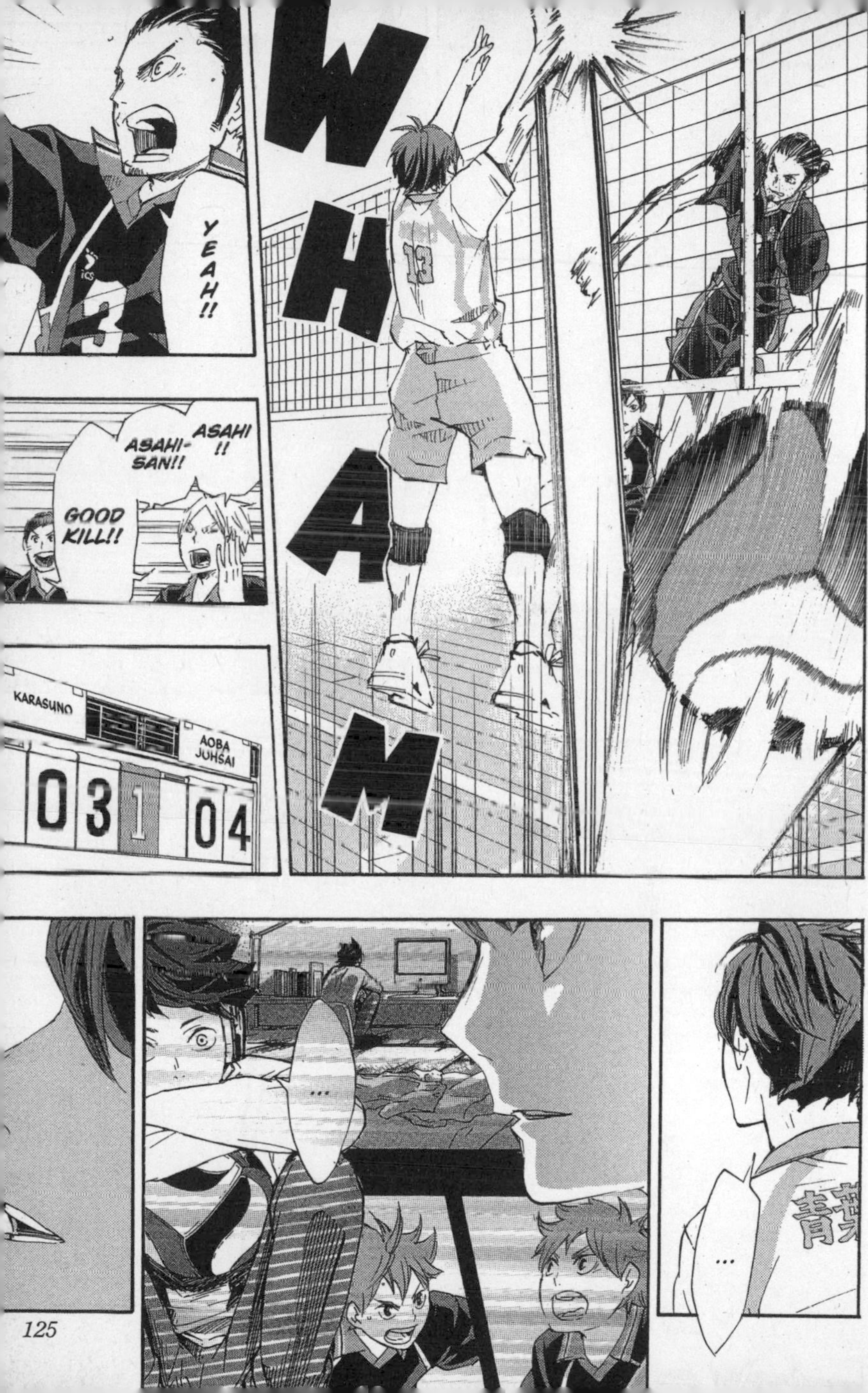
WHAM
YEAH!!
ASAHI!!
ASAHI-SAN!!
GOOD KILL!!
KARASUNO
AOBA JUHSAI
03 1 04
...
...

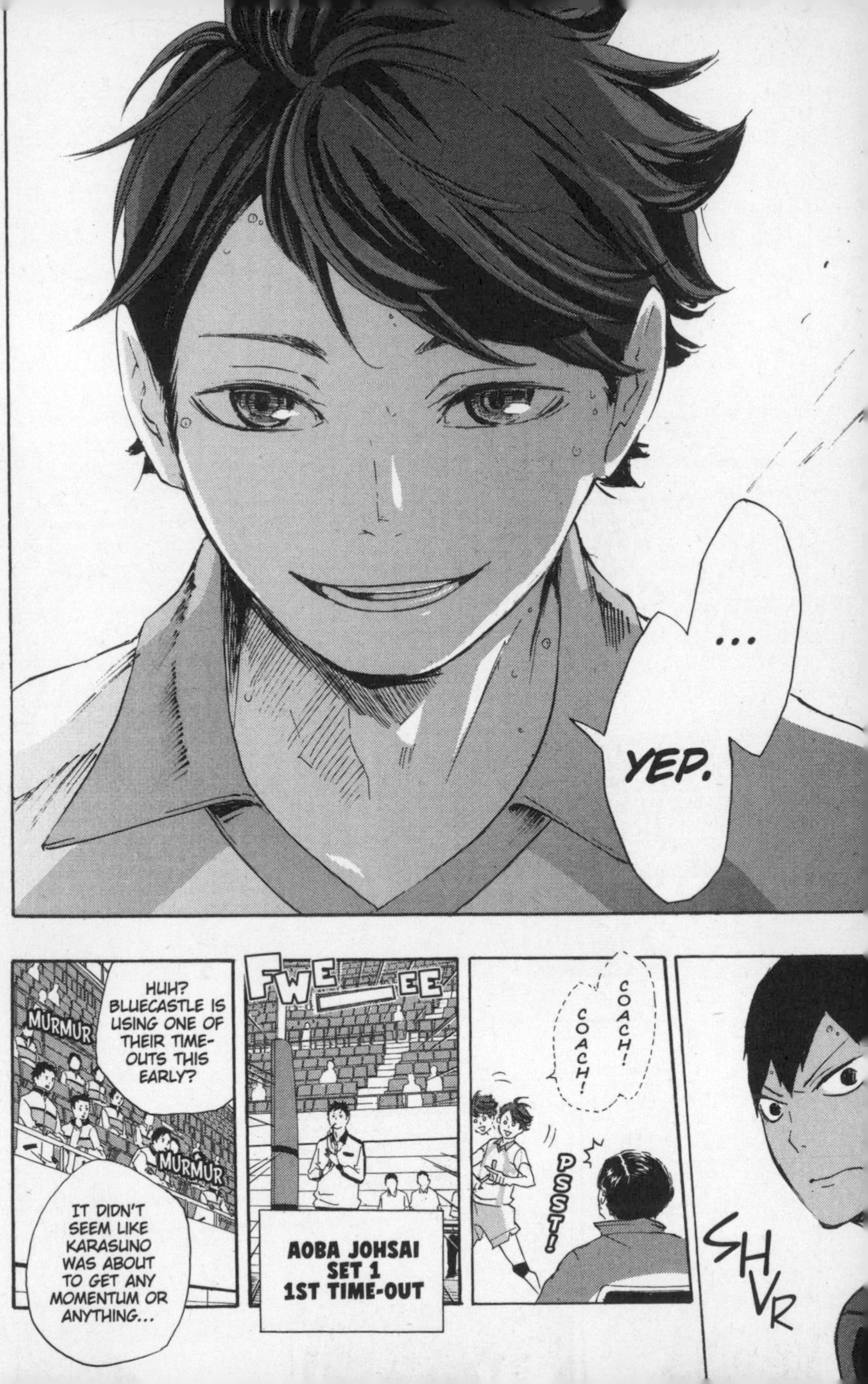
...
YEP.
SHVR
COACH!
COACH!
PSST!
FWE——EE
AOBA JOHSAI SET 1 1ST TIME-OUT
HUH? BLUECASTLE IS USING ONE OF THEIR TIME-OUTS THIS EARLY?
MURMUR
MURMUR
IT DIDN'T SEEM LIKE KARASUNO WAS ABOUT TO GET ANY MOMENTUM OR ANYTHING...

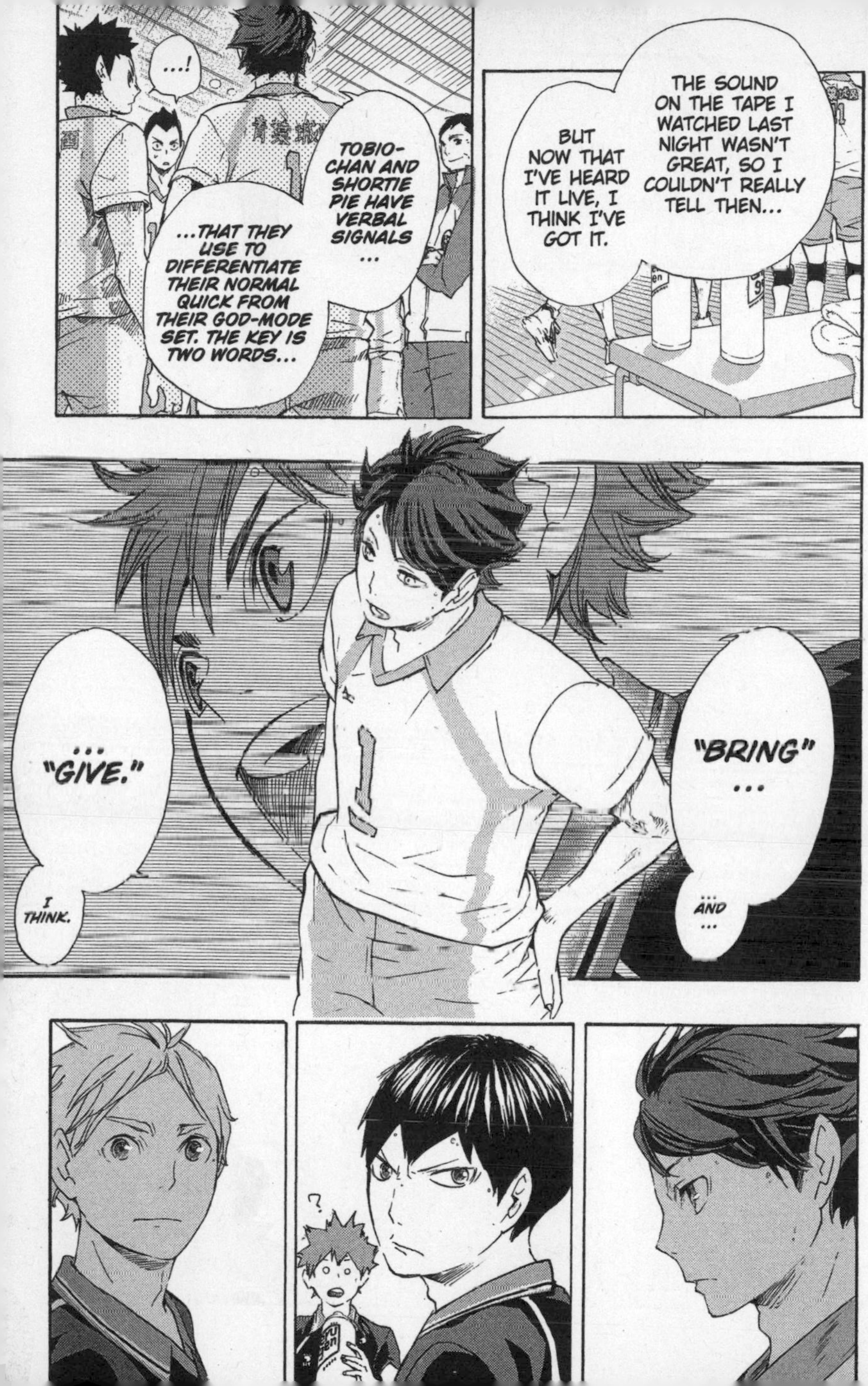

THE SOUND ON THE TAPE I WATCHED LAST NIGHT WASN'T GREAT, SO I COULDN'T REALLY TELL THEN...
BUT NOW THAT I'VE HEARD IT LIVE, I THINK I'VE GOT IT.
...!
TOBIO-CHAN AND SHORTIE PIE HAVE VERBAL SIGNALS...
...THAT THEY USE TO DIFFERENTIATE THEIR NORMAL QUICK FROM THEIR GOD-MODE SET. THE KEY IS TWO WORDS...
"BRING"...
...AND...
..."GIVE."
I THINK.
?

NOBUTERU IRIHATA

AOBA JOHSAI HIGH SCHOOL

VOLLEYBALL TEAM
HEAD COACH

AGE: 52

CURRENT WORRY:
HE'S STARTING TO GET A
BIT OF A BEER BELLY, BUT
DRINKING IS JUST TOO
GOOD TO GIVE UP.

SADAYUKI MIZOGUCHI

DATE TECHNICAL
HIGH SCHOOL

VOLLEYBALL TEAM
ASSISTANT COACH

AGE: 31

CURRENT WORRY:
HE CAUGHT HIMSELF
SAYING, "KIDS THESE
DAYS" ONCE. IT MADE
HIM FEEL REALLY OLD.

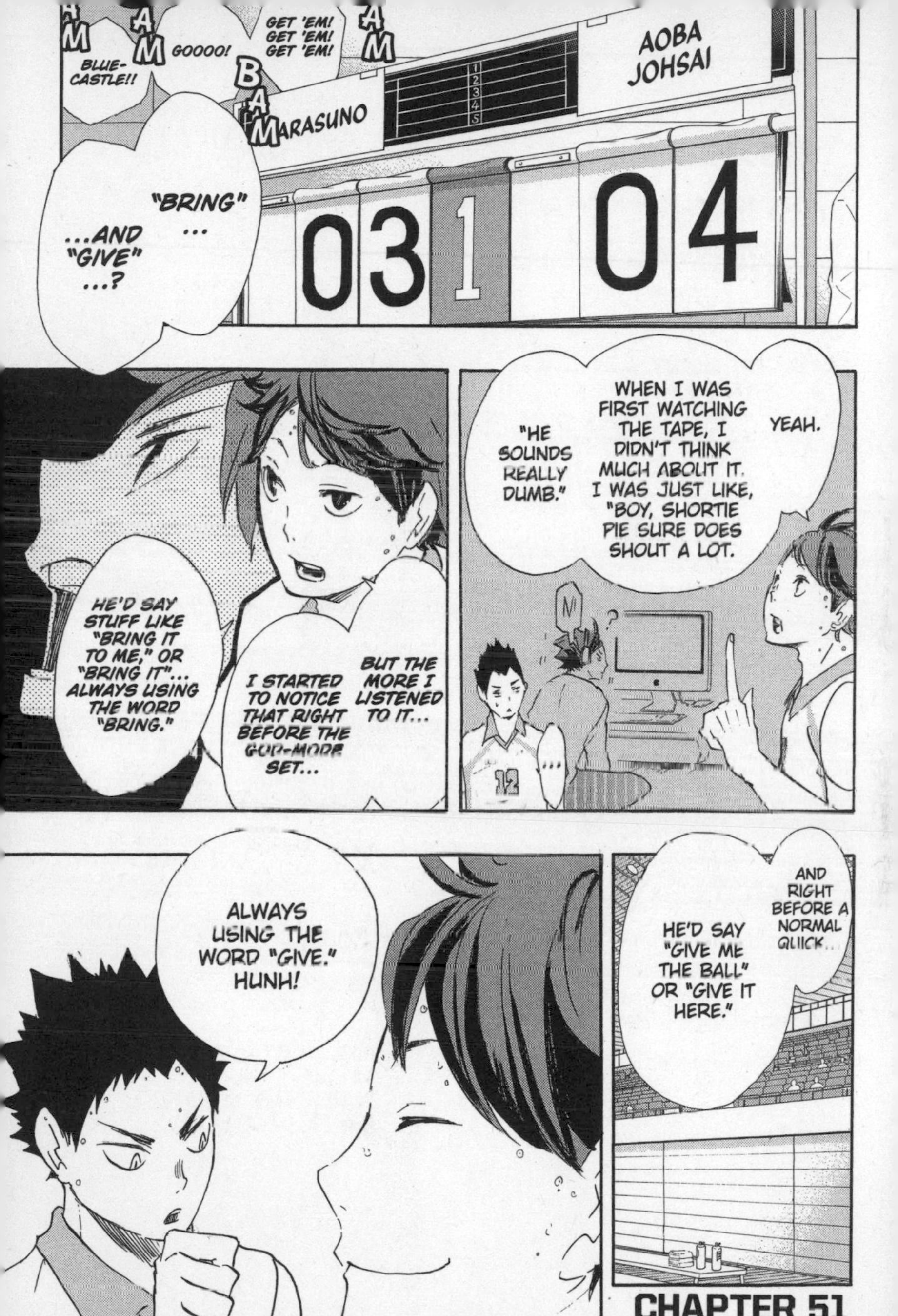
AOBA JOHSAI
GET 'EM! GET 'EM! GET 'EM!
BAM
GOOOO!
BLUE-CASTLE!!
BAM
KARASUNO
03
1
04
"BRING" ...
...AND "GIVE" ...?
YEAH.
WHEN I WAS FIRST WATCHING THE TAPE, I DIDN'T THINK MUCH ABOUT IT. I WAS JUST LIKE, "BOY, SHORTIE PIE SURE DOES SHOUT A LOT.
"HE SOUNDS REALLY DUMB."
BUT THE MORE I LISTENED TO IT...
I STARTED TO NOTICE THAT RIGHT BEFORE THE GOD-MODE SET...
HE'D SAY STUFF LIKE "BRING IT TO ME," OR "BRING IT"... ALWAYS USING THE WORD "BRING."
AND RIGHT BEFORE A NORMAL QUICK...
HE'D SAY "GIVE ME THE BALL" OR "GIVE IT HERE."
ALWAYS USING THE WORD "GIVE." HUNH!

CHAPTER 51

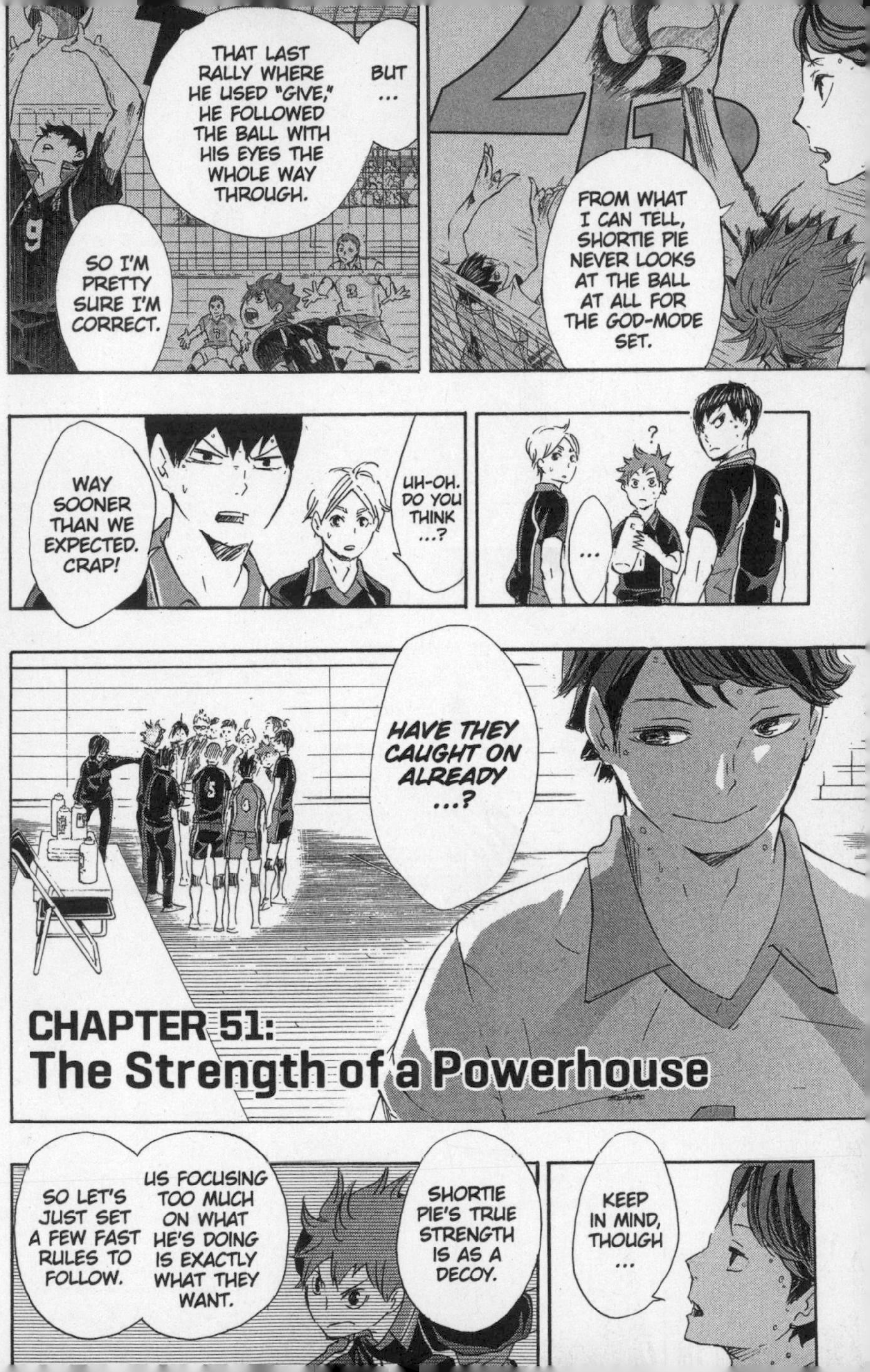
FROM WHAT I CAN TELL, SHORTIE PIE NEVER LOOKS AT THE BALL AT ALL FOR THE GOD-MODE SET.
BUT ...
THAT LAST RALLY WHERE HE USED "GIVE," HE FOLLOWED THE BALL WITH HIS EYES THE WHOLE WAY THROUGH.
SO I'M PRETTY SURE I'M CORRECT.
?
...
UH-OH. DO YOU THINK ...?
WAY SOONER THAN WE EXPECTED. CRAP!
HAVE THEY CAUGHT ON ALREADY ...?
CHAPTER 51:
The Strength of a Powerhouse
KEEP IN MIND, THOUGH ...
SHORTIE PIE'S TRUE STRENGTH IS AS A DECOY.
US FOCUSING TOO MUCH ON WHAT HE'S DOING IS EXACTLY WHAT THEY WANT.
SO LET'S JUST SET A FEW FAST RULES TO FOLLOW.

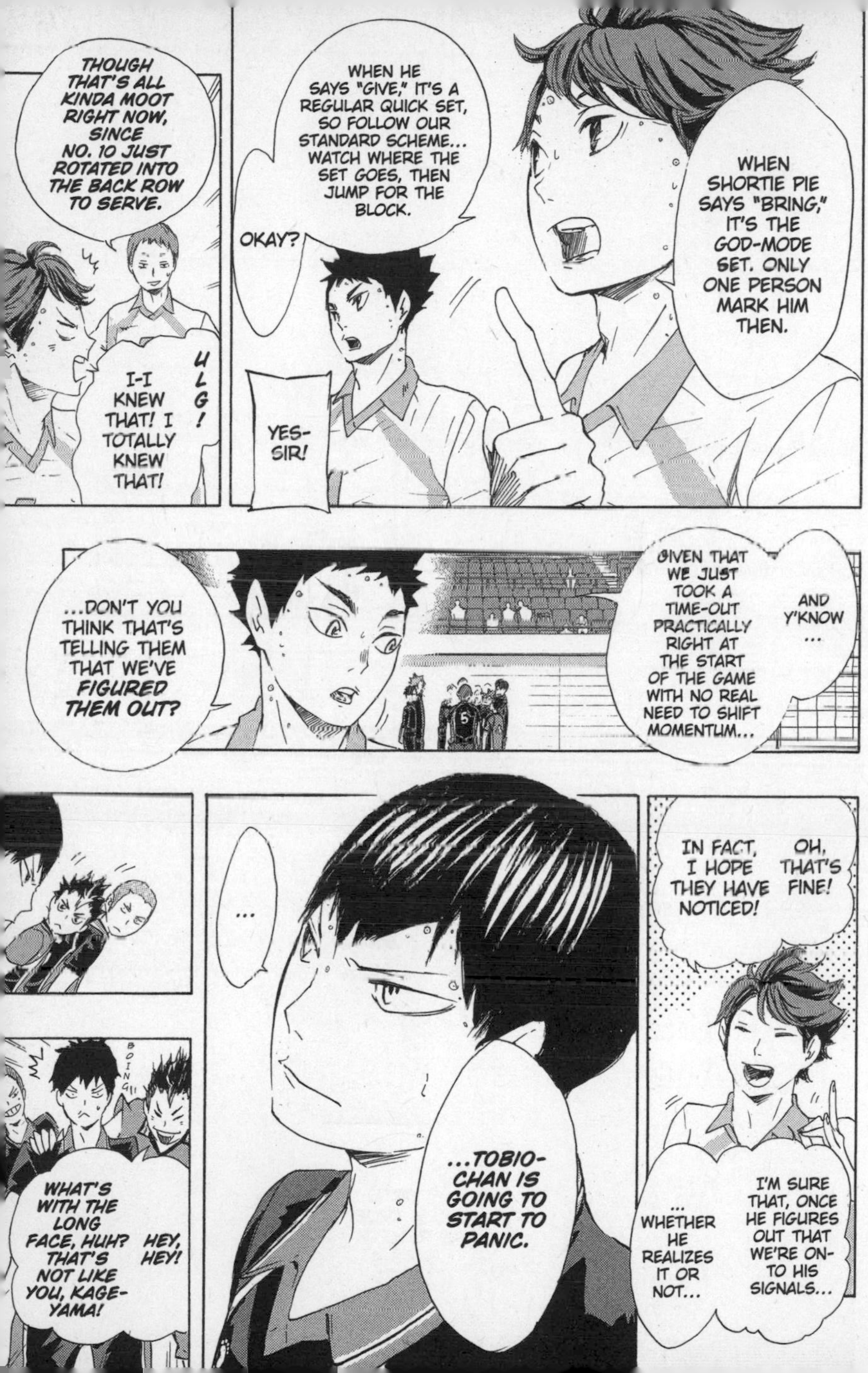
WHEN SHORTIE PIE SAYS "BRING," IT'S THE GOD-MODE SET. ONLY ONE PERSON MARK HIM THEN.
WHEN HE SAYS "GIVE," IT'S A REGULAR QUICK SET, SO FOLLOW OUR STANDARD SCHEME... WATCH WHERE THE SET GOES, THEN JUMP FOR THE BLOCK.
OKAY?
YES-SIR!
THOUGH THAT'S ALL KINDA MOOT RIGHT NOW, SINCE NO. 10 JUST ROTATED INTO THE BACK ROW TO SERVE.
ULG!
I-I KNEW THAT! I TOTALLY KNEW THAT!
AND Y'KNOW...
GIVEN THAT WE JUST TOOK A TIME-OUT PRACTICALLY RIGHT AT THE START OF THE GAME WITH NO REAL NEED TO SHIFT MOMENTUM...
...DON'T YOU THINK THAT'S TELLING THEM THAT WE'VE FIGURED THEM OUT?
OH, THAT'S FINE!
IN FACT, I HOPE THEY HAVE NOTICED!
I'M SURE THAT, ONCE HE FIGURES OUT THAT WE'RE ON-TO HIS SIGNALS...
...WHETHER HE REALIZES IT OR NOT...
...
...TOBIO-CHAN IS GOING TO START TO PANIC.
BOING
HEY, HEY!
WHAT'S WITH THE LONG FACE, HUH? THAT'S NOT LIKE YOU, KAGE-YAMA!

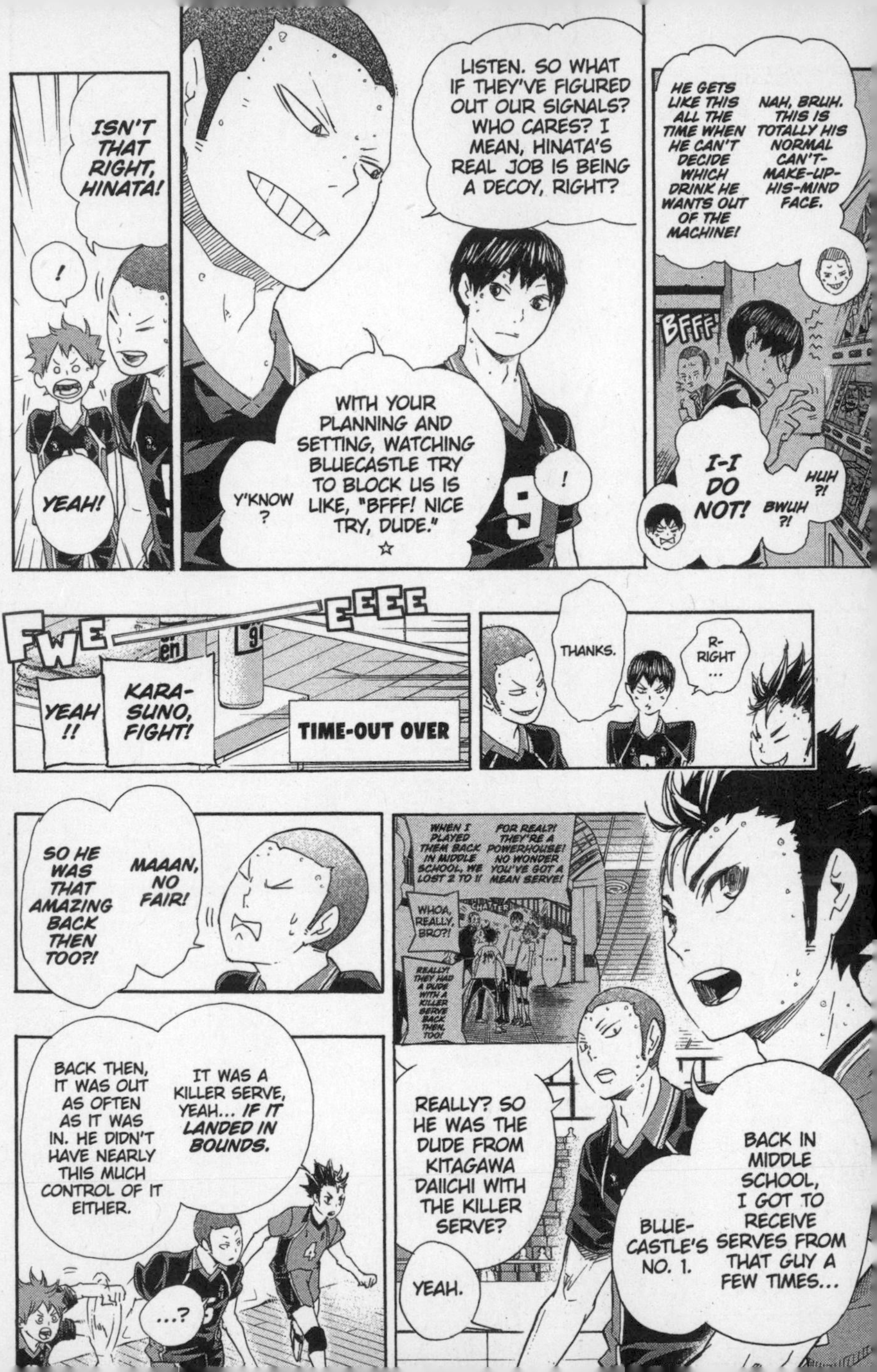
NAH, BRUH. THIS IS TOTALLY HIS NORMAL CAN'T-MAKE-UP-HIS-MIND FACE.
HE GETS LIKE THIS ALL THE TIME WHEN HE CAN'T DECIDE WHICH DRINK HE WANTS OUT OF THE MACHINE!
BFFF
I-I DO NOT!
HUH ?!
BWUH ?!
LISTEN. SO WHAT IF THEY'VE FIGURED OUT OUR SIGNALS? WHO CARES? I MEAN, HINATA'S REAL JOB IS BEING A DECOY, RIGHT?
WITH YOUR PLANNING AND SETTING, WATCHING BLUECASTLE TRY TO BLOCK US IS LIKE, "BFFF! NICE TRY, DUDE." ☆
Y'KNOW ?
!
ISN'T THAT RIGHT, HINATA!
!
YEAH!
R-RIGHT ...
THANKS.
FWEEEE
TIME-OUT OVER
KARA-SUNO, FIGHT!
YEAH !!
WHEN I PLAYED THEM BACK IN MIDDLE SCHOOL, WE LOST 2 TO 1!
FOR REAL?! THEY'RE A POWERHOUSE! NO WONDER YOU'VE GOT A MEAN SERVE!
WHOA, REALLY, BRO?!
CHATTER
REALLY! THEY HAD A DUDE WITH A KILLER SERVE BACK THEN, TOO!
...
MAAAN, NO FAIR!
SO HE WAS THAT AMAZING BACK THEN TOO?!
BACK IN MIDDLE SCHOOL, I GOT TO RECEIVE SERVES FROM THAT GUY A FEW TIMES...
BLUE-CASTLE'S NO. 1.
REALLY? SO HE WAS THE DUDE FROM KITAGAWA DAIICHI WITH THE KILLER SERVE?
YEAH.
IT WAS A KILLER SERVE, YEAH... IF IT LANDED IN BOUNDS.
BACK THEN, IT WAS OUT AS OFTEN AS IT WAS IN. HE DIDN'T HAVE NEARLY THIS MUCH CONTROL OF IT EITHER.
...?

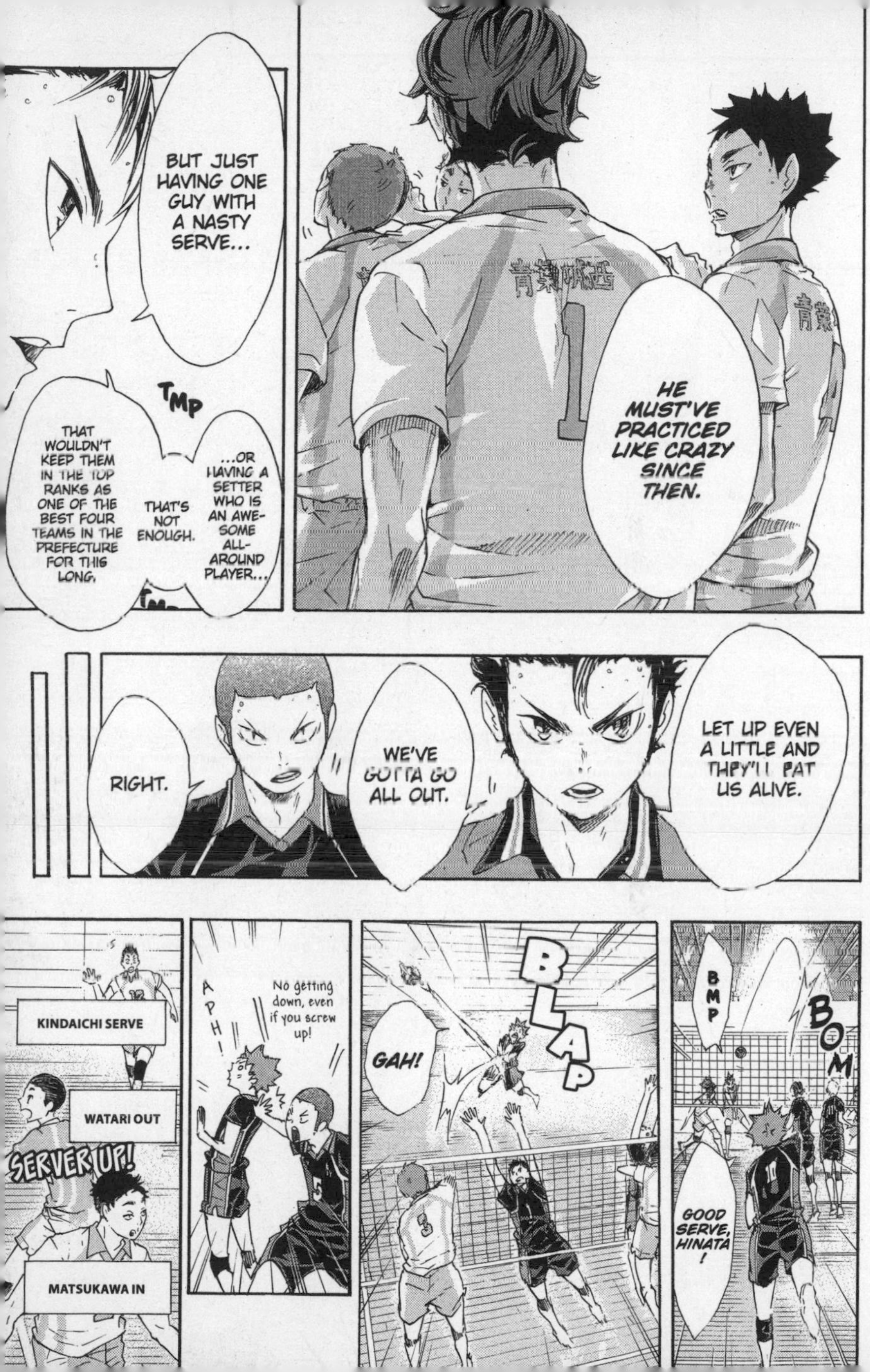
HE MUST'VE PRACTICED LIKE CRAZY SINCE THEN.
BUT JUST HAVING ONE GUY WITH A NASTY SERVE...
TMP
...OR HAVING A SETTER WHO IS AN AWESOME ALL-AROUND PLAYER...
THAT'S NOT ENOUGH.
THAT WOULDN'T KEEP THEM IN THE TOP RANKS AS ONE OF THE BEST FOUR TEAMS IN THE PREFECTURE FOR THIS LONG.
LET UP EVEN A LITTLE AND THEY'LL EAT US ALIVE.
WE'VE GOTTA GO ALL OUT.
RIGHT.
BMP
BOM
GOOD SERVE, HINATA!
BLAP
GAH!
APH!
No getting down, even if you screw up!
KINDAICHI SERVE
WATARI OUT
SERVER UP!
MATSUKAWA IN

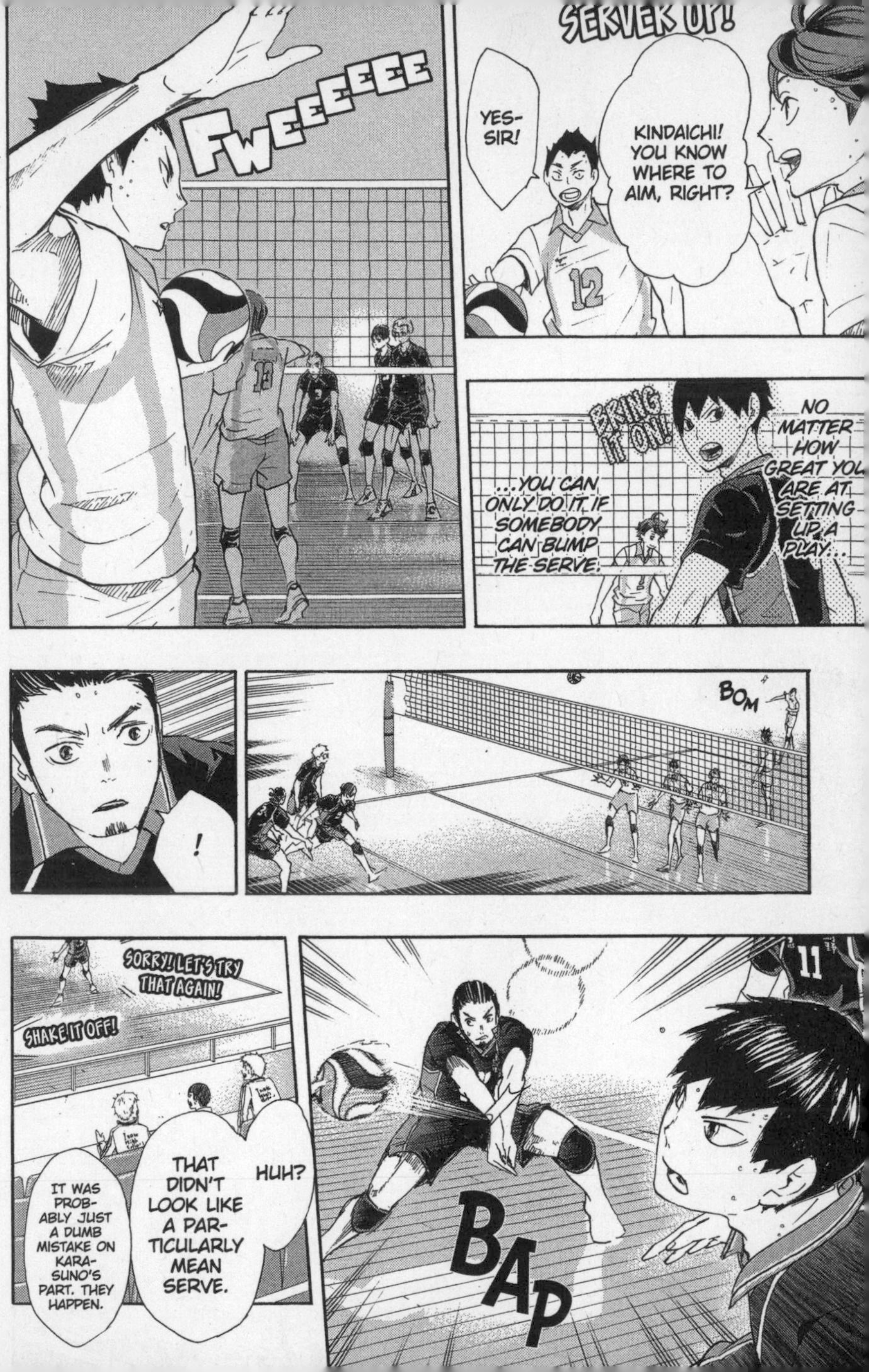
SERVER UP!
KINDAICHI! YOU KNOW WHERE TO AIM, RIGHT?
YES-SIR!
NO MATTER HOW GREAT YOU ARE AT SETTING UP A PLAY...
BRING IT ON!
...YOU CAN ONLY DO IT IF SOMEBODY CAN BUMP THE SERVE.
FWEEEEEE
BOM
!
BAP
SORRY! LET'S TRY THAT AGAIN!
SHAKE IT OFF!
HUH?
THAT DIDN'T LOOK LIKE A PAR-TICULARLY MEAN SERVE.
IT WAS PROB-ABLY JUST A DUMB MISTAKE ON KARA-SUNO'S PART. THEY HAPPEN.

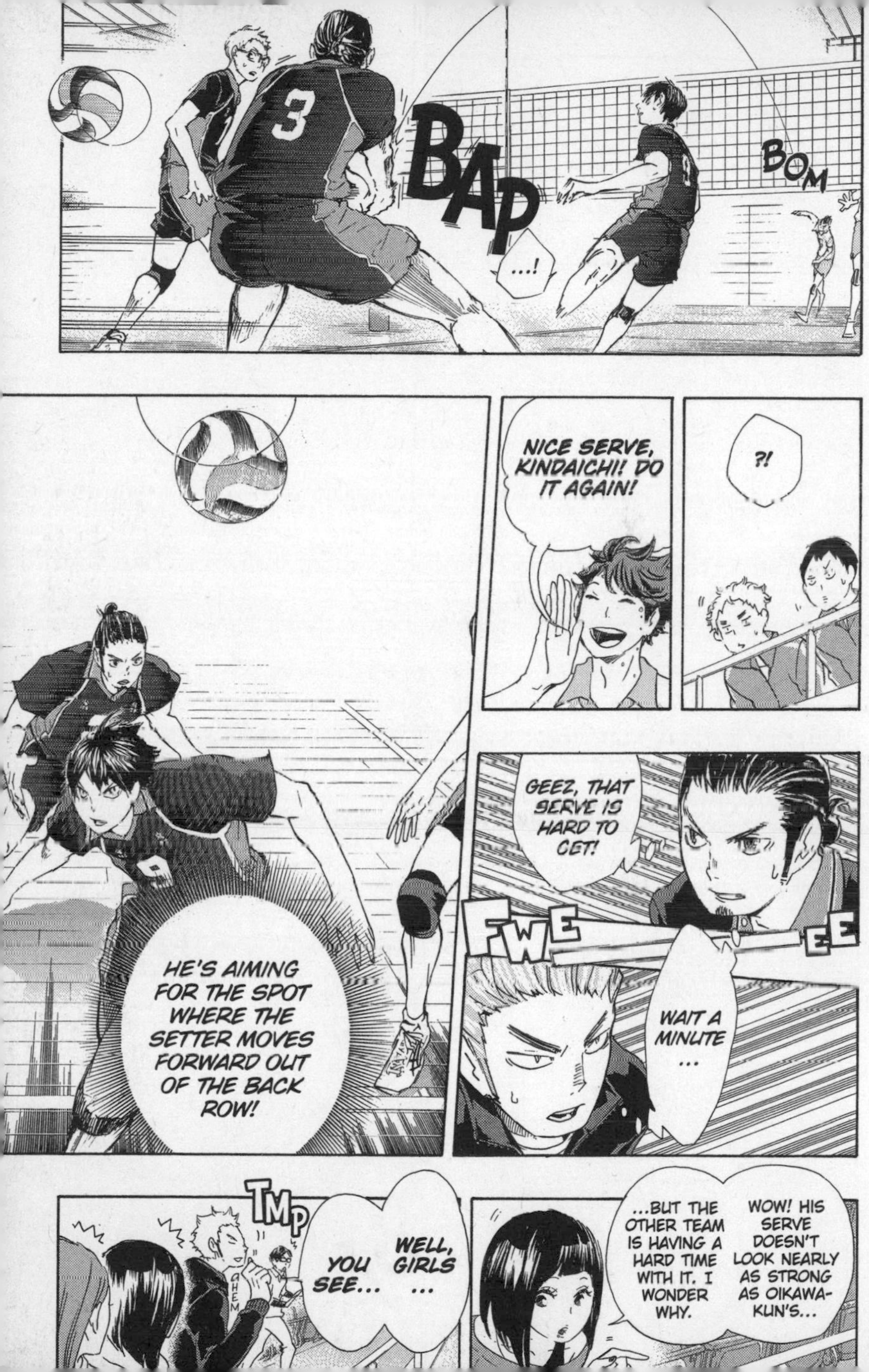
BOM
BAP
...!
?!
NICE SERVE, KINDAICHI! DO IT AGAIN!
GEEZ, THAT SERVE IS HARD TO GET!
FWEEE
WAIT A MINUTE ...
HE'S AIMING FOR THE SPOT WHERE THE SETTER MOVES FORWARD OUT OF THE BACK ROW!
WOW! HIS SERVE DOESN'T LOOK NEARLY AS STRONG AS OIKAWA-KUN'S...
...BUT THE OTHER TEAM IS HAVING A HARD TIME WITH IT. I WONDER WHY.
TMP
WELL, GIRLS ...
YOU SEE...
AHEM

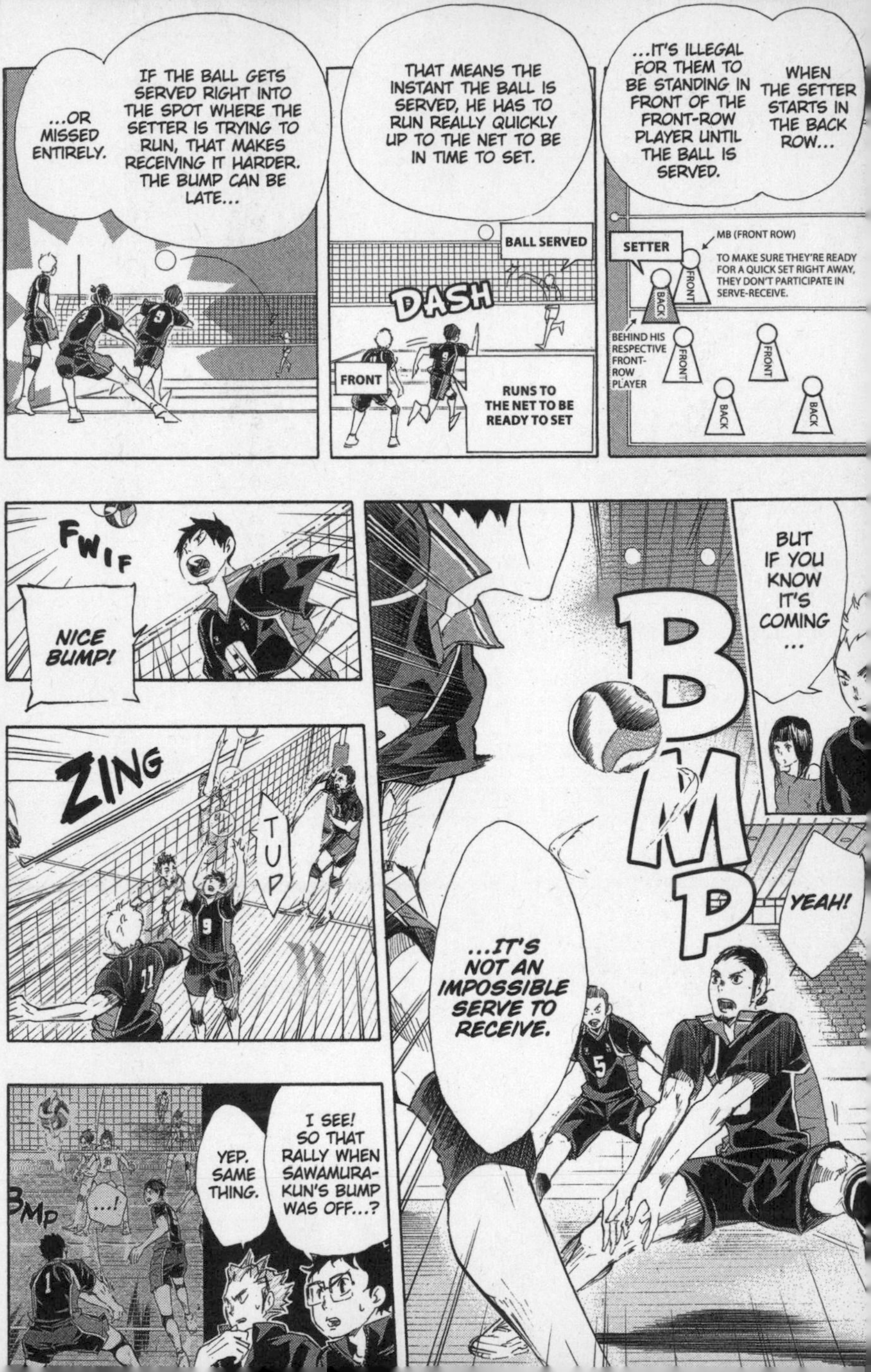
WHEN THE SETTER STARTS IN THE BACK ROW...
...IT'S ILLEGAL FOR THEM TO BE STANDING IN FRONT OF THE FRONT-ROW PLAYER UNTIL THE BALL IS SERVED.
MB (FRONT ROW)
TO MAKE SURE THEY'RE READY FOR A QUICK SET RIGHT AWAY, THEY DON'T PARTICIPATE IN SERVE-RECEIVE.
SETTER
FRONT
BACK
BEHIND HIS RESPECTIVE FRONT-ROW PLAYER
FRONT
FRONT
BACK
BACK
THAT MEANS THE INSTANT THE BALL IS SERVED, HE HAS TO RUN REALLY QUICKLY UP TO THE NET TO BE IN TIME TO SET.
BALL SERVED
DASH
FRONT
RUNS TO THE NET TO BE READY TO SET
IF THE BALL GETS SERVED RIGHT INTO THE SPOT WHERE THE SETTER IS TRYING TO RUN, THAT MAKES RECEIVING IT HARDER. THE BUMP CAN BE LATE...
...OR MISSED ENTIRELY.
BUT IF YOU KNOW IT'S COMING...
BMP
YEAH!
...IT'S NOT AN IMPOSSIBLE SERVE TO RECEIVE.
FWIF
NICE BUMP!
ZING
TUP
I SEE! SO THAT RALLY WHEN SAWAMURA-KUN'S BUMP WAS OFF...?
YEP. SAME THING.
...!
BMP

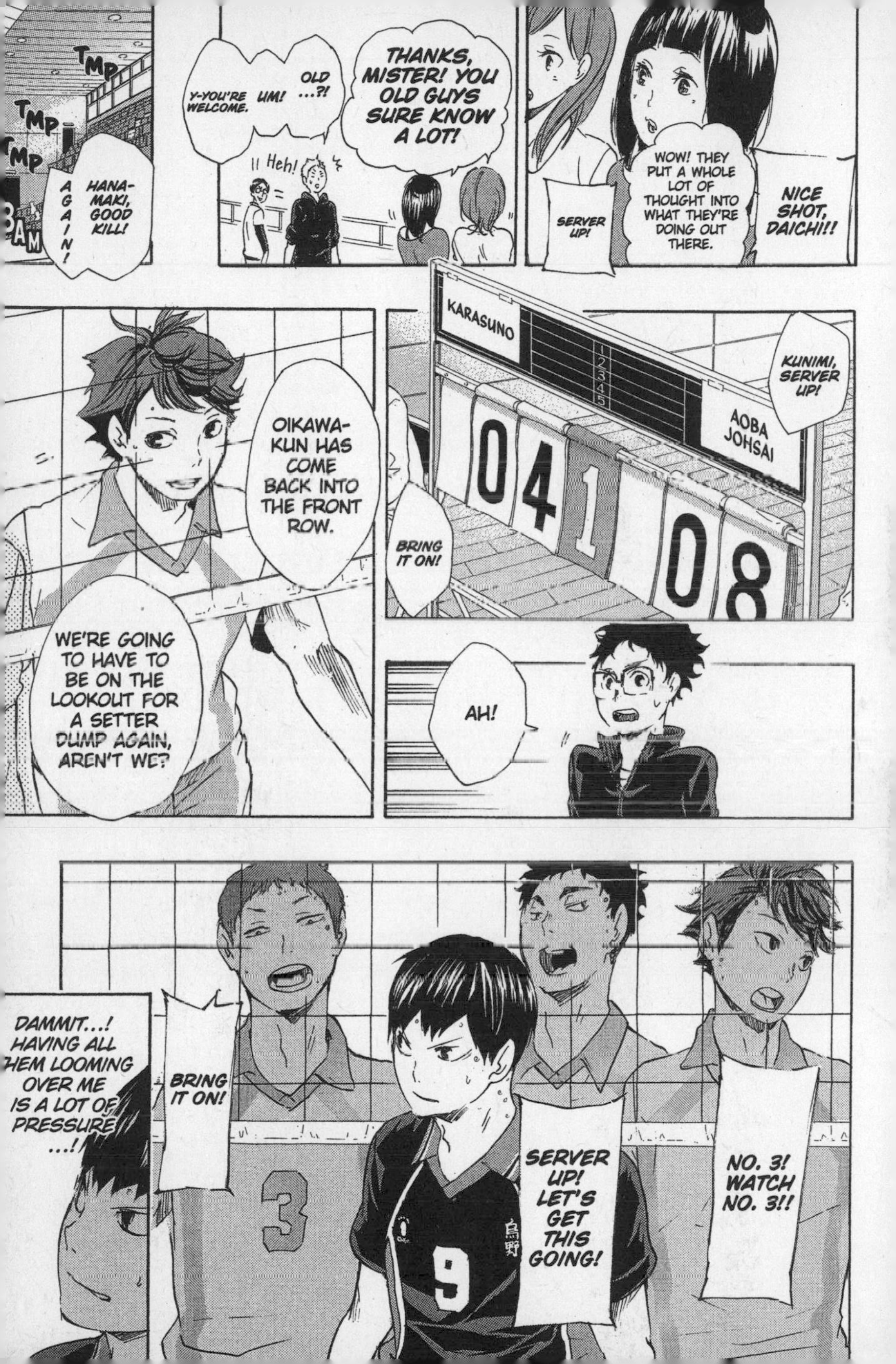
NICE SHOT, DAICHI!!
WOW! THEY PUT A WHOLE LOT OF THOUGHT INTO WHAT THEY'RE DOING OUT THERE.
SERVER UP!
THANKS, MISTER! YOU OLD GUYS SURE KNOW A LOT!
OLD ...?!
UM!
Y-YOU'RE WELCOME.
Heh!
TMP
TMP
TMP
BAM
HANA-MAKI, GOOD KILL!
AGAIN!
KUNIMI, SERVER UP!
KARASUNO
AOBA JOHSAI
04 1 08
BRING IT ON!
AH!
OIKAWA-KUN HAS COME BACK INTO THE FRONT ROW.
WE'RE GOING TO HAVE TO BE ON THE LOOKOUT FOR A SETTER DUMP AGAIN, AREN'T WE?
NO. 3! WATCH NO. 3!!
SERVER UP! LET'S GET THIS GOING!
BRING IT ON!
DAMMIT...! HAVING ALL THEM LOOMING OVER ME IS A LOT OF PRESSURE...!

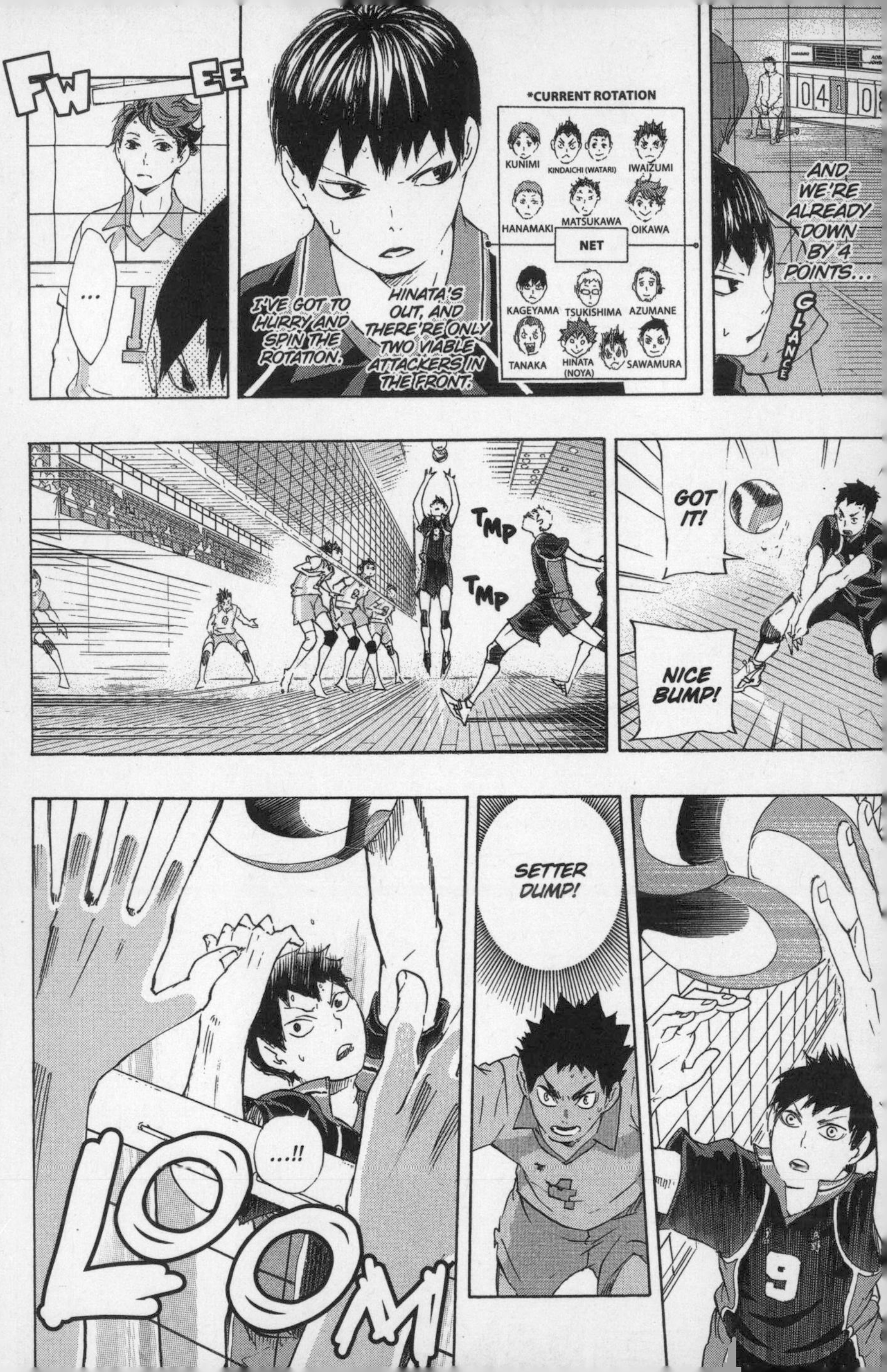
AND WE'RE ALREADY DOWN BY 4 POINTS...
GLANCE
*CURRENT ROTATION
KUNIMI
KINDAICHI (WATARI)
IWAIZUMI
HANAMAKI
MATSUKAWA
OIKAWA
NET
KAGEYAMA
TSUKISHIMA
AZUMANE
TANAKA
HINATA (NOYA)
SAWAMURA
HINATA'S OUT, AND THERE'RE ONLY TWO VIABLE ATTACKERS IN THE FRONT.
I'VE GOT TO HURRY AND SPIN THE ROTATION.
FWEE
...
GOT IT!
NICE BUMP!
TMP
TMP
SETTER DUMP!
...!!
LOOM

RRRGH!!

SWAT

Nice block!

THERE'S NOTHING EASIER TO BLOCK THAN A TELEGRAPHED SETTER DUMP.

SORRY ...!!

IT'S OKAY, IT'S OKAY! RELAX AND TAKE A DEEP BREATH. EASY DOES IT!

NICE PASS!

FRONT! FRONT!

TUMP

KARASUNO	AOBA JOHSAI
5	10

...

...

...

GOOD ONE, TSUKISHIMA!

KARASUNO	AOBA JOHSAI
5	9

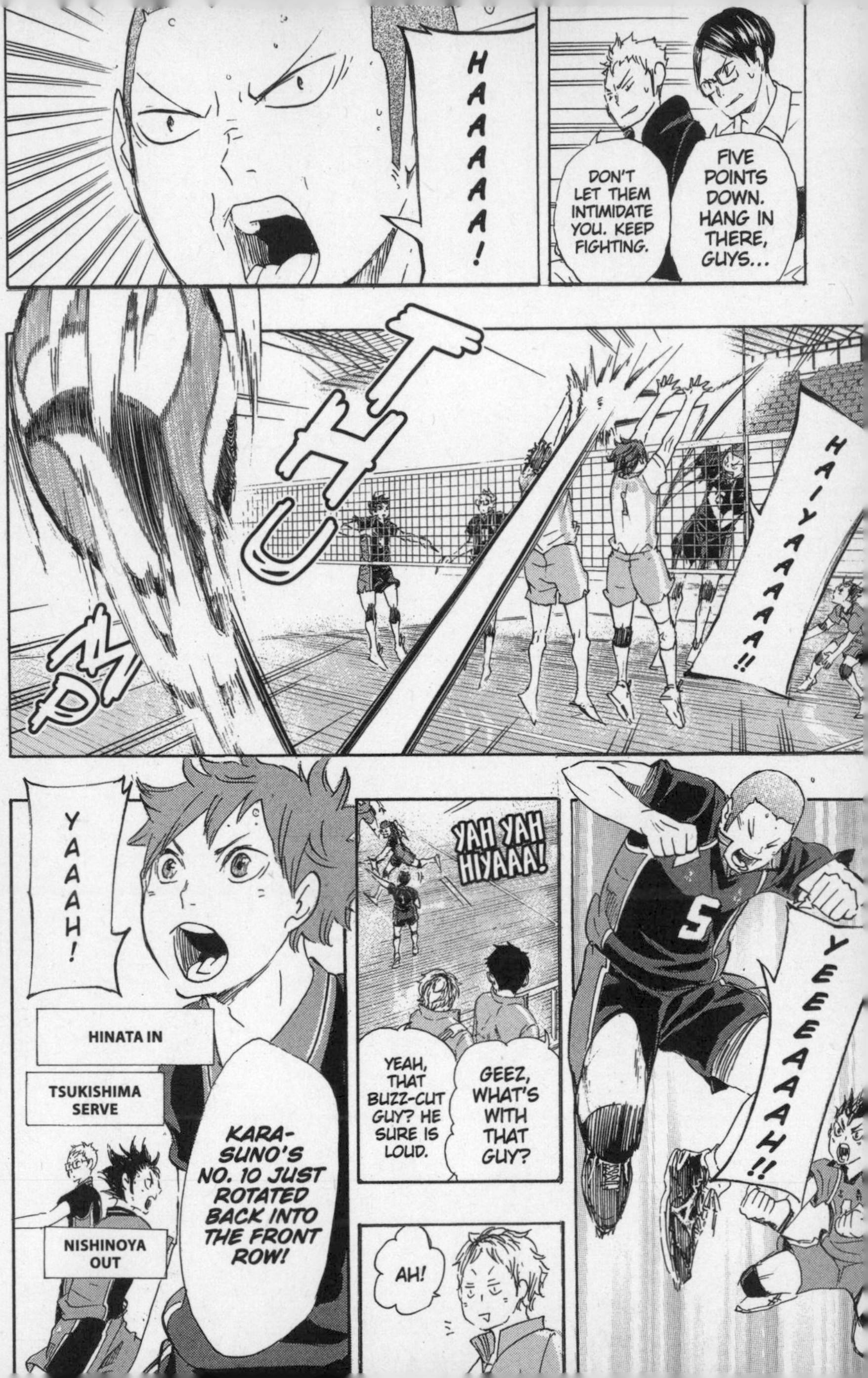
FIVE POINTS DOWN. HANG IN THERE, GUYS...
DON'T LET THEM INTIMIDATE YOU. KEEP FIGHTING.
HAAAAAA!
HAIYAAAAAAA!!
THUMP
YEEEAAAAH!!
YAH YAH HIYAAA!
GEEZ, WHAT'S WITH THAT GUY?
YEAH, THAT BUZZ-CUT GUY? HE SURE IS LOUD.
AH!
YAAAAH!
HINATA IN
TSUKISHIMA SERVE
KARA-SUNO'S NO. 10 JUST ROTATED BACK INTO THE FRONT ROW!
NISHINOYA OUT

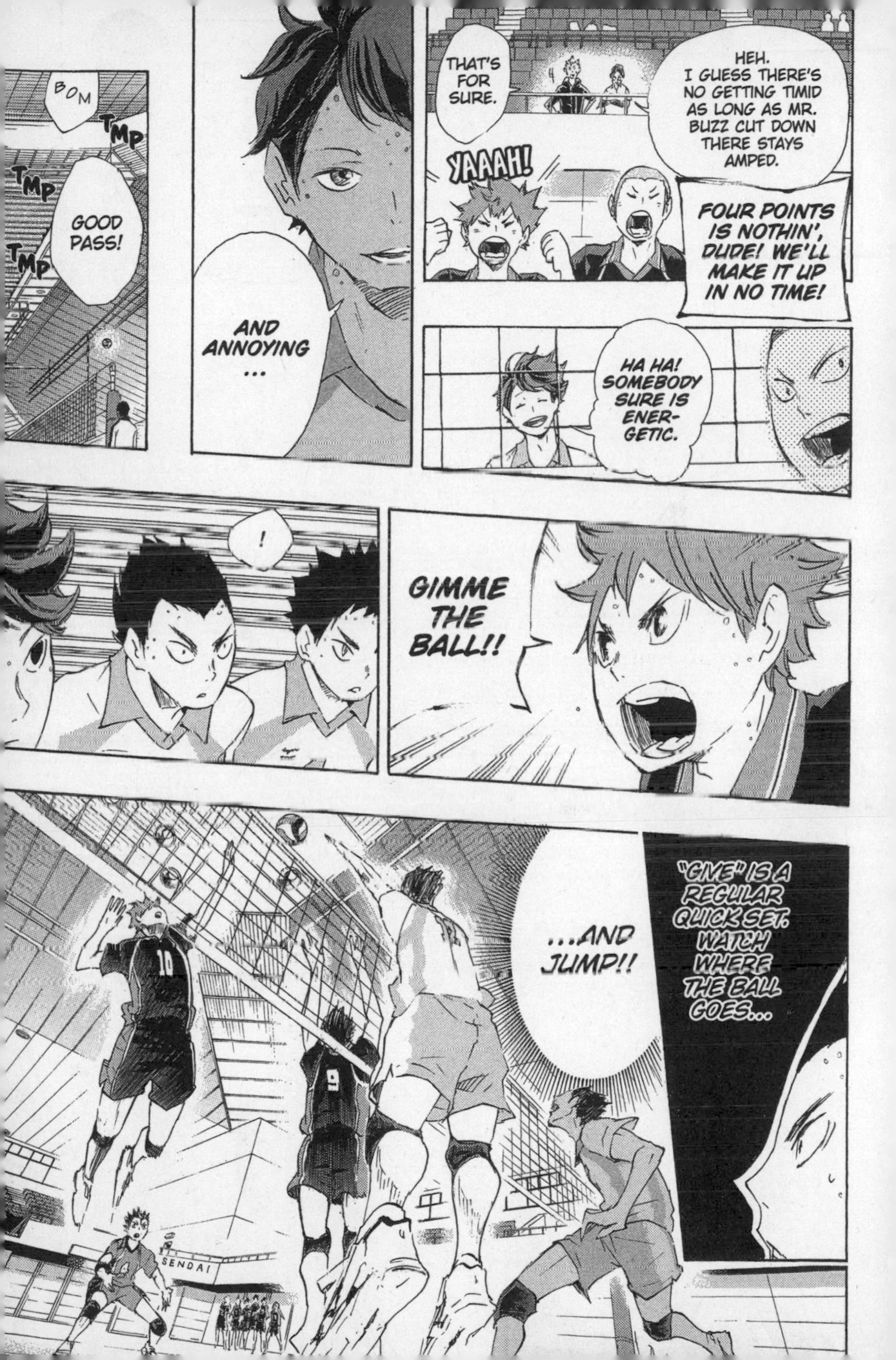
HEH. I GUESS THERE'S NO GETTING TIMID AS LONG AS MR. BUZZ CUT DOWN THERE STAYS AMPED.
THAT'S FOR SURE.
YAAAH!
FOUR POINTS IS NOTHIN', DUDE! WE'LL MAKE IT UP IN NO TIME!
HA HA! SOMEBODY SURE IS ENER-GETIC.
AND ANNOYING...
BOM
TMP
TMP
TMP
GOOD PASS!
GIMME THE BALL!!
!
"GIVE" IS A REGULAR QUICK SET. WATCH WHERE THE BALL GOES...
...AND JUMP!!
10
9
SENDAI

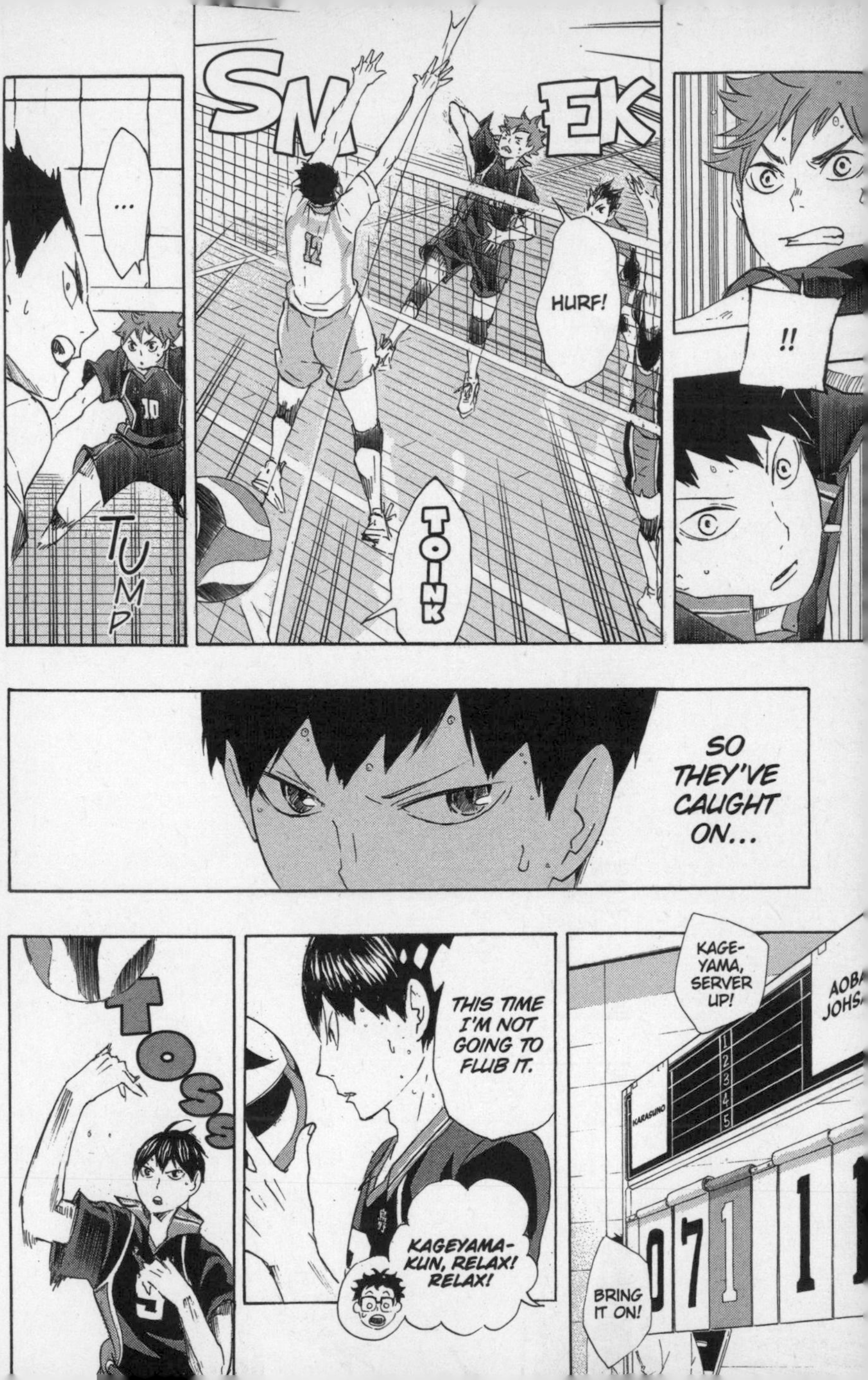
!!
SMEK
HURF!
TOINK
...
TUMP
SO THEY'VE CAUGHT ON...
KAGE-YAMA, SERVER UP!
BRING IT ON!
KARASUNO
THIS TIME I'M NOT GOING TO FLUB IT.
KAGEYAMA-KUN, RELAX! RELAX!
TOSS

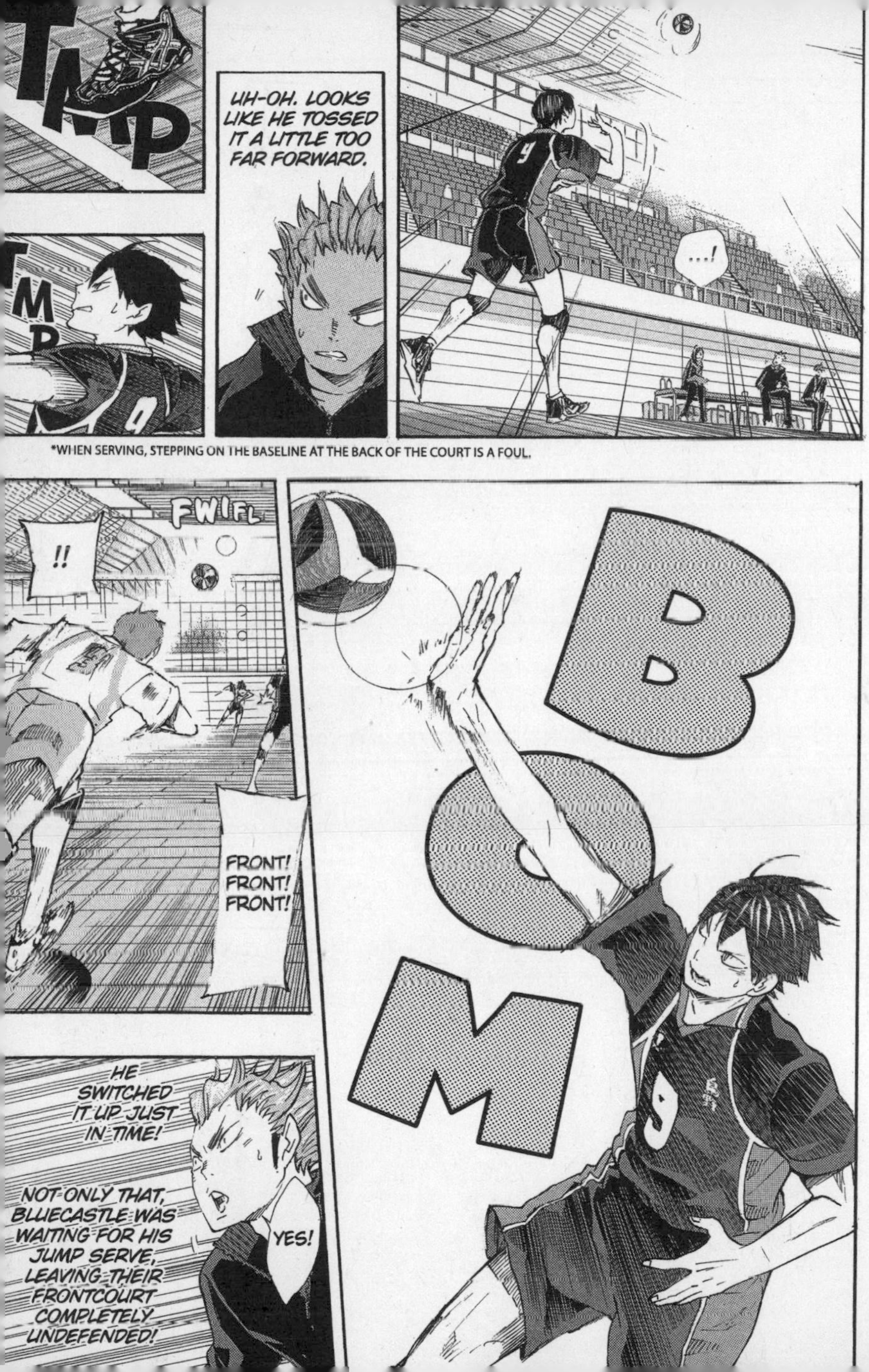
...!
UH-OH. LOOKS LIKE HE TOSSED IT A LITTLE TOO FAR FORWARD.
TMP
TMP
BOOM
FWIFL
!!
FRONT! FRONT! FRONT!
HE SWITCHED IT UP JUST IN TIME!
NOT ONLY THAT, BLUECASTLE WAS WAITING FOR HIS JUMP SERVE, LEAVING THEIR FRONTCOURT COMPLETELY UNDEFENDED!
YES!

*WHEN SERVING, STEPPING ON THE BASELINE AT THE BACK OF THE COURT IS A FOUL.

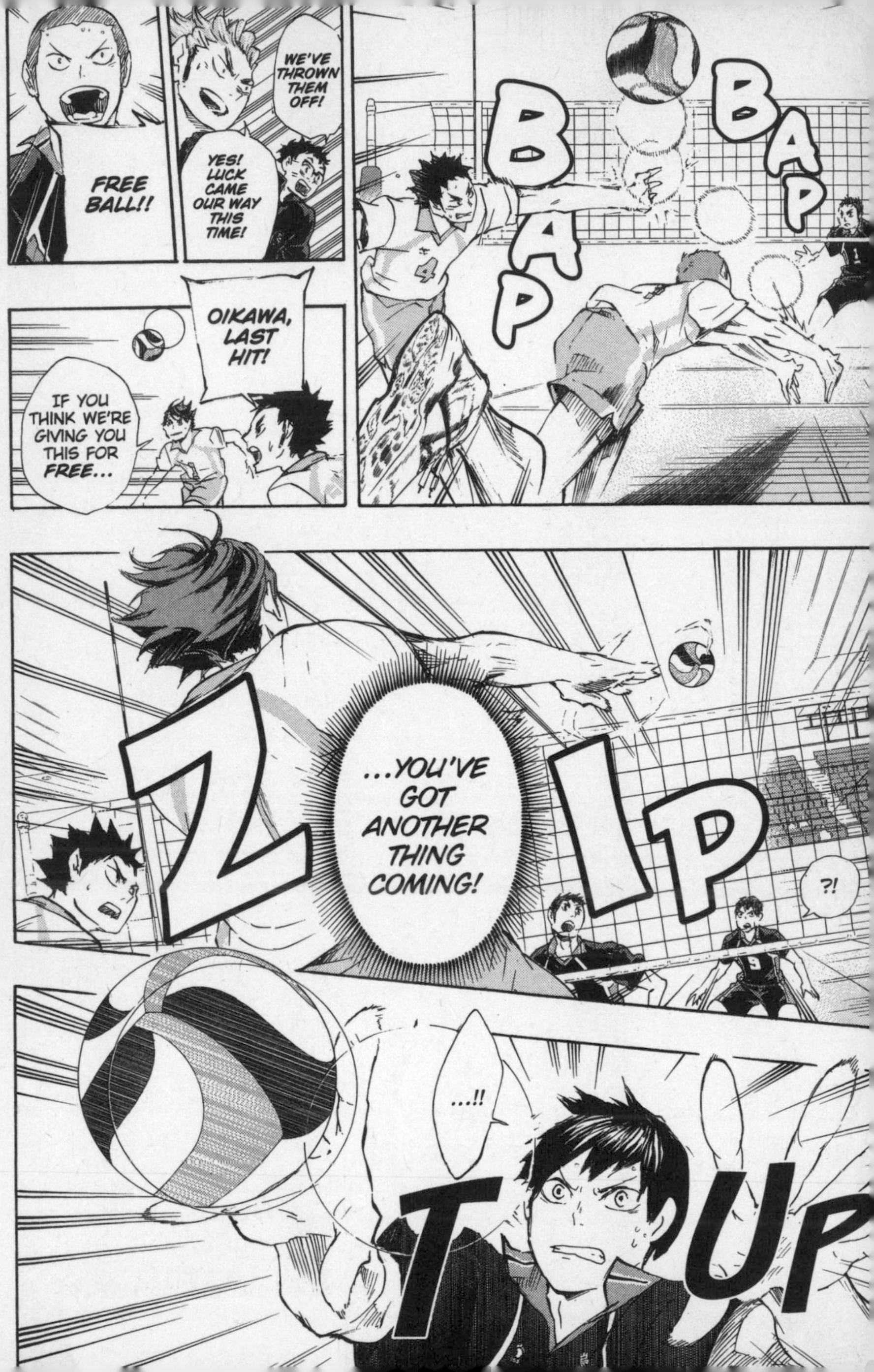

BAP
BAP
WE'VE THROWN THEM OFF!
YES! LUCK CAME OUR WAY THIS TIME!
FREE BALL!!
OIKAWA, LAST HIT!
IF YOU THINK WE'RE GIVING YOU THIS FOR FREE...
...YOU'VE GOT ANOTHER THING COMING!
ZIP
?!
...!!
TUP

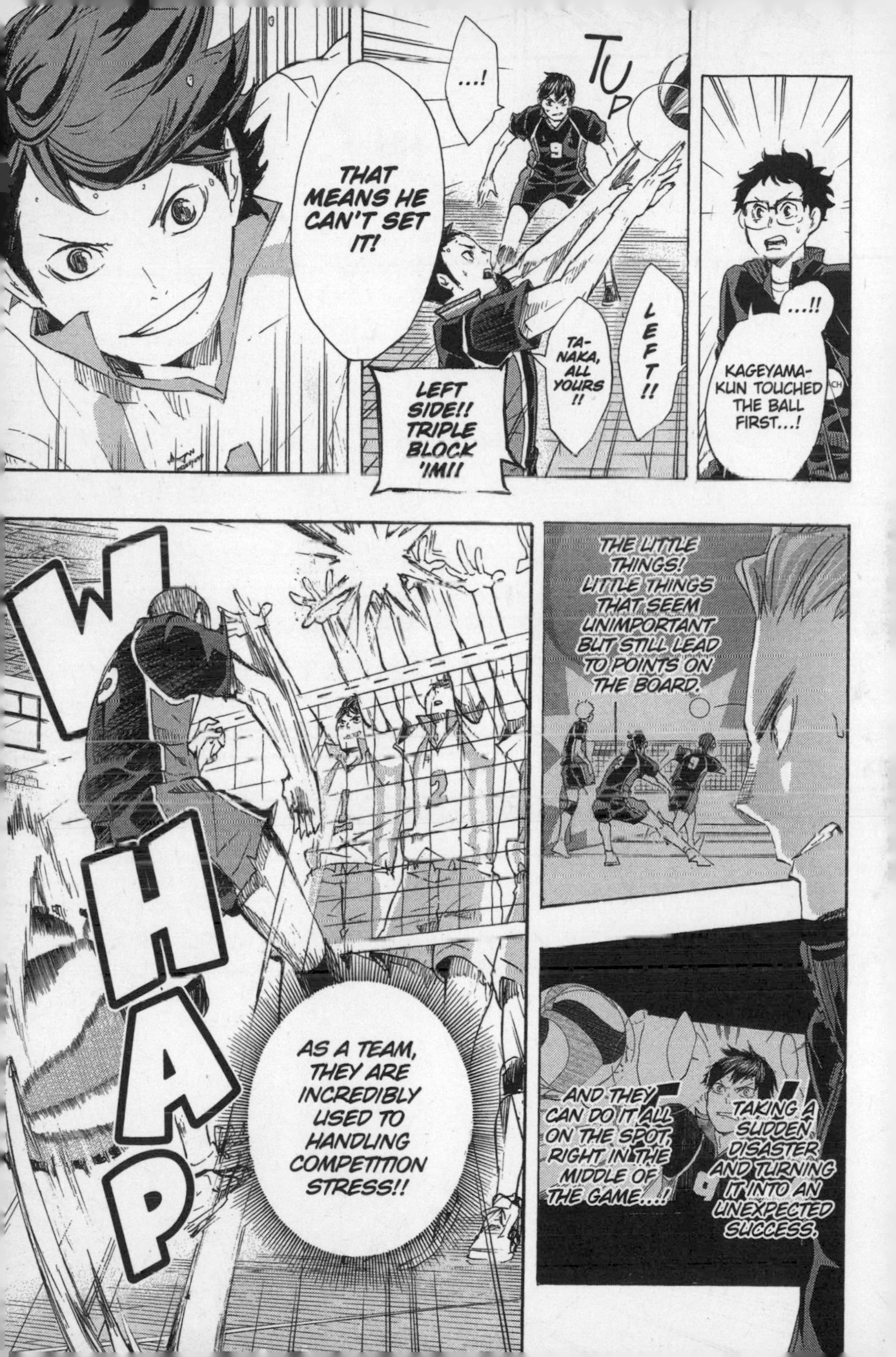
...!!
KAGEYAMA-KUN TOUCHED THE BALL FIRST...!
TUP
...!
LEFT!!
TA-NAKA, ALL YOURS!!
LEFT SIDE!! TRIPLE BLOCK 'IM!!
THAT MEANS HE CAN'T SET IT!
THE LITTLE THINGS! LITTLE THINGS THAT SEEM UNIMPORTANT BUT STILL LEAD TO POINTS ON THE BOARD.
TAKING A SUDDEN DISASTER AND TURNING IT INTO AN UNEXPECTED SUCCESS.
AND THEY CAN DO IT ALL ON THE SPOT, RIGHT IN THE MIDDLE OF THE GAME...!
WHAP
AS A TEAM, THEY ARE INCREDIBLY USED TO HANDLING COMPETITION STRESS!!

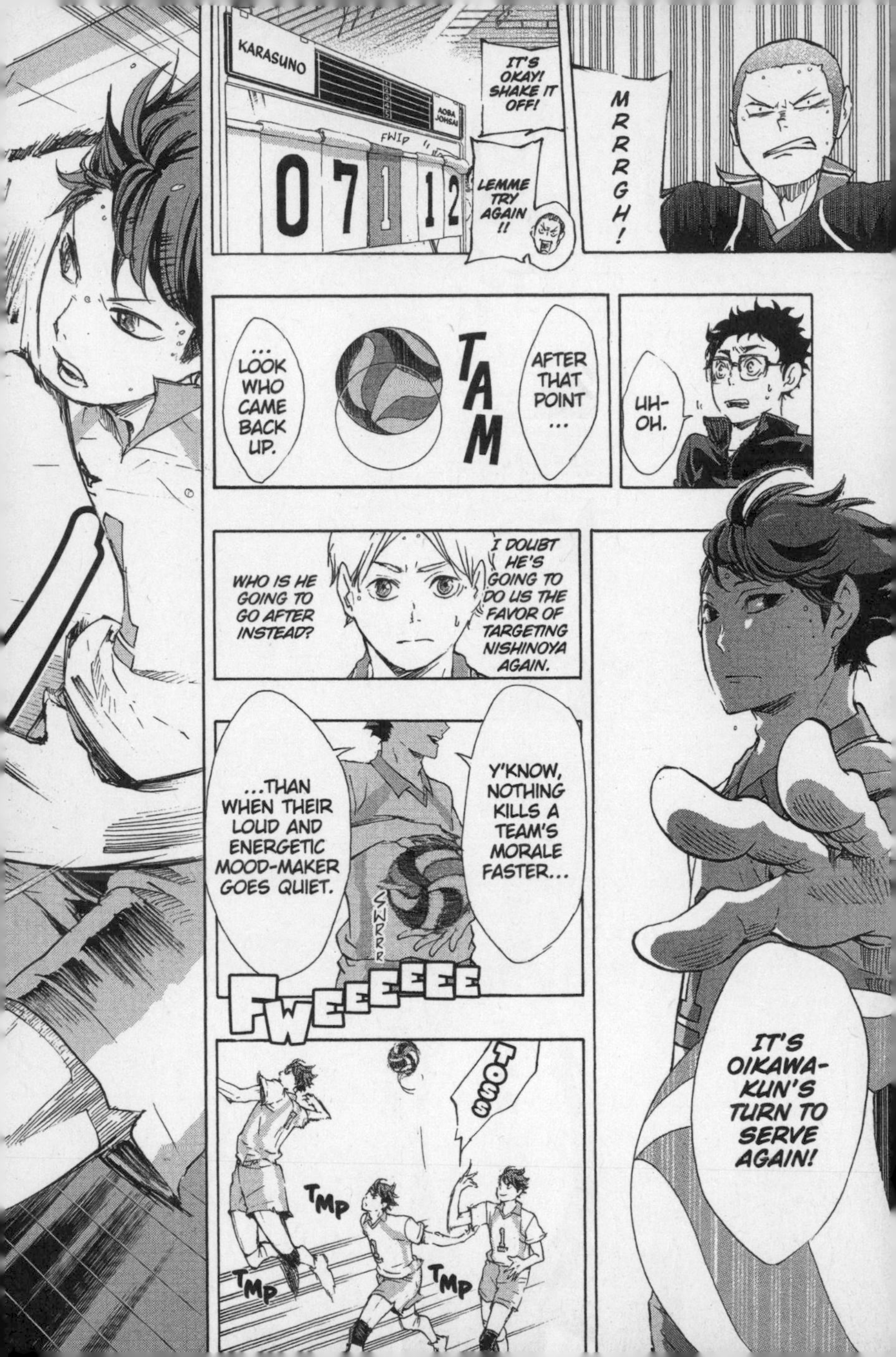
MRRRGH!
KARASUNO
AOBA JOHSAI
0 7 1 12
FWIP
IT'S OKAY! SHAKE IT OFF!
LEMME TRY AGAIN!!
UH-OH.
AFTER THAT POINT...
TAM
...LOOK WHO CAME BACK UP.
IT'S OIKAWA-KUN'S TURN TO SERVE AGAIN!
I DOUBT HE'S GOING TO DO US THE FAVOR OF TARGETING NISHINOYA AGAIN.
WHO IS HE GOING TO GO AFTER INSTEAD?
Y'KNOW, NOTHING KILLS A TEAM'S MORALE FASTER...
...THAN WHEN THEIR LOUD AND ENERGETIC MOOD-MAKER GOES QUIET.
SWRRR
FWEEEEEE
TOSS
TMP
TMP
TMP

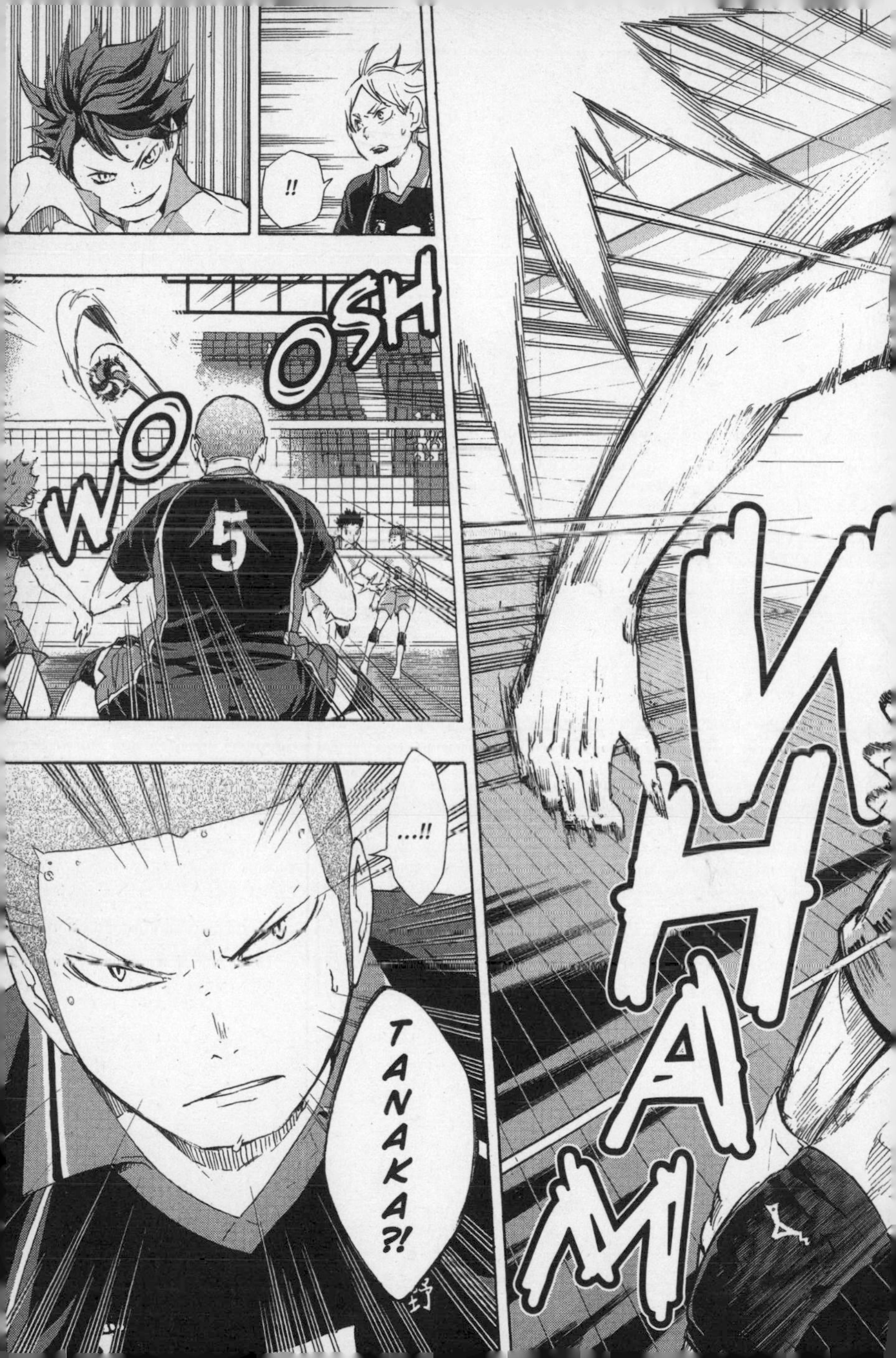
WHAM
!!
WOOSH
...!!
TANAKA?!

IN CELEBRATION OF ONE FULL YEAR OF SERIALIZATION, MY ASSISTANTS DREW THIS ILLUSTRATION. THANK YOU, EVERYONE!!

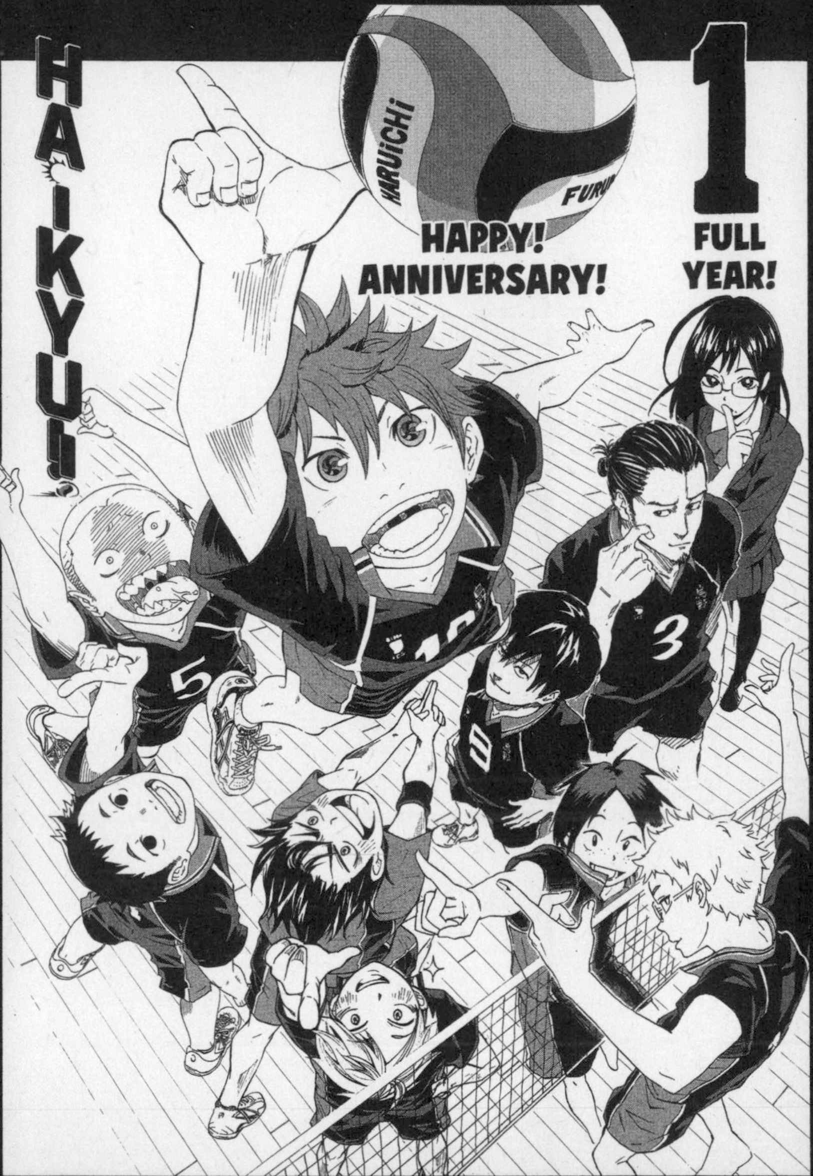
HAIKYU!!
HARUICHI
FURU
HAPPY! ANNIVERSARY!
1 FULL YEAR!
5
10
3
8

ASSISTANT ART STAFF

ATSUSHI NAMIKIRI | SAKUJO KOIZUMI | RYOTARO OGURA | MIYAKO WATAHASHI

CHAPTER 52: Makings of an Ace

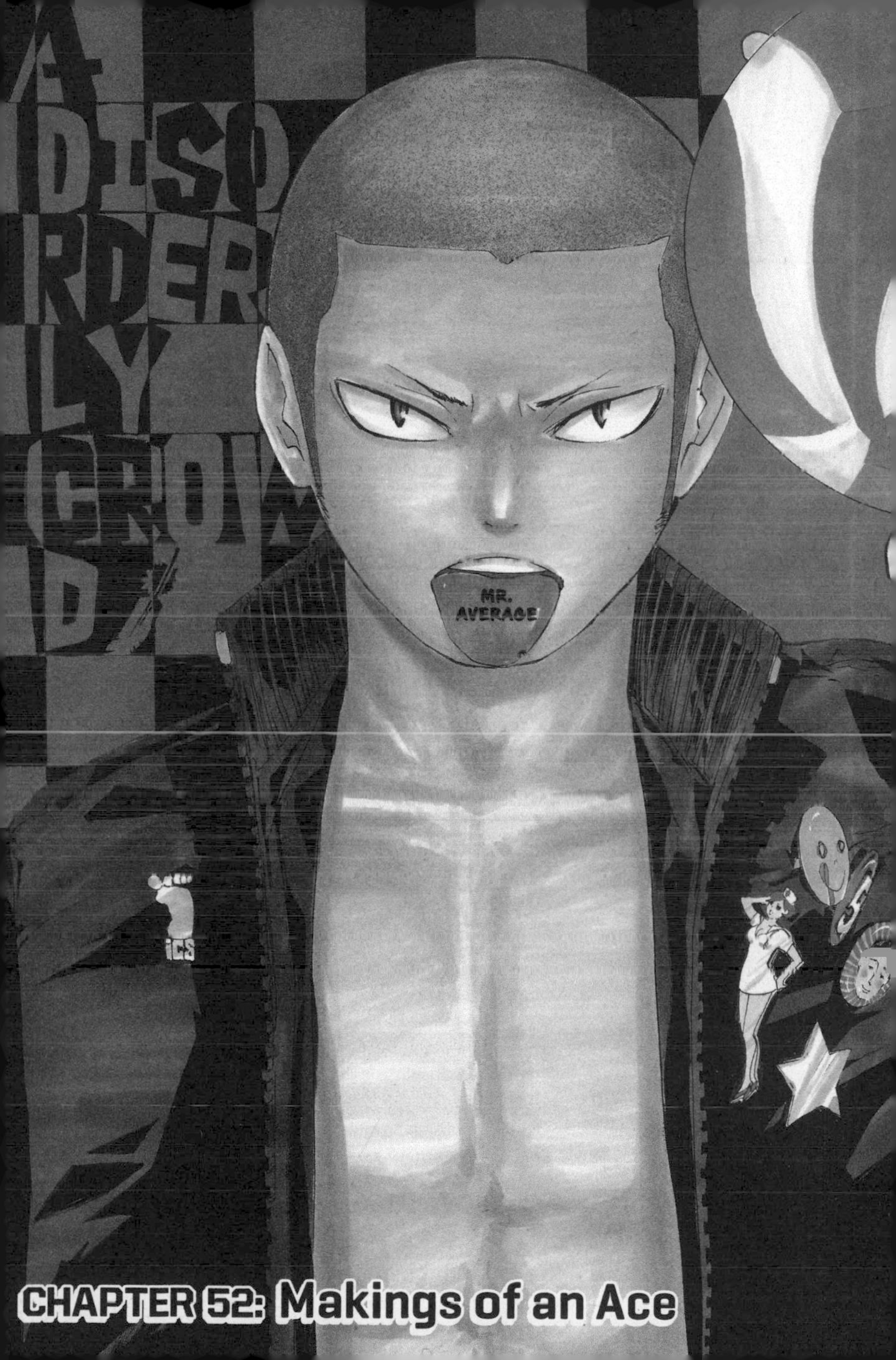
A DISORDERLY CROWD
MR. AVERAGE

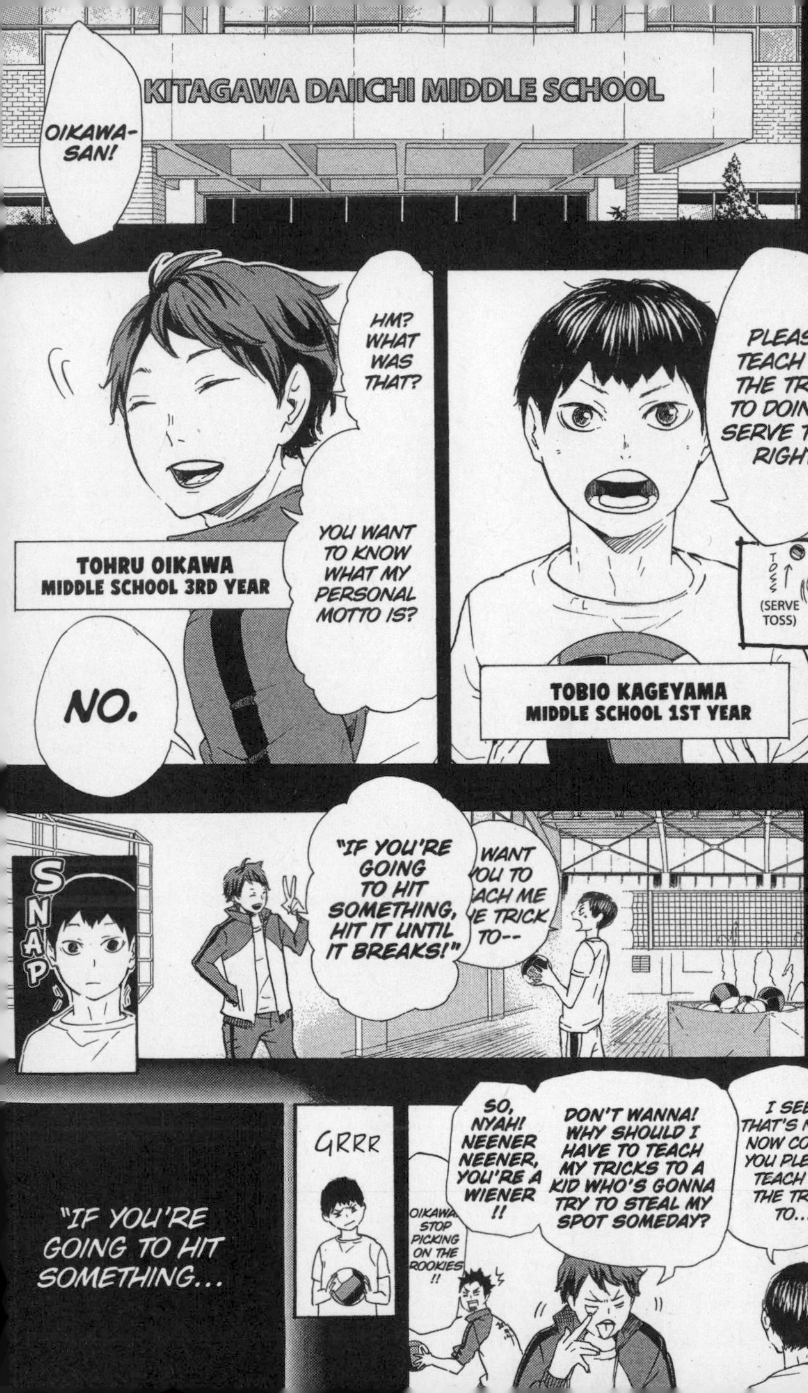
KITAGAWA DAIICHI MIDDLE SCHOOL
OIKAWA-SAN!
PLEASE TEACH ME THE TRICK TO DOING A SERVE TOSS RIGHT!
TOSS (SERVE TOSS)
TOBIO KAGEYAMA MIDDLE SCHOOL 1ST YEAR
HM? WHAT WAS THAT?
TOHRU OIKAWA MIDDLE SCHOOL 3RD YEAR
YOU WANT TO KNOW WHAT MY PERSONAL MOTTO IS?
NO.
WANT YOU TO ACH ME E TRICK TO--
"IF YOU'RE GOING TO HIT SOMETHING, HIT IT UNTIL IT BREAKS!"
SNAP
I SEE. THAT'S NICE. NOW COULD YOU PLEASE TEACH ME THE TRICK TO...
DON'T WANNA! WHY SHOULD I HAVE TO TEACH MY TRICKS TO A KID WHO'S GONNA TRY TO STEAL MY SPOT SOMEDAY?
SO, NYAH! NEENER NEENER, YOU'RE A WIENER !!
OIKAWA STOP PICKING ON THE ROOKIES !!
GRRR
"IF YOU'RE GOING TO HIT SOMETHING...

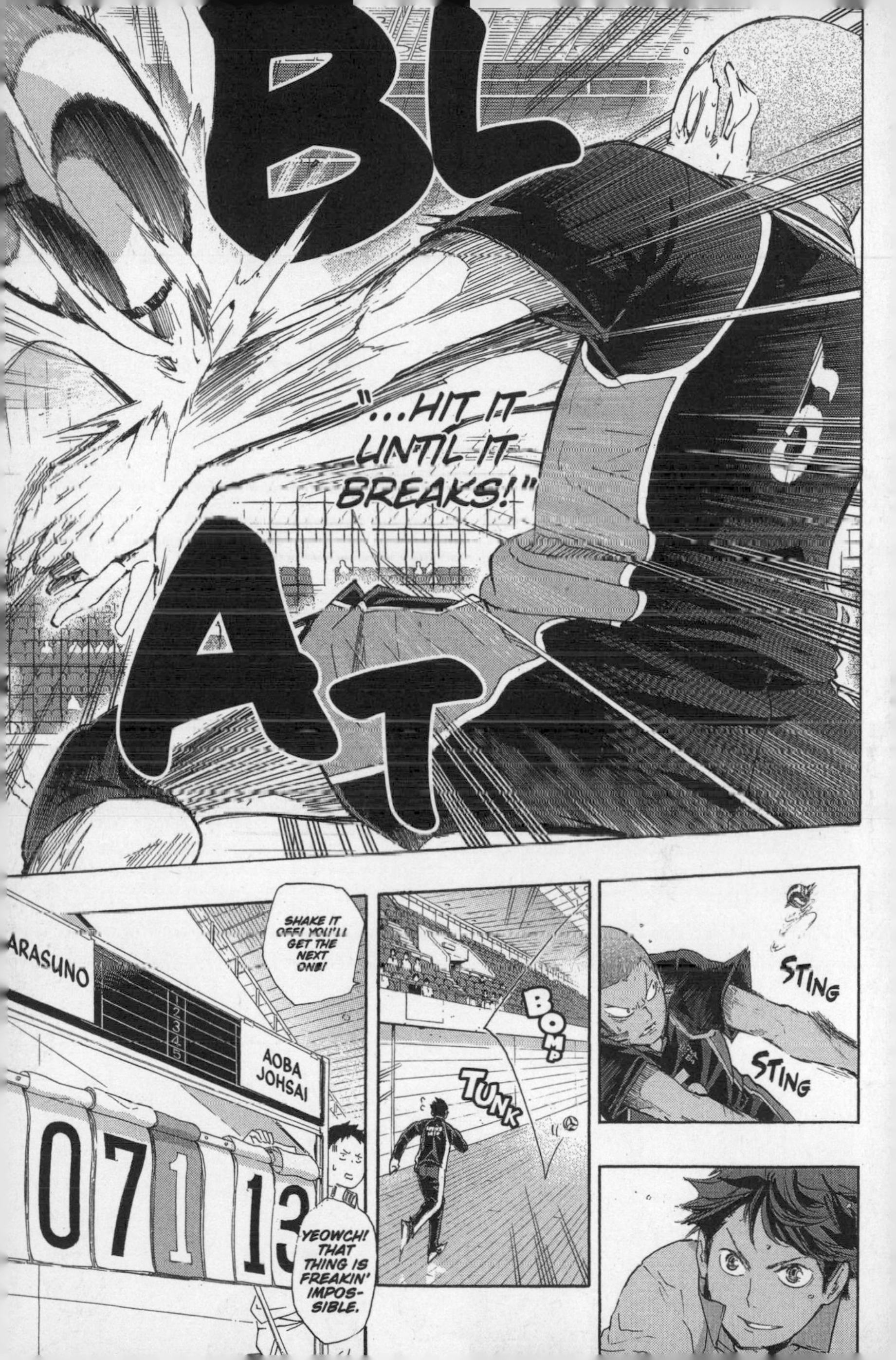
BLAT
"...HIT IT UNTIL IT BREAKS!"
STING
STING
BOMP
TUNK
SHAKE IT OFF! YOU'LL GET THE NEXT ONE!
KARASUNO
1 2 3 4 5
AOBA JOHSAI
07 1 13
YEOWCH! THAT THING IS FREAKIN' IMPOSSIBLE.

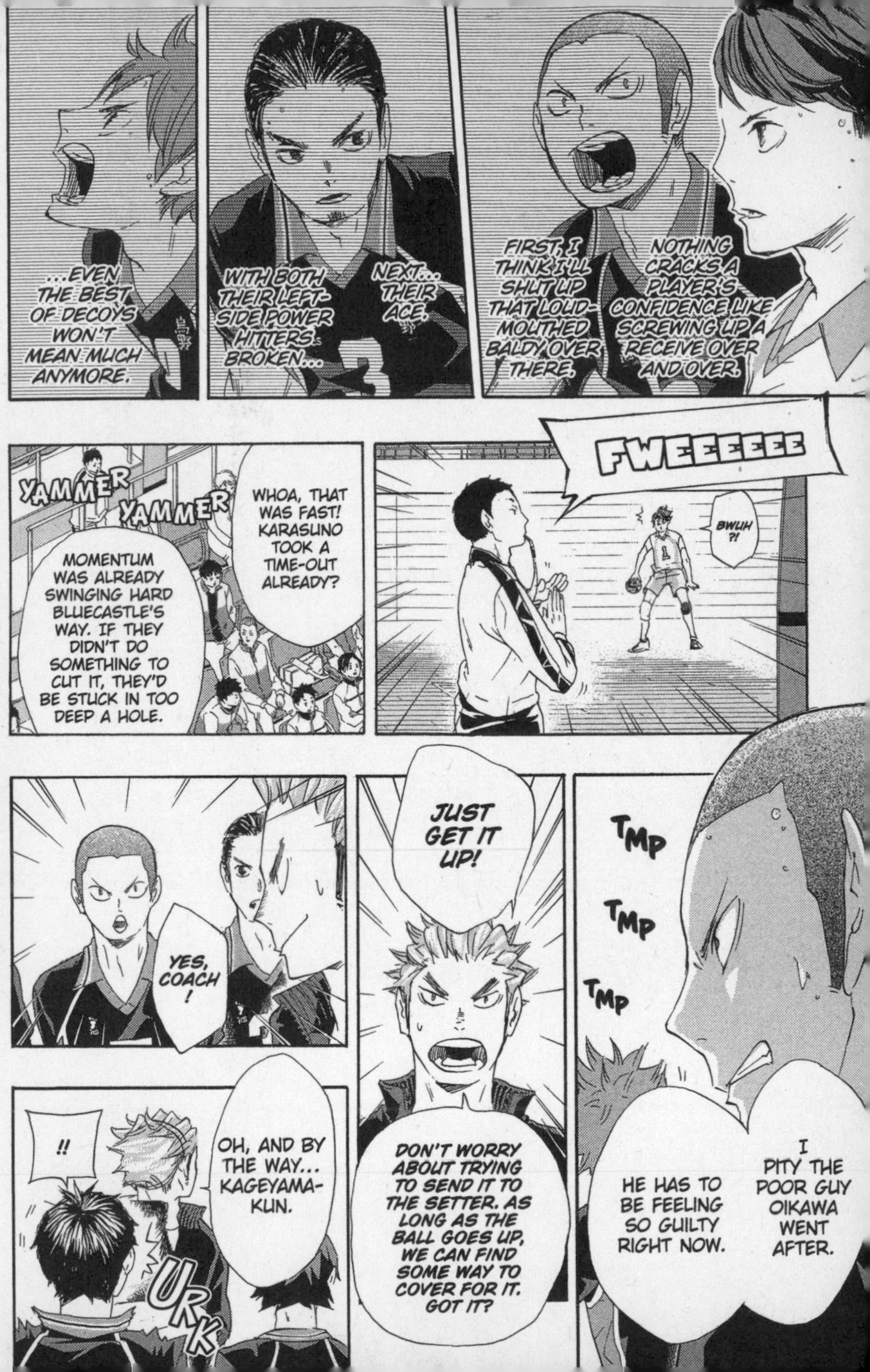
NOTHING CRACKS A PLAYER'S CONFIDENCE LIKE SCREWING UP A RECEIVE OVER AND OVER.
FIRST, I THINK I'LL SHUT UP THAT LOUD-MOUTHED BALDY OVER THERE.
NEXT... THEIR ACE.
WITH BOTH THEIR LEFT-SIDE POWER HITTERS BROKEN...
...EVEN THE BEST OF DECOYS WON'T MEAN MUCH ANYMORE.
FWEEEEEE
BWUH ?!
WHOA, THAT WAS FAST! KARASUNO TOOK A TIME-OUT ALREADY?
YAMMER
YAMMER
MOMENTUM WAS ALREADY SWINGING HARD BLUECASTLE'S WAY. IF THEY DIDN'T DO SOMETHING TO CUT IT, THEY'D BE STUCK IN TOO DEEP A HOLE.
TMP
TMP
TMP
I PITY THE POOR GUY OIKAWA WENT AFTER.
HE HAS TO BE FEELING SO GUILTY RIGHT NOW.
JUST GET IT UP!
DON'T WORRY ABOUT TRYING TO SEND IT TO THE SETTER. AS LONG AS THE BALL GOES UP, WE CAN FIND SOME WAY TO COVER FOR IT. GOT IT?
YES, COACH!
OH, AND BY THE WAY... KAGEYAMA-KUN.
!!
URK

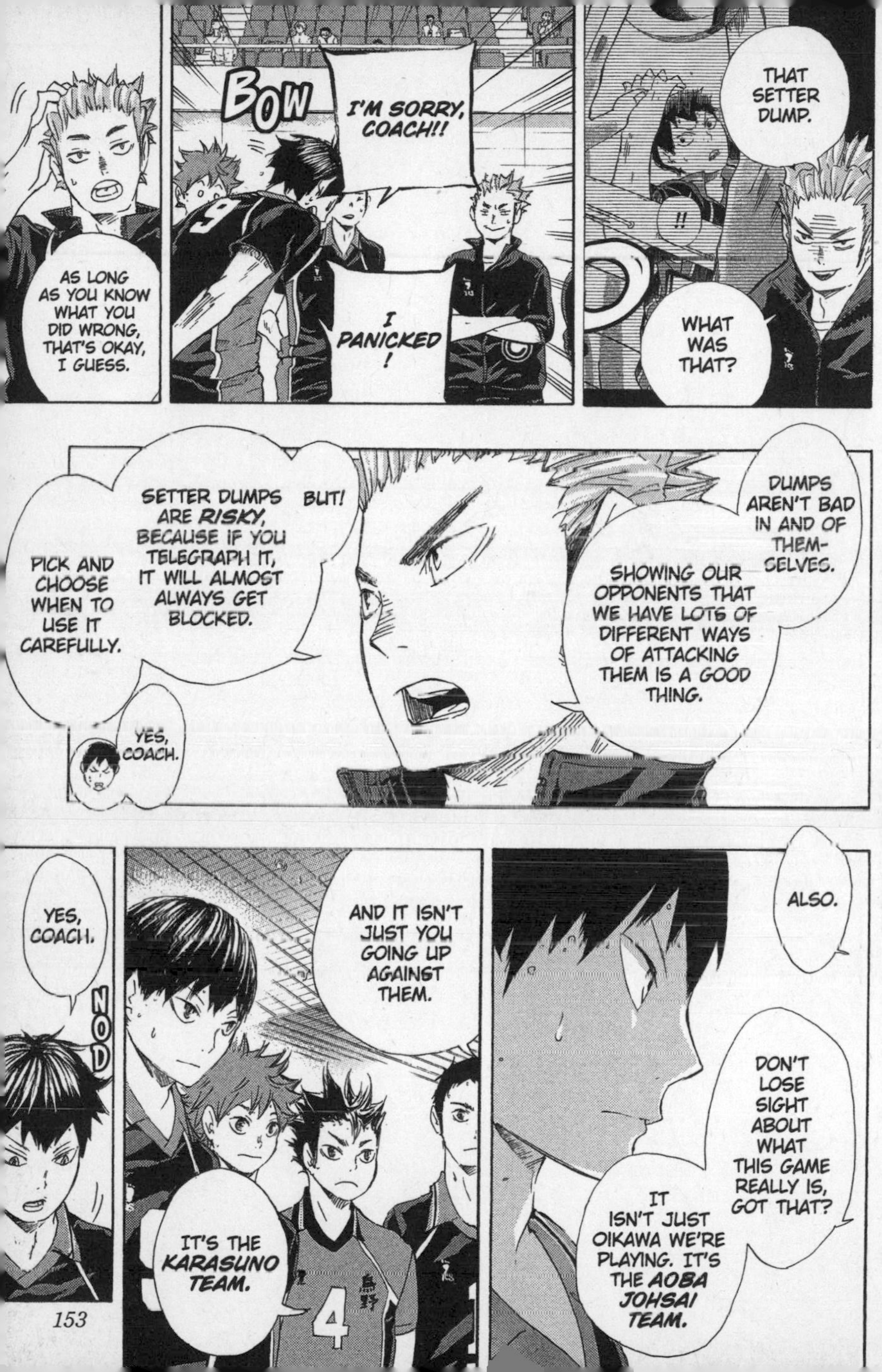
THAT SETTER DUMP.
!!
WHAT WAS THAT?
BOW
I'M SORRY, COACH!!
I PANICKED!
AS LONG AS YOU KNOW WHAT YOU DID WRONG, THAT'S OKAY, I GUESS.
DUMPS AREN'T BAD IN AND OF THEMSELVES.
SHOWING OUR OPPONENTS THAT WE HAVE LOTS OF DIFFERENT WAYS OF ATTACKING THEM IS A GOOD THING.
BUT!
SETTER DUMPS ARE RISKY, BECAUSE IF YOU TELEGRAPH IT, IT WILL ALMOST ALWAYS GET BLOCKED.
PICK AND CHOOSE WHEN TO USE IT CAREFULLY.
YES, COACH.
ALSO.
DON'T LOSE SIGHT ABOUT WHAT THIS GAME REALLY IS, GOT THAT?
IT ISN'T JUST OIKAWA WE'RE PLAYING. IT'S THE AOBA JOHSAI TEAM.
AND IT ISN'T JUST YOU GOING UP AGAINST THEM.
IT'S THE KARASUNO TEAM.
YES, COACH.
NOD

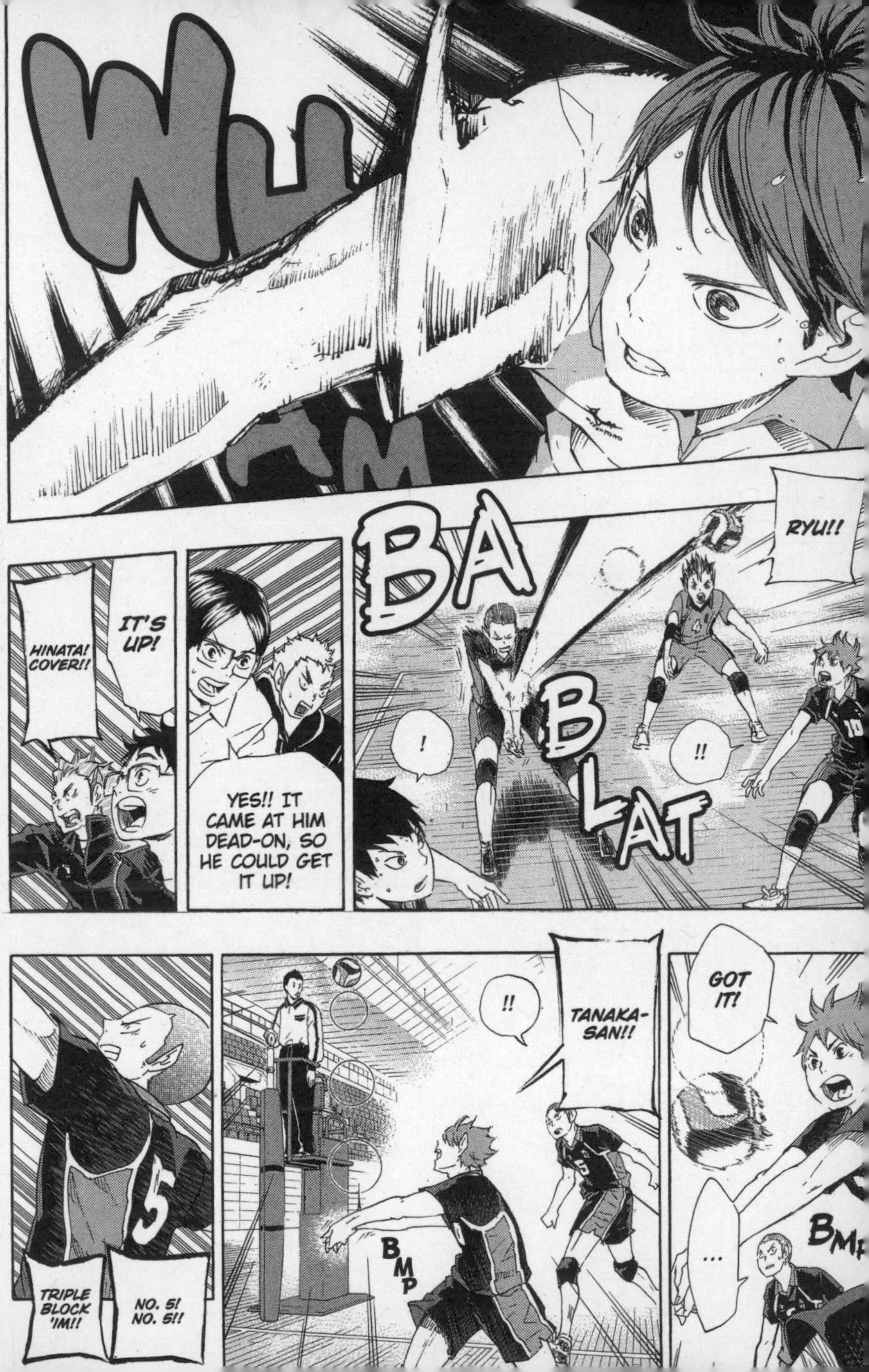
RYU!!
BA
B
LAT
!!
!
YES!! IT CAME AT HIM DEAD-ON, SO HE COULD GET IT UP!
IT'S UP!
HINATA! COVER!!
GOT IT!
...
BMP
TANAKA-SAN!!
!!
BMP
NO. 5! NO. 5!!
TRIPLE BLOCK 'IM!!

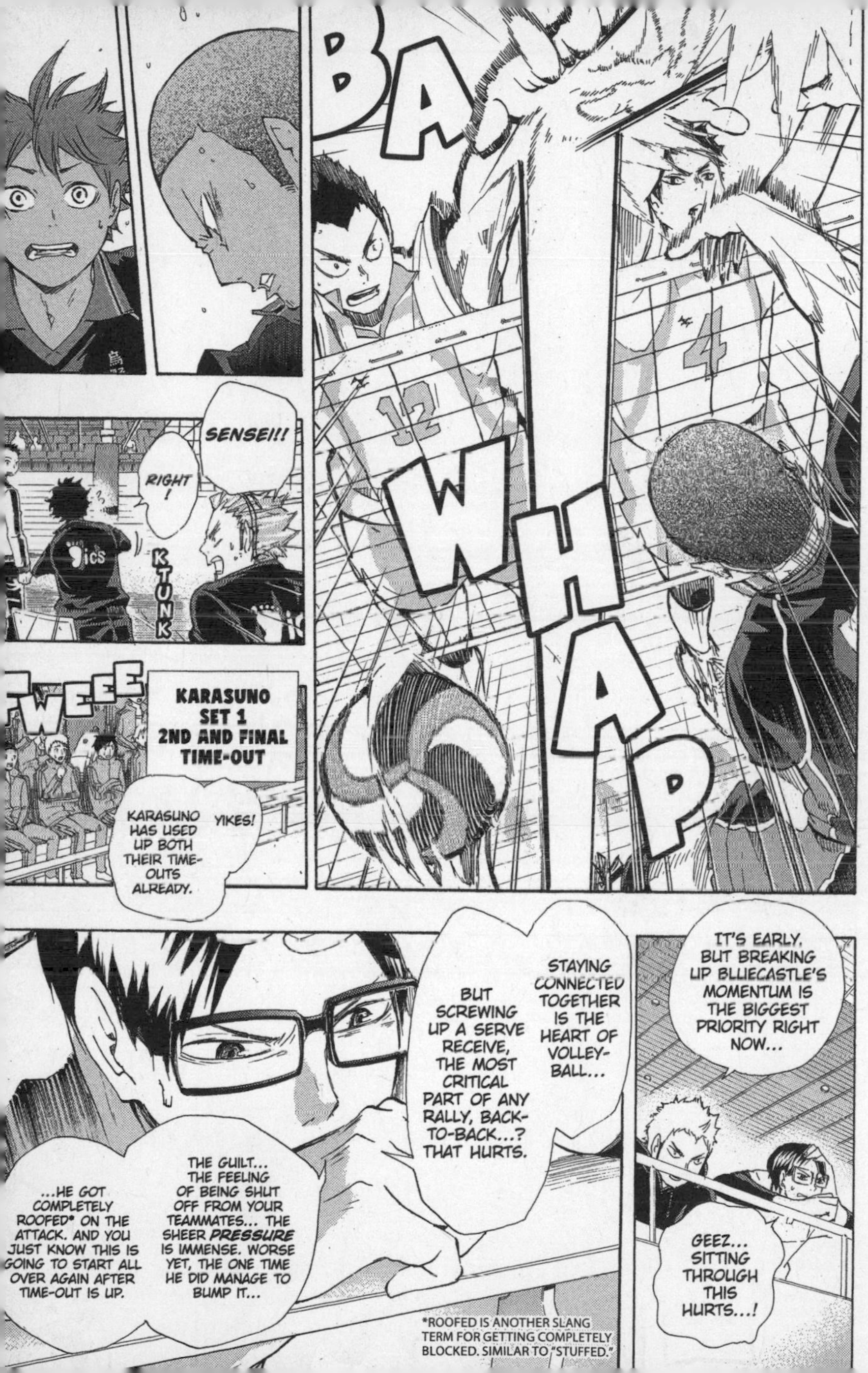
BA
WHAP
SENSEI!!!
RIGHT!
KTUNK
KARASUNO SET 1 2ND AND FINAL TIME-OUT
FWEEE
YIKES!
KARASUNO HAS USED UP BOTH THEIR TIME-OUTS ALREADY.
IT'S EARLY, BUT BREAKING UP BLUECASTLE'S MOMENTUM IS THE BIGGEST PRIORITY RIGHT NOW...
GEEZ... SITTING THROUGH THIS HURTS...!
STAYING CONNECTED TOGETHER IS THE HEART OF VOLLEY-BALL...
BUT SCREWING UP A SERVE RECEIVE, THE MOST CRITICAL PART OF ANY RALLY, BACK-TO-BACK...? THAT HURTS.
THE GUILT... THE FEELING OF BEING SHUT OFF FROM YOUR TEAMMATES... THE SHEER PRESSURE IS IMMENSE. WORSE YET, THE ONE TIME HE DID MANAGE TO BUMP IT...
...HE GOT COMPLETELY ROOFED* ON THE ATTACK. AND YOU JUST KNOW THIS IS GOING TO START ALL OVER AGAIN AFTER TIME-OUT IS UP.
*ROOFED IS ANOTHER SLANG TERM FOR GETTING COMPLETELY BLOCKED. SIMILAR TO "STUFFED."

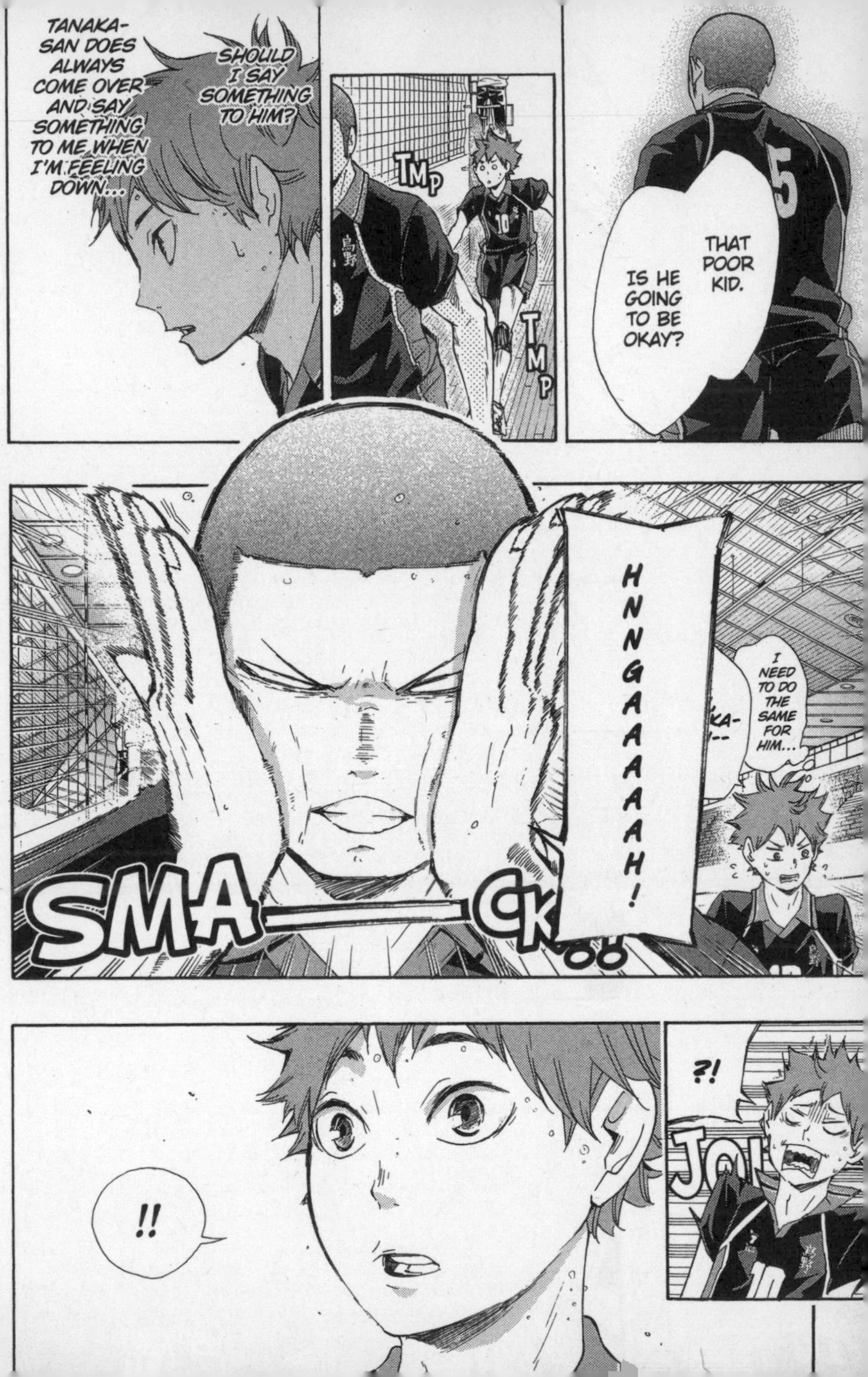

THAT POOR KID.
IS HE GOING TO BE OKAY?
TMP
TMP
TANAKA-SAN DOES ALWAYS COME OVER AND SAY SOMETHING TO ME WHEN I'M FEELING DOWN...
SHOULD I SAY SOMETHING TO HIM?
I NEED TO DO THE SAME FOR HIM...
HNNGAAAAAAAH!
SMA——CK..!!
?!
!!

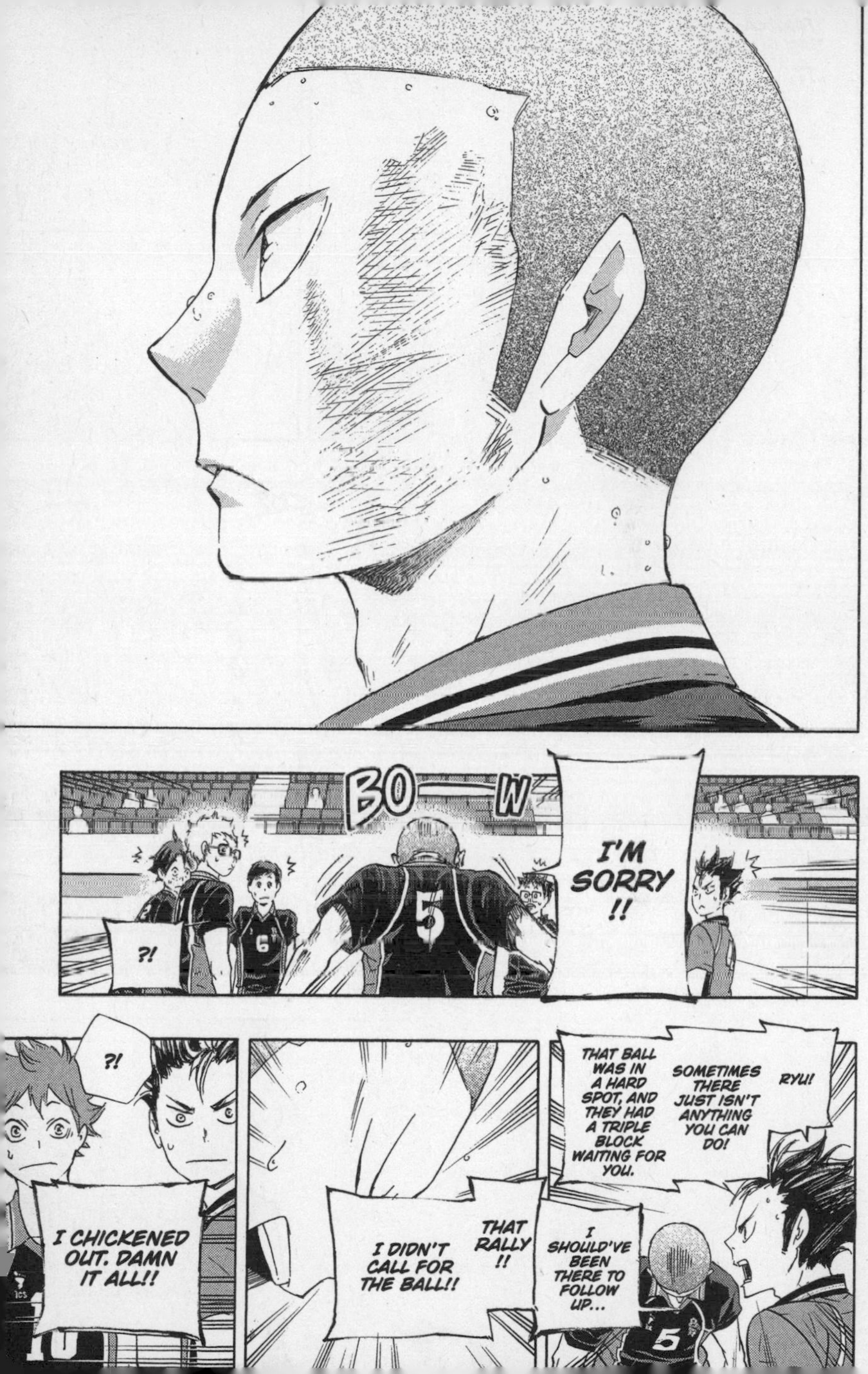

I'M SORRY!!
BO—W
?!
RYU!
SOMETIMES THERE JUST ISN'T ANYTHING YOU CAN DO!
THAT BALL WAS IN A HARD SPOT, AND THEY HAD A TRIPLE BLOCK WAITING FOR YOU.
I SHOULD'VE BEEN THERE TO FOLLOW UP...
THAT RALLY!!
I DIDN'T CALL FOR THE BALL!!
?!
I CHICKENED OUT. DAMN IT ALL!!

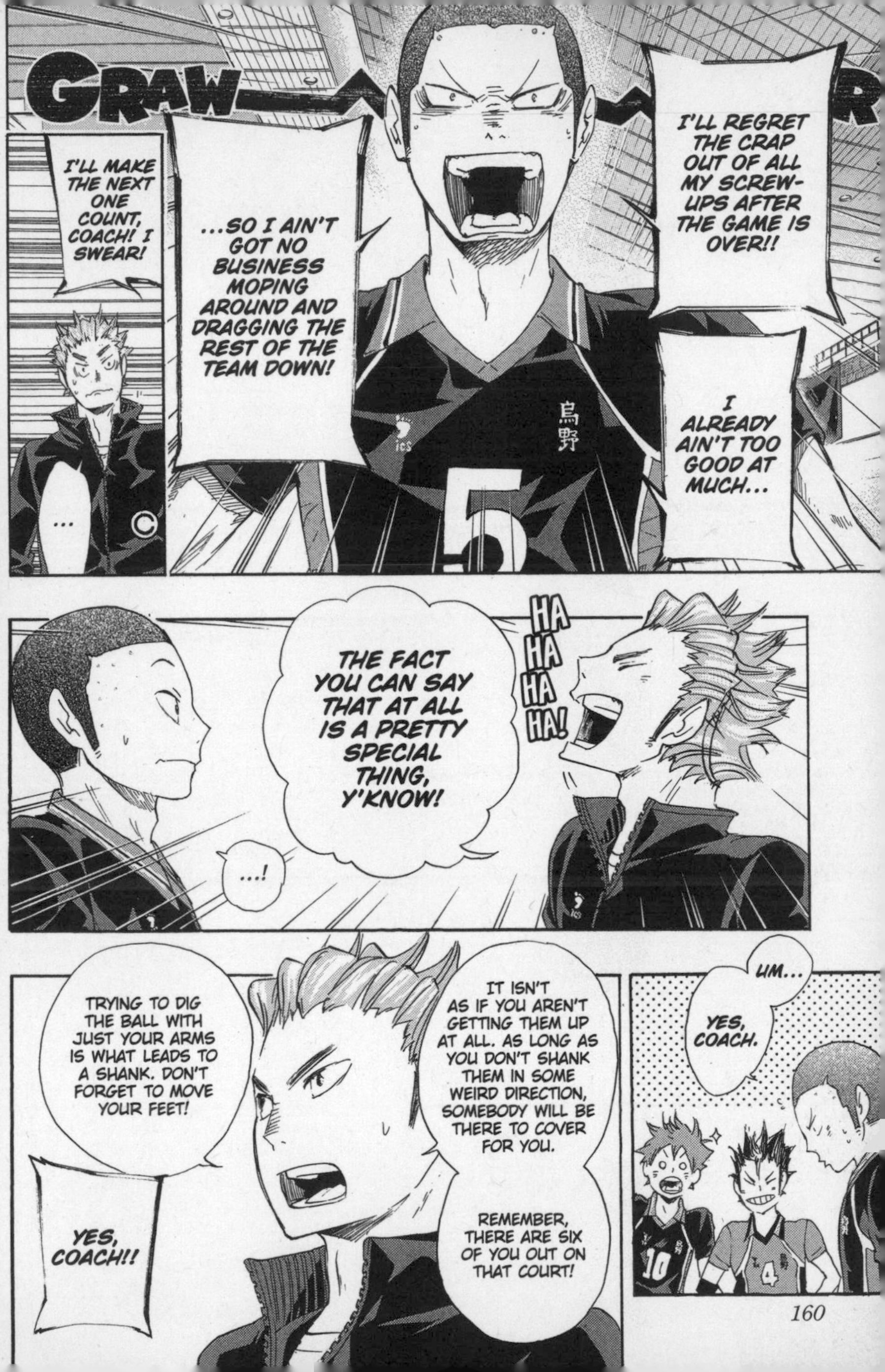
GRAW
R
I'LL REGRET THE CRAP OUT OF ALL MY SCREW-UPS AFTER THE GAME IS OVER!!
I ALREADY AIN'T TOO GOOD AT MUCH...
...SO I AIN'T GOT NO BUSINESS MOPING AROUND AND DRAGGING THE REST OF THE TEAM DOWN!
I'LL MAKE THE NEXT ONE COUNT, COACH! I SWEAR!
...
HA HA HA HA!
THE FACT YOU CAN SAY THAT AT ALL IS A PRETTY SPECIAL THING, Y'KNOW!
...!
UM...
YES, COACH.
IT ISN'T AS IF YOU AREN'T GETTING THEM UP AT ALL. AS LONG AS YOU DON'T SHANK THEM IN SOME WEIRD DIRECTION, SOMEBODY WILL BE THERE TO COVER FOR YOU.
TRYING TO DIG THE BALL WITH JUST YOUR ARMS IS WHAT LEADS TO A SHANK. DON'T FORGET TO MOVE YOUR FEET!
REMEMBER, THERE ARE SIX OF YOU OUT ON THAT COURT!
YES, COACH!!

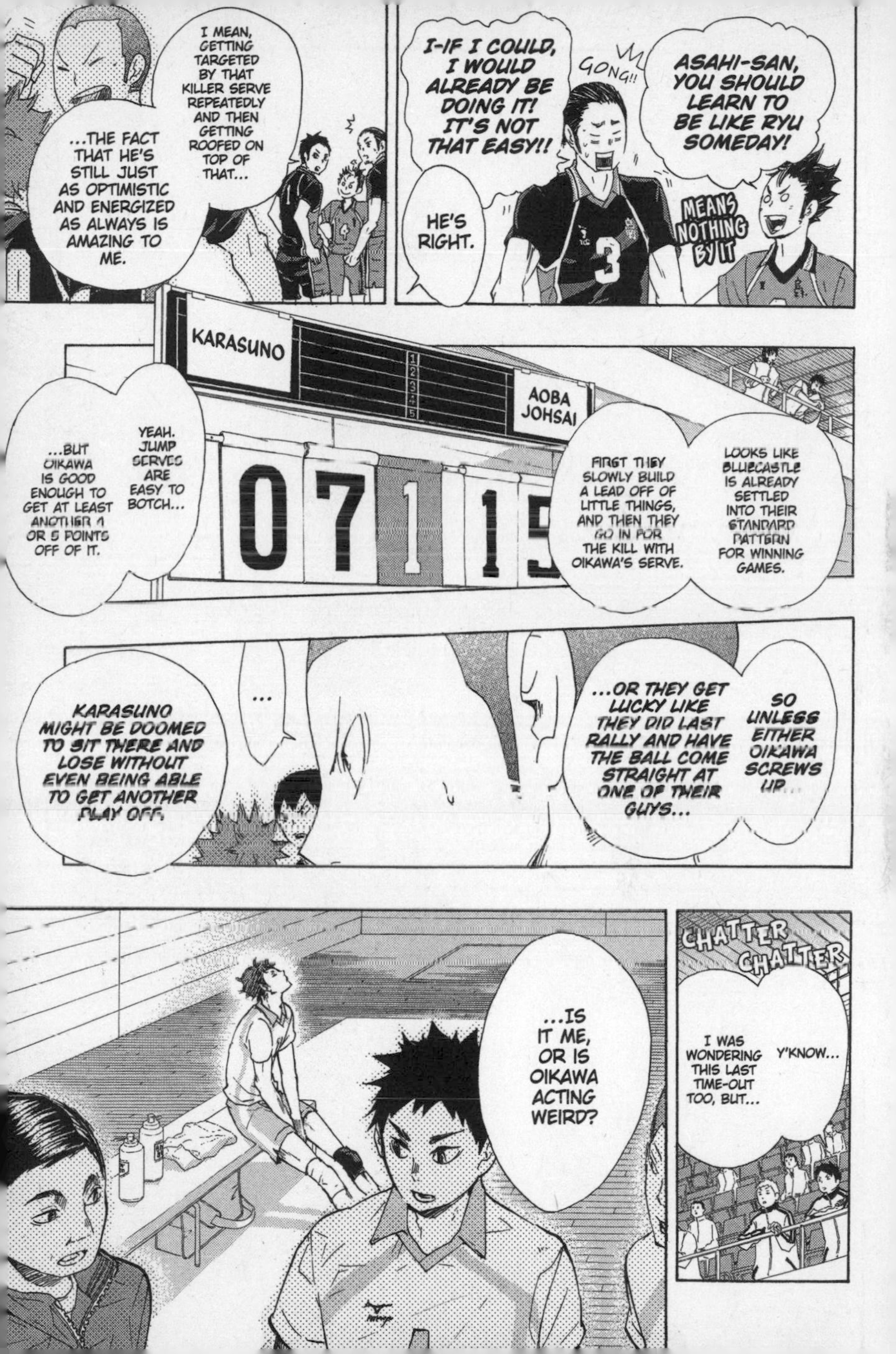
ASAHI-SAN, YOU SHOULD LEARN TO BE LIKE RYU SOMEDAY!
MEANS NOTHING BY IT
GONG!!
I-IF I COULD, I WOULD ALREADY BE DOING IT! IT'S NOT THAT EASY!!
HE'S RIGHT.
I MEAN, GETTING TARGETED BY THAT KILLER SERVE REPEATEDLY AND THEN GETTING ROOFED ON TOP OF THAT...
...THE FACT THAT HE'S STILL JUST AS OPTIMISTIC AND ENERGIZED AS ALWAYS IS AMAZING TO ME.
KARASUNO
AOBA JOHSAI
LOOKS LIKE BLUECASTLE IS ALREADY SETTLED INTO THEIR STANDARD PATTERN FOR WINNING GAMES.
FIRST THEY SLOWLY BUILD A LEAD OFF OF LITTLE THINGS, AND THEN THEY GO IN FOR THE KILL WITH OIKAWA'S SERVE.
YEAH. JUMP SERVES ARE EASY TO BOTCH...
...BUT OIKAWA IS GOOD ENOUGH TO GET AT LEAST ANOTHER 4 OR 5 POINTS OFF OF IT.
SO UNLESS EITHER OIKAWA SCREWS UP...
...OR THEY GET LUCKY LIKE THEY DID LAST RALLY AND HAVE THE BALL COME STRAIGHT AT ONE OF THEIR GUYS...
...
KARASUNO MIGHT BE DOOMED TO SIT THERE AND LOSE WITHOUT EVEN BEING ABLE TO GET ANOTHER PLAY OFF.
CHATTER CHATTER
Y'KNOW...
I WAS WONDERING THIS LAST TIME-OUT TOO, BUT...
...IS IT ME, OR IS OIKAWA ACTING WEIRD?

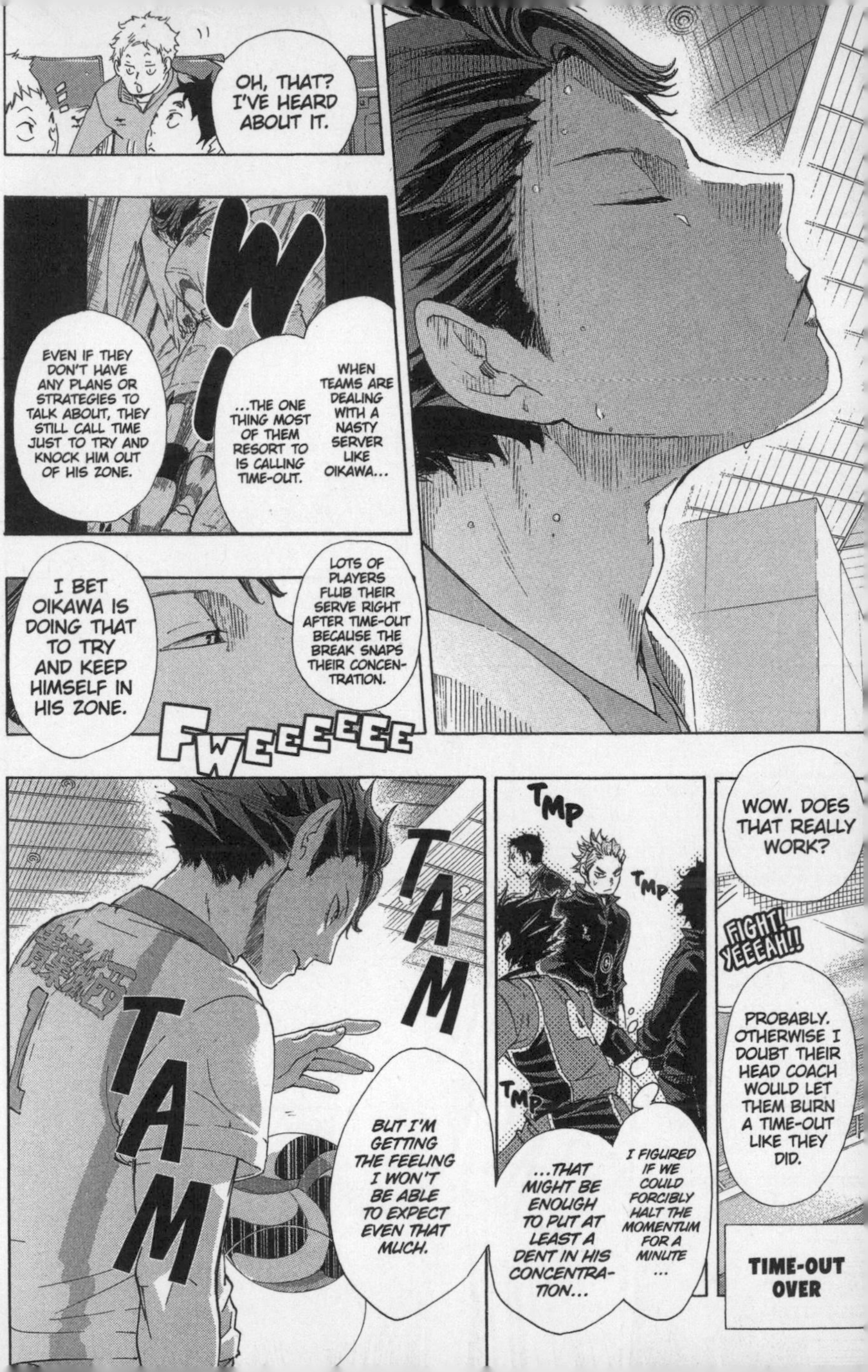
OH, THAT? I'VE HEARD ABOUT IT.
W
WHEN TEAMS ARE DEALING WITH A NASTY SERVER LIKE OIKAWA...
...THE ONE THING MOST OF THEM RESORT TO IS CALLING TIME-OUT.
EVEN IF THEY DON'T HAVE ANY PLANS OR STRATEGIES TO TALK ABOUT, THEY STILL CALL TIME JUST TO TRY AND KNOCK HIM OUT OF HIS ZONE.
LOTS OF PLAYERS FLUB THEIR SERVE RIGHT AFTER TIME-OUT BECAUSE THE BREAK SNAPS THEIR CONCEN-TRATION.
I BET OIKAWA IS DOING THAT TO TRY AND KEEP HIMSELF IN HIS ZONE.
FWEEEEEE
WOW. DOES THAT REALLY WORK?
FIGHT! YEEEAH!!
PROBABLY. OTHERWISE I DOUBT THEIR HEAD COACH WOULD LET THEM BURN A TIME-OUT LIKE THEY DID.
TIME-OUT OVER
TMP
TMP
TMP
I FIGURED IF WE COULD FORCIBLY HALT THE MOMENTUM FOR A MINUTE...
...THAT MIGHT BE ENOUGH TO PUT AT LEAST A DENT IN HIS CONCENTRA-TION...
BUT I'M GETTING THE FEELING I WON'T BE ABLE TO EXPECT EVEN THAT MUCH.
TAM
TAM

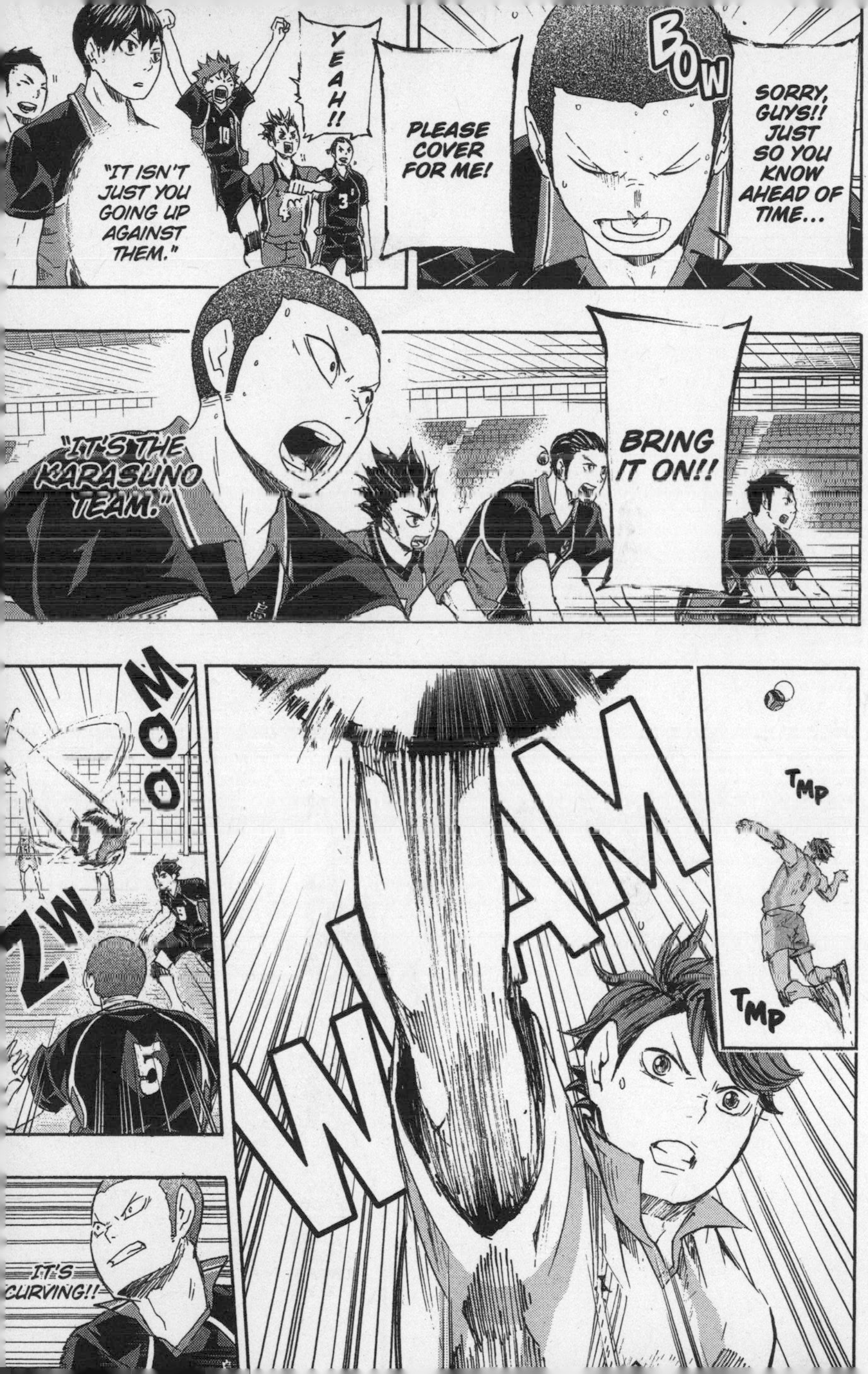
BOW
SORRY, GUYS!! JUST SO YOU KNOW AHEAD OF TIME...
PLEASE COVER FOR ME!
YEAH!!
"IT ISN'T JUST YOU GOING UP AGAINST THEM."
BRING IT ON!!
"IT'S THE KARASUNO TEAM."
TMP
TMP
WHAM
ZWOOM
IT'S CURVING!!

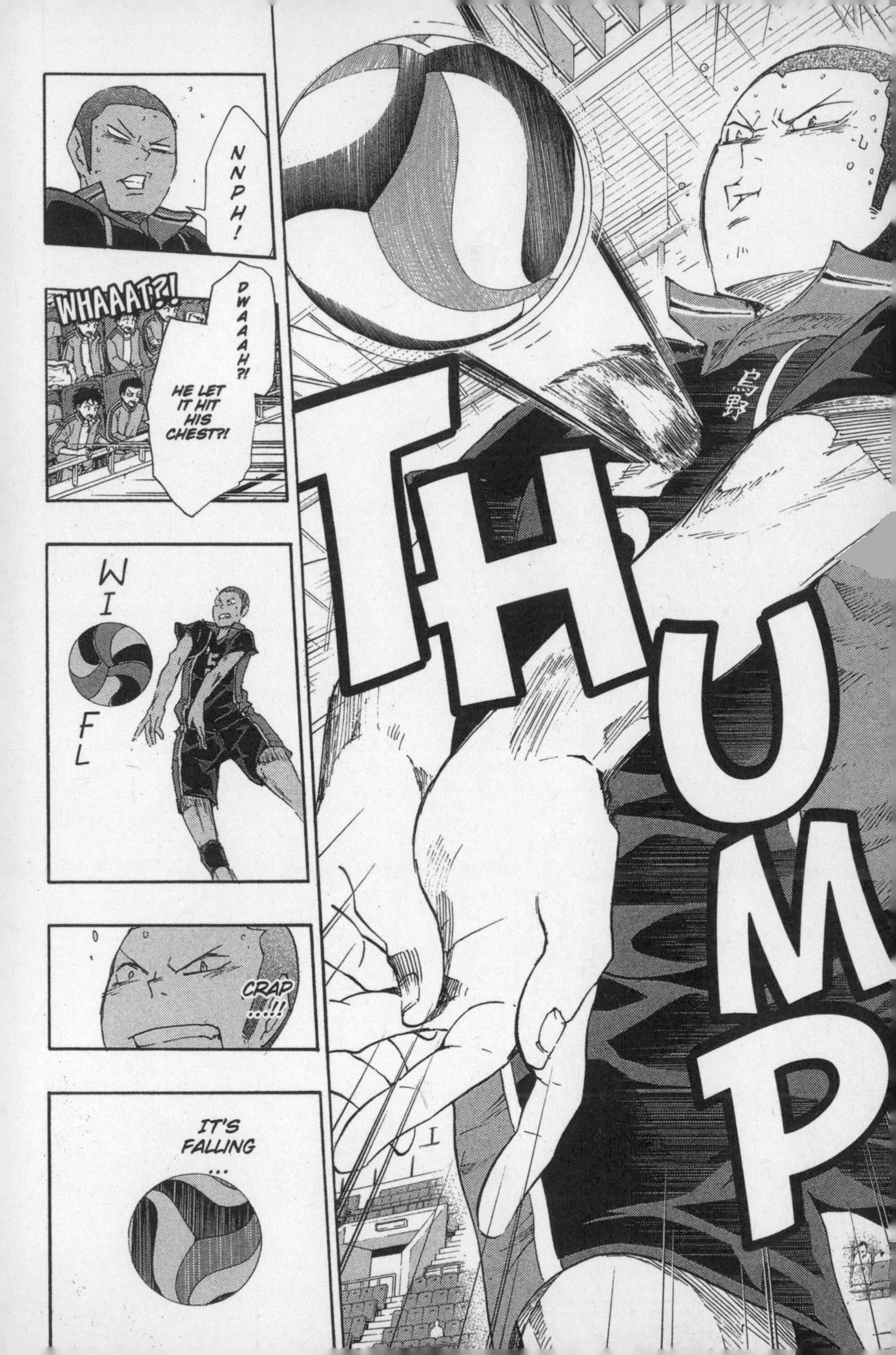
烏野
THUMP
NNPH!
DWAAAAH?!
HE LET IT HIT HIS CHEST?!
WHAAAT?!
WIFL
CRAP...!!
IT'S FALLING...

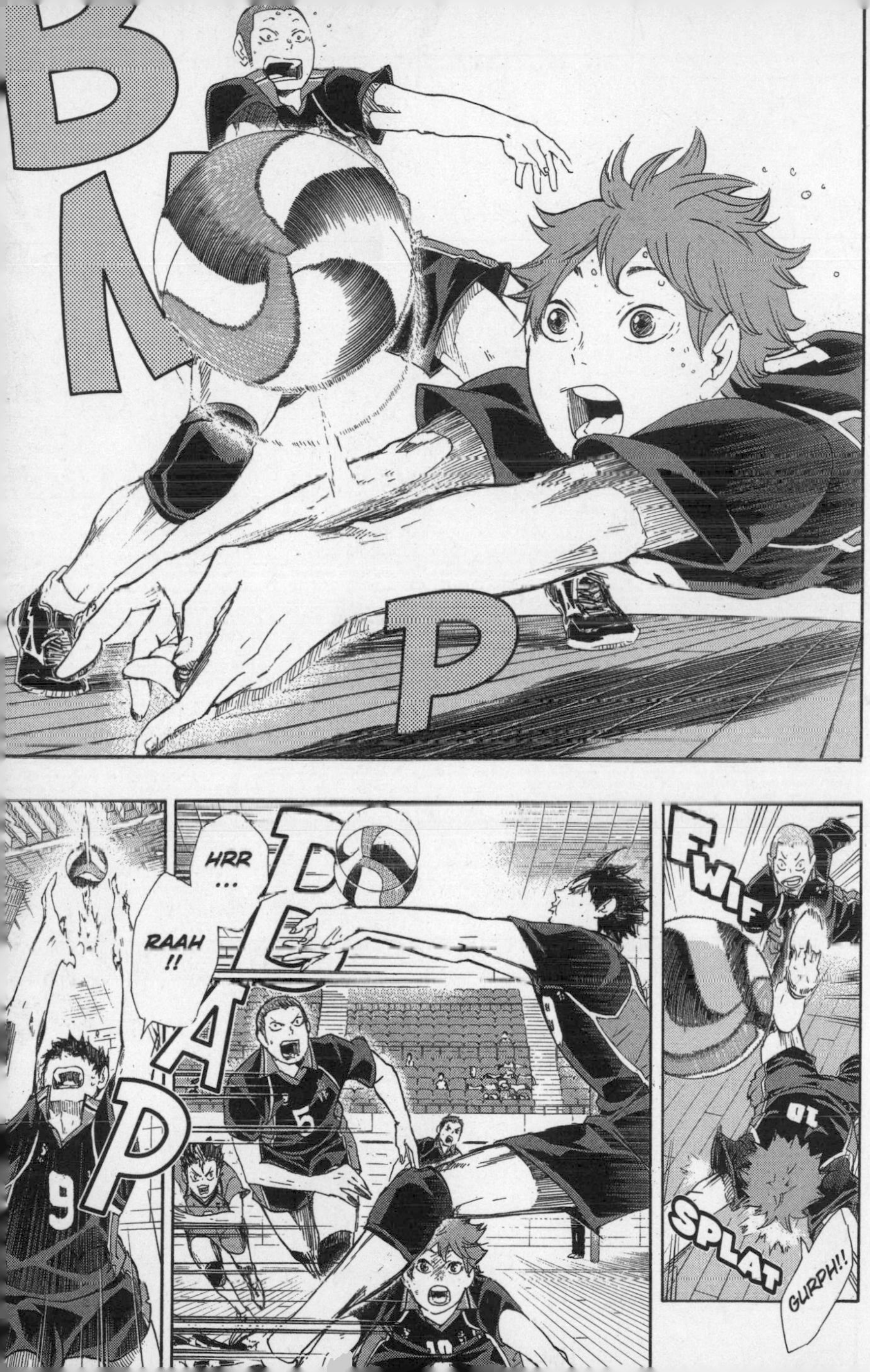

FWIF
SPLAT
GURPH!!
HRR ...
RAAH !!

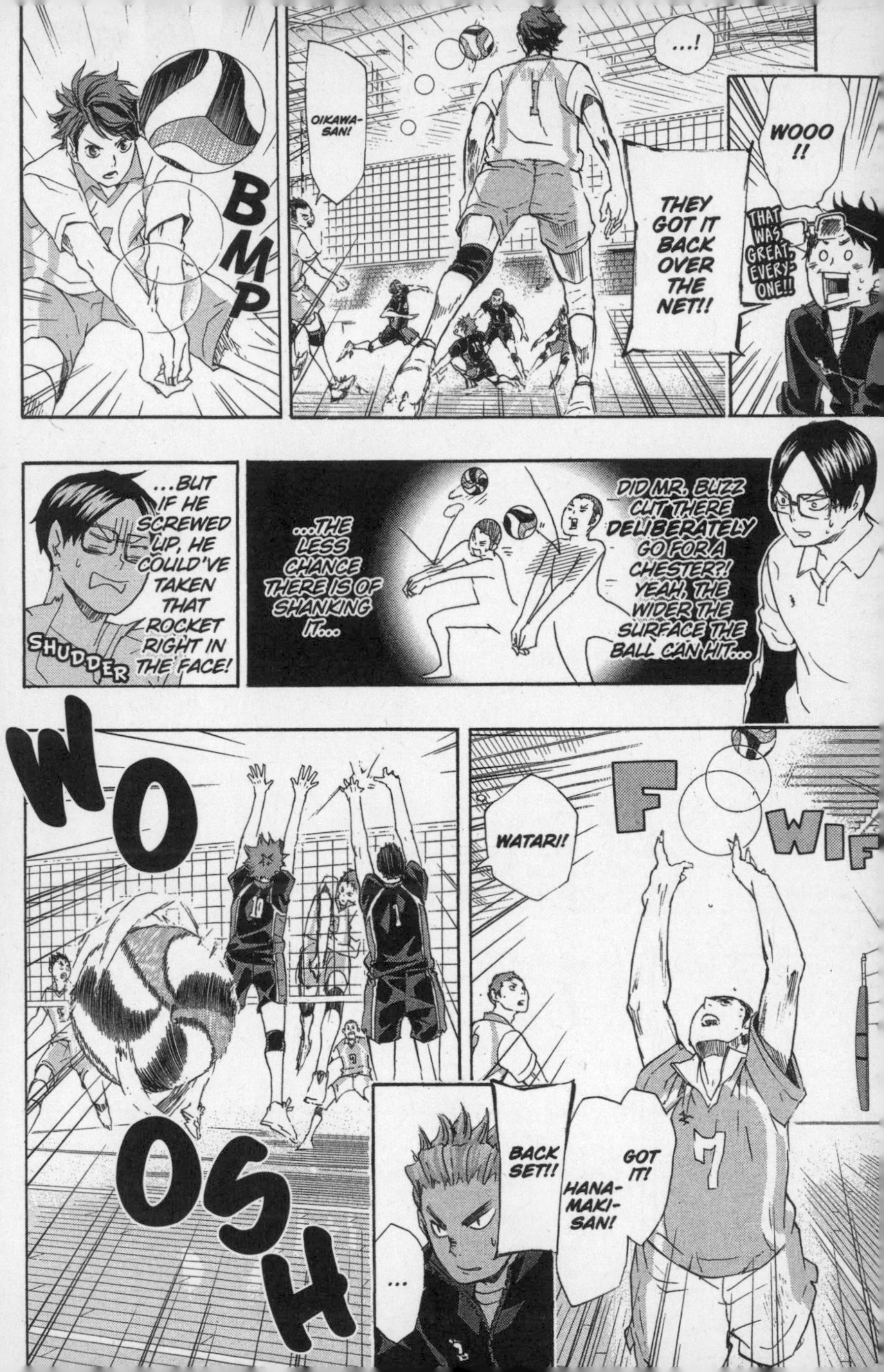
WOOO!!
THAT WAS GREAT, EVERYONE!!
THEY GOT IT BACK OVER THE NET!!
...!
OIKAWA-SAN!
BMP
DID MR. BUZZ CUT THERE DELIBERATELY GO FOR A CHESTER?! YEAH, THE WIDER THE SURFACE THE BALL CAN HIT...
...THE LESS CHANCE THERE IS OF SHANKING IT...
...BUT IF HE SCREWED UP, HE COULD'VE TAKEN THAT ROCKET RIGHT IN THE FACE!
SHUDDER
FWIF
WATARI!
GOT IT!
HANA-MAKI-SAN!
BACK SET!!
...
WOOSH

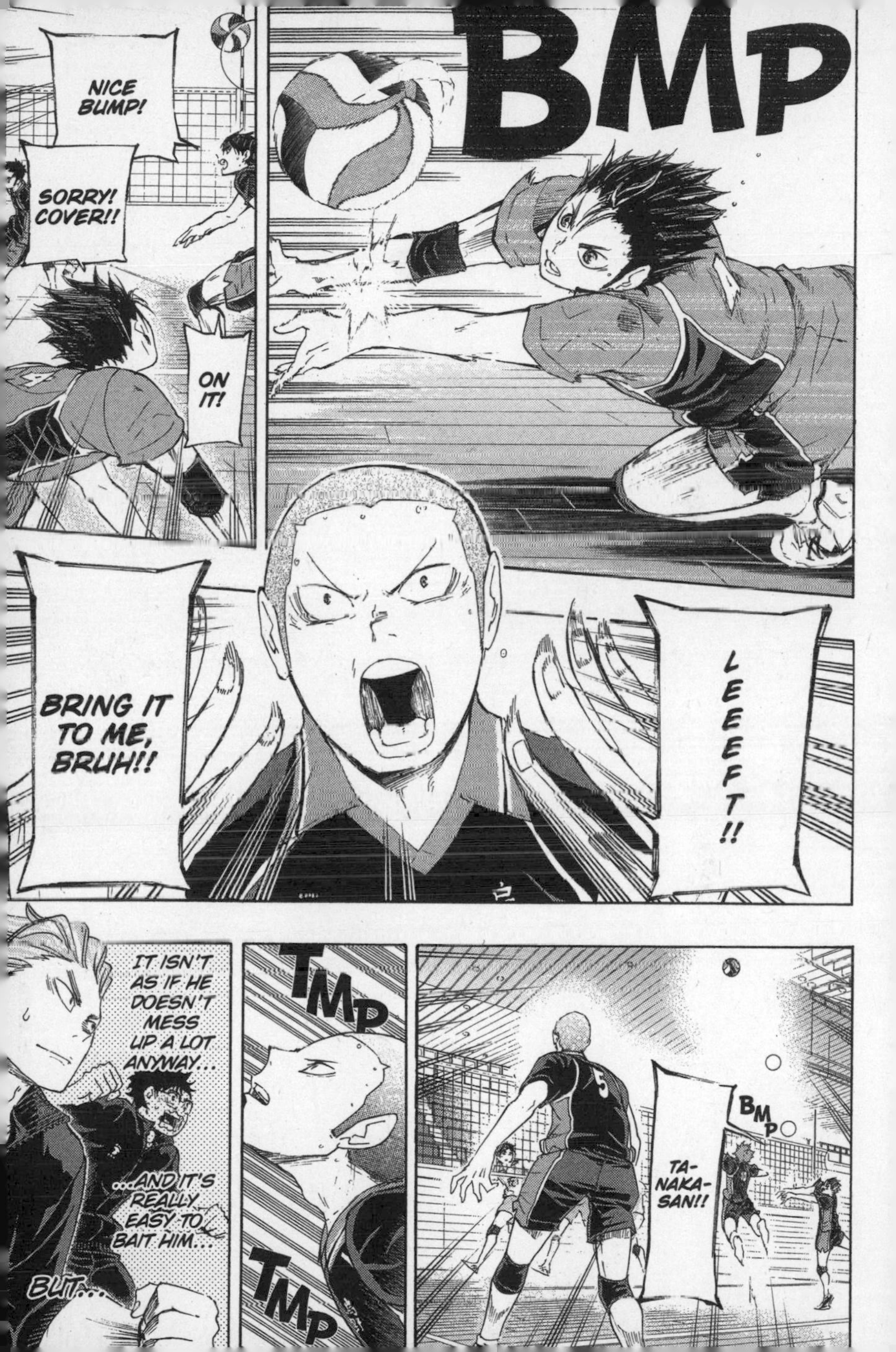
BMP
NICE BUMP!
SORRY! COVER!!
ON IT!
LEEEFT!!
BRING IT TO ME, BRUH!!
BMP
TA-NAKA-SAN!!
TMP
TMP
IT ISN'T AS IF HE DOESN'T MESS UP A LOT ANYWAY...
...AND IT'S REALLY EASY TO BAIT HIM...
BUT...

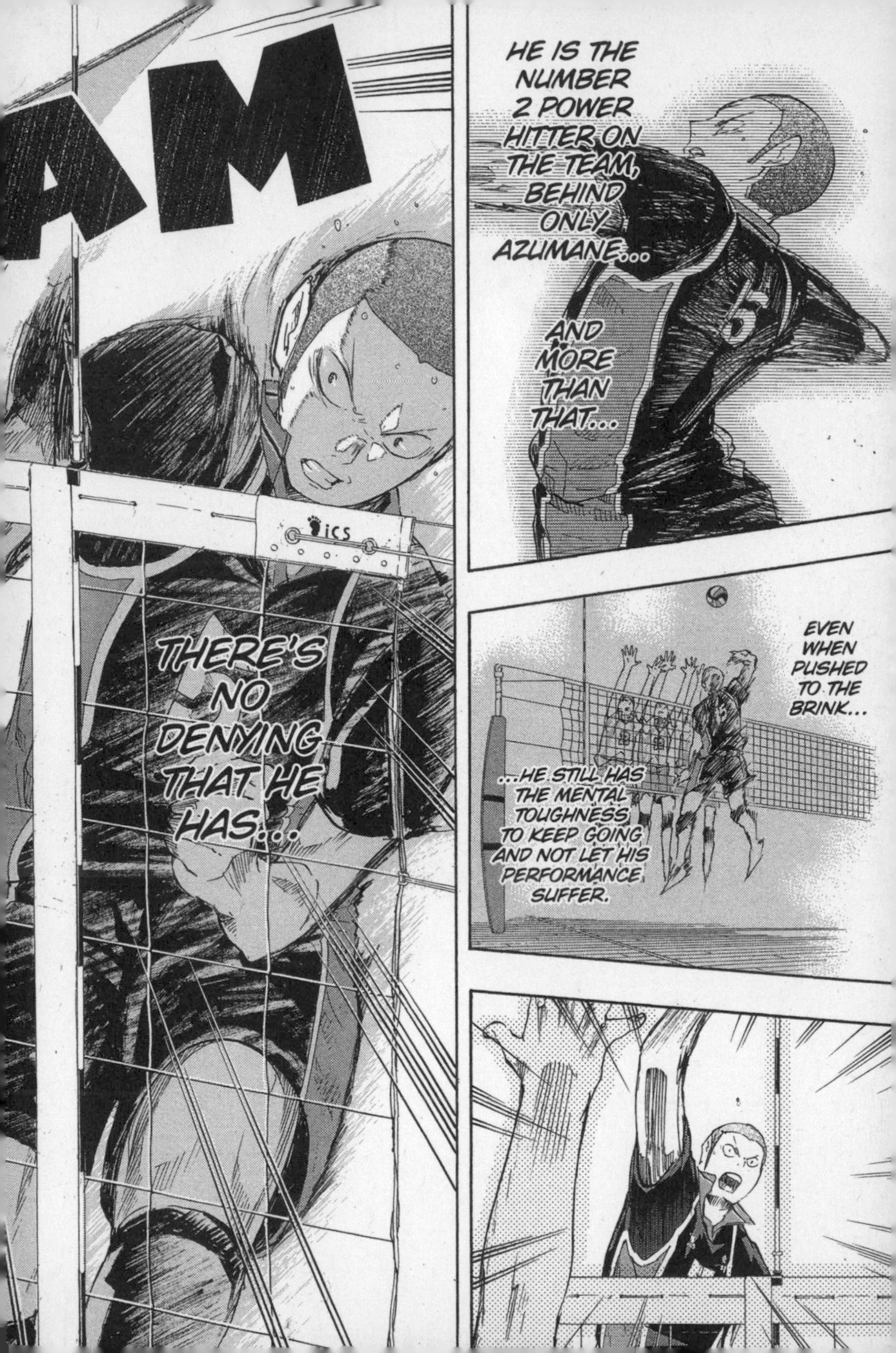
HE IS THE NUMBER 2 POWER HITTER ON THE TEAM, BEHIND ONLY AZUMANE...
AND MORE THAN THAT...
EVEN WHEN PUSHED TO THE BRINK...
...HE STILL HAS THE MENTAL TOUGHNESS TO KEEP GOING AND NOT LET HIS PERFORMANCE SUFFER.
AM
THERE'S NO DENYING THAT HE HAS...

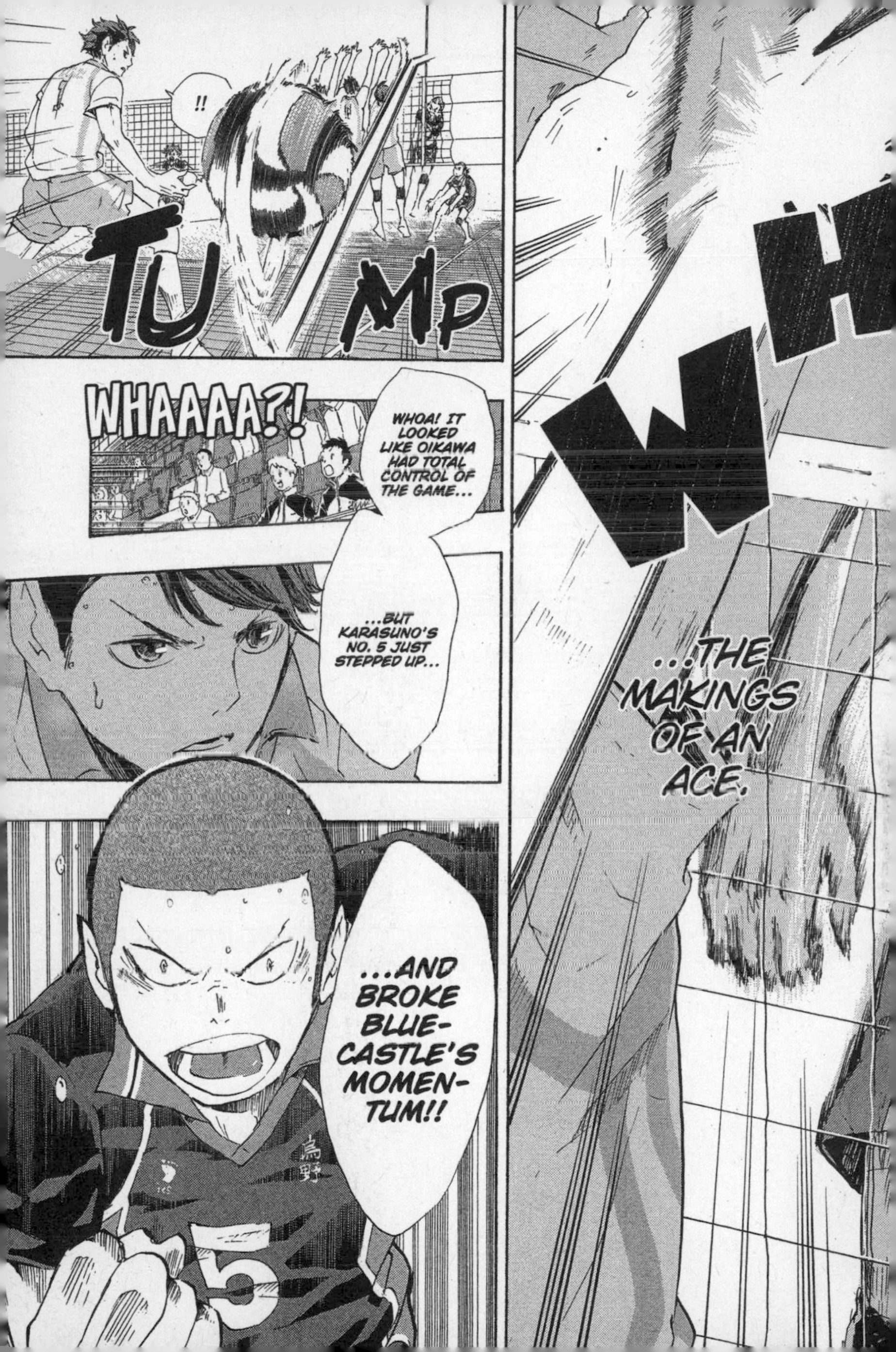
WHH
...THE MAKINGS OF AN ACE.
!!
TUMP
WHAAAA?!
WHOA! IT LOOKED LIKE OIKAWA HAD TOTAL CONTROL OF THE GAME...
...BUT KARASUNO'S NO. 5 JUST STEPPED UP...
...AND BROKE BLUE-CASTLE'S MOMEN-TUM!!

THIS IS ANOTHER ILLUSTRATION MY AWESOME STAFF DREW IN CELEBRATION OF ONE FULL YEAR OF SERIALIZATION.

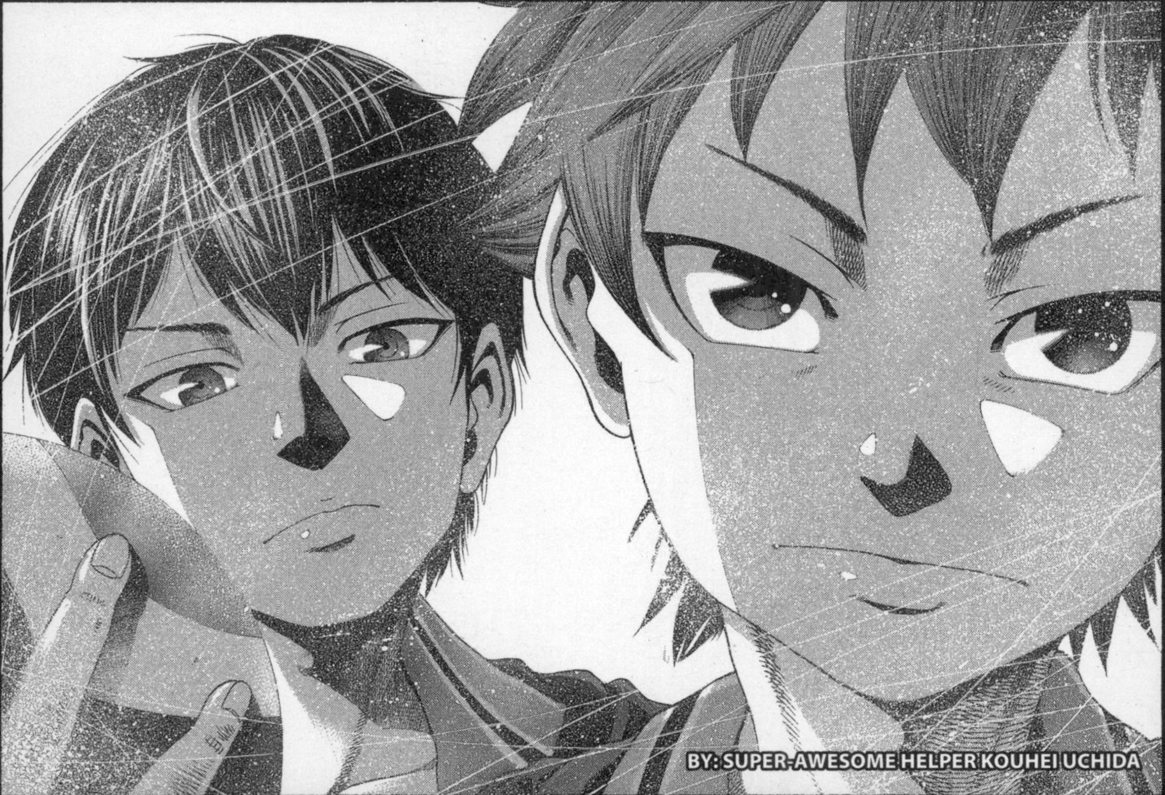
BY: SUPER-AWESOME HELPER KOUHEI UCHIDA

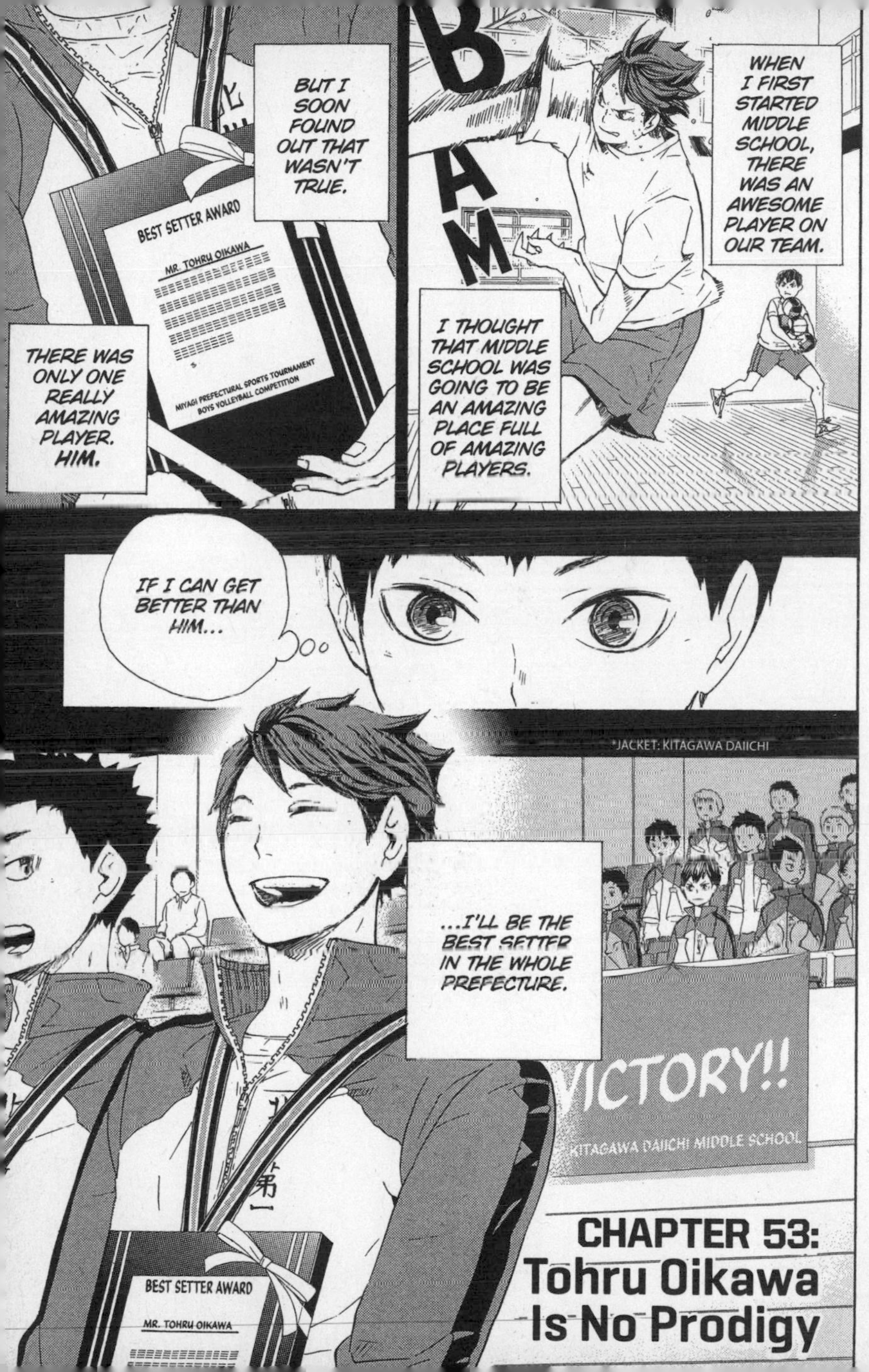
BAM
WHEN I FIRST STARTED MIDDLE SCHOOL, THERE WAS AN AWESOME PLAYER ON OUR TEAM.
I THOUGHT THAT MIDDLE SCHOOL WAS GOING TO BE AN AMAZING PLACE FULL OF AMAZING PLAYERS.
BUT I SOON FOUND OUT THAT WASN'T TRUE.
BEST SETTER AWARD
MR. TOHRU OIKAWA
MIYAGI PREFECTURAL SPORTS TOURNAMENT BOYS VOLLEYBALL COMPETITION
THERE WAS ONLY ONE REALLY AMAZING PLAYER. HIM.
IF I CAN GET BETTER THAN HIM...
*JACKET: KITAGAWA DAIICHI
...I'LL BE THE BEST SETTER IN THE WHOLE PREFECTURE.
VICTORY!!
KITAGAWA DAIICHI MIDDLE SCHOOL
BEST SETTER AWARD
MR. TOHRU OIKAWA

CHAPTER 53: Tohru Oikawa Is No Prodigy

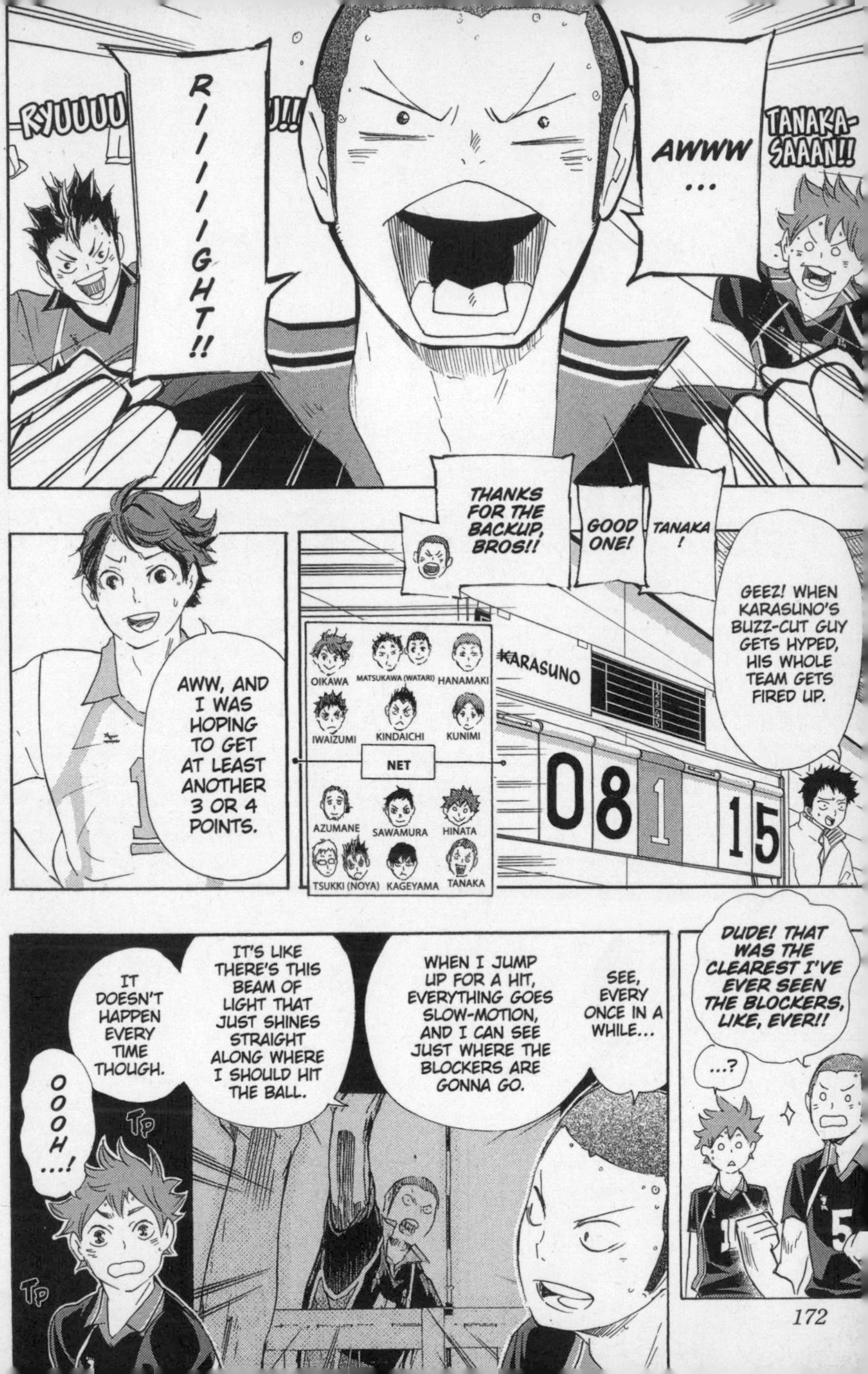
TANAKA-SAAAN!!
AWWW ...
RIIIIIGHT!!
RYUUUU
U!!
GEEZ! WHEN KARASUNO'S BUZZ-CUT GUY GETS HYPED, HIS WHOLE TEAM GETS FIRED UP.
TANAKA!
GOOD ONE!
THANKS FOR THE BACKUP, BROS!!
KARASUNO
08
1
15
OIKAWA
MATSUKAWA (WATARI)
HANAMAKI
IWAIZUMI
KINDAICHI
KUNIMI
NET
AZUMANE
SAWAMURA
HINATA
TSUKKI (NOYA)
KAGEYAMA
TANAKA
AWW, AND I WAS HOPING TO GET AT LEAST ANOTHER 3 OR 4 POINTS.
DUDE! THAT WAS THE CLEAREST I'VE EVER SEEN THE BLOCKERS, LIKE, EVER!!
...?
SEE, EVERY ONCE IN A WHILE...
WHEN I JUMP UP FOR A HIT, EVERYTHING GOES SLOW-MOTION, AND I CAN SEE JUST WHERE THE BLOCKERS ARE GONNA GO.
IT'S LIKE THERE'S THIS BEAM OF LIGHT THAT JUST SHINES STRAIGHT ALONG WHERE I SHOULD HIT THE BALL.
IT DOESN'T HAPPEN EVERY TIME THOUGH.
OOOH...!
Tp
Tp

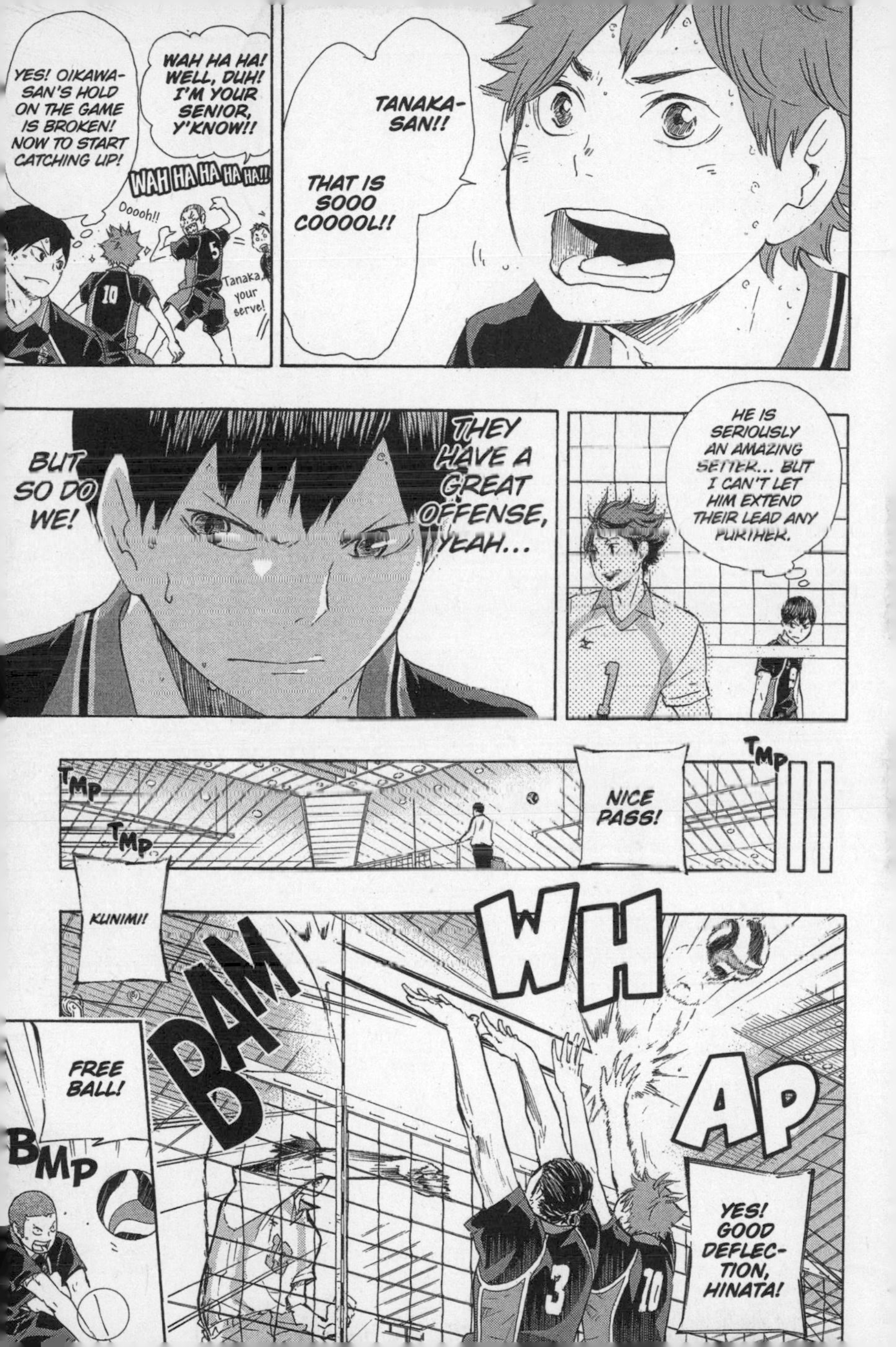
TANAKA-SAN!!
THAT IS SOOO COOOOL!!
WAH HA HA! WELL, DUH! I'M YOUR SENIOR, Y'KNOW!!
YES! OIKAWA-SAN'S HOLD ON THE GAME IS BROKEN! NOW TO START CATCHING UP!
WAH HA HA HA HA!!
Ooooh!!
Tanaka, your serve!
HE IS SERIOUSLY AN AMAZING SETTER... BUT I CAN'T LET HIM EXTEND THEIR LEAD ANY FURTHER.
THEY HAVE A GREAT OFFENSE, YEAH...
BUT SO DO WE!
TMP
NICE PASS!
TMP
TMP
WHAP
KUNIMI!
BAM
YES! GOOD DEFLECTION, HINATA!
FREE BALL!
BMP

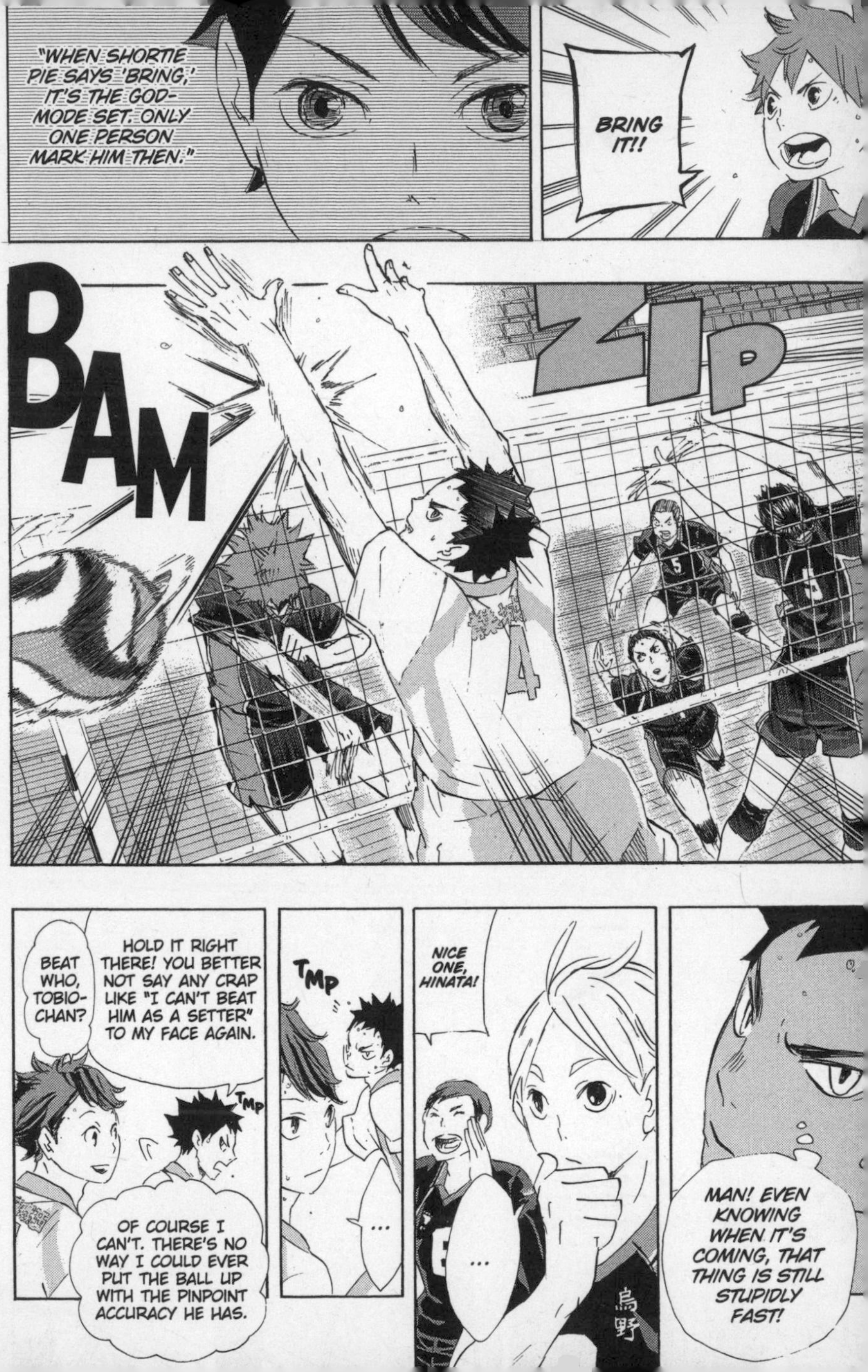
BRING IT!!
"WHEN SHORTIE PIE SAYS 'BRING,' IT'S THE GOD-MODE SET. ONLY ONE PERSON MARK HIM THEN."
ZIP
BAM
MAN! EVEN KNOWING WHEN IT'S COMING, THAT THING IS STILL STUPIDLY FAST!
NICE ONE, HINATA!
...
TMP
...
BEAT WHO, TOBIO-CHAN?
HOLD IT RIGHT THERE! YOU BETTER NOT SAY ANY CRAP LIKE "I CAN'T BEAT HIM AS A SETTER" TO MY FACE AGAIN.
TMP
OF COURSE I CAN'T. THERE'S NO WAY I COULD EVER PUT THE BALL UP WITH THE PINPOINT ACCURACY HE HAS.

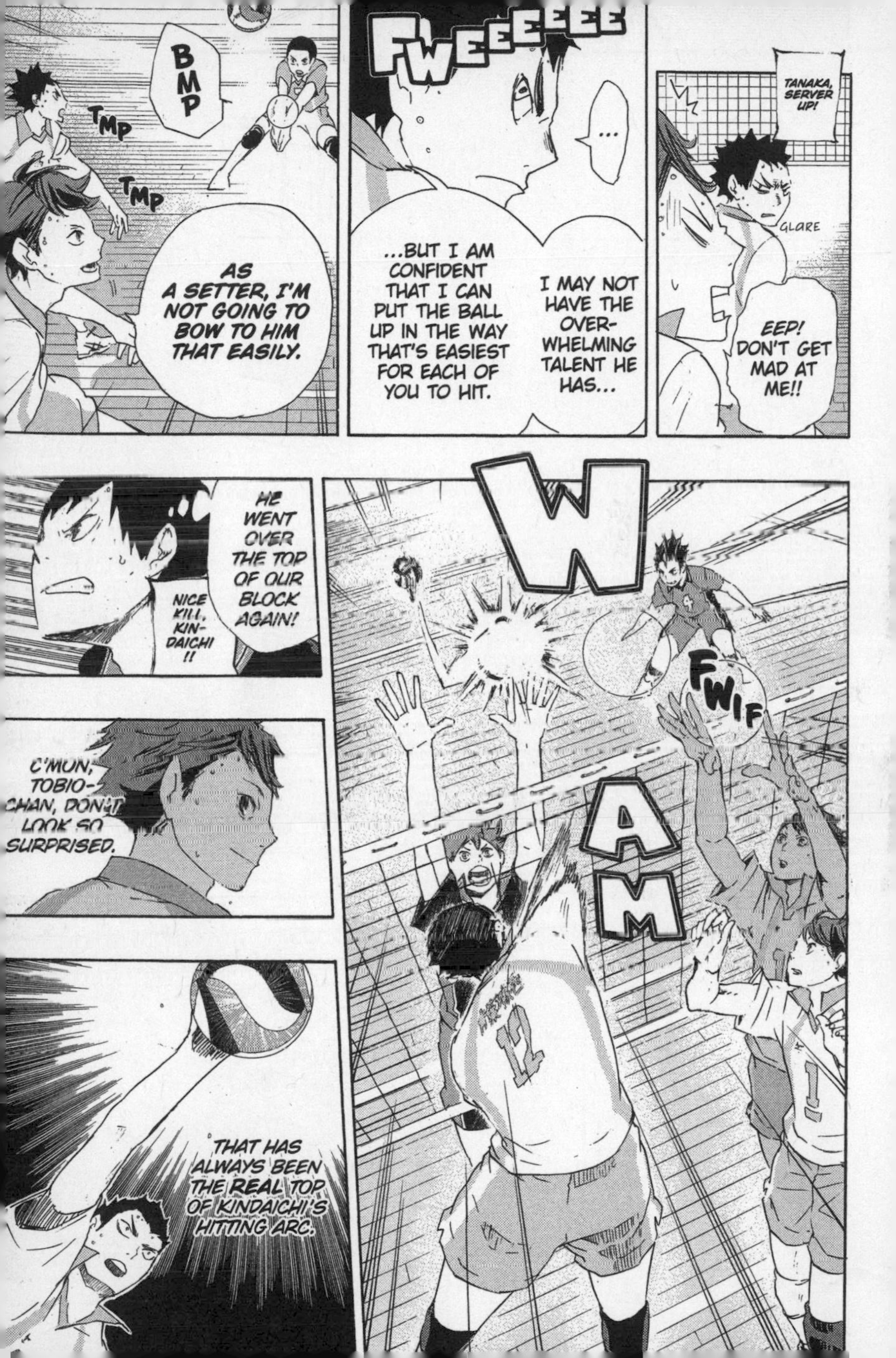
TANAKA, SERVER UP!
GLARE
EEP! DON'T GET MAD AT ME!!
FWEEEEEE
...
I MAY NOT HAVE THE OVER-WHELMING TALENT HE HAS...
...BUT I AM CONFIDENT THAT I CAN PUT THE BALL UP IN THE WAY THAT'S EASIEST FOR EACH OF YOU TO HIT.
BMP
TMP
TMP
AS A SETTER, I'M NOT GOING TO BOW TO HIM THAT EASILY.
WHAM
FWIF
HE WENT OVER THE TOP OF OUR BLOCK AGAIN!
NICE KILL, KINDAICHI!!
C'MON, TOBIO-CHAN, DON'T LOOK SO SURPRISED.
THAT HAS ALWAYS BEEN THE REAL TOP OF KINDAICHI'S HITTING ARC.

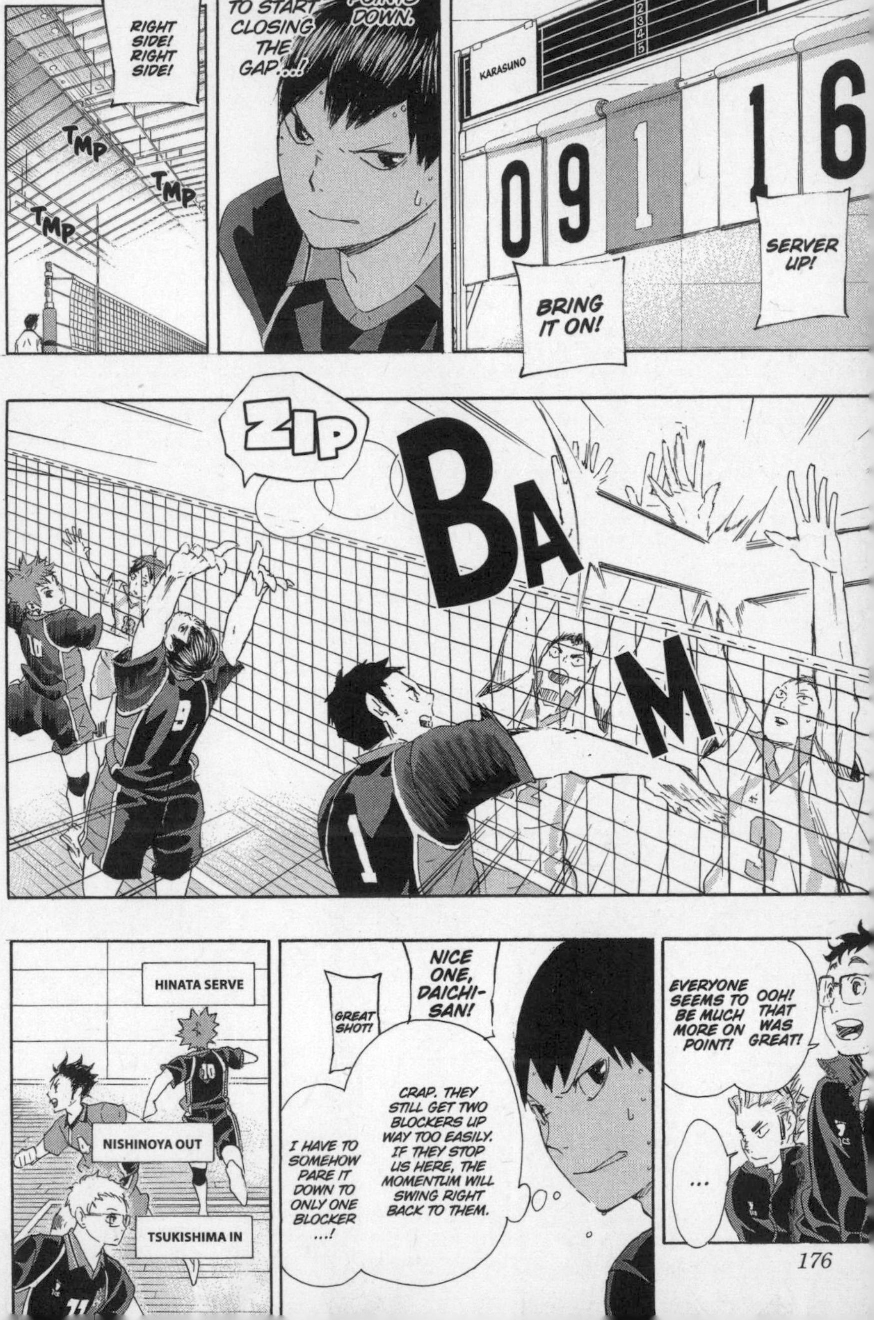
AOBA JOHSAI
KARASUNO
SERVER UP!
BRING IT ON!
SEVEN POINTS DOWN.
I HAVE TO START CLOSING THE GAP...!
RIGHT SIDE! RIGHT SIDE!
TMP
TMP
TMP
BAM
ZIP
OOH! THAT WAS GREAT!
EVERYONE SEEMS TO BE MUCH MORE ON POINT!
...
NICE ONE, DAICHI-SAN!
GREAT SHOT!
CRAP. THEY STILL GET TWO BLOCKERS UP WAY TOO EASILY. IF THEY STOP US HERE, THE MOMENTUM WILL SWING RIGHT BACK TO THEM.
I HAVE TO SOMEHOW PARE IT DOWN TO ONLY ONE BLOCKER ...!
HINATA SERVE
NISHINOYA OUT
TSUKISHIMA IN

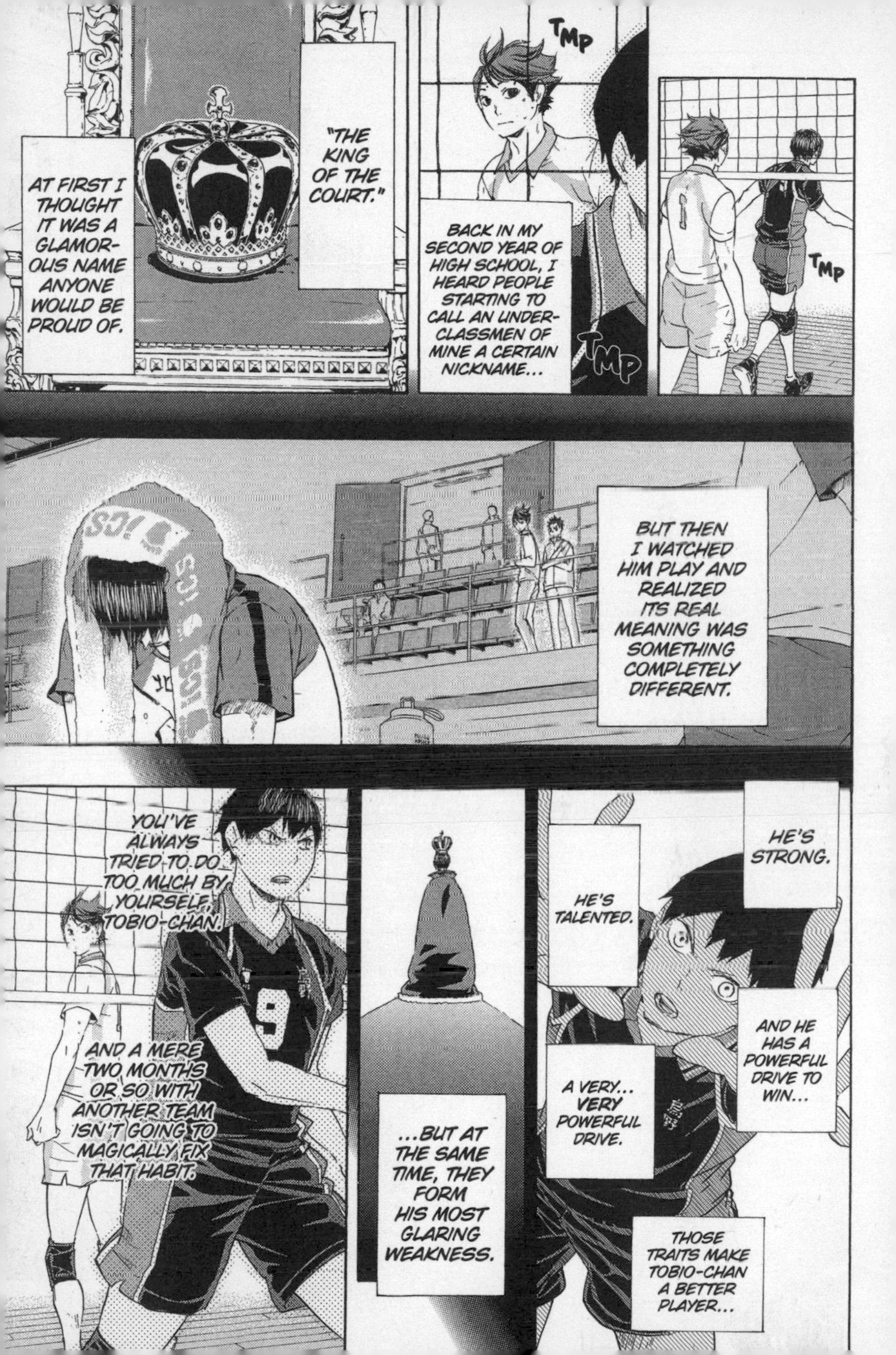
TMP
TMP
BACK IN MY SECOND YEAR OF HIGH SCHOOL, I HEARD PEOPLE STARTING TO CALL AN UNDER-CLASSMEN OF MINE A CERTAIN NICKNAME...
TMP
"THE KING OF THE COURT."
AT FIRST I THOUGHT IT WAS A GLAMOR-OUS NAME ANYONE WOULD BE PROUD OF.
BUT THEN I WATCHED HIM PLAY AND REALIZED ITS REAL MEANING WAS SOMETHING COMPLETELY DIFFERENT.
HE'S STRONG.
HE'S TALENTED.
AND HE HAS A POWERFUL DRIVE TO WIN...
A VERY... VERY POWERFUL DRIVE.
THOSE TRAITS MAKE TOBIO-CHAN A BETTER PLAYER...
...BUT AT THE SAME TIME, THEY FORM HIS MOST GLARING WEAKNESS.
YOU'VE ALWAYS TRIED TO DO TOO MUCH BY YOURSELF, TOBIO-CHAN.
AND A MERE TWO MONTHS OR SO WITH ANOTHER TEAM ISN'T GOING TO MAGICALLY FIX THAT HABIT.

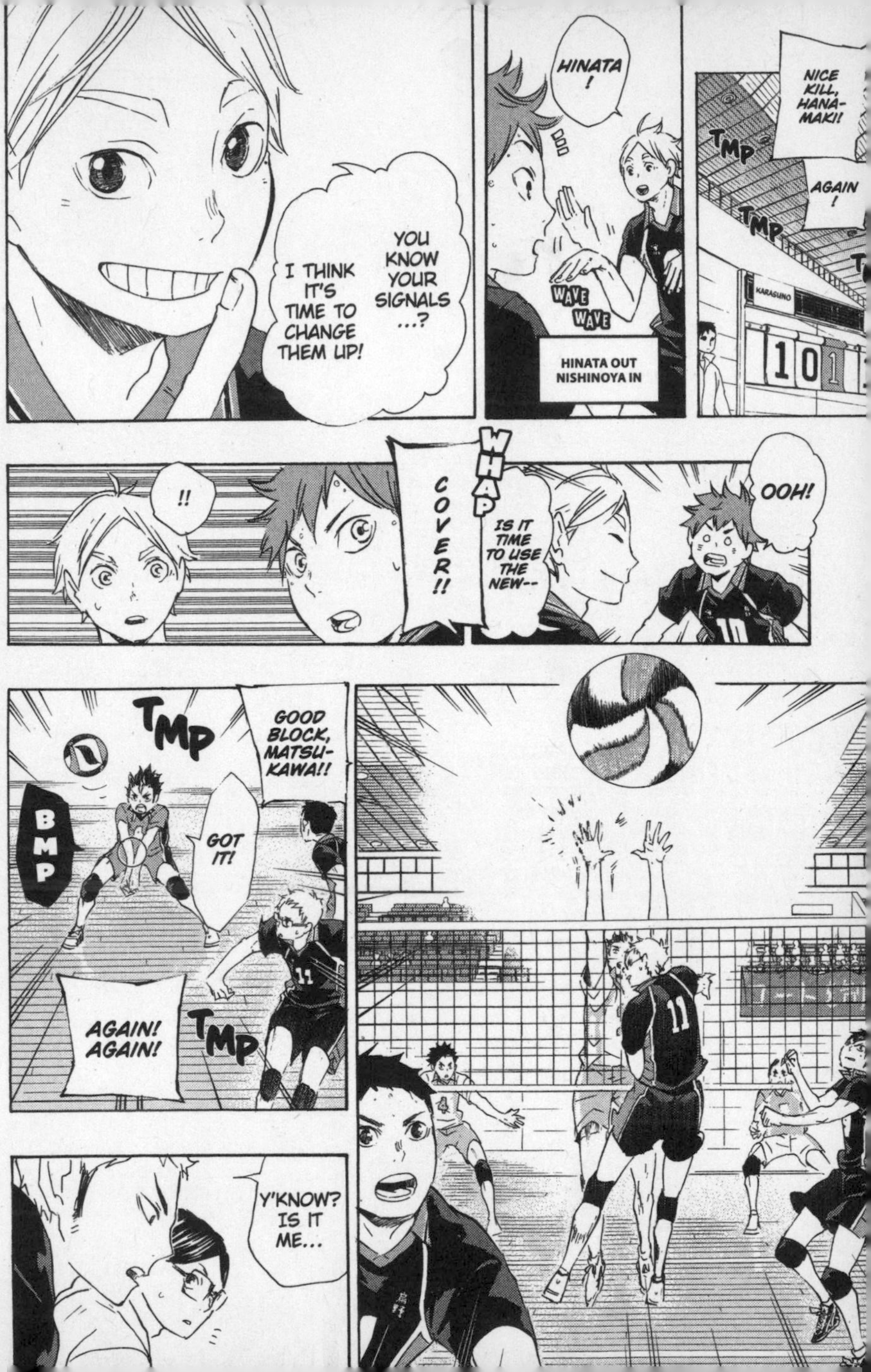
NICE KILL, HANAMAKI!
TMP
AGAIN!
TMP
KARASUNO
HINATA!
WAVE
WAVE
HINATA OUT NISHINOYA IN
YOU KNOW YOUR SIGNALS ...?
I THINK IT'S TIME TO CHANGE THEM UP!
OOH!
IS IT TIME TO USE THE NEW--
WHAP
COVER!!
!!
GOOD BLOCK, MATSUKAWA!!
TMP
GOT IT!
BMP
AGAIN! AGAIN!
TMP
Y'KNOW? IS IT ME...

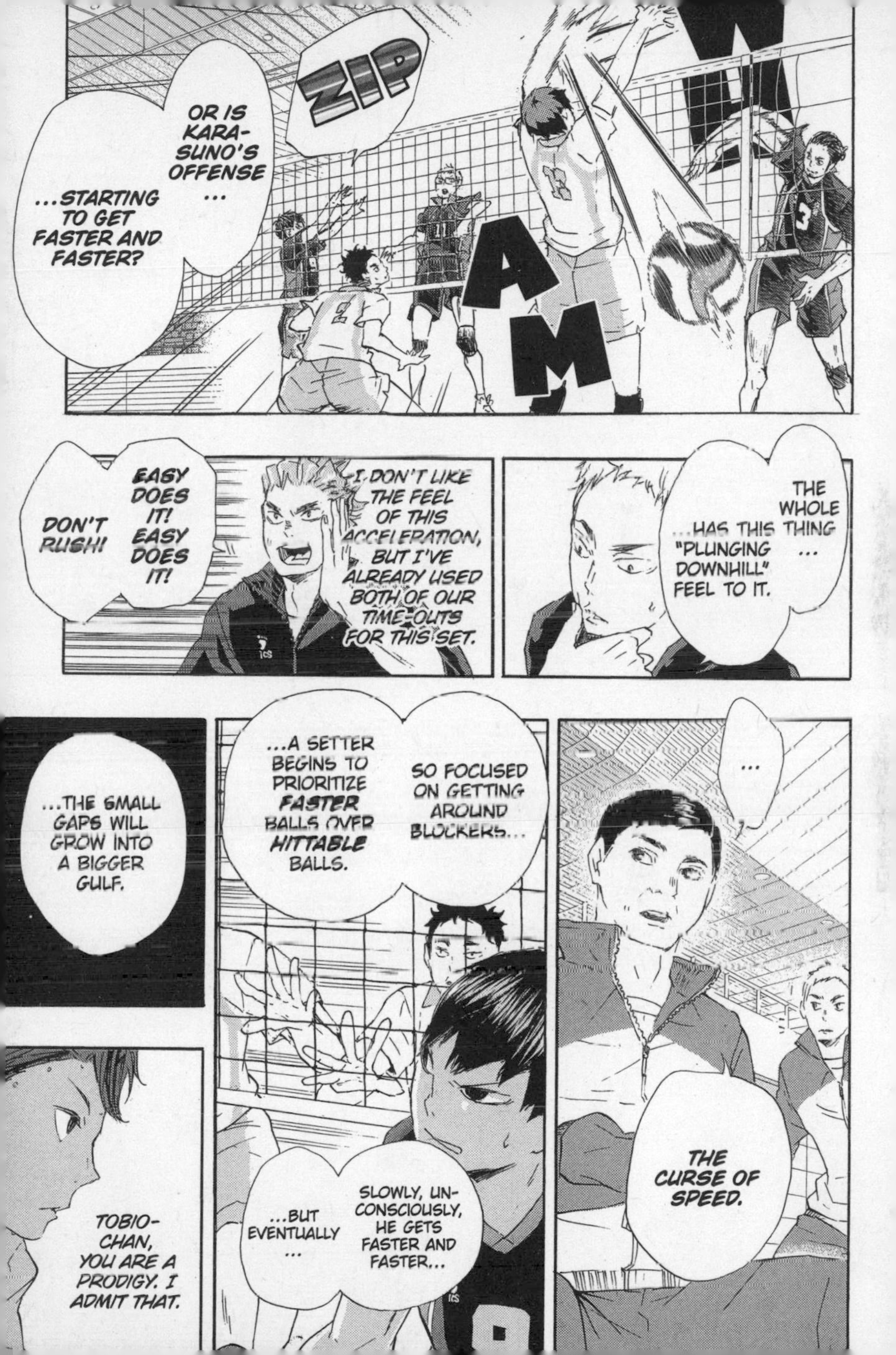
ZIP
OR IS KARA-SUNO'S OFFENSE ...
...STARTING TO GET FASTER AND FASTER?
W
A
M
THE WHOLE ...HAS THIS THING ... "PLUNGING DOWNHILL" FEEL TO IT.
I DON'T LIKE THE FEEL OF THIS ACCELERATION, BUT I'VE ALREADY USED BOTH OF OUR TIME-OUTS FOR THIS SET.
EASY DOES IT! EASY DOES IT!
DON'T RUSH!
...
THE CURSE OF SPEED.
SO FOCUSED ON GETTING AROUND BLOCKERS...
...A SETTER BEGINS TO PRIORITIZE FASTER BALLS OVER HITTABLE BALLS.
SLOWLY, UN-CONSCIOUSLY, HE GETS FASTER AND FASTER...
...BUT EVENTUALLY ...
...THE SMALL GAPS WILL GROW INTO A BIGGER GULF.
TOBIO-CHAN, YOU ARE A PRODIGY. I ADMIT THAT.

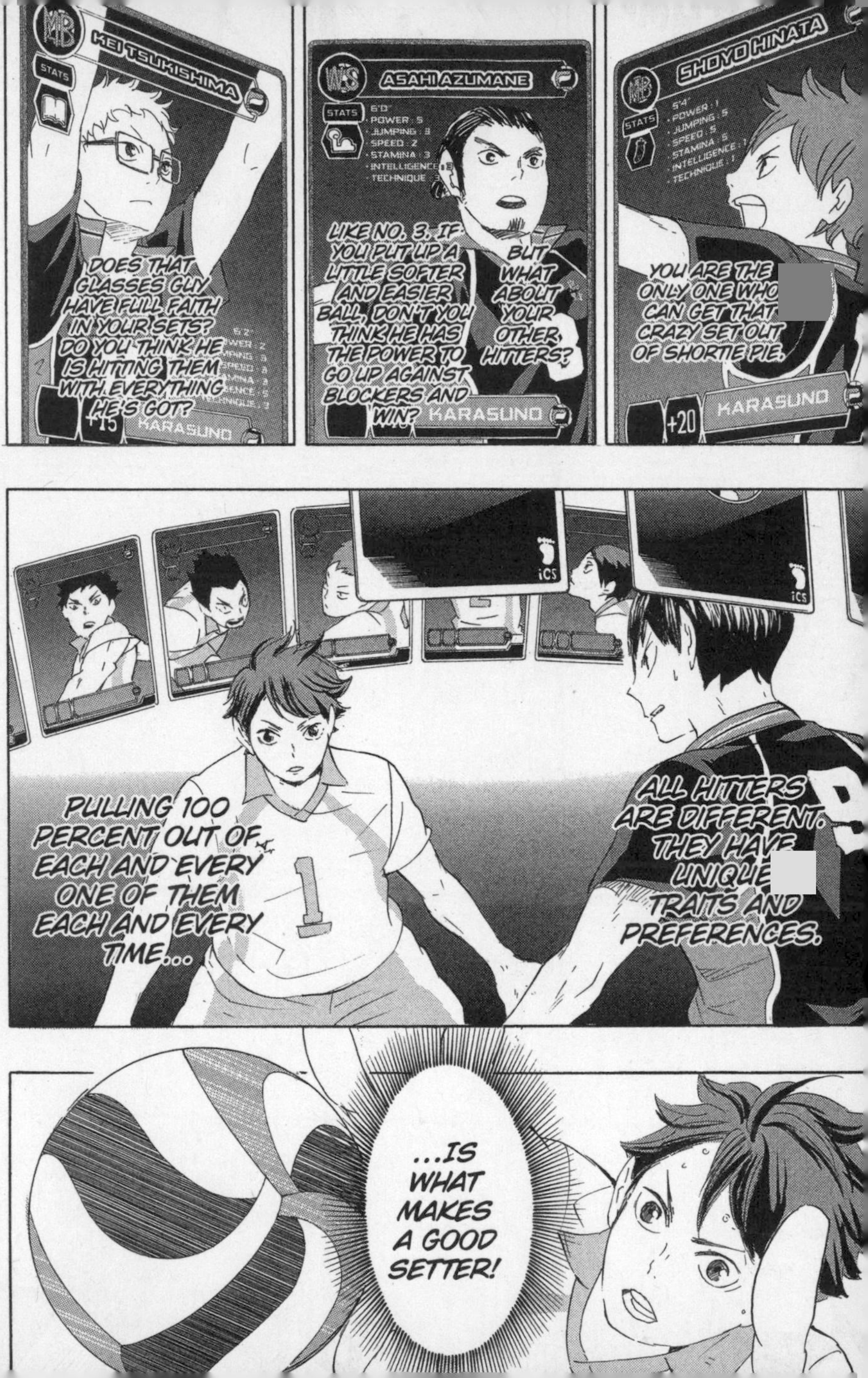
SHOYO HINATA
STATS
5'4"
POWER: 1
JUMPING: 5
SPEED: 5
STAMINA: 5
INTELLIGENCE: 1
TECHNIQUE: 1
+20
KARASUNO
YOU ARE THE ONLY ONE WHO CAN GET THAT CRAZY SET OUT OF SHORTIE PIE.
ASAHI AZUMANE
STATS
6'0"
POWER: 5
JUMPING: 3
SPEED: 2
STAMINA: 3
KARASUNO
BUT WHAT ABOUT YOUR OTHER HITTERS?
LIKE NO. 3. IF YOU PUT UP A LITTLE SOFTER AND EASIER BALL, DON'T YOU THINK HE HAS THE POWER TO GO UP AGAINST BLOCKERS AND WIN?
KEI TSUKISHIMA
STATS
+15
KARASUNO
DOES THAT GLASSES GUY HAVE FULL FAITH IN YOUR SETS? DO YOU THINK HE IS HITTING THEM WITH EVERYTHING HE'S GOT?
ALL HITTERS ARE DIFFERENT. THEY HAVE UNIQUE TRAITS AND PREFERENCES.
PULLING 100 PERCENT OUT OF EACH AND EVERY ONE OF THEM EACH AND EVERY TIME...
...IS WHAT MAKES A GOOD SETTER!

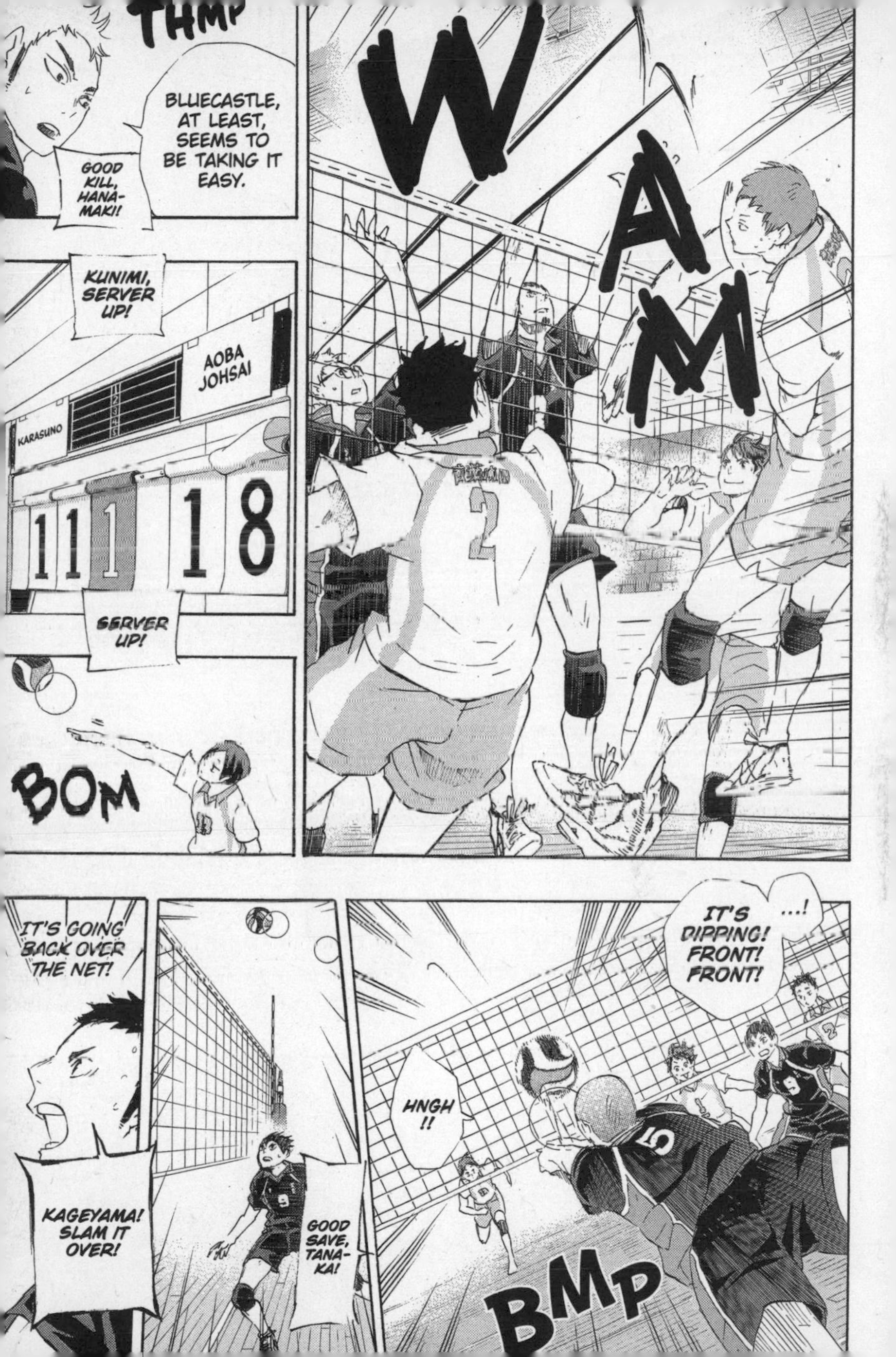
WAM
THMP
BLUECASTLE, AT LEAST, SEEMS TO BE TAKING IT EASY.
GOOD KILL, HANA-MAKI!
KUNIMI, SERVER UP!
AOBA JOHSAI
KARASUNO
11 1 18
SERVER UP!
BOM
...!
IT'S DIPPING! FRONT! FRONT!
HNGH !!
BMP
GOOD SAVE, TANAKA!
IT'S GOING BACK OVER THE NET!
KAGEYAMA! SLAM IT OVER!

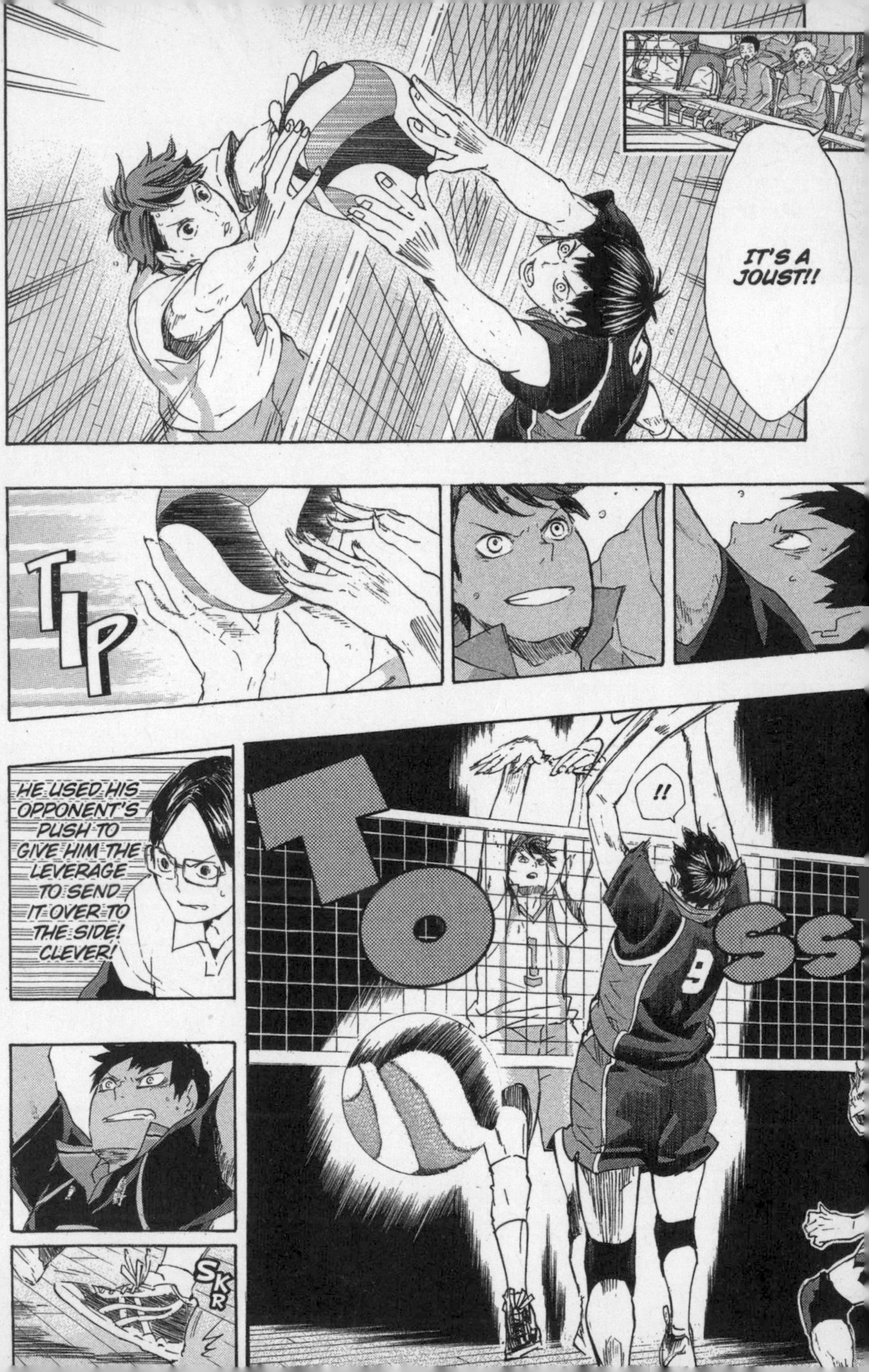
IT'S A JOUST!!
TIP
!!
TOSS
HE USED HIS OPPONENT'S PUSH TO GIVE HIM THE LEVERAGE TO SEND IT OVER TO THE SIDE! CLEVER!
SKR

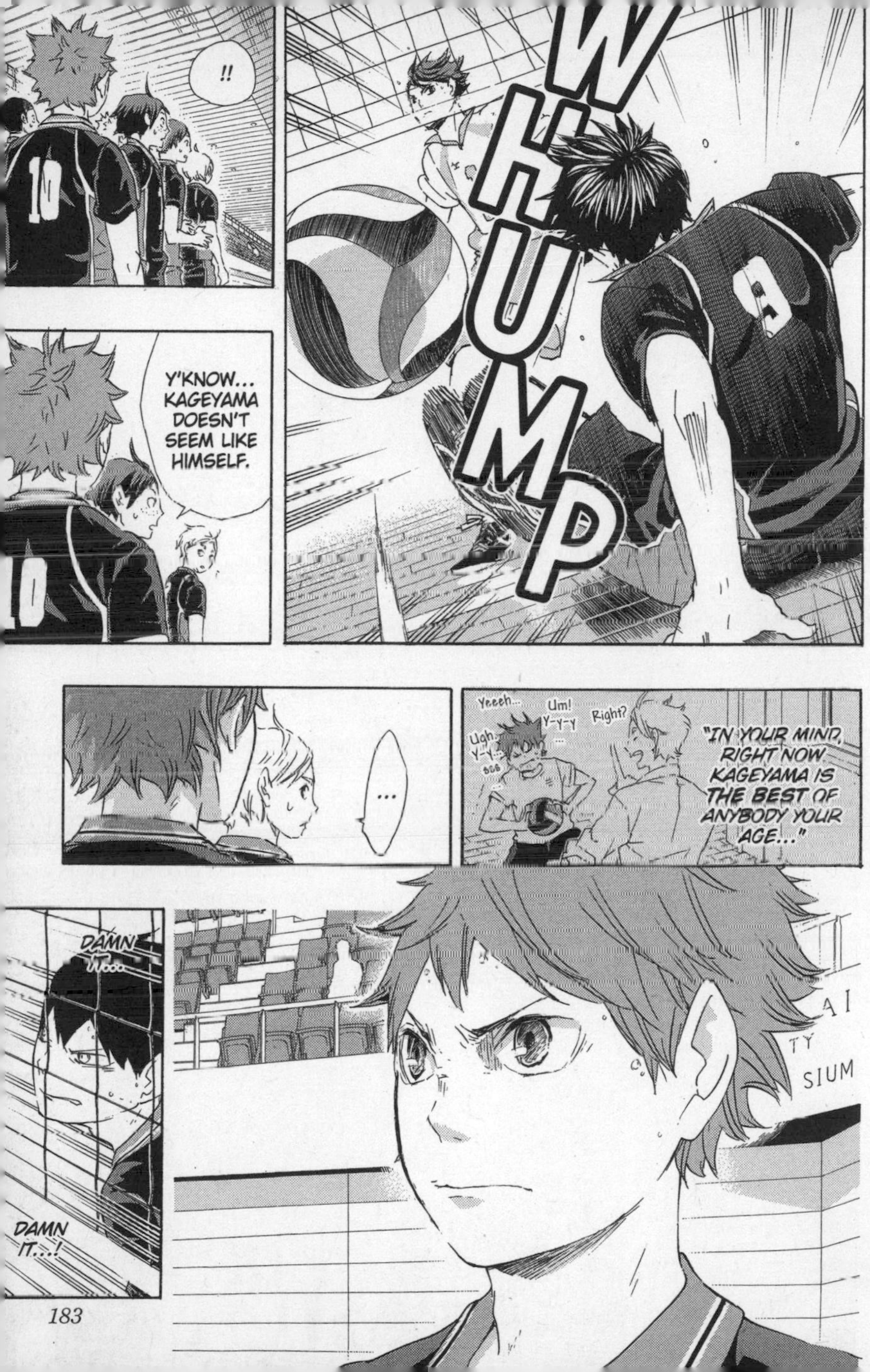
WHUMP
!!
Y'KNOW... KAGEYAMA DOESN'T SEEM LIKE HIMSELF.
"IN YOUR MIND, RIGHT NOW KAGEYAMA IS THE BEST OF ANYBODY YOUR AGE..."
Right?
Um! Y-y-y ...
Yeeeh...
Ugh. Y-y...
...
AI
TY
SIUM
DAMN IT...
DAMN IT...!

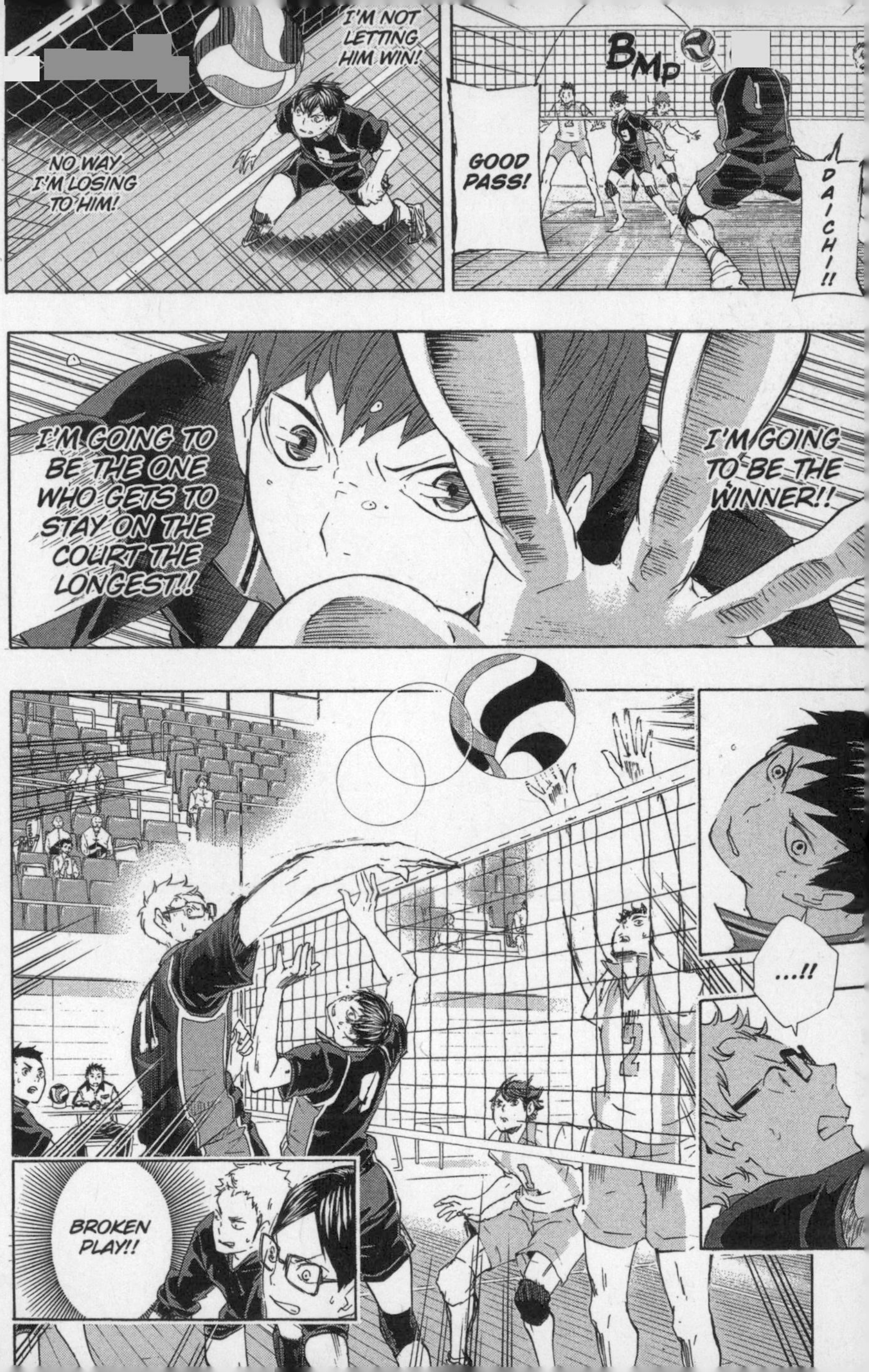
DAICHI!!
BMP
GOOD PASS!
I'M NOT LETTING HIM WIN!
NO WAY I'M LOSING TO HIM!
I'M GOING TO BE THE WINNER!!
I'M GOING TO BE THE ONE WHO GETS TO STAY ON THE COURT THE LONGEST!!
...!!
BROKEN PLAY!!

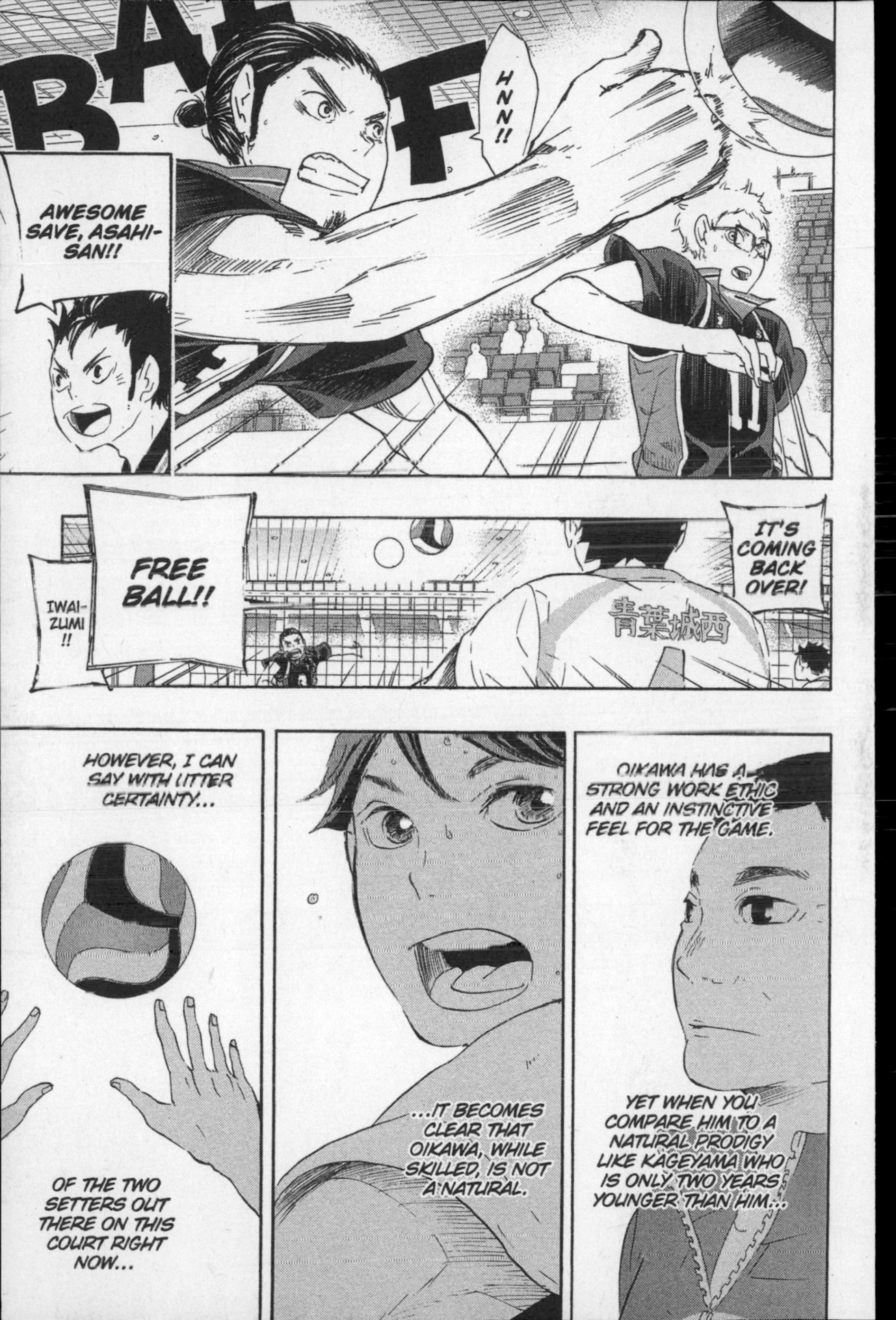
BAFF
HNN!!
AWESOME SAVE, ASAHI-SAN!!
IT'S COMING BACK OVER!
青葉城西
FREE BALL!!
IWAI-ZUMI!!
OIKAWA HAS A STRONG WORK ETHIC AND AN INSTINCTIVE FEEL FOR THE GAME.
YET WHEN YOU COMPARE HIM TO A NATURAL PRODIGY LIKE KAGEYAMA WHO IS ONLY TWO YEARS YOUNGER THAN HIM...
...IT BECOMES CLEAR THAT OIKAWA, WHILE SKILLED, IS NOT A NATURAL.
HOWEVER, I CAN SAY WITH UTTER CERTAINTY...
OF THE TWO SETTERS OUT THERE ON THIS COURT RIGHT NOW...

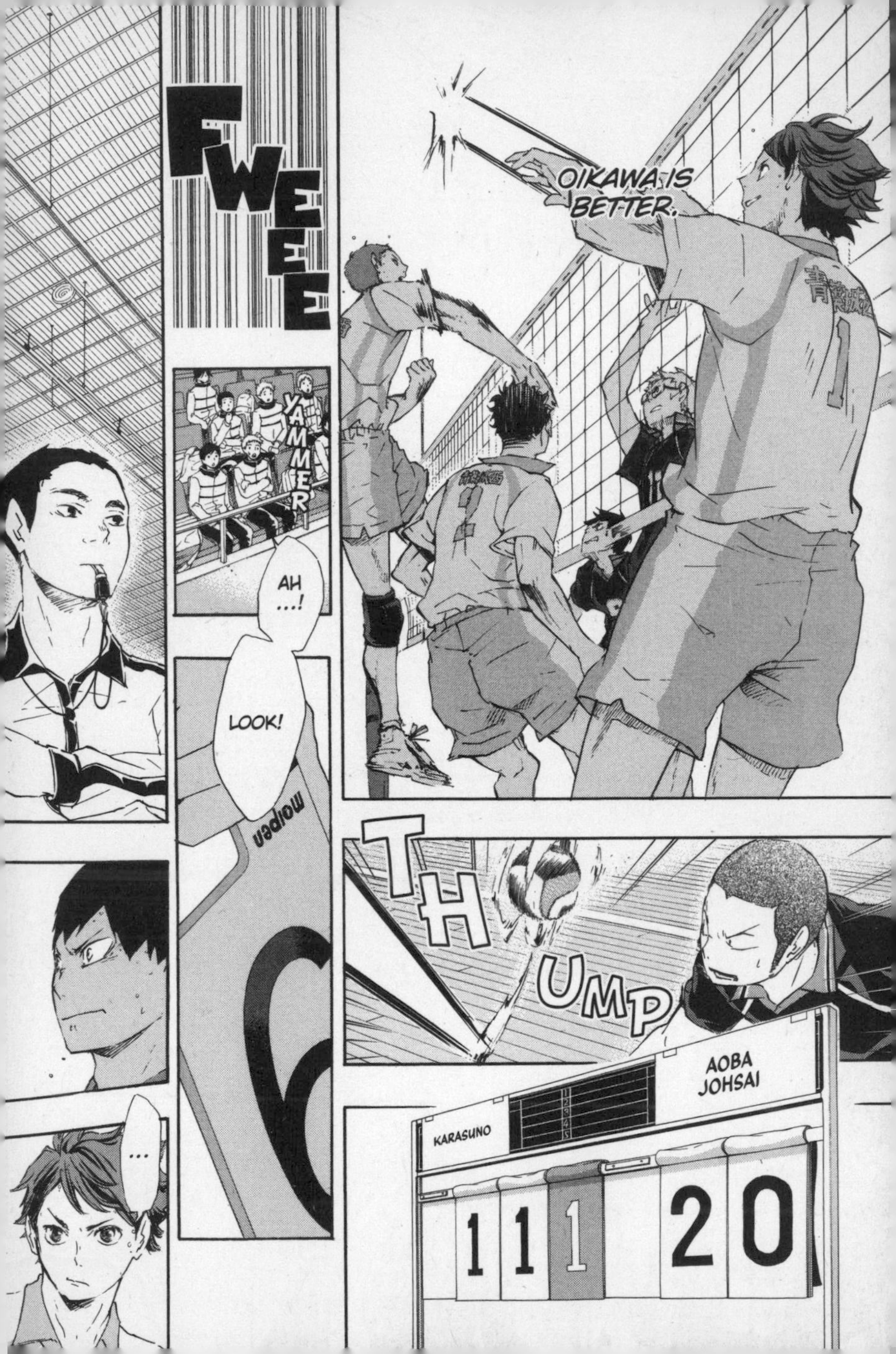
OIKAWA IS BETTER.
FWEEE
YAMMER
AH ...!
LOOK!
THUMP
moipen
AOBA JOHSAI
KARASUNO
11 1 20
...

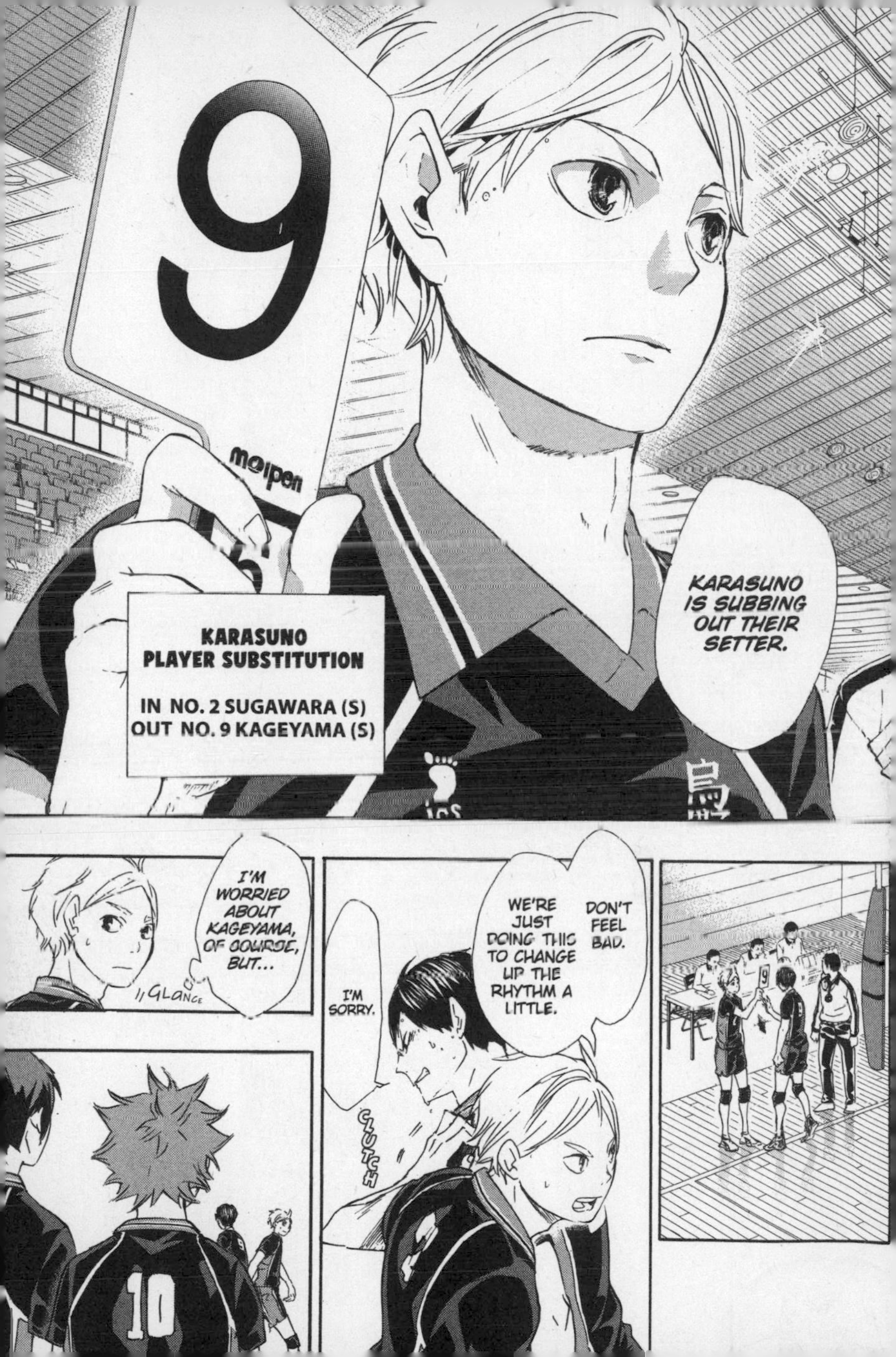
KARASUNO IS SUBBING OUT THEIR SETTER.
KARASUNO PLAYER SUBSTITUTION
IN NO. 2 SUGAWARA (S)
OUT NO. 9 KAGEYAMA (S)
DON'T FEEL BAD.
WE'RE JUST DOING THIS TO CHANGE UP THE RHYTHM A LITTLE.
I'M SORRY.
CLUTCH
I'M WORRIED ABOUT KAGEYAMA, OF COURSE, BUT...
GLANCE

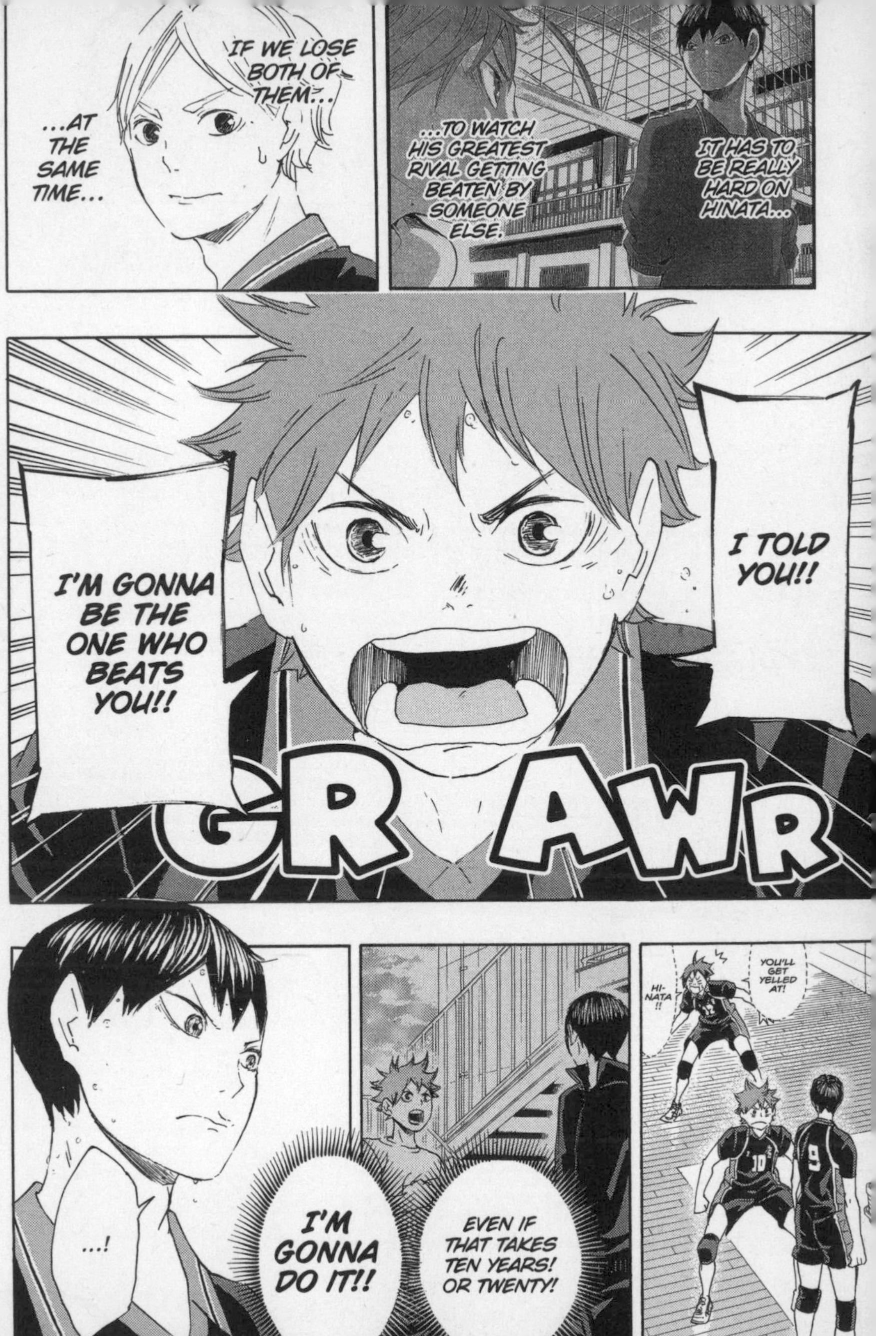
IT HAS TO BE REALLY HARD ON HINATA...
...TO WATCH HIS GREATEST RIVAL GETTING BEATEN BY SOMEONE ELSE.
IF WE LOSE BOTH OF THEM...
...AT THE SAME TIME...
I TOLD YOU!!
I'M GONNA BE THE ONE WHO BEATS YOU!!
GRAWR
YOU'LL GET YELLED AT!
HI-NATA!!
EVEN IF THAT TAKES TEN YEARS! OR TWENTY!
I'M GONNA DO IT!!
...!

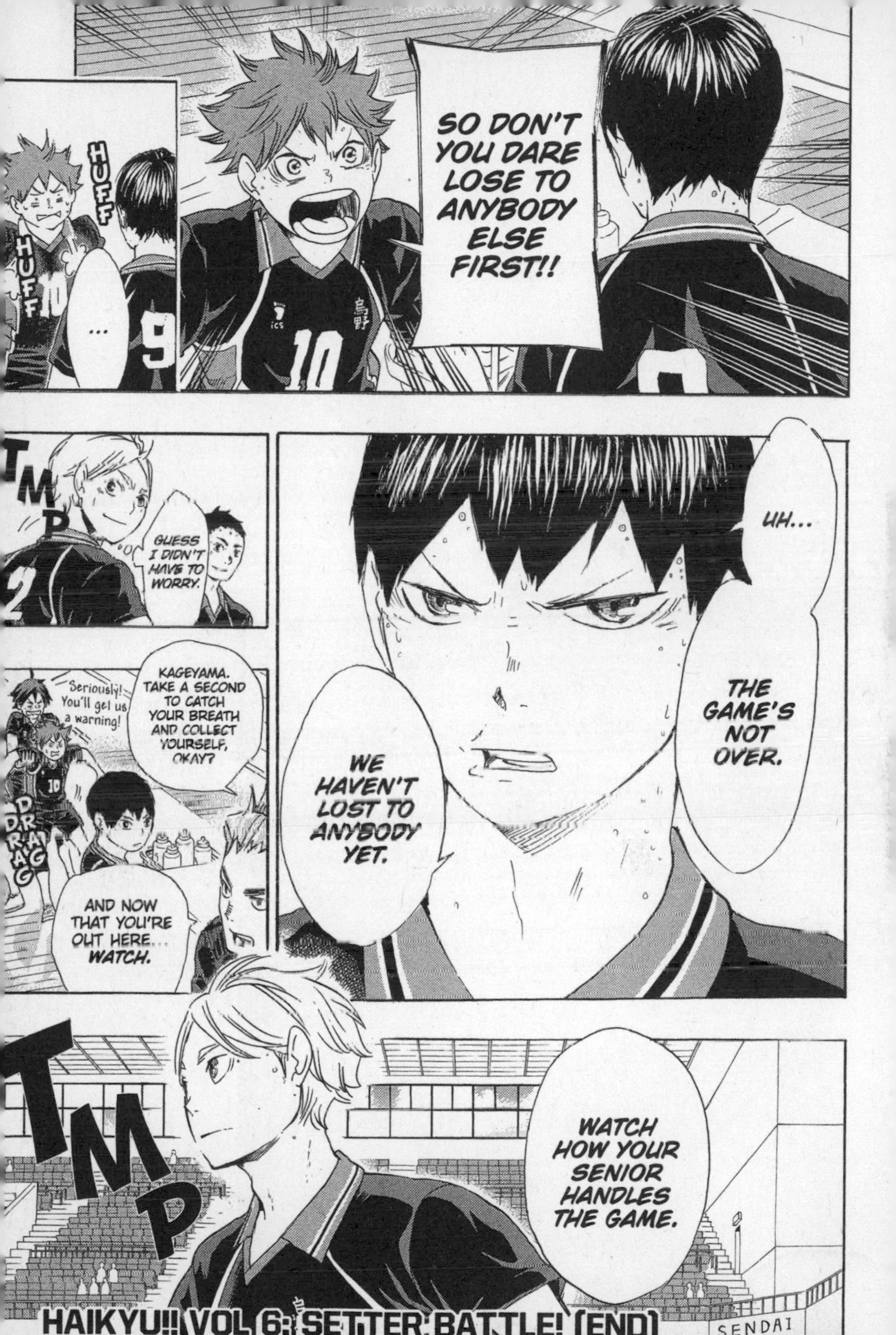
SO DON'T YOU DARE LOSE TO ANYBODY ELSE FIRST!!
HUFF
HUFF
HUFF
...
UH...
THE GAME'S NOT OVER.
WE HAVEN'T LOST TO ANYBODY YET.
TMP
GUESS I DIDN'T HAVE TO WORRY.
KAGEYAMA. TAKE A SECOND TO CATCH YOUR BREATH AND COLLECT YOURSELF, OKAY?
Seriously! You'll get us a warning!
DRAG
DRAG
AND NOW THAT YOU'RE OUT HERE... WATCH.
TMP
WATCH HOW YOUR SENIOR HANDLES THE GAME.
SENDAI

HAIKYU!! VOL 6: SETTER BATTLE! (END)

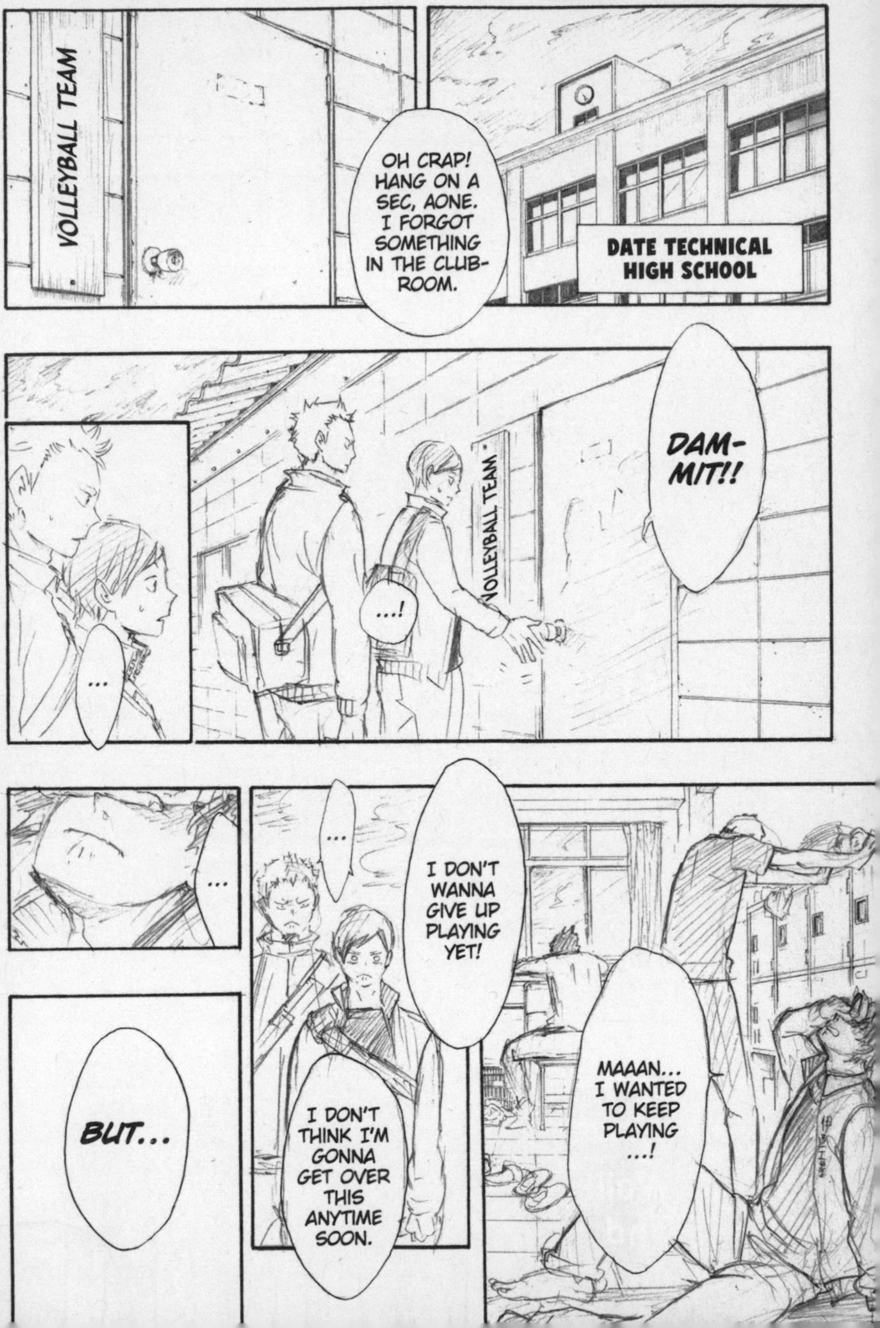
DATE TECHNICAL HIGH SCHOOL
OH CRAP! HANG ON A SEC, AONE. I FORGOT SOMETHING IN THE CLUB-ROOM.
VOLLEYBALL TEAM
DAM-MIT!!
VOLLEYBALL TEAM
...!
...
MAAAN... I WANTED TO KEEP PLAYING ...!
I DON'T WANNA GIVE UP PLAYING YET!
...
I DON'T THINK I'M GONNA GET OVER THIS ANYTIME SOON.
...
BUT...

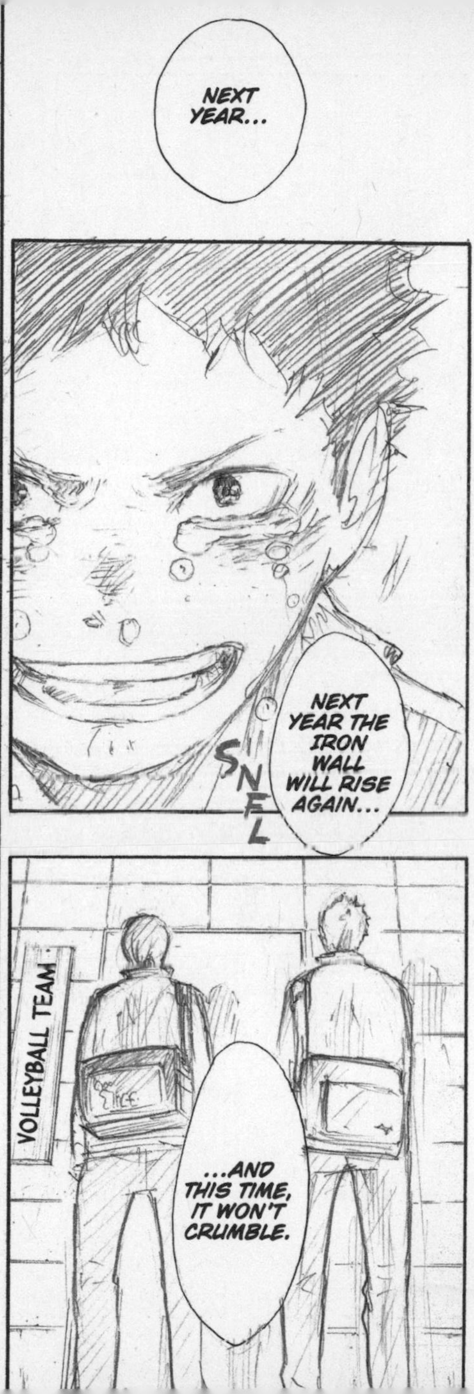
NEXT YEAR...
SNFL
NEXT YEAR THE IRON WALL WILL RISE AGAIN...
VOLLEYBALL TEAM
...AND THIS TIME, IT WON'T CRUMBLE.

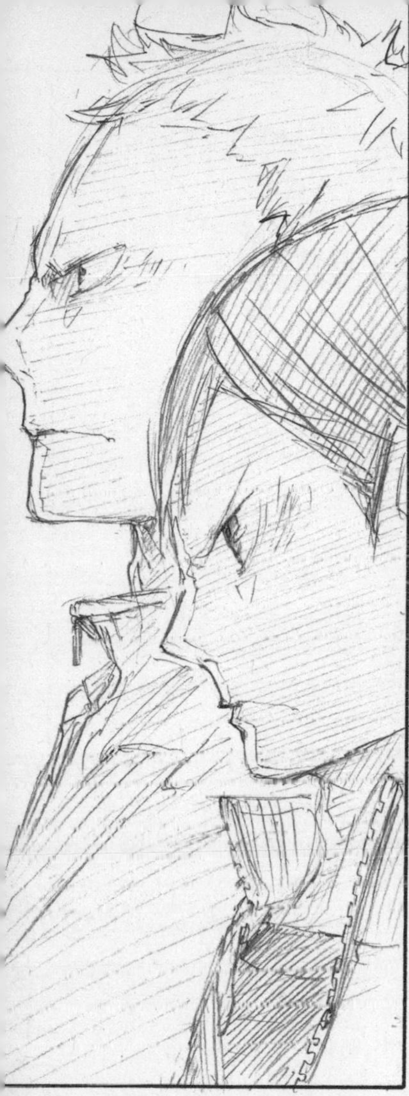

HAIKYU!! BONUS STORY

The Iron Wall will rise and rise again.

EDITOR'S NOTES

The English edition of Haikyu!! maintains the honorifics used in the original Japanese version. For those of you who are new to these terms, here's a brief explanation to help with your reading experience!

When saying someone's name in Japanese, a suffix is often attached to indicate how familiar the speaker is with the person. Some are more polite and respectful, while others are endearing.

1. **-kun** is often used for young men or boys, usually someone you are familiar with.

2. **-chan** is used for young children and can be used as a term of endearment.

3. **-san** is used for someone you respect or are not close to, or to be polite.

4. **Senpai** is used for someone who is older than you or in a higher position or grade in school.

5. **Kohai** is used for someone who is younger than you or in a lower position or grade in school.

6. **Sensei** means teacher.

7. **Bluecastle** is a nickname for Aoba Johsai. It is a combination of *Ao* (blue) and *Joh* (castle).

LOCK ON!!

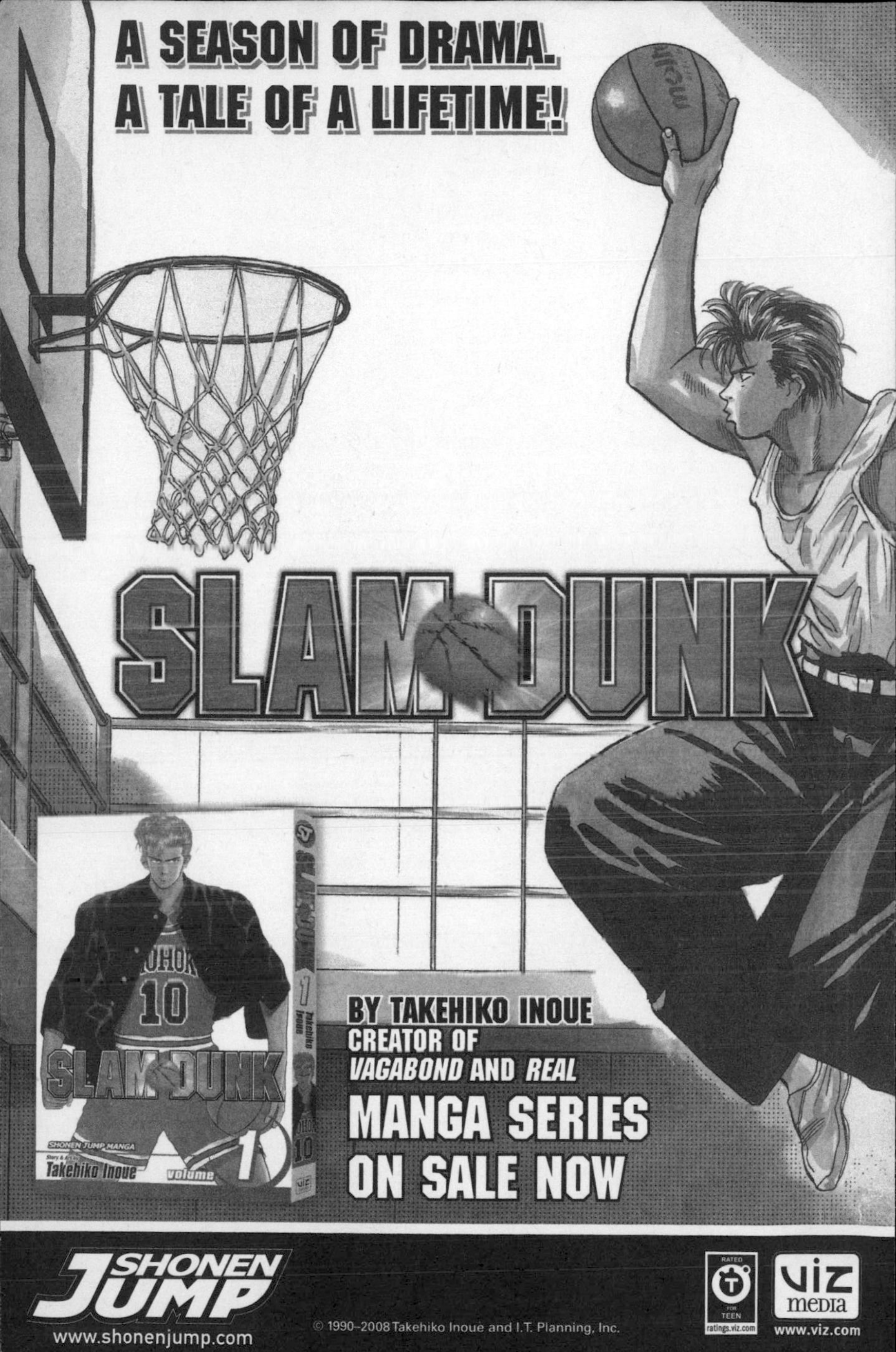

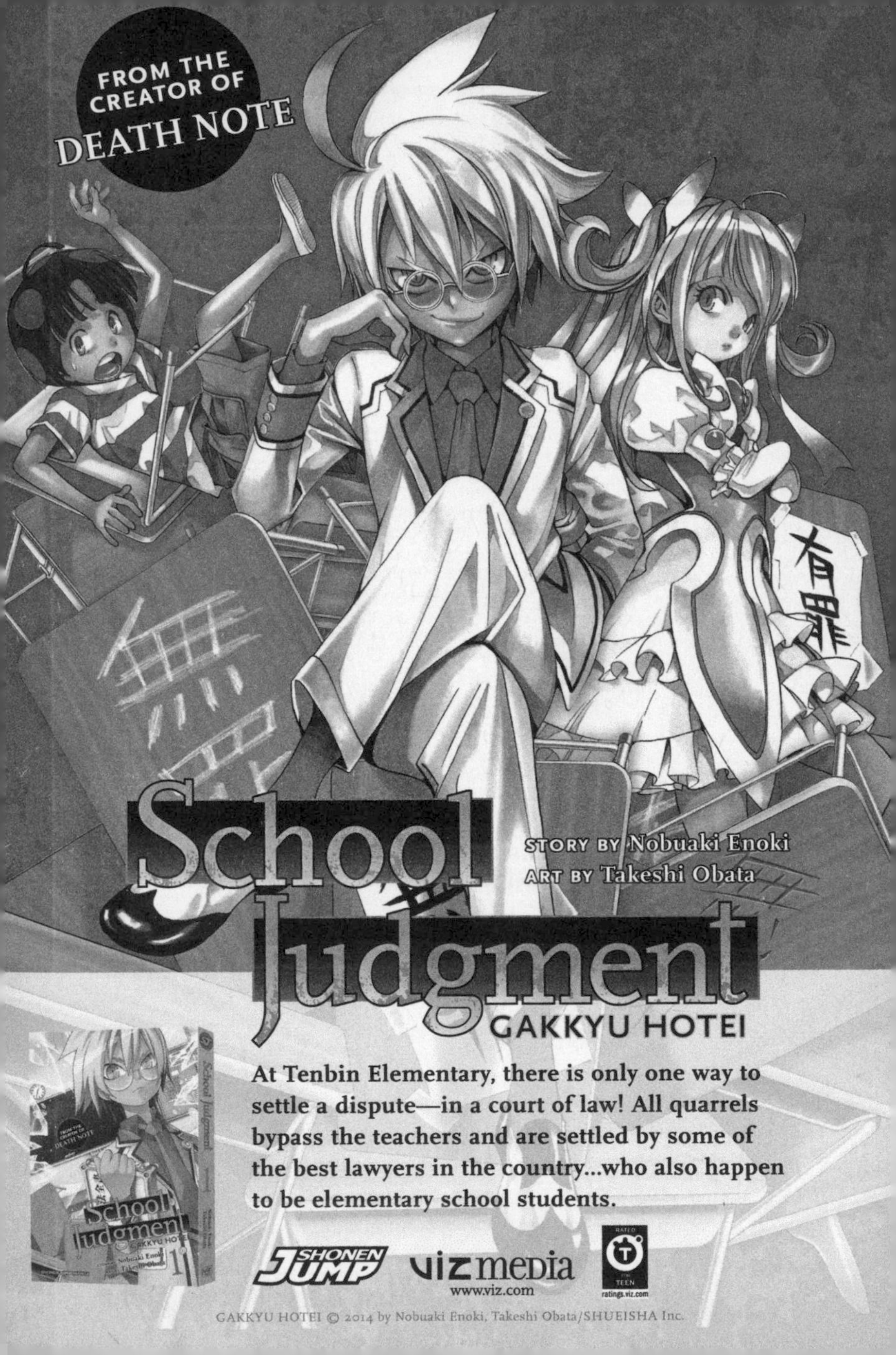

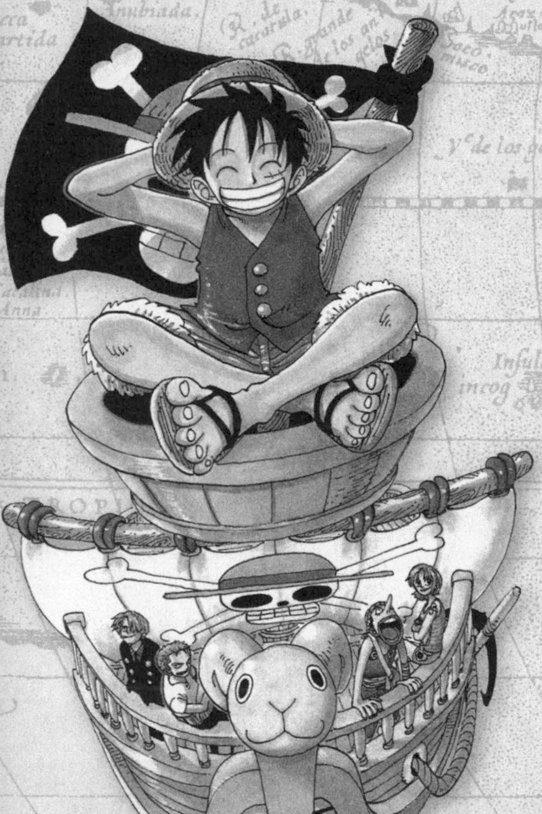

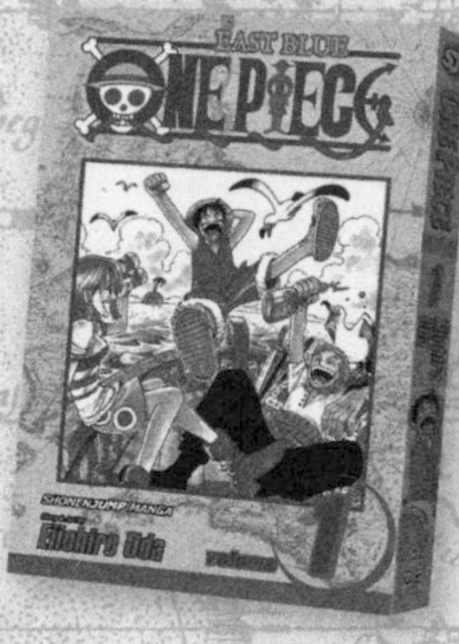
EAST BLUE
ONE PIECE
SHONEN JUMP MANGA
Eiichiro Oda

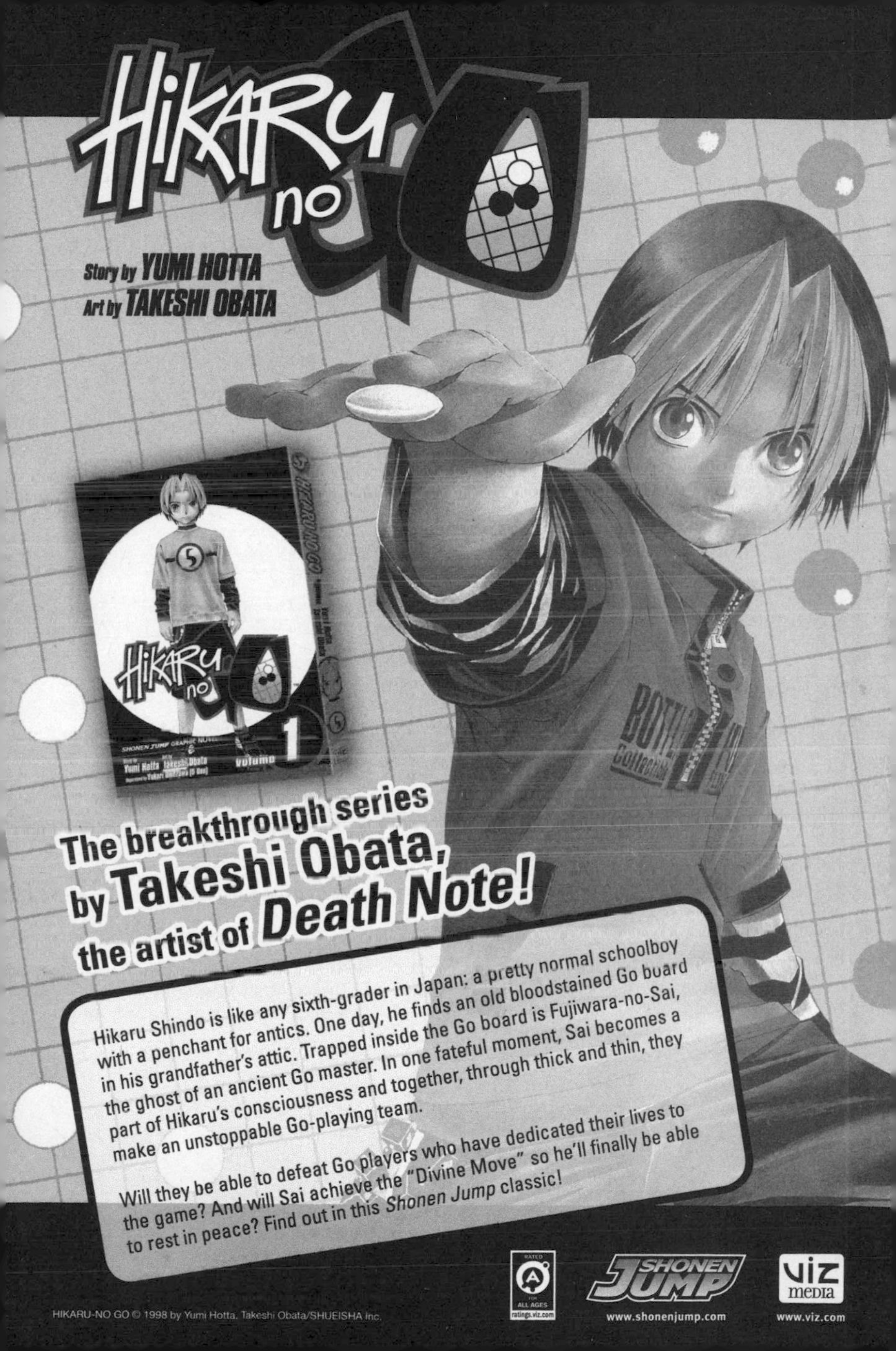
HIKARU no GO
Story by YUMI HOTTA
Art by TAKESHI OBATA
The breakthrough series by Takeshi Obata, the artist of Death Note!
Hikaru Shindo is like any sixth-grader in Japan: a pretty normal schoolboy with a penchant for antics. One day, he finds an old bloodstained Go board in his grandfather's attic. Trapped inside the Go board is Fujiwara-no-Sai, the ghost of an ancient Go master. In one fateful moment, Sai becomes a part of Hikaru's consciousness and together, through thick and thin, they make an unstoppable Go-playing team.
Will they be able to defeat Go players who have dedicated their lives to the game? And will Sai achieve the "Divine Move" so he'll finally be able to rest in peace? Find out in this Shonen Jump classic!
RATED A FOR ALL AGES ratings.viz.com
SHONEN JUMP
www.shonenjump.com
VIZ MEDIA
www.viz.com
HIKARU-NO GO © 1998 by Yumi Hotta, Takeshi Obata/SHUEISHA Inc.

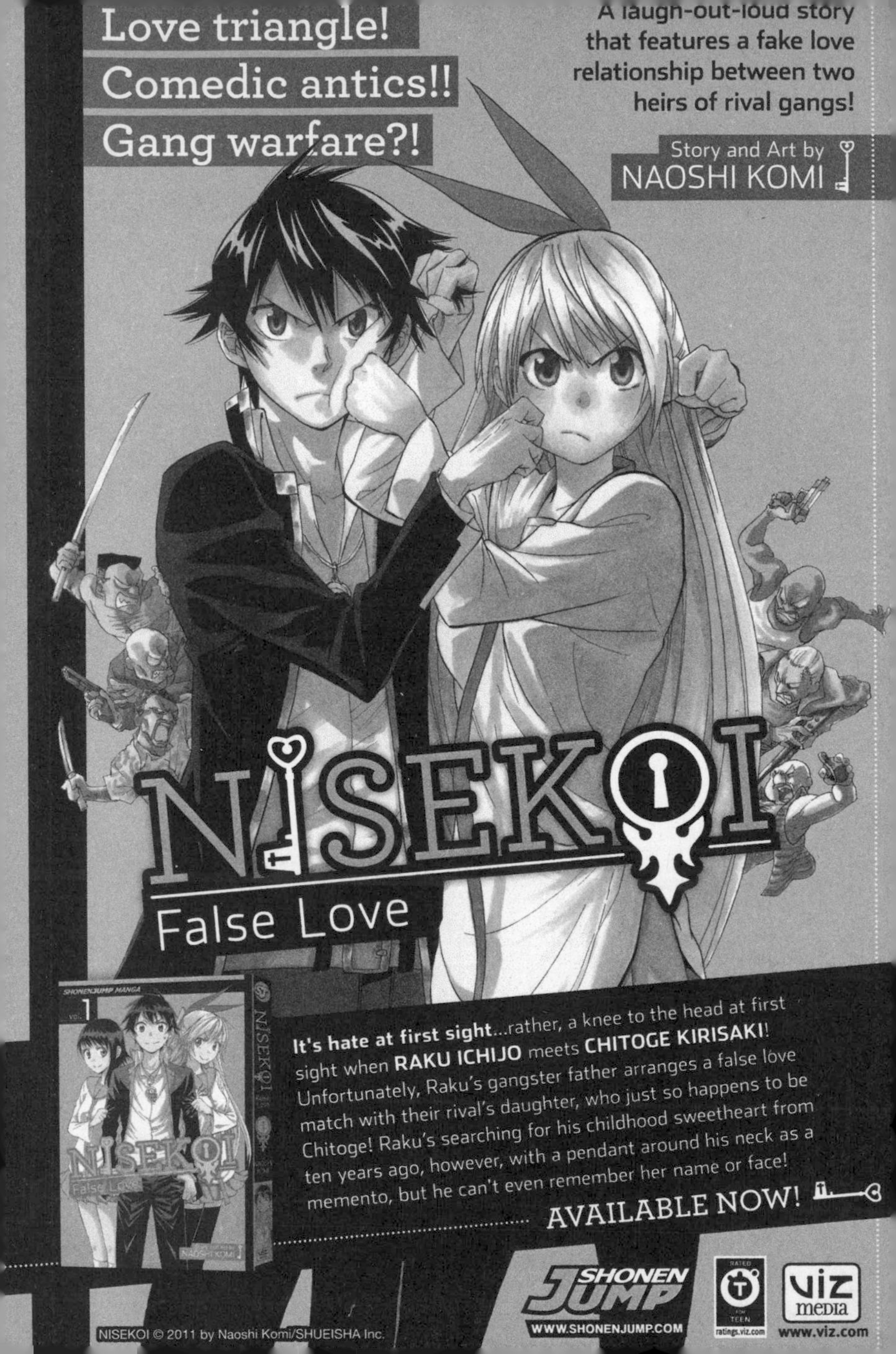

Love triangle!
Comedic antics!!
Gang warfare?!
A laugh-out-loud story that features a fake love relationship between two heirs of rival gangs!
Story and Art by
NAOSHI KOMI
NISEKOI
False Love
SHONENJUMP MANGA
VOL. 1
NISEKOI
False Love
NAOSHI KOMI
It's hate at first sight...rather, a knee to the head at first sight when RAKU ICHIJO meets CHITOGE KIRISAKI! Unfortunately, Raku's gangster father arranges a false love match with their rival's daughter, who just so happens to be Chitoge! Raku's searching for his childhood sweetheart from ten years ago, however, with a pendant around his neck as a memento, but he can't even remember her name or face!
AVAILABLE NOW!
SHONEN JUMP
WWW.SHONENJUMP.COM
RATED T FOR TEEN
ratings.viz.com
VIZ media
www.viz.com
NISEKOI © 2011 by Naoshi Komi/SHUEISHA Inc.

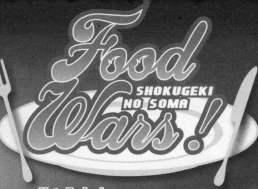

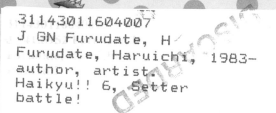

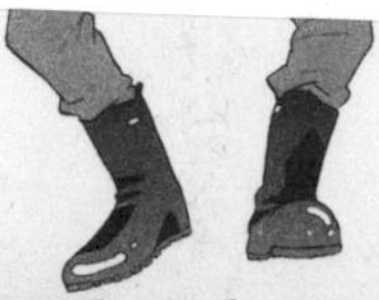

You're Reading the WRONG WAY!

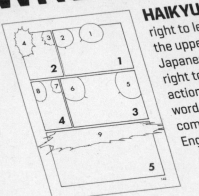

HAIKYU!! reads from right to left, starting in the upper-right corner. Japanese is read from right to left, meaning that action, sound effects and word-balloon order are completely reversed from English order.